The Power to Destroy

The Power to Destroy

How the Antitax Movement Hijacked America

Michael J. Graetz

PRINCETON UNIVERSITY PRESS

PRINCETON & OXFORD

Published by Princeton University Press
41 William Street, Princeton, New Jersey 08540
99 Banbury Road, Oxford OX2 6JX

press.princeton.edu

All Rights Reserved
ISBN: 978-0-691-22554-8
ISBN (e-book): 978-0-691-22555-5

British Library Cataloging-in-Publication Data is available

Editorial: Bridget Flannery-McCoy and Alena Chekanov
Production Editorial: Jenny Wolkowicki
Text and jacket design: Karl Spurzem
Production: Erin Suydam
Publicity: James Schneider and Kathryn Stevens

This book has been composed in Arno Pro and Neue Haas Grotesk

Printed on acid-free paper. ∞

Printed in the United States of America

10 9 8 7 6 5 4 3 2 1

For our grandchildren, Jordan, Edison, Eliot,
The little boy on his way,
And those to come

Contents

Chapter 1

Reset from the Right

The year 1978 was a remarkable turning point. Almost unconsciously it seemed the body politic rejected the gestalt that had dominated tax policy.

—ROBERT BARTLEY, EDITOR, *WALL STREET JOURNAL*

In 1897 Charles Dudley Warner, the editor of the *Hartford Courant*, said, in an observation frequently attributed to Mark Twain, "Everybody talks about the weather, but nobody does anything about it."[1] During the half century from the late 1920s until the late 1970s, much the same could be said about taxes: people across the land complained about taxes but did nothing about it. In 1978, starting in California, people sprang into action—galvanizing an antitax, antigovernment movement that remains remarkably strong more than a generation later. What started as an obsessive fringe movement to cut taxes, bolstered by spurious economic claims and camouflaged racist rhetoric, grew into a powerful force that transformed American politics and undermined the nation's financial strength.

The modern antitax movement is the most overlooked social and political movement in recent American history. It has impeded the nation's ability to protect its people from the vicissitudes of life, produced massive public debt, and contributed to the country's exceptional inequality. Like all social movements, some antitax protagonists have acted out of self-interest, others out of deep-seated ideological commitments; many have been motivated by both.

American Taxes and Resistance to Them

All governments—including the United States—are financed by some combination of four kinds of taxes: taxes on consumption, income, wages, or wealth. These taxes are sufficiently robust to produce adequate revenues to finance a modern government and may also be described as fair—connected to people's ability to pay.

Resistance to taxes in the United States has a long pedigree: it is as American as apple pie and fried catfish.[2] Taxes are the primary link between the people and their government: in the United States, more people file tax returns than vote in presidential elections. Antitax efforts are necessarily about the public's relationship to their government. Debates over "fair" taxation involve disputes over what constitutes a just society. Issues of whom and what to tax and how much necessarily involve fundamental cultural, social, and economic decisions. The nation's founders understood taxation as a "means for shaping the national economy, bringing foreign nations to fair commercial terms, regulating morals, and realizing . . . social reforms."[3]

The Boston Tea Party in 1773 was a response to legislation of the British Parliament providing a tax advantage for tea sold in the American colonies by the British East India Company. It remains the most iconic antitax symbol: ratifying the principle of "no taxation without representation" and helping trigger the American Revolution.[4] Attacking the tax collector—always a prominent feature of the antitax movement—also has a long history: Samuel Adams, frequently called the "Father of the American Revolution," was elected Boston tax collector before the revolution on a platform of not collecting taxes.[5]

During the nation's early years, antitax protests were sometimes violent. In 1786 and 1787, after America had secured its independence from Great Britain, armed Massachusetts rebels attempted to overthrow the state government because of its attempts to collect higher taxes than the British had. This uprising, known as Shays' Rebellion, is frequently credited with inducing the Constitutional Convention to create a stronger national government with the power to tax. In 1791 the Whiskey Rebellion—a violent protest against the first tax levied by the new federal government on a product produced domestically—began in western Pennsylvania and lasted for three years during George Washington's presidency. After concluding that tariffs on imported goods would not suffice, Alexander Hamilton decided taxing whiskey was essential to pay off the nation's Revolutionary War debts and to validate the new federal government's authority to tax. (The whiskey tax was repealed in 1801 after Thomas Jefferson became president.) In 1799 Pennsylvania Dutch farmers, in what became known as Fries's Rebellion, began an armed rebellion against a new federal tax on real estate and slaves to help pay for a naval war with France.[6] Like the Whiskey Rebellion, this protest was halted by the federal government, costing the Federalists support in Pennsylvania in the 1800 election.

The United States first enacted an income tax because the country needed the money to finance the Civil War after Treasury Secretary Salmon P. Chase told President Lincoln the Union government could not borrow enough money, a doleful truth that eluded the Confederacy until it was too late. After the war, the income tax was allowed to lapse. By 1893 when the federal government again moved to tax income, revenue needs no longer solely justified the tax. An income tax was viewed as necessary for economic justice in an industrializing nation. The 1893 income tax was struck down by the Supreme Court two years later, but in 1913 the nation overcame the difficulty of amending the Constitution to enact the Sixteenth Amendment, enabling the federal government to tax income.[7]

Before World War I and to a lesser extent after, the United States relied heavily on tariffs, taxes imposed on imported goods. Tariffs typically produce higher prices for imported and domestically produced goods that are subject to them, much like excise or retail sales taxes. After World War II until 2017, the United States (along with much of the rest of the world) decreased and eliminated tariffs to reduce barriers to international trade.

The modern income tax was initially limited to high-income Americans and corporations with the tax's scope and rates varying depending on the nation's need for revenues. When our nation faced massive challenges to finance World War II, Congress transformed the income tax from a class tax to one on the masses. Then, for the first time, our nation became full of income taxpayers. In 1939 fewer than four million Americans paid income tax, but by 1945 that number had increased tenfold to more than forty million people. By the time World War II ended, individual income taxes accounted for 40 percent of federal revenues, and corporate income taxes contributed another third. In the decades since, the individual income tax has remained the centerpiece of the federal tax system.

In 2021 more than half of all U.S. federal revenues were supplied by income taxes on individuals. About 9 percent came from the corporate income tax, which typically applies only to publicly traded businesses. (Unlike most countries, about half of U.S. business income is earned by partnerships and privately held companies, the income of which is taxed only to its owners.) Taxes on wages and earnings from self-employment finance Social Security, Medicare's hospital insurance, and unemployment insurance and accounted for another 31 percent. Together, these payroll and income taxes comprised more than 90 percent of the total. Excise taxes on the consumption of specified goods, such as fuels, alcohol, and tobacco, added another 2 percent, as did tariffs on imported goods. The estate and gift taxes—the only federal taxes on wealth, imposed when very rich people transfer their wealth by gift or at death—supplied only a fraction of 1 percent of federal receipts.[8]

Consumption taxes, such as retail sales taxes, are prevalent in states and localities, which also impose property taxes on real estate, automobiles, and sometimes securities. The United States relies much less heavily on consumption taxes than does the rest of the world. About 170 countries worldwide impose national value-added taxes (sometimes called goods and services taxes) on purchases of goods and services. These taxes are a type of sales tax with withholding required from producers and wholesalers so that collection does not depend solely on compliance by retailers. An income tax includes income whether saved or consumed, while a consumption tax exempts income people save.

Income taxes are typically imposed with progressive rates, which means the tax rate goes up as income increases. Consumption and wage taxes are typically levied at flat rates without any personal exemptions or thresholds, and are often regressive, which means they impose greater burdens on the poor than the rich, but flat-rate sales and value-added taxes can be made proportional to income. For a long time, Americans viewed the income tax as the fairest tax, but beginning in the 1970s, polling showed the public considered income taxes to be the least fair and approval of sales taxes rose.[9]

Distrust of Government

When the modern antitax movement began in 1978 with a property tax limitation referendum in California, economic and social conditions were ripe for a populist antitax movement. The economy was stagnant, inflation was raging, and American society was ripping apart. As the historian Dominic Sandbrook wrote, the "single most compelling theme of the 1970s" was the "notion of the virtuous citizen locked in battle against big government, big business, and a decadent elite."[10]

From the end of World War II until the mid-1970s, fortune smiled on the United States. The U.S. economy expanded for nearly a generation—fulfilling America's promise as a land of exceptional opportunity. For young (white) men back from the war, the government offered a free college education. Even unskilled workers without a college degree typically had good jobs that could last a lifetime or started small businesses with excellent chances of success given the coming years of robust, broadly distributed economic growth. One salary could finance a family's living expenses and frequently the purchase of a federally subsidized home.

Public and private institutions were strong. Public education provided a ladder up for white children nationwide. Unions represented more than a third of all private-sector workers—negotiating good wage and benefit packages and providing middle-class workers and their families an effective voice in federal and state legislatures. Churches and synagogues, along with other religious and secular civic organizations, offered substantial social supports. Having defeated Hitler in the war and enjoying the fruits of robust economic growth, Americans generally had confidence in their government and believed their children's lives would be better than their own.

This happy picture, of course, was dominated by the color white. In the South, Jim Crow ruled. Black Americans were ghettoized in American cities everywhere. Public schools rarely created economic opportunities for Black children.

Together, the civil rights revolution and the women's movement challenged long-standing social and political arrangements. Efforts by Black families to desegregate public schools met resistance across the country. White men were threatened by new competition for jobs from minority and women workers. Long-standing family arrangements suddenly became contested. Historian Ruth Rosen aptly titled her modern history of the women's movement *The World Split Open.*[11] President Lyndon Johnson asserted in his June 1965 commencement address at the historically Black Howard University, "You do not take a person who, for years, has been hobbled by chains and liberate him, bring him up to the starting line of a race and then say, 'you are free to compete with all the others,' and still justly believe that you have been completely fair," indicating his support for affirmative action.[12] While both movements achieved important progress, turmoil became palpable in the 1960s, and confidence in government eroded during the 1970s.

The 1970s was a hinge decade, a time of dramatic change. The era of individualism and isolation described by Harvard political scientist Robert

Putnam in his 2000 book *Bowling Alone* emerged in the 1970s.[13] The seeds of disquiet and distrust of government and other institutions planted in the 1960s blossomed in the 1970s, setting the agenda for much of what transpired over the rest of the twentieth century and well into the twenty-first—an effect well documented once the decade became a fit subject for historians.[14] The 1970s was a time of divisiveness and upheaval, a period of cultural clashes, racial division, and economic distress. The 1970s began, as historian Daniel T. Rodgers put it, a long "age of fracture" in America.[15]

Epic government failures, such as Watergate (along with corruption by other government officials), the disastrous Vietnam War, and illegal domestic intelligence operations by the CIA and FBI against antiwar protestors and other dissident groups, along with more common deficiencies, fueled disdain for and distrust of government that had been suppressed by more than two decades of postwar prosperity and U.S. global dominance.[16] Antigovernment skepticism pervaded the nation.

As World War II became more distant and the Vietnam War more costly and less popular, antitax sentiment grew. Tax increases to support widely accepted wars have long been supported by the American people, but public support for tax increases to fund controversial military ventures abroad or increases in domestic spending has been more difficult to muster.[17]

After Richard Nixon resigned the presidency in disgrace, Gerald Ford, a long-time Michigan congressman who replaced Spiro Agnew as vice president after Agnew pled nolo contendere to a felony charge of tax evasion and resigned, became the first vice president to become president without having been elected. On September 8, 1974, President Ford issued an unpopular, controversial "full, free and absolute" pardon of Nixon for any crimes he committed while in office.

Two months later, on November 5, 1974, Democrats won 49 seats in the House of Representatives, producing more than a two-thirds majority. Democrats also gained 4 Senate seats, giving them a 60-vote majority, and 4 governorships. Democrats mistook these victories as public endorsement of liberal government policies rather than the temporary repudiation of Republicans they were. Many Democrats failed to recognize that their New Deal coalition of blue-collar workers, racial minorities, white southerners, and urban intellectuals was disintegrating.

In his State of the Union Address on January 19, 1976, the beginning of the nation's bicentennial year, President Ford said, "We must introduce a new balance in the relationship between the individual and the government—a balance that favors greater individual freedom and self-reliance. . . . The Government must stop spending so much and stop borrowing so much of our money. More money must remain in private hands where it will do the most good. To hold down the cost of living, we must hold down the cost of government." He also called for about $10 billion in tax cuts in an effort to stimulate the economy.[18] Ford presided over a weak economy that had not fully recovered by January 1977, when Jimmy Carter, a former Georgia governor and "born-again" Christian, moved into the White House.

Stagflation

From 1973 through 1975, the United States experienced its most severe recession since the end of World War II. Unlike previous recessions, this downturn was accompanied by double-digit inflation that did not abate until the 1980s. The toxic mix of unemployment and inflation, known as "stagflation," was a major catalyst for the antitax movement and inculcated widespread beliefs that government no longer worked.

In his most feckless effort to battle inflation, President Ford urged Americans to wear "WIN" buttons, standing for "Whip Inflation Now." Alan Greenspan, Ford's chairman of the Council of Economic Advisers, later described this idea as "unbelievably stupid."[19] President Carter fared no better in his efforts to control inflation.

Making matters worse, productivity growth—the most important contributor to wage growth and rising standards of living, which had been strong for nearly thirty years following World War II—began to decline and disappeared for many workers by the end of the 1970s. Beliefs that the nation's economy would continue to expand robustly, producing many winners and few losers, vanished simultaneously.[20]

The unprecedented stagflation of the 1970s energized the antitax movement. Rising prices took more out of families' pockets, just as wages were flattening and job security disappearing. Income and property taxes made matters worse. As housing prices rose, so did property taxes, increasing costs for both homeowners and renters without providing corresponding benefits. Progressive income taxes increased as inflation pushed people into higher tax brackets even though their wages purchased fewer goods and services. Fixed dollar allowances for standard deductions and personal exemptions became less valuable as the dollar's purchasing power declined. Inflation also overtaxes investment income when it measures current year's income by subtracting historical costs from current receipts, such as with capital gains. Inflation makes people appear richer to property and income taxes than they actually are.

In 1980 MIT economist Lester Thurow published a gloomy bestseller, *The Zero-Sum Society*, relating the nation's economic decline during the 1970s. Thurow emphasized the slippage in U.S. standards of living relative to the rest of the world and observed how such a decline engendered dissatisfaction with government. He rejected the "hard-core conservative solution" of deregulation, cuts in "social expenditures," and tax cuts for "those who save, the rich." Any solution to the nation's economic ills, he wrote, "requires that some large group . . . be willing to tolerate a large reduction in their real standard of living." The United States, Thurow contended, had entered a "zero-sum game," where the stakes are over the distribution of costs and benefits, and each group wants government to protect it from losses and push costs onto others.[21]

The time was ripe for an antitax movement. Economic challenges and insecurities, however, were not the only disruptions confronting the United States. Social and cultural turmoil also helped incite antitax fervor. Contrary to common views, taxation is not solely about economics: cultural values are also at stake. In the 1970s, racial conflict was manifest.

An American Dilemma

In 1938 Swedish Nobel Laureate in economics Gunnar Myrdal undertook a comprehensive study of social and economic problems of African Americans in the United States, famously leading him to describe race relations as "An American Dilemma."[22] Over nearly 1,500 pages Myrdal and his colleagues detailed "an ever-raging conflict" between the "American Creed" of "national and Christian precepts"—including belief that all people are created equal and a commitment to equality of opportunity—and personal and local economic and social interests limiting the education of Black children and job opportunities of Black workers, a conflict that persists.[23] Racial divisions played an important role in advancing the modern antitax movement. This was not new.

The Constitution's constraints on federal taxation were shaped in part by political compromises over how slaves should be counted in determining the size of the population for representation in Congress. The absence of federal taxing power under the Articles of Confederation, which preceded the Constitutional Convention, rendered the national government helpless when the states ignored the Continental Congress's requests for revenue.[24] To correct that shortcoming, the Constitution grants Congress the power "to lay and collect Taxes, Duties, Imposts and Excises" so long as all "Duties, Imposts and Excises shall be uniform throughout the United States."[25] The Constitution also requires any "Capitation, or other direct Tax" to be apportioned among the states based on population.[26] The phrase "other direct tax" is not defined in the Constitution but clearly includes taxes on land.[27] Slaveholding and racial prejudice were important components of arguments on behalf of strong "states' rights" and a weak national government. The limitation on direct taxes was part of the Constitution's original three-fifths compromise over slavery, which determined how slaves should be counted in apportioning seats in the House of Representatives and how capitation or other direct taxes were to be distributed among the states.[28]

After the Civil War, rising public expenditures in the South by new biracial governments responding to the expansion in the number of free citizens demanding public services, such as public education, hospitals, railroad construction, and law enforcement, required rising taxes to finance substantial growth in the costs of government. The increasing tax burdens, in turn, inflamed white opposition, exacerbated by falling property values, especially when they weakened plantations and promoted Black ownership. Rising taxes, especially property taxes, became a rallying cry for Reconstruction's opponents.[29]

Beginning in the 1890s, poll taxes were used to keep African Americans from voting. Some poor whites were exempted from these taxes if they had an ancestor who voted before the Civil War. Not until 1964 did the Twenty-Fourth Amendment to the Constitution prohibit poll taxes for federal elections. In 1966 the Supreme Court struck down the remaining poll taxes used by some southern states for state elections.[30] Jim Crow and ongoing racial animus also elicited calls for strong states' rights and a weak national government. Racial conflicts have long played a central role in American tax politics and policy.

Support for taxes to pay for social insurance, including to alleviate poverty, is lower when nations are more racially heterogeneous. Racial animosity makes paying for redistribution to the poor, who are disproportionately Black in the United States, objectionable for many voters.[31] Beginning in the mid-1960s, the U.S. population became even more heterogeneous due to changes in immigration policies. By the 1970s conflicts over race were conspicuous.

In 1954, in *Brown v. Board of Education*, the Supreme Court issued perhaps its most important decision of the twentieth century—requiring desegregation of public schools in America. Federal appellate judge J. Harvie Wilkinson captured its momentousness, writing, "Its greatness lay in the enormity of injustice it condemned, in the entrenched sentiment it challenged, in the immensity of how it both created and overthrew."[32] But the Court underestimated the intransigence of school segregation.

It took until May 1968, fourteen years after the *Brown* decision and a month after Martin Luther King's assassination, before the Court ruled delays in desegregating schools were "no longer tolerable."[33] Three years later, the Court approved busing students as the main method for integrating schools.[34] Public opposition to busing for desegregation intensified, producing violent clashes in cities across America and exacerbating anger of working-class whites toward poor Blacks. The transformation of the composition of public schools fueled antipathy to property taxes, the main source for financing public schools, and for income taxes paying for other government expenditures, especially welfare.

Concurrently, the Immigration and Naturalization Act of 1965 added fuel to the anti-property-tax and anti-income-tax fires by transforming immigration into the United States. From the 1920s until 1965, the United States based immigration quotas on national origin, favoring immigrants from northern and western Europe. The 1965 legislation made unification of families an immigration priority. Massachusetts senator Edward Kennedy, a strong supporter of the changes, assured his Senate colleagues that immigration would remain "substantially the same" and the "ethnic mix of this country will not be upset."[35] But that did not happen.

In the 1950s more than 70 percent of U.S. immigrants came from Canada and Europe, but by the 1980s immigration from these regions had dropped to 11 percent. More than 85 percent came from Latin America, the Caribbean, and Asia. By the late 1970s, particularly in southwestern states, Latino children of immigrants were flooding into public schools.[36] The new immigration law changed the composition of public schools and the workforce, fomenting anti-immigrant, antigovernment, and antitax attitudes that profoundly affected the nation's tax policies and politics.[37]

Simultaneously, efforts by colleges and universities to admit African Americans and other minority students fomented further discord, intensifying antigovernment sentiments. Affirmative action in admissions by colleges and universities and by employers—initially for African Americans and expanded in the 1970s to include Native Americans, Puerto Ricans, Mexican Americans, and some Asian Americans—splintered the nation. Many white Americans came to believe that others were "cutting in line" and blamed the government.[38] They did not want to pay taxes to finance expanding public benefits for Black or Latino people or the salaries of government workers distributing them.

Government Spending on the Poor

President Lyndon Johnson pushed the 1964 Civil Rights Act and the 1965 Immigration Act through Congress. In Johnson's "war on poverty" and "Great Society" programs, Congress during the 1960s also greatly expanded government spending on the poor and elderly, through Medicaid, Medicare, food stamps, housing, education, and welfare. This induced backlash from middle-class whites who believed most of the money was going to poor urban African Americans and Latinos. Although the majority of spending on welfare, food stamps, and subsidized housing assistance went to whites, these minorities, whose median family income was less than 60 percent that of whites and were disparately poor and unemployed, received a disproportionate share of these benefits.[39] Resentment over paying taxes to support growing transfers to the poor grew as inflation eroded paychecks' values and the economy struggled during the 1970s.

In his 1976 presidential campaign, Ronald Reagan famously complained at nearly every stop of a "welfare queen" with "80 names, 30 addresses, and 12 Social Security cards" who drove a Cadillac and was collecting "veterans' benefits on four nonexistent deceased husbands," along with Social Security, Medicaid, food stamps, and welfare "under each of her names." Reagan said, "Her tax-free cash income alone is over $150,000." He continued speaking about this woman during the next four years in his popular radio shows and in his successful 1980 campaign for president.[40] Reagan never mentioned the recipient's race, but his diatribes intensified anti-poor, antigovernment, and anti-Black sentiment, reinforcing widespread views that government spending on the poor was riddled with fraud and abuse. No one had volunteered to pay higher taxes to support crooked "welfare queens."

Few foresaw the political toxicity of the combination of a massive increase in Latino immigration and the expansion of civil rights for African Americans. One who did was Kevin Phillips, a young, controversial, Republican strategist. In his 1969 book, *The Emerging Republican Majority*, Phillips predicted much of what happened. "All the talk about Republicans making inroads into the Negro vote is persiflage," Phillips said. "The more Negroes who register as Democrats in the South, the sooner the Negrophobe whites will quit the

Democrats and become Republicans. That's where the voters are." Phillips concluded, "for a long time, the liberal-conservative split was on economic issues. That favored the Democrats until the focus shifted from programs which taxed the few for the many to things like 'welfare' that taxed the many for the few."[41]

In a 1981 interview with Alexander Lamis, a political scientist from Case Western Reserve University, Lee Atwater, a notoriously brutal Republican political strategist from South Carolina working in Reagan's White House, dispelled any doubts about the relationship of the antitax movement to racial resentment. Here's what Atwater said:

> You start out in 1954 by saying [the n-word three times]. By 1968 you can't say [the n-word] . . . so you say stuff like forced busing, states' rights, and all that stuff and you're getting so abstract. Now, you're talking about cutting taxes and all these things you're talking about are totally economic things and a byproduct of them is blacks get hurt worse than whites . . . "we want to cut this," is much more abstract than even the busing thing, and a hell of a lot more abstract than "[the n-word twice]."[42]

Social Upheaval

Racial resentment was not the only division among Americans in the late 1970s. Books and movies that would have been banned as obscene became commonplace. Attitudes and arrangements concerning sex were changing; by the late 1970s so many unmarried couples were living together that the Census Bureau coined the designation "POSSLQ" for persons of opposite sex sharing living quarters.[43] Efforts to secure rights for same-sex couples moved into the mainstream. Religious conservatives and their allies saw their "family values" being threatened. Each of these generated antigovernment political engagement from the right.

The women's movement produced distinct enmity toward the income tax. Although the Equal Rights Amendment (ERA) never made it into the Constitution, the 1964 Civil Rights Act prohibited employment discrimination against women, and during the 1970s the Supreme Court extended constitutional rights to women in a series of decisions that some legal scholars called a "de facto ERA."[44]

The income tax has long struggled with how to tax married couples. From its inception in 1913 until World War II, when the tax was transformed from a tax on the rich into a tax on the masses, income tax turned on each individual's income without regard to marital status. Because of the progressive rate schedule, this meant married couples with the same income would often pay very different taxes—more if most of the income belonged to one spouse, as was most often the case, less whenever the spouses' incomes were more equal.

In 1948 Congress adopted joint returns, which allowed married couples to treat their separate incomes as if equal and pay twice the tax that a single person would pay on one-half the couples' total income. This is the most advantageous division of income with progressive rates, and it provided great benefits to married couples. But it meant two single people might pay much greater taxes than a married couple with the same income. In the late 1960s, Vivien Kellems, an unmarried, successful Connecticut businesswoman, inspired thousands of Americans to mail teabags to their representatives in Congress to protest what she regarded as the excessive taxation of single people—and remind senators and congressmen of the Boston Tea Party.

In 1969 Congress narrowed the gap for singles but in the process created "marriage penalties" for married couples earning roughly equal incomes.[45] This prompted some couples to postpone marrying and impelled some married couples to divorce to save income taxes.[46] In the early 1970s, when marriage penalties first occurred, they happened infrequently, but as women's employment opportunities expanded and married couples with more equal incomes became common, the number of married couples facing income tax penalties grew. Between 1981 and 2017, Congress frequently changed the income tax treatment of married couples, often endeavoring to reduce penalties on marrying.

Single people and married couples who suffered tax disadvantages were frequently angry about their treatment under progressive income taxes. After singles got relief from Congress, one married couple divorced during Caribbean vacations each December in the late 1970s and remarried the beginning of the next year to avoid the income tax marriage penalties. The *Washington Post* called them "contemporary American heroes." In 1980 one member of the couple told a congressional tax committee, "In America today the fastest ways to become a national hero are to hit a home run in the World Series or to fight the IRS."[47]

Additionally, when not permitted to marry, wealthy same-sex couples faced substantially larger estate taxes than married couples. In 2015 the Supreme Court, in a challenge to the estate tax disadvantage, concluded that prohibiting same-sex marriages was unconstitutional.[48]

The tax law is laden with fundamental cultural, social, economic, and political judgments. For example, the income tax favors homeowners over renters, promotes charitable gifts over family transfers, and provides substantial benefits for savings for higher education or retirement. The tax also advantages certain forms of business organizations over others and frequently rewards specified investments, such as for real estate. Individual income tax rates are lower for capital gains and dividends than for wages. Alcohol excise taxes favor wine drinkers over beer drinkers, and both over people who sip whiskey. These political choices please some people and foment antitax attitudes in others.

Clashing Interests and Ideologies

For the antitax movement to succeed, public support would not suffice. Although some states allow referendums, changing the tax law usually requires mustering a legislative majority and securing support from the president or relevant governor.

In his 1927 presidential address to the American Economic Association, the economist Thomas Sewall Adams, who served as the Treasury Department's principal advisor on tax policy and its spokesman before Congress on tax legislation from 1917 until 1923, said, "Modern taxation or tax-making . . . is a group contest in which powerful interests vigorously endeavor to rid themselves of present or proposed tax burdens. It is . . . a hard game in which he who trusts wholly to economics, reason, and justice, will in the end retire beaten and disillusioned."[49] His description remains apt a century later.

Achieving legislative success is not an evenhanded exercise.[50] Money to organize meetings, produce favorable polls, generate supporting research by friendly experts, and contribute to political campaigns is more readily available to those who want to reduce their taxes than it is to their opponents. Politicians are more responsive to their wealthy constituents.[51] Constitutional decisions treat money in politics as equivalent to speech and protected under the First Amendment even when political contributions create the potential for corruption.[52] A constitutional amendment restricting campaign contributions and spending, however, would not eliminate the advantage of monied interests in legislatures: lobbying, creating data and arguments, publicizing them, and presenting them to legislators will always be constitutionally protected speech. Unsurprisingly, the hallways outside the tax-writing committees' rooms became known as "Gucci Gulch."[53]

The decline of private-s 𝑒 𝑐tor labor unions also shifted political power in federal and state legislatures toward high-income contributors and business owners and away from middle-class workers—who have never found a substitute to argue effectively for their economic interests.

During the 1970s, businesses became more active, better coordinated, more powerful, and more effective at mobilizing support for their legislative agendas. Business political action committees (PACs) began to greatly increase their contributions to congressional candidates.[54] In 1974, large businesses organized the Business Roundtable, an organization of CEOs of about two hundred of the largest U.S. businesses, enhancing their ability to coordinate access to Congress. The National Federation of Independent Businesses (NFIB), founded in 1943 as the legislative advocate for small businesses, became one of Washington's most powerful lobbying groups. Like the Chamber of Commerce and the National Association of Manufacturers, it is able to generate thousands of phone calls and emails to members of Congress overnight.

In the tax arena, businesses typically lobby for rate cuts or tax breaks for particular industries. In a 2013 analysis of the long decline in the social responsibility of corporate leaders, University of Michigan sociologist Mark Mizruchi wrote that the "corporate elite" contributed "to an extremism in politics that the country has not seen in a century" and "retreated into narrow self-interest."[55]

Important as they are, arguments based solely on self-interest often fail in distributional politics. Moral and ideological commitments play an essential role in motivating legislators and holding coalitions together. As the Washington tax lawyer Louis Eisenstein wrote in *The Ideologies of Taxation*, advocates for tax changes need to "convey a vital sense of some immutable principle that rises majestically above partisan preferences."[56]

In *The Great Tax Wars*, the journalist Steven Weisman describes the struggles leading up to the 1913 constitutional amendment permitting income taxation as a battle between proponents of "justice" on one side and "virtue" on the other, with advocates for the former insisting "it is fair for society to tax income at graduated rates, according to ability to pay, because of a need to establish some level of social equity and to curb the power of great wealth over government." Champions on the other side countered that allowing citizens to keep the wealth they earned is vital to the spirit of free enterprise. Income tax opponents insisted that "taxing wealth wrecks the incentives that have fueled the engine of American prosperity."[57] This debate has never ceased, although the two sides revised their language, typically by substituting "fair-ness" for "justice" and "economic efficiency" and "economic growth" for "virtue."

One common thread among many antitax elites is their admiration for Ayn Rand—and in the case of the influential economist Alan Greenspan, a close friendship with her. Her widely read novels, *The Fountainhead* (1943) and *Atlas Shrugged* (1957), are paeans to individualism and self-interest; celebrations of capitalism, especially entrepreneurs; and portraits of government as inevitably destructive of individual initiative and freedom. Rand's ideas inspired "an ideological explosion on the right" and greatly influenced numerous powerful Republican conservatives. As her biographer, the historian Jennifer Burns, observed, "for over half a century Rand has been the ultimate gateway drug to life on the right."[58] Her novels have sold more than thirty million copies; thirty years after her death they continued to sell a million or more annually.

The Harvard political philosopher Robert Nozick reached fewer public readers and policymakers, but he was widely read in academic circles and important to some antitax advocates. His 1974 book, *Anarchy, State, and Utopia*, offered a sophisticated counterargument to his Harvard colleague John Rawls's momentous *A Theory of Justice*, published three years earlier.[59] Rawls prioritized liberty but argued that inequalities should be permitted only if they benefit the worst off in society. Nozick, a committed antigovernment libertarian, claimed "the minimal state is the most extensive state that can be justified."[60] Nozick's ideal state is one that protects only against force, theft, and fraud and enforces voluntary contracts. He insisted that taxation is equivalent to slavery, writing that "taxation of earnings from labor is on a par with forced labor."[61] He maintained that taxing a person on their labor income is equivalent to forcing someone to work. Nozick's arguments are consistent with attacks on progressive taxation as discriminating against the wealthy by the influential Austrian economist Friedrich Hayek, but Nozick goes further, opposing any taxation of labor income. Nozick's book won the 1975 National Book Award in Philosophy and Religion and was named by the *London Times* one of "The Hundred Most Influential Books since the Second World War" and one of the fifteen most influential of the 1970s.[62]

In the legislative process, the philosophical propositions of writers like Rand and Nozick typically are offered as assertions that tax cuts are necessary to advance or preserve freedom, bolstered by claims they will produce desir-able economic results and be good for the country. The latter contentions are typically grounded in economic analyses insisting tax reductions will enlarge the economy, stimulate productive investments, and produce more jobs and higher wages. Economists advancing such claims are frequently from business coalitions, think tanks, or universities.

Policy-oriented research institutions have long played important roles in advancing antitax agendas. Until the 1970s, Washington think tanks mostly leaned left, but beginning in the 1970s, conservatives changed this profile. Between 1976 and 1995, almost twice as many conservative think tanks emerged as liberal ones.[63] With a few exceptions, conservative think tanks are better funded than liberal ones—and generally have been more effective in Congress. In 1973 conservative Republicans Paul Weyrich and Edwin Feulner founded the Heritage Foundation with funds from ultraconservative millionaires Richard Mellon Scaife and Joseph Coors. In an understatement, *The Economist* described Weyrich as "one of the conservative movement's more vigorous thinkers." Weyrich was not as modest, insisting, "we are radicals, working to overturn the present power structure of this country."[64] From 1981 when Ronald Reagan became president until 2017 when Donald Trump took office, Heritage was the most important activist right-wing think tank.

In 1977 Kansas billionaire Charles Koch founded and funded the libertarian CATO Institute, led by the former National Libertarian Party chair Edward Crane. While substantially smaller than Heritage, CATO has long been an important tentacle of a group of right-wing organizations constituting what is now frequently called the "Kochtopus."

Other conservative organizations, such as the American Enterprise Institute, California's Hoover Institution, and the American Council for Capital Formation, also played large roles in the antitax movement beginning in the late 1970s.

Which Taxes Have Been Targeted?

Virtually any product or transaction can be taxed, and politicians enjoy great discretion over whom and what to tax. The tax law is tortuous in its complexity, and tax-policy debates and changes are often cloaked with misdirection. This allows legislatures to provide special benefits or burdens and produce unfairness and economic waste, all of which may bolster antitax sentiments.

The distribution of income in the United States has grown much more unequal since the 1970s as increasing shares of wages have gone to highly educated and skilled workers at the top. Changes in family composition have also contributed to inequality, as affluent single people have become more likely to marry one another and single-parent households have grown, especially among parents with only a high school education. Wealth is even more skewed toward the top than income. The wealthiest 10 percent of U.S. households own nearly three-fourths of the nation's wealth, while the bottom half of the population owns just 1 or 2 percent.[65]

Antitax advocates have not treated all taxes as equally important to attack. Nor are the gains from winning equivalent. As discussed above, businesses and wealthy individuals enjoy important advantages in the legislative process. This increases the vulnerability of taxes they pay: individual income taxes at the top, the corporate income tax, and taxes on property and wealth have been the most vulnerable antitax targets. Eliminating or greatly reducing the only national tax on wealth, the estate and gift tax, has been a conspicuous goal of antitax advocates.

———

The first major success of the modern antitax movement occurred in June 1978 with a referendum to cut property taxes and limit their future growth. The movement soon enjoyed additional successes in other states, then began to reduce federal income and estate taxes. Opposition to any and all tax increases and ongoing support of tax cuts became the indispensable cornerstone of the Republican Party's economic policy—no matter the economic circumstances or the government's financial condition. Democrats began collaborating with the antitax movement, then fundamentally surrendered. The story of how that happened begins in California.

Part I

Takeoff

1978–1981

Chapter 2

A Political Earthquake

That sound roaring out of the West—what was it? A California earthquake?
A Pacific tidal wave threatening to sweep across the country? Literally, it was
neither; figuratively, it was both. That angry noise was the sound of a middle
class tax revolt erupting, and its tremors are shaking public officials from
Sacramento to Washington, D.C. Suddenly all kinds of candidates in election
year 1978 are joining the chorus of seductive anti-tax sentiment, assailing high
taxes, inflation and government spending.

—*TIME*, JUNE 19, 1978

June 6, 1978, seemed like any other day that month in Los Angeles with the
gloomy cloud cover slowly breaking up in late morning leading to another
sunny, if surprisingly humid, day. But that day California voters triggered a
political earthquake, enacting by a 63 to 34 percent margin Proposition 13, a
constitutional limitation on the state's property taxes: 4,300,000 voters supported Proposition 13 with only 2,300,000 opposed, despite efforts to kill it by
Governor Jerry Brown, most of the state's political leaders, the League of
Women Voters, labor unions, and many large businesses, including Bank of
America, the state's utility companies, and the majority of California's major
newspapers.[1]

Proposition 13 amended the California constitution to constrain the financing of state and local governments. First, it limited local property taxes to
1 percent of the property's assessed valuation and rolled back assessed property values to their 1975–76 levels. Second, it limited increases in property tax
assessments to 2 percent a year, except on a sale when property could be re-
valued at market value for property tax purposes. Finally, Proposition 13

required a two-thirds vote by the state legislature to create or raise any state or local taxes.

Proposition 13 saved California businesses and homeowners—and cost the state and local governments—$228 billion in the decade that followed, half a trillion dollars by the turn of the century. California's largest businesses saved millions: the next year Pacific Telephone saved $130 million, Pacific Gas and Electric more than $90 million; California Edison, nearly $54 million; Standard Oil, more than $13 million in one county alone.[2] Homeowners received less than a quarter of the total taxes saved despite supplying most of the votes. People who owned the most expensive homes saved the most: residents of Beverly Hills, Bel Air, and Malibu in Los Angeles; San Francisco (and later Silicon Valley) in Northern California. Property taxes on average homes were immediately reduced by about 60 percent, saving middle-class homeowners hundreds and the rich thousands of dollars each year.[3] Warren Buffett bought his Laguna Hills, California, beach house in 1971 for $150,000; in 2003 when the house was worth $4 million, his property taxes were just $2,264.[4] In 2018, he sold the house for $7.5 million. Many homeowners enjoyed lower property taxes for decades due to Proposition 13, notwithstanding large boosts in their homes' values.

Proposition 13's proponents promised landlords would pass their tax savings on to their tenants by lowering rents, but that did not happen. Proposition 13 benefited homeowners and landlords but typically not tenants. In about a dozen cities, such as Santa Monica, the backlash from renters produced stringent rent controls, limiting rents to below-market levels, but across most of the state, renters failed to obtain the tax benefits homeowners enjoyed.[5] Renters are not only poorer than homeowners: they are disproportionately people of color. Nor did business owners, who saved many millions in property taxes annually from Proposition 13, cut prices. As the journalist Robert Kuttner, author of the most influential book on Proposition 13, concluded: the "distributional consequences of Proposition 13 mark it as a striking bonanza for the haves."[6]

Proposition 13 mobilized the modern antitax movement. Pat Caddell, President Jimmy Carter's pollster, described Proposition 13 as not just a tax revolt but "a revolution against government." *Newsweek*'s Meg Greenfield wrote that it heralded a national conservative movement just as the New Deal had launched big government. Ronald Reagan dubbed Proposition 13 a second American Revolution, insisting it was "a little bit like dumping those cases of tea off the boat in Boston harbor."[7]

An Unlikely Populist

Proposition 13 was the brainchild of the indefatigable Howard Jarvis, a cantankerous, cigar-chomping, jowly, seventy-five-year-old, right-wing Republican. Its enactment made him the hero of 13 and "the messiah of an American tax revolt."[8] Jarvis described the vote for 13 as "a revolution with fountain pens rather than rifles."[9]

"Crazy Howard Jarvis," as he was known in Southern California, was an improbable revolutionary. He had grown up in Magna, Utah, a tiny town nearly twenty miles west of Salt Lake City, milking cows, shooting hogs, and cutting the heads off chickens on his family's farm. Jarvis was battle-tested: he was a young boxer in twenty-one professional bouts in Utah and sparred with Jack Dempsey, the legendary heavyweight champion of the 1920s—good preparation for his battles to remake California and American politics.[10] At age seventy-five, people still described him as pugnacious.

Jarvis's fascination with politics came naturally: his father, a Democrat, had been the county treasurer and then a judge. Howard Jarvis studied law at the University of Utah while working nights at the local copper mill but decided the law "wasn't for me."[11] In 1925 he bought the local newspaper, the *Magna Times*, and within five years he owned five small-town Utah papers with a total circulation of about thirty thousand. All the papers reported the same stories, rearranged and with different headlines. Jarvis soon became president of the Utah State Press Association and the Young Republicans of Salt Lake City. He served briefly as the "press man" on Herbert Hoover's 1932 campaign train. Hoover carried only six states. Howard Jarvis fared no better in his campaign as a Republican that year for state representative. He lost to his father.

In 1935 Howard Jarvis moved to Hollywood—he claimed at the urging of Earl Warren—where he began dabbling in real estate, manufacturing, and Republican politics. He led the Los Angeles County Republican Assembly, chaired the local speakers' bureau, and served as Republican precinct chairman for Los Angeles County.

Soon after the Japanese bombed Pearl Harbor, the U.S. government confiscated all the latex of Jarvis's rubber padding plant near downtown Los Angeles for the war effort, putting him out of business. The government never used the latex and took several years to compensate Jarvis for commandeering it. That triggered his future as an antigovernment activist. A subsequent confrontation with a union boss turned him against unions with similar fervor. An angry dispute with the IRS over the amount of his business taxes added the tax collector to Jarvis's shitlist. Nearly two decades later when the Supreme Court decided against him in a patent case involving his claim to have invented push-button radios, his antigovernment dogmatism hardened.[12]

By the time he sold his last manufacturing businesses—a chain of home appliance factories—Jarvis had accumulated a small fortune. He retired from business and ran for the Republican Senate nomination in 1962, finishing a distant third. He fared no better in two subsequent attempts at elective office.[13] He then founded his own Conservative Party, which soon dissolved. He also started a local anti-union right-to-work committee, and became a member of the national board of the Liberty Amendment Committee, a right-wing group urging repeal of the federal income and estate and gift taxes. Before Proposition 13, Howard Jarvis was never taken seriously in California politics.

By all accounts but his own, Jarvis used his political dabbling to line his pockets. In 1964 he and two associates set up an "independent" Los Angeles Campaign Committee called Businessmen for Goldwater. The committee raised $115,000, but none of that money ever reached the Goldwater campaign. After Goldwater and his allies sued to shut the operation down, Jarvis's group disbanded. A decade later, Jarvis and a colleague created a similar scam ostensibly to raise funds for the successful Senate campaign of S. I. Hayakawa. Once Hayakawa discovered his campaign had not gotten any of the $60,000 they raised, Hayakawa sued, and Jarvis's organization again quietly shut down. *Washington Post* muckraker Jack Anderson uncovered a similar Jarvis scam in Arizona where his anti-union effort mimicked the National Right to Work Committee. Jarvis dismissed the allegations as "manure."[14]

In the mid-1960s, after his failures at electoral politics, Jarvis assembled a group of Los Angeles antitax protesters and formed the United Organization of Taxpayers, which experienced a decade of failed efforts. In 1968 and again in 1971, Jarvis and his organization failed to gather enough petition signatures to qualify for a statewide tax-limitation referendum. Having noticed his vehement opposition to property taxes, the Los Angeles Apartment Owners Association hired Jarvis as its executive director in 1972. The *Los Angeles Times* in the early 1970s described Jarvis as "the chief spokesman for a large group of disgruntled California property owners who are convinced simply that they pay too much of the costs of government."[15]

In 1973 Jarvis and his United Organization of Taxpayers supported Governor Ronald Reagan's Proposition 1, an initiative to reduce the state's income taxes by 7.5 percent and over a fifteen-year period to limit the total percentage of income that the state could tax, except for future tax increases ratified by

Howard Jarvis rallying the vote for Proposition 13.

public referendums. Proposition 1 garnered almost two million votes but was defeated 54 to 46 percent. Governor Reagan attributed this loss to its opponents' "false claim that it would increase, not reduce, taxes." He predicted limiting the government's tax take "will become a reality." That idea must prevail, Reagan continued, "because if it does not, the free society we have known for two hundred years, the ideal of a government by consent of the governed, will simply cease to exist."[16]

On June 6, 1978, Howard Jarvis succeeded where Reagan had failed. Jarvis started the day with his usual morning drink: a mixture of apple and cranberry juice. He then went for a haircut, looking forward to an ebullient night before the television cameras, and began polishing the victory speech he expected to give.[17] That night in the ballroom of the Biltmore Hotel, Howard Jarvis shouted to his fans: "Now we know how it felt when we dumped tea in Boston harbor." Later he said, "We have a new revolution. We are telling the government, 'screw you.'"[18] After the enactment of Proposition 13, *Time* magazine featured a fist-clenched, shouting Howard Jarvis on its cover with "Tax Revolt!" emblazoned in large yellow type over his suit and tie. Jarvis began traveling the country preaching his antitax creed.

Housing Inflation

In the mid-1960s, housing prices in California increased by 2 to 3 percent a year, as they did throughout the country. By 1976 they were rising 2 to 3 percent *a month*. During the late 1970s housing prices doubled and, in many cases, doubled again, along with soaring property tax bills. Between 1974 and 1978, the average price of a single-family home in Los Angeles rose from $37,800 to $83,000, an increase of 120 percent, compared to 48 percent nationally. Further south in Orange County, homes for less than $100,000 became nearly impossible to find.[19] The astounding inflation in California home prices in the 1970s, particularly in Southern California, spurred the vote for 13. Housing prices were rising so rapidly that homeowners were simultaneously bragging about their newfound wealth and complaining about accelerating property taxes.

The spike in housing prices made many a real estate speculator rich, but for homeowners living and working in booming California cities, rising housing prices meant only increasing property taxes. Their homes were no nicer or larger. Elderly homeowners and others living on fixed incomes became fearful ongoing property tax increases might cause them to lose their homes. City and county revenues were going up, but homeowners did not believe their government's services were improving. The doubling and tripling of property taxes due to the unprecedented surge in California housing values undoubtedly propelled the success of 13. Princeton political scientist Martin Gilens cites Proposition 13 as an important exception to his judgment that "most people, most of the time, do not base their political preferences on calculations of self-interest."[20] But inflation was not the only incitement for 13.

Corruption and Inequities

Homeowners were also repulsed by the lingering stench from corrupt property tax assessors. In the 1960s, assessors from San Francisco and Alameda County (across the Bay Bridge from San Francisco) responsible for valuing property for local tax purposes were imprisoned for taking campaign contributions and bribes in exchange for reduced property valuations. In Los Angeles County, the property tax assessor was indicted but not convicted. A crooked San Diego assessor died by suicide.[21] Revelations of businesses' bribes of tax assessors demolished public confidence in the fairness of their property tax determinations.

In response the California legislature passed AB80, the Assessment Reform Act of 1966, which required all property to be assessed at 25 percent of its market value as periodically redetermined. Even with bribes, assessors had been valuing business property at higher percentages of their value than homes. As a result, this "reform" shifted about $500 million in property tax burdens from businesses to homeowners.[22] After homeowners squealed, the California legislature in 1968 adopted a homeowners' exemption, which it increased substantially in 1972. This meant that most of the tax shifts to homeowners under AB80 were postponed until the mid-1970s—just when housing prices began to spike. In the years leading up to the vote for 13, bumper stickers in San Francisco urged: "Bring back the crooked assessor."[23]

Proposition 13 did not produce evenhanded property tax assessments: instead it produced large disparities in property taxes among neighbors. If you owned your home in 1978 and did not sell it, your property tax was based on its value in 1975 or 1976 and its value could be increased for property tax purposes only by 2 percent a year. But California home prices increased much faster than that, and assessments for property taxes are adjusted to market value whenever homes are sold. Neighbors pay radically different property taxes depending on when they bought their homes. On the west side of Los Angeles or in San Francisco, it became common for long-time homeowners to pay property taxes based on 2 percent increases from a 1975 valuation of around $60,000, while the family next door paid taxes based on the millions of dollars they recently spent to buy their home. The *San Francisco Examiner* in 1990 described two neighboring suburban homes of the same quality and size built in 1963. The original owners of one paid $742 in property taxes while their neighbors, who had bought their home in 1986, paid $3,280.[24] Between 1980 and 2018, median home prices in California increased sevenfold. Even with Proposition 13's ceiling of 1 percent of value, the differences in tax burdens are very large.[25]

Howard Jarvis and his wife enjoyed an immediate property tax reduction on their West Los Angeles home, assessed at $80,000 in 1976.[26] He died in 1986, and his widow, Estelle Jarvis, died in the home twenty years later. Proposition 13 limited their property tax increases for nearly three decades. Warren

Buffett bought his Laguna beach house in 1971. His property taxes on what became a multimillion-dollar second home were low despite its value and his wealth—a fraction of the taxes on the beach house next door.[27] In 1992 the 44 percent of California homeowners who owned their homes since 1975 were paying less than a quarter of the state's residential property taxes. The U.S. Supreme Court upheld the disparate treatment, even though it might "frustrate the 'American Dream' of home ownership for many younger and poorer families."[28] Beneficiaries of the disparities were disproportionately white and newcomers disproportionately Latino and Asian.

Similar differences among California businesses, benefiting long-time owners over new competitors, make even less sense. The California Supreme Court agreed to hear a case challenging these distinctions brought by Macy's of California, but after Jarvis's group and other Proposition 13 advocates threatened boycotts and Macy's had thousands of credit cards canceled, the company dropped the lawsuit.[29] Disneyland is still taxed based on its value in the 1970s.

Race and Immigration

The United States is unique in its heavy reliance on local property taxes to fund public schools. In 1971 the California Supreme Court decided the state's reliance on property taxes for public school finance violated both the state and federal constitutions because the schools' resources depended on the wealth of the residents of the local school district.[30] In a momentous 1973 decision, however, the U.S. Supreme Court concluded there is no federal constitutional right to education and socioeconomic disadvantages in education do not violate the federal constitution—even though there is no way for parents in poor school districts to levy property taxes sufficient to finance an education close to the quality in wealthier districts.[31]

Undeterred by the federal decision, in December 1976 the California Supreme Court, which had not yet fashioned a remedy for the state constitutional violation, required California's legislature to ensure the combination of state and local spending per pupil for public education not vary by more than $100 across the state.[32] This requirement was the most stringent in the nation: most states required only adequate educational funding, not equality. The following year Governor Jerry Brown signed legislation to take effect in July 1978 that limited wealthy districts' school spending and transferred a portion of wealthy districts' property tax revenues to the state treasury for redistribution to poorer districts.[33]

This infuriated wealthier homeowners, many of whom had purchased their homes to take advantage of well-funded high-quality schools in their neighborhoods. They lost their very large edge in funding their children's public education, and, adding insult to injury, their homes lost value. Many state courts elsewhere concluded financing public schools with local property taxes violated the state's constitutional guarantees of a right to education and equal protection but were less aggressive than California in redistributing revenues from wealthy to poor school districts.

Dartmouth economics professor William Fischel attributes Proposition 13's success to the dramatic changes in California's school financing, speculating that if the California court had left property tax financing of public schools alone, as the New York Court of Appeals and the Supreme Court did, "Proposition 13 might not have passed."[34] That is likely an overstatement, but the California Supreme Court's school finance decisions and the legislature's response surely incited many wealthy homeowners to vote for Proposition 13.

In addition, the composition of public schools was changing. Because of the transformation of immigration policy, students in California's public schools were increasingly Latino and Asian—a circumstance that increased support for Proposition 13.[35] Howard Jarvis described many Latino children as illegal aliens "who had just come . . . to get on the taxpayers' gravy train."[36] In the late 1970s, for the first time in California, less than half of the state's households had children in public schools. Along with the changes in school finance and the composition of public school classrooms, this meant rising property taxes were paying for someone else's children's schools—and increasingly for children of color.

In addition to the California Supreme Court's mandated redistribution of property tax revenues to poorer communities, busing school children to desegregate public schools had become a controversial and highly salient issue in the years leading up to the vote for 13. In 1972 California voters, by a 63 to 37 percent majority, passed a proposition that prohibited busing of students to any school on the basis of race, creed, or color and repealed the state law making desegregation state policy. But this proposition was ruled unconstitutional by the California courts. Between 1971 and 1978, 72,000 white students left Los Angeles public schools, making white students a minority in the city's school system. In 1979 Proposition 1 was enacted, prohibiting busing except when intended to remedy intentional discrimination. This change was upheld by the California courts.[37]

Affirmative action for minorities in higher education and the workplace was also conspicuous. Alan Bakke, a white Vietnam War veteran whose application to the medical school of the University of California at Davis had been denied, challenged the school's special admissions program for minority applicants (specifically for Black, Chicano, Asian, and American Indian applicants) as an unconstitutional racial quota. His case was awaiting decision by the Supreme Court when voters went to the polls for Proposition 13. (Twenty days later in a 5–4 vote the Supreme Court ordered Bakke's admission.)[38]

Howard Jarvis used welfare as his prime example of wasteful government spending, complaining repeatedly about taxing the few "to pay for social services, food stamp recipients, and aid to dependent children programs" (as welfare was then known). "*They*," he said, "are the ones who want more services—not the ones who pay the bills.[39] Governor Jerry Brown's director of social services observed, "Proposition 13 was intended to cut welfare costs. I thought that was what the people were voting for."[40] Welfare was the trope for "others," who lived off the taxes "we" pay.

During a debate in Orange County, Jarvis said he did not care "if his proposal harms government affirmative action programs" because putting women and minorities in such jobs "makes work for people at the taxpayers' expense." He said property owners would not only receive a significant tax cut but would also strike back at California hiring programs targeted at Blacks, feminists, and others.[41]

Proposition 13 passed at a time when white Californians were worried about the state's demographic transformation from an overwhelmingly white population to one where Latino, Asian, and Black residents were increasing dramatically—and accounted for most of the enrollment in the state's public schools. Minorities, in contrast, were worried that Proposition 13 would eliminate many state and local government jobs with the more recently hired Black and Latino workers the first fired. A report by the Los Angeles County Office of Affirmative Action Compliance predicted Black workers, who comprised just under 30 percent of the Los Angeles County workforce, would see their numbers drop by 63 percent and 83 percent of Latino employees would be laid off.[42] Willie Brown, chairman of the California legislature's Black Caucus, said all of the constituents he talked to were voting "no on 13—even the black apartment-house owners." "It will cause a real depression in the black community," he added.[43]

Exit polls revealed a majority of Black voters opposed Proposition 13, while white voters overwhelmingly supported it. When asked what services they would like to see cut, 69 percent of voters for 13 answered "welfare."[44] Another poll reported 91 percent of the voters for 13 were willing to have expenditures on welfare reduced.[45]

Syndicated columnist Jimmy Breslin wrote, "Blacks are one of the reasons for the tax revolt but almost nobody mentions them . . . because this could cause charges of racism to be aimed at the tax revolt and, once again, the poor would have ruined everybody's pleasure."[46] South Dakota senator George McGovern, the 1972 Democratic presidential nominee, said the antitax, antigovernment proponents who propelled Proposition 13 had "undertones of racism."[47] In their 1991 bestseller, *Chain Reaction: The Impact of Race, Rights, and Taxes on American Politics,* Tom and Mary Edsall agreed, emphasizing the "coded" racist language of Jarvis and other advocates. The NAACP insisted at its 1978 annual convention that racism was involved in Proposition 13.[48]

As those who followed the Supreme Court's decisions concerning claims of racial discrimination know, it is far more difficult to prove that an action was motivated by racial animus than to show the action had a disparate adverse impact on minorities—as Proposition 13 did.[49] In the case of 13, there may have been enough self-interest in reducing property taxes and "sticking it to the man" to generate majority support.[50] But the antigovernment, antitax movement that began with Proposition 13 was substantially abetted by racial enmity.

Consequences of 13

Polls showed a majority of voters regarded both their state and local governments as inefficient and unresponsive.[51] Several property tax relief bills floundered in the California legislature while it failed to deal with a 1978 budget surplus of nearly $6 billion, expected to grow to $10 billion annually if Proposition 13 failed. The legislature's discord and inaction clearly contributed to the support for 13, and Proposition 13's impact was initially softened by the large state surpluses.[52] Like many of its antitax successors, Proposition 13 seemed to offer substantial tax relief without imposing hardships—something for nothing. But that did not happen.

California's constitution, like nearly all state constitutions, requires a balanced budget (with California's restrictions among the most stringent). Proposition 13 required substantial cutbacks in public spending. School districts lost half their revenues, some fire districts as much as 40 percent, and the general governments of cities and counties about one-third. San Francisco fired a thousand teachers, doubled its transit fares, and, along with other cities including Los Angeles, closed some public health centers and libraries. Larger public school classes with fewer teachers, elimination of important summer programs, and neglect of school facilities also followed. California ranked fourth among the states in per capita income, but after the enactment of Proposition 13, the state dropped to thirty-first in public school spending per child. Other services also suffered: community colleges, police departments, public hospitals and health programs, public works, local parks, and welfare and social services.[53] Parks became dirty. Community colleges struggled to stay open.

Although the voters for 13 did not necessarily intend it, its enactment shifted power from local governments to state legislators in Sacramento. Fees and user charges climbed, with large increases for new schools, parks, sewers, sidewalks, street lighting, and similar activities. Local governments tried to improve their finances by shifting from property taxes to income and sales taxes. They favored shopping malls, car dealerships, and superstores contributing local sales tax revenues over manufacturing businesses providing better-paying jobs without generating new sales taxes.

In a 2014 speech bemoaning the trends in inequality of wealth and income in the United States, Janet L. Yellen, then chair of the Federal Reserve, identified the "building blocks" of economic opportunity. One of the building blocks was elementary and secondary schooling. Yellen emphasized the crucial role of public education funding for "families below the top." "Public funding for education," she said, "is [a] way governments can help offset the advantages some households have in resources available for children." "The United States," she added, "is one of the few advanced economies in which public education spending is often lower for students in lower-income households than for students in higher income households. . . . A major reason the United States is different is that we are one of the few advanced nations that fund primary and secondary public education mainly through subnational taxation. Half of U.S. public school funding comes from local property taxes, a much higher share than in other advanced countries, and thus the inequalities in housing wealth and income . . . enhance the ability of more affluent school districts to spend more on public schools."[54]

Proposition 13 increased the structural barriers and economic disadvantages faced by minorities. Economic inequality—especially the gap between the rich and the poor—increased faster in California than anywhere else in America. In 2018 Proposition 13 saved California homeowners an estimated $30 billion in property taxes—an amount equal to about 15 percent of the state budget—and saved businesses more than $11 billion.[55]

One frequently overlooked irony of Proposition 13 is that California voters in a referendum—frequently described as an occasion of "direct democracy" because the public, rather than the legislature, votes on a change—restricted majority rule for any increase in the state's taxes by requiring a two-thirds vote in the legislature to increase taxes.[56] Cutting taxes continued, of course, to require only a majority vote. Pushing for asymmetrical voting requirements making tax cuts easier to enact than tax increases has been a hallmark aspiration of the antitax movement, sometimes with success, sometimes not.

Because some of its causes seem California-centric—corrupt assessors, extraordinary housing inflation, stringent school-finance decisions—some observers viewed Proposition 13 as a one-off, California phenomenon. Writing in 1980, Robert Kuttner described "California's great revolt" as sputtering out that June, when Howard Jarvis's Proposition 9—an initiative that would have reduced California's income tax by half—was rejected by a 61 to 39 percent vote. Kuttner writes that this failure should "puzzle only those who insist on seeing in Proposition 13 the antigovernment revolt that it never was."[57]

But Kuttner was wrong. California's Proposition 13 spurred many imitators. In the four years following its enactment, thirty-four additional states enacted property tax cuts. Nineteen states base their property taxes on the purchase price and, like Proposition 13, limit the rate at which its assessed values can increase.[58] Seventeen states require a supermajority to override state property tax limitations. Altogether, forty-six states have some sort of constitutional or statutory limitation on financing their local governments, about half of which were adopted after 1977.[59] By 2013, only four states—Hawaii, New Hampshire, Tennessee, and Vermont—had not enacted significant state limitations on property taxes.[60]

In 1986, with a 75 percent majority, California voters permitted children who inherit homes from their parents to retain their parents' property tax advantages. A decade later, voters extended the same privilege to grandchildren.[61] Another 1986 proposition allowed homeowners after age fifty-five to transfer their low property tax assessments to a new home of equal or lesser value.[62]

On November 3, 2020, California voters rejected Proposition 15, which would have modified Proposition 13 to tax commercial properties worth more than $3 million based on fair market value rather than their costs. Agricultural land, small-business owners, and residential properties would have been exempted from the change. According to its proponents, 92 percent of the additional revenue would have been paid by 10 percent of the highest-value commercial properties. Almost half would have come from business properties that had not been reassessed in the twenty-first century.[63] The proposed changes were defeated by 52 to 48 percent. [64] Despite its shortcomings, Proposition 13 has had remarkable staying power.

Proposition 13 animated a copious, vigorous, sustainable antitax and anti-government movement. In 1980 antitax forces targeted the federal income tax. In 1982, two years after Robert Kuttner's book was published, Californians voted by nearly two to one to repeal the state's inheritance tax, its most progressive levy. On the night before Proposition 13 passed, NBC News anchor David Brinkley said, "It seems nobody loves government anymore."[65] Writing two decades later, journalist Peter Schrag described Proposition 13 as having "set in motion the holy crusade against taxes in which most of the country now seems irretrievably stuck."[66]

———

Howard Jarvis savored his long-sought victory. He became a national hero for the antitax movement. In the eighteen months following the vote for 13 he spoke in every state but Alaska and Hawaii, netting $150,000 between September and the end of 1978 (nearly $675,000 in 2021 dollars). He spoke to 250,000 people and reached another 80 million on television. He also wrote a regular column syndicated in nearly 50 newspapers. Jarvis insisted he had not changed. "I've still got the same number of suits, and I still eat bread and milk for dinner three times a week," he said. He claimed politicians had not changed either. "Politicians are basically cowardly," he said. "They go with the wind."[67]

The reverberations from Proposition 13 were heard in statehouses across the country and in state and national elections. Proposition 13 kicked off an antitax social movement that has transformed American politics and policy for more than a generation—and remains strong nearly a half century later. It brought new energy, new recruits, new money, and anti-elite momentum to the Republican Party. As National Urban League president Vernon Jordan said, "Proposition 13 has become the new spirit of America."[68]

Three years after the vote for 13, the newly elected president—former California governor Ronald Reagan—extended the antitax revolution to federal income and estate taxes. In the interim the movement gained unanticipated popular support from an unlikely source: southern Christian evangelicals. Some may dispute the role racial enmity played in the vote for 13, but the role of race in the antitax movement's second generative event of 1978 was unmistakable.

Chapter 3

Christian Evangelicals Join the Antitax Movement

What galvanized the Christian community was not abortion, school prayer, or the ERA [Equal Rights Amendment]. . . . What changed their mind was Jimmy Carter's intervention against the Christian schools, trying to deny them their tax-exempt status on the basis of so-called de facto segregation.

—PAUL WEYRICH

It didn't cross my mind that segregation and its consequences for the human family were evil.

—JERRY FALWELL SR.

In June 1978, Howard Jarvis's Proposition 13 recruited millions of middle- and upper-class Californians into the antitax movement and inspired imitations across the country. Subsequent state tax referendums confirmed this was no temporary phenomenon. The principal target of these measures was property taxes, which finance only state and local governments. For the antitax movement to succeed at the national level, the income tax had to become its quarry.

Public approval of the income tax had deteriorated by the mid to late 1970s, but widespread resentment had not yet blossomed into politically meaningful animus. In November 1978, however, the antitax constituency expanded unexpectedly. Efforts by the Internal Revenue Service to eliminate income tax benefits for racially segregated private schools angered Christian evangelical leaders, propelling their entry into the antitax crusade—and into a powerful and abiding force in Republican politics. Recalling the difficulties in desegregating public schools in the South illuminates how racial conflict prompted Christian evangelicals to clash with the IRS and enlist in the antitax movement.

Racial Conflict in Prince Edward County

On April 23, 1951, Barbara Rose Johns, a quiet, brave high school junior, stood before a packed auditorium at Robert Russa Moton High School in Farmville, Virginia, the county seat of Prince Edward County, to lead a strike of 450 Black students. The strike was triggered by the horrific physical condition of the school, built 70 years earlier to house 300 fewer students. Three recently added classrooms were tar paper shacks that leaked when it rained. The school had no central heating, no gym, no cafeteria, no science labs, and no lockers. John Stokes, Moton's senior class president, said, "The cows I milk are better sheltered than the Moton students."[1] Moton's conditions could not have been more different from those at nearby Farmville High School where 400 white students were enrolled.

The students urged only better physical conditions, but their NAACP lawyers transformed the strike into a fight for desegregation—a quest to enroll Black students at all-white Farmville High. Two weeks later when the students resumed their classes at Moton, NAACP lawyers filed a desegregation lawsuit in *Davis v. County School Board of Prince Edward County* on behalf of ninth-grader Dorothy Davis and 117 other Moton students. The suit prompted Prince Edward County's school board to build a new high school for Black students in an effort to get the lawsuit dropped or dismissed, but that didn't happen.

In 1951 and 1952 the Supreme Court agreed to hear Dorothy Davis's case, along with four others challenging segregated schools. Chief Justice Warren, speaking for a unanimous court in these cases known as *Brown v. Board of Education*, wrote that "segregation . . . in public schools has a detrimental effect upon the colored children . . . denoting the inferiority of the negro group," a consequence that violates the equal protection requirement of the Fourteenth Amendment adopted after the Civil War to make equal those who were slaves.[2]

Warren's short opinion, issued on May 17, 1954, did not specify a desegregation remedy. The next year Thurgood Marshall, arguing for Black schoolchildren, urged the Court to desegregate schools promptly when they opened in September 1956.[3] The Court, however, in what became known as *Brown II*, prescribed no deadline, instead instructing federal district court judges to weigh the interest "in admission to public schools as soon as practicable on a nondiscriminatory basis" against "the public interest" in "systematic and effective" desegregation, which should occur "with deliberate speed."[4] Justice Hugo Black, a former Alabama senator, told his colleagues that enforcing desegregation in the South would be as difficult as enforcing prohibition in New York City.[5] This was an understatement.

Most white southern political leaders treated "deliberate speed" as an invitation to resistance.[6] In Prince Edward County, hours after the Supreme Court's decision in *Brown II*, the board of supervisors voted to allocate only $150,000 to the county's public schools, the minimum allowed by the state. Edward Carter, the board's chairman, described why: "I don't believe integration will serve to elevate or make better citizens of either race."[7] A few days later, community leaders and white parents formed the Prince Edward School Foundation to found Prince Edward Academy, a private all-white elementary and high school.

In January 1956, with the support of the governor and state legislature, Virginia voters amended the state constitution to allow public funding of private schools. The legislature also authorized the governor to close public schools subject to desegregation orders. In his inaugural address in January 1958, governor J. Lindsay Almond Jr. said, "There will be no enforced integration in Virginia." In September he shut down schools in Charlottesville, Front Royal, and Norfolk, which were under court orders to integrate. Several months later those schools reopened and integrated pursuant to the court orders.[8]

In May 1959, eight years after Moton students filed their lawsuit, the court of appeals ordered desegregation of Prince Edward County schools the following September (overruling a lower court decision that would have given the county until 1965 to desegregate). The Prince Edward County Board of Supervisors—with support from the governor—then voted to eliminate the entire school budget and close all of the county's twenty-one public schools. Volunteers provided temporary facilities for white students in church basements and social clubs. Soon Prince Edward Academy opened for them.

Most Black students—1,500 of the county's 1,800—had no school until September 1963 when a privately funded free school opened. Barbara Johns left to live with an uncle in Montgomery, Alabama. The illiteracy rate of Black youth ages three to twenty-two rose from 3 percent to 23 percent while the Prince Edward County public schools were closed.[9] The county's public schools remained shuttered until 1964—a decade after *Brown*—when the Supreme Court unanimously required them to reopen.[10]

When the Prince Edward County public schools reopened in the fall of 1964, eight of the 1,500 students were white. All the other white students attended Prince Edward Academy. In 1961 the academy's tuition was $240 a year in the elementary school and $265 in the high school, with tuition allowed to relieve the parents' property taxes. The academy also received tuition grants from the county and tax-deductible donations that provided $265,000 ($2,400,000 in 2021 dollars) in operating funds in its first year of operation.[11]

Farmville's Prince Edward Academy was just one of many all-white "segregation academies" opened throughout the South in response to court-ordered integration. The exodus of white children to private segregated schools and white families to the suburbs left the South's public schools almost entirely with only Black students. By 1969 nearly 300,000 students were enrolled in all-white private schools across eleven southern states; by 1974 the South's 3,500 private academies taught 750,000 white children.[12]

The Legal Battle over Tax Benefits for Private Segregated Schools

After the 1964 Civil Rights Act barred the use of federal funds to support segregation, the IRS temporarily stopped granting tax exemptions and charitable deductions to segregated private schools, but in 1967 it resumed providing these tax benefits except when the schools received government aid. This supplied crucial financial support for all-white segregation academies.

In 1968 Mississippi granted $240 per pupil annually to help fund the 49 private segregated schools then operating in the state. One of these schools had only Black students, the other 48 only whites. Between 1964 and 1970, the number of non-Catholic private schools in Mississippi increased from 17 to 155. As elsewhere in the South, the new private schools replicated formerly segregated public schools.

In January 1969 a federal district court halted payment of Mississippi's tuition grants as an unconstitutional effort "to perpetuate segregation," describing Holmes County—a poor, rural, predominately Black county—as a place where the link between the desegregation effort and the growth of private schools was "particularly evident."[13] After a federal court in July 1965 ordered desegregation of the county's public schools, three private schools opened in the county, and white public school enrollment dropped from 771 to 28. No white students were left in the remaining two public schools by the 1968–69 school year.[14]

In May 1969 a group of Black Holmes County parents and students filed a class action lawsuit, *Green v. Kennedy*, to halt federal tax benefits for private segregated schools. The tax breaks—exempting the schools from both income and payroll taxes and permitting contributions to be deducted from donors' income taxes—had become financial lifeblood for private segregated schools.

An April 1969 fundraising letter soliciting donations for scholarships and new buildings for Central Holmes Academy, a private segregated school, stressed the importance of tax-deductible contributions. Without the dona-tions, the letter warned, the county's poor white children "for financial reasons alone, will be forced into one of the intolerable and repugnant other schools . . . or into dropping out of school entirely." The letter emphasized, "donations to the school are deductible from your gross income for tax purposes."[15]

In January 1970, the *Green* court issued an order temporarily prohibiting the Internal Revenue Service from issuing new rulings providing tax exemp-tions or deductible contributions to private racially segregated schools that served as "an alternative to white students seeking to avoid desegregated pub-lic schools."[16] Eighteen months later, the district court made the injunction permanent. The injunction applied only to private schools in Mississippi, but the court indicated its interpretation of the tax law applied nationally.[17] The court set forth guidelines requiring private schools to publicize racially non-discriminatory policies. In January 1971, the Supreme Court affirmed the lower court's decision.[18]

It was nonsensical to have one set of federal tax rules for Mississippi and more lenient rules elsewhere, so the *Green* decision impelled the IRS to deny tax exemptions and charitable deductions for segregated private schools throughout the country. With the reluctant approval of President Nixon, the IRS in July 1970 announced it would deny tax exemptions and tax-deductible charitable contributions to segregated private schools.[19] In 1971 the IRS offi-cially confirmed the policy, stating, "racial discrimination in education is contrary to federal public policy. Therefore, a school not having a racially non-discriminatory policy for students is not 'charitable' . . . and accordingly does not qualify as an organization exempt from federal tax."[20] The IRS required private schools to announce they were open to students of all races, but Ran-dolph Thrower, Nixon's Commissioner of Internal Revenue, later told Con-gress this did not create "any large movement of minority students into private schools which theretofore had barred their admission."[21]

Some Christian segregated school leaders claimed mixing the races was forbid-den by the Bible. North Carolina's Goldsboro Christian Schools prohibited the admission of Black students since its founding in 1963 and insisted God "separated mankind into various nations and races" and such separation "should be preserved in the fear of the Lord."[22]

In 1975 the IRS clarified its requirements for making nondiscriminatory admissions policies of private schools known to the public and announced it would revoke the tax exemptions of noncomplying schools. The IRS concluded the nondiscrimination requirements also applied to private segregated schools founded or operated by churches or segregated because of religious beliefs.[23] The U.S. Commission on Civil Rights criticized the IRS guidelines as inadequate to identify racially discriminatory schools.[24] On July 23, 1976, the *Green* plaintiffs went back to court claiming the IRS action failed to comply with the court's order against racially discriminatory private schools in Mississippi. The next week parents of Black children in eight states filed a lawsuit seeking a nationwide injunction similar to the *Green* court's Mississippi injunction.[25]

In August 1978 Jimmy Carter's IRS commissioner proposed much tougher rules, indicating that any private school formed or expanded when desegregation was ordered or occurring locally would be presumed racially discriminatory unless its minority enrollment was equal to at least one-fifth of the proportion of the minority schoolwide population in the local community. Schools could rebut this presumption only through specified activities to attract minority students.[26]

"The *Infernal* Revenue Service has been questioning the taxability, the exempt status of Christian schools. Why? Because they're motivated by the devil in this business, that's why," Jerry Falwell ranted on his television show.[27] In 1956 Falwell (now known as Jerry Falwell Sr.) and thirty-five parishioners had founded the Thomas Road Baptist Church in Lynchburg, Virginia, an hour's drive west of Prince Edward County. In 1958 he preached a sermon denouncing the *Brown* decision, claiming if Earl Warren "had known God's word" the *Brown* decision "would never have been made." Integration was "the work of the Devil," Falwell said, and would lead to the destruction of the white race. "The true Negro," he said, "does not want integration. We see the hand of Moscow in the background. . . . It boils down to whether we are going to take God's word as final."[28]

Falwell became chaplain of the Defenders of State Sovereignty and Individual Liberties, a group helping the Virginia governor and others resist desegregation orders. In 1964, when President Lyndon Johnson asked the nation's clergy to support the Civil Rights Act, Falwell responded: "It's a terrible violation of human and private property rights. It should be called civil wrongs rather than civil rights."[29] In 1967 Falwell founded the Lynchburg Christian

Academy as "a local school for whites."[30] A year later, the school accepted three Black students, and one Black family joined Falwell's church. By 1972 his church had 16,000 members in a city of 60,000 with 123 other churches.[31] He became the most important leader of the Christian Right, largely through his *Old Time Gospel Hour*, which began as a local radio show and was broadcast on more than 300 television stations nationwide. By 1979, Falwell had two million people on his mailing lists and was raising $35 million a year.[32]

Jerry Falwell was not the only Christian evangelical cleric to object to the new IRS policy. Other evangelical ministers with large television audiences, including Pat Robertson, founder of the successful Christian Broadcasting Network (CBN); Jim Bakker, a televangelist who had left CBN to found his own network; and James Dobson, founder of Focus on the Family and one of the most influential conservative evangelical leaders, all echoed Falwell's complaints. Bob Jones III, the third president of Bob Jones University and grandson of its founder, observed that the hearing on the proposed regulations occurred on December 7, the anniversary of the bombing of Pearl Harbor and insisted Americans now gathered "to defend our freedoms from a different enemy, the IRS."[33] Robert Billings, an important organizer of the Christian school movement, said the IRS might next seek to crush the Quakers for their commitment to pacifism and order Catholic doctors to perform abortions. Christian evangelicals stimulated a backlash unprecedented in IRS history.

Seventy-eight congressional conservatives signed a letter complaining, "If these regulations are accepted as valid, . . . we can be found . . . to conform to the notion of social good proclaimed in Washington, not just as to race but to any matter." Three Catholic Democratic senators, including Joe Biden, complained that the regulations would affect a number of non-white-flight schools. Biden threatened to withhold any IRS funds for enforcing the regulations.[34] The Conservative Republican organizer Paul Weyrich wrote that the IRS was "pronouncing a death penalty on wrong thoughts," adding he could not "think of anything more totalitarian."[35]

The IRS received more than 150,000 comments, nearly all opposed to the changes, mostly generated by evangelical leaders and the American Conservative Union. Many witnesses objected that the new guidelines required numerical quotas and affirmative action. The IRS held four days of angry public hearings in Washington, D.C., in early December. The first seven witnesses were senators and representatives, all opposing the regulations. The last of these, South Carolina senator Strom Thurmond, claimed there was not a "shred of authority" for the proposed regulations. Witnesses from the North and Northwest testified on behalf of Catholic, Jewish, and Protestant private schools with no links to desegregation controversies.

The IRS retreated in February 1979, eliminating all numerical requirements and telling agents to review schools on a "case-by-case" basis. The agency also eased the ability of schools to rebut any presumption of discrimination.[36]

But these changes failed to appease the opposition. The IRS commissioner was called before Congress for two days of denouncements. At the initiative of Ohio Republican congressman John Ashbrook, California's Robert Dornan, and North Carolina senator Jesse Helms, Congress prohibited enforcement of the 1978 and 1979 IRS regulations, but not enforcement of the more lenient requirements previously in effect.

In May 1980 the federal district court in *Green* required the IRS to implement substantially tougher procedures than those it had used before 1978 without compelling any specific number of minority students.[37] As before, the *Green* court's order was limited to Mississippi. To obey both the court and Congress, the IRS was required to apply one set of guidelines to Mississippi private schools and less stringent rules elsewhere, even where the schools were formed under similar circumstances and behaved identically. Former IRS commissioner Thrower said the IRS was in a "thorny thicket."[38]

While controversy raged, the IRS denied the tax exemption of some racially discriminatory private schools under its pre-1978 guidelines. In October 1978, more than three decades after its founding, the IRS finally revoked the tax exemption of Prince Edward Academy. George Leonard, the lawyer representing the school, told the federal district court, "We're discriminatory as hell." "We're goddamned if we're going to tell everyone that we were hypocrites all these years" by claiming now that the school does not discriminate. Leonard added: "Fundamentally, we believe blacks deserve a different type of education than whites. We strongly believe whites among whites and blacks among blacks get a better education." The Justice Department lawyer told the court that donors could continue to deduct up to $1,000 a year without challenge while the litigation was pending.[39] In 1979 the district court ruled in favor of the IRS. In 1980 the appellate court agreed, and in 1981 the Supreme Court refused to hear the case.[40]

Republican Recruitment of the Christian Right

Most Americans have never heard of Paul Weyrich, but he was one of the most important unelected Republicans of the late twentieth century. He came to Washington in 1967 as a twenty-five-year-old press secretary to Colorado

Republican senator Gordon Allott, resembling a young spectacled Clark Kent. Weyrich was raised in Wisconsin by a German Catholic father who cherished religion and politics. "Religion determines your eternal life," his father said, "and politics determines your temporal life. So what else is there to talk about?"[41]

In 1973 Paul Weyrich cofounded the Heritage Foundation, and in 1977 he became Heritage's first president. Heritage soon became the nation's most influential conservative think tank. Weyrich also cofounded the American Legislative Exchange Council (ALEC), a potent organization of conservative state legislators committed to limited government and the free market.[42] He later became copublisher of *Conservative Digest* magazine and launched a conservative television station.

To recruit Christian evangelicals to Republican politics, Weyrich joined forces with Richard Viguerie, a soft-spoken Texan, who early in his career worked for the segregationist Christian televangelist Billy James Hargis and was the executive secretary of Young Americans for Freedom where he began to master the art of political fundraising. In 1965 Viguerie created a direct-mail fundraising company based on a right-wing mailing list. By the 1970s he accumulated ten million names and addresses and produced more than fifty million direct-mail fundraising requests. He founded *Conservative Digest* magazine in 1975 and supported Alabama's segregationist governor George Wallace in his 1976 presidential campaign.

After the Supreme Court's 1973 *Roe v. Wade* decision, Weyrich and Viguerie tried to recruit southern Protestants to join the growing Republican anti-abortion movement. But most southern evangelical Protestants then viewed abortion as a "Catholic issue."[43] In 1976 the Southern Baptist Convention supported abortion in cases of "rape, incest, and fetal deformity" or threats to the "emotional, mental, or physical health of the mother."[44]

In 1976 Viguerie told a leftist evangelical magazine, "The next real major area of growth for the conservative ideology and philosophy is among evangelical people."[45] That year Weyrich, Viguerie, and Robert Billings met with Jerry Falwell and urged him to create an organization to mobilize the Christian evangelical community politically. Falwell refused.[46] When Falwell criticized a 1976 interview by Jimmy Carter with *Playboy* magazine and the next year invited to his *Old Time Gospel Hour* Anita Bryant, who led a campaign to repeal a gay rights ordinance enacted by Dade County, Florida, he insisted these were moral, not political, issues. According to Weyrich, Falwell "didn't know what he wanted to do and he certainly didn't know how to do it." "If I am too political," Falwell said, "it will dilute my effectiveness."[47]

Two years later, Falwell changed his mind. Paul Weyrich explained why: "What galvanized the Christian community was not abortion, school prayer, or the ERA [Equal Rights Amendment]. I am living witness to that because I was trying to get those people interested in those issues and I utterly failed. What changed their mind was Jimmy Carter's intervention against the Christian schools, trying to deny them their tax-exempt status on the basis of so-called de facto segregation."[48]

In 1979 Weyrich, Billings, and others met with Jerry Falwell at a Lynchburg Holiday Inn to tell Falwell how he might play an important role in Republican politics. Weyrich began the meeting, saying, "Out there is what one might call a moral majority. . . . The key to any kind of political impact is to get these people united in some way." After an awkward back-and-forth, Falwell said "that's it!" "That's the name of the organization."[49] The Holiday Inn conversation then turned to issues on which a Christian organization should focus. Abortion was at the top of the list. Segregation was not mentioned. The Moral Majority became the most important political organization of the Christian Right and Jerry Falwell its most politically influential and best-known leader.

In his newsletter, which became the *Moral Majority Report* (and soon had more than a million subscribers thanks in part to Viguerie's mailing lists), Falwell announced a political crusade against "abortion-on-demand, pornography, sex and violence on television, and government intervention." "But," he added, "I am especially concerned about the IRS attempt to legislate regulations that will control Christian schools."[50] In 1980 Falwell published his manifesto in a book called *Listen America!*—an ode to the free market, patriotism, anti-communism, and personal morality. Among his list of the "sins of America," he identified abortion, homosexuality, pornography, humanism, "the fractured family," and "the feminist revolution."[51] In *Listen America*, Falwell described the IRS as attacking "Christian schools," noting it is sometimes "easier to open a massage parlor than a Christian school." He failed to mention the IRS was challenging racially discriminatory schools. "Christians," Falwell added, "simply want to educate their children in the way they see fit."[52]

Toward the end of his book, Falwell lists "minimum moral standards" (originally promulgated by evangelical minister and Moral Majority board member Tim LaHaye) that Falwell claimed are dictated by the Bible and are to be "used to evaluate the stand of candidates on moral issues." Question 12 asks, "Do you favor removal of the tax-exempt status of Churches?" Question 13 asks: "Do you favor removal of the tax-exempt status of church-related schools?" Questions 17 and 18 ask, "Do you favor a reduction in taxes to allow families more spendable income?" and "Do you favor a reduction in government?"[53] Falwell's Moral Majority was becoming an important component of the antitax movement.

Political scientists Sidney Milkis and Daniel Tichenor, in a rich account of the relationship between social movements and presidents, conclude that controversies over tax exemptions for private segregated schools "played a decidedly pivotal role in mobilizing conservative evangelicals against the liberal state."[54] Robert Billings, who became the first executive director of the Moral Majority in 1979, said, "Jerome Kurtz [the IRS commissioner] has done more to bring Christians together than any man since the Apostle Paul."[55]

Efforts by Christian Right evangelical leaders, like Jerry Falwell, to attribute their political engagement to a response to the Supreme Court's 1973 abortion decision, rather than the IRS's 1978 effort to strengthen enforcement of denials of tax benefits to racially discriminatory schools, are hardly surprising. Creating an effective national grassroots coalition of evangelical Christians on a foundation of keeping Black children out of schools for whites was inconceivable. The movement needed to emphasize different goals and values important to conservative Christians: the sanctity of life; preservation of the family; protection of Christian values; opposition to pornography, gay rights, and feminism. It had to be about freedom to raise children as parents chose, freedom from overbearing government bureaucrats. Antitax attitudes were invoked in the service of righteous causes. As Yale historian C. Vann Woodward observed, "Every self-conscious group of any size fabricates myths about its past: about its origins, its mission, its righteousness, its benevolence, its general superiority."[56] Anti-IRS, antitax, and antigovernment commitments, wrapped in arguments for freedom and liberty, became enduring elements of the Christian Right's political creed.[57] And attacking the IRS became an indispensable call to arms for the antitax movement.

Ronald Reagan's Enticement of Christian Evangelicals

In the 1976 presidential campaign, most evangelical Christians voted for Jimmy Carter. He was a proud, born-again Southern Baptist who frequently said so. Carter viewed politics as a "vehicle to advancing God's kingdom on earth by alleviating human suffering and despair."[58] But by 1980 when he was running for reelection, Carter had alienated evangelical Christians. He opposed a constitutional amendment to ban abortion, failed to reject feminists or gays, and reneged on a promise to appoint evangelicals to his cabinet. Moreover, the 1978 IRS effort concerning private segregated schools outraged and mobilized southern Christian evangelicals, who blamed President Carter.[59]

Looking toward his upcoming presidential campaign, Ronald Reagan railed against the 1978 IRS announcement. In a nationally syndicated radio address Reagan said the IRS commissioner "from his granite and marble palace" was "driving a large number of private schools out of business." Reagan insisted that "virtually all of [the private] schools are presently desegregated" and the IRS action "threatens the destruction of religious freedom itself."[60] To attract votes from the Christian Right in his 1980 campaign, Reagan attacked the IRS efforts to deny tax exemptions to racially discriminatory schools. In January he gave a speech at Bob Jones University calling for a "spiritual revival" and denouncing the 1978 IRS proposals as an instance of government bureaucrats establishing "racial quotas."[61]

In Dallas on August 22, 1980, Reagan gave a famous campaign speech at a two-day "National Affairs Briefing." His audience included fifteen thousand Christian conservatives, preachers from forty-one states, and a host of right-wing political operatives. The charismatic Texas televangelist James Robison introduced Reagan in a fiery antigovernment address, holding his Bible high and shouting: "Not voting is a sin against almighty God. . . . Government is a complicator! And a consumer! And a disperser of your wealth! It produces nothing! And it functions best when it functions least!"[62]

Reagan began by saying to scattered laughter, "I know this is a nonpartisan gathering," "I know that you can't endorse me, but I want you to know that I endorse you and what you are doing."[63] He continued:

> Fully backed by the White House, the Internal Revenue Service was prepared to proclaim, without approval of Congress, that tax exemption constitutes federal funding. The purpose was to force all tax-exempt schools—including church schools—to abide by affirmative action orders drawn up by—who else?—I.R.S. bureaucrats.

> On that particular point, I would like to read you a line from a certain political platform, written in Detroit about a month ago. It goes like this:

> "We will halt the unconstitutional regulatory vendetta launched by Mr. Carter's IRS Commissioner against independent schools."[64]

In attributing the IRS policy to unelected bureaucrats, Reagan ignored the inconvenient fact that the policy of denying tax exemptions to private segregated schools had been approved by Republican presidents Nixon and Ford.

President Reagan with Jerry Falwell in the Oval Office.

In 1980 Christian evangelicals mobilized and, for the first time, voted for a Republican candidate for president.

The Segregated Private School Controversy
Reaches the Supreme Court

In October 1981—more than a decade after the IRS first attempted to deny tax benefits to racially discriminatory schools—the Supreme Court agreed to hear controversies over tax exemptions and charitable deductions for Bob Jones University and Goldsboro Christian Schools. Bob Jones University was founded in 1927 by the Reverend Bob Jones Sr., one of the most famous Christian evangelists in America.[65] He was succeeded as university president in 1948 by his son Bob Jones Jr. and his grandson Bob Jones III in 1971. From its founding as a school "giving special emphasis to the Christian religion and the ethics revealed in the Holy Scriptures," Bob Jones University excluded Black students, claiming that the Bible forbade "intermingling" of the races.[66] In response to a November 1970 inquiry from the IRS, the university replied it did not admit Black students and would not change its policy. In 1973 the university somewhat loosened its racially discriminatory policies by allowing enrollment of any Black staff member employed there for four years or more.

In April 1975 the IRS revoked the university's tax exemption retroactively to December 1, 1970. A month later, after an appellate court decision that private schools denying admission to Black students violated the law, the university changed its admissions policy to allow Black students but prohibited interracial dating or marriage. The IRS was unmoved, viewing the ban on interracial dating as an integral part of the school's admissions policy.[67]

Goldsboro Christian Schools had explicitly maintained a racially discriminatory policy since its inception. On audit the IRS rejected the school's exemption. A federal district court in North Carolina upheld the denial.[68] Fifteen months after the IRS won the *Goldsboro Christian Schools* case, a South Carolina district court ruled for Bob Jones University.[69] In 1980 the appellate court reversed the *Bob Jones University* decision and subsequently, in February 1981, upheld the lower court's decision in the *Goldsboro Christian Schools* case.[70]

Fulfilling President Reagan's campaign promise, his administration on January 8, 1982—two days before its Supreme Court brief was due—reversed the long-standing IRS prohibition of tax benefits for racially discriminatory private schools and announced it was going to restore Bob Jones University's tax exemption. The Justice Department urged the Supreme Court to dismiss both cases because there was no longer a controversy between the federal government and the schools.[71] The Reagan administration insisted Congress had to decide the issue.[72]

Christian evangelicals were exuberant that President Reagan kept his campaign promise. Bob Jones III, said, "We rejoice that God in his own way has allowed this to happen and He gets all the glory for it."[73] President Reagan and his White House staff underestimated the censure from reversing the IRS position. Despite White House efforts to limit controversy, the Associated Press report of Reagan's policy reversal began: "The Internal Revenue Service plans to allow tax-exempt status to private schools that discriminate against blacks"—a description echoed in front-page stories in the *New York Times*, *Washington Post*, and newspapers throughout the country.[74] The *Los Angeles Times* described the Reagan administration's legal position as claiming the "IRS Commissioner could not know, without legislation passed by Congress, that national policy opposed racial discrimination."[75] New York Democratic senator Daniel Patrick Moynihan warned "a quarter century's achievement could unravel in months." Editorial writers and political cartoonists berated what the *New York Times* called "tax-exempt hate." When Justice Department officials said anyone against the policy reversal was "welcome to leave," twenty lawyers resigned.[76]

Nor did President Reagan apprehend the difference between reversing the 1978 enforcement rules and reversing the decade-old policy denying exemptions and charitable deductions to segregated private schools. He was surprised to learn that rather than prohibiting tax collectors from threatening schools obeying the law, he was providing tax exemptions for schools still practicing segregation. Apparently no one told him Goldsboro Christian Schools was crystal clear about its ongoing refusal to admit Blacks or that Bob Jones University explicitly retained racially discriminatory policies.

After the unanticipated blowback, President Reagan said he was "unalterably opposed to racial discrimination in any form" and announced he would propose legislation to deny tax exemptions and charitable deductions for segregated private schools.[77] The Treasury Department said it would not grant new tax exemptions to segregated schools while the legislation was pending. These steps appeased neither the administration's critics nor the press, which accused Reagan of cynicism and hypocrisy.

Bob Dole, chairman of the Senate Finance Committee, told Treasury's tax policy head that President Reagan was not going to move "that skunk" onto his committee's doorstep. At a February hearing on the proposed legislation, Dole told administration witnesses, "we may want to send it back," adding, "hopefully [the Supreme Court] reads the papers" and "will go ahead and make [the] decision."[78] Dole got his wish.

On February 18, 1982, the federal court of appeals in the District of Columbia enjoined the IRS from granting or restoring any tax exemption to racially discriminatory private schools.[79] This made it impossible for the Supreme Court to duck the issue. The Justice Department then filed a brief arguing the IRS had erred in denying tax exemptions to racially discriminatory schools. That left no lawyer to argue for the IRS and lower-court decisions denying the tax benefits.

In April 1982 the Supreme Court appointed William T. Coleman to support the court of appeals decision upholding the IRS's denials of tax exemption to racially discriminatory schools. Coleman, a Harvard Law graduate, had broken the color barrier as a clerk for Justice Felix Frankfurter, and was Gerald Ford's secretary of transportation, the second African American appointed to a president's cabinet. He was chairman of the NAACP Legal Defense and Education Fund and practicing law in Philadelphia when the Court appointed him.[80]

On May 24, 1983, the Supreme Court ruled 8 to 1 that the IRS had the authority under the tax law to deny tax exemptions to racially discriminatory schools and that it did not violate the Constitution by denying exemptions to segregated religious schools.[81] The sole dissenter was William Rehnquist (whom Ronald Reagan nominated to become Chief Justice in 1986). The *New York Times* wrote, "President Reagan and the lawyers he has put in charge of civil rights should stand ashamed."[82]

Christian evangelicals condemned the Court's decision. The *Biblical Evangelist* headline screamed: "IRS Wins 'Hunting License'! Supreme Court Grants 'Open Season' on Fundamentalist Schools and Churches." Jerry Falwell described the decision as "a broad-based attack on religious liberty."[83] Bob Jones University lowered its flags to half-mast.

Ronald Reagan escaped criticism from the Christian Right because he refused to support the IRS position in the Supreme Court. His proposed legislation, which would have produced a similar result, was ignored.

Goldsboro Christian Schools paid its back taxes and changed its admission policies to become open to Black students. In 1987 it closed. "We will never change beliefs that we base on the Word of God," Bob Jones III said after the Court's decision.[84] But in March 2000 he told the audience of the *Larry King Show* the university would permit interracial dating. Bob Jones University's website then apologized for its failure "to accurately represent the Lord and to fulfill the commandment to love others as ourselves."[85]

What Happened to Prince Edward Academy?

In 1985, more than three decades after the *Brown* decision and four years after its challenges to the IRS's denial of its tax exemption failed in court, Prince Edward Academy told the IRS its board had adopted a policy of "open admissions" and had Native American, French, German, Spanish, and Vietnamese students, but no Black students because none had ever applied. Contrary to all evidence, the Board of Directors said "nothing in [the school's] constitution or by-laws is discriminatory, nor has the school practiced racial discrimination in admission practices in its 25-year history." On August 21, 1985, the IRS restored the academy's tax exemption, retroactive to October 3, 1984, even though the school had no Black students and never had. James Ghee, president of the Virginia NAACP, expressed surprise that simply by saying it does not discriminate, the school got its exemption back. "Nothing has changed in the policies or procedures of Prince Edward Academy," he said. The director of the Virginia Civil Liberties Union said the new ruling was "laughable."[86]

Even though segregated private schools in the South lost the legal battle over their tax benefits, they prevailed. Prince Edward Academy, the most notorious segregation academy in America—formed in 1959 to educate white students in a county that litigated and lost in the *Brown* case and closed its public schools to avoid integrating them—received federal financial support in the form of tax benefits for nearly its entire thirty-four-year existence.[87] The Supreme Court decided the tax law prohibits exemptions and charitable deductions for racially discriminatory schools, but all a school needed to do was declare an "open admissions policy." The Reagan administration never imposed a more aggressive enforcement policy.

In the early 1990s, with the approval of the Supreme Court (then headed by William Rehnquist) and George H. W. Bush's Justice Department, federal courts began terminating court-supervised desegregation orders for public schools. Throughout America, public and private schools remain largely separate and starkly unequal.

———

Battles of Christian evangelicals with the IRS over tax exemptions for segregated private schools transformed American politics. The failed 1978 IRS enforcement efforts provided the spark that enabled Paul Weyrich and his conservative allies to engage Christian evangelicals as a powerful component of the Republican coalition.

Before long, antitax, anti-IRS, antigovernment attitudes would become the linchpin holding together the diverse interests of the Republican coalition. Some evangelicals even came to see tax cuts as a manifestation of God's will. During the Reagan years, a "prosperity gospel"—the notion that God will reward true believers with wealth—took hold in some quarters.[88] As Jerry Falwell put it, material wealth is "God's way of blessing people who put him first."[89] But gospel alone would not convince a majority of Americans to embrace Ronald Reagan's tax-cutting passions. For that he needed help from secular humanists.

Chapter 4

Prophets of the Supply-Side Gospel

The decline and fall of the GOP since 1930 resulted not from its lack of passion, but from its failure to understand the nature of the Laffer Curve.

—JUDE WANNISKI, *THE WAY THE WORLD WORKS*

Neither the garrulous California populist Howard Jarvis nor the preachers of the Christian Right enjoyed constituencies broad enough to turn their anti-government, antitax efforts into successful national legislation. For that they needed a charismatic leader in the White House. In 1981 the former governor of California Ronald Reagan played that role. But for Reagan to build the necessary support for his tax-cutting agenda in Congress, he needed a comprehensible, secular economic story. He also needed to be confident an antitax, antigovernment agenda would generate widespread support from voters. By the end of 1978, he had both.

Nature Abhors a Vacuum

From the Depression in the 1930s through the early 1970s, the economic ideas of John Maynard Keynes dominated policymaking. Keynes's masterpiece, *The General Theory of Employment, Interest and Money*, served as the economic playbook for the United States and Europe for more than two decades after Keynes died from a heart attack in 1946 at age sixty-three. At the end of 1965, *Time* magazine published a cover story titled "We Are All Keynesians Now," a phrase attributed to Milton Friedman and later made famous by President

Richard Nixon in January 1971 when he said, "I am now a Keynesian in economics."[1]

In August 1971, Nixon, with eyes on his reelection prospects, attempted to halt inflation by a temporary freeze of wages and prices. He soon let the wage and price controls expire with the notable exception of a decade of failed energy price controls.[2] This gambit postponed price increases until after Nixon's reelection.

In the mid-1970s, the stubborn period of stagflation, with its devastating combination of high unemployment and soaring inflation, undermined the most famous visual representation of Keynesianism: the "Phillips Curve," which insisted when unemployment was high, inflation would be low and vice versa. Until the 1970s, the inverse relationship between unemployment and inflation seemed to hold. Leading Keynesian economists, such as MIT's Nobel Laureates Paul Samuelson and Robert Solow, produced precise estimates of the trade-offs between unemployment and inflation and based economic prescriptions on them.

Keynesian remedies were straightforward: all one needed to do was mix the right cocktail of fiscal and monetary policies. When inflation was high, tighten monetary policy. When unemployment was high, loosen fiscal policy to stimulate demand for goods and services by increasing government spending or cutting taxes. Wise economists were ready and available to supply advice about the proper blend of these policies. This worked quite well in the United States from the end of World War II into the late 1960s. But in the 1970s, when inflation rose so did unemployment. In 1975, 1976, and 1977, Congress reduced taxes and expanded federal spending in classic Keynesian countercyclical efforts to stimulate demand (and thereby economic growth) in response to a recession—but failed to solve stagflation.

In 1977 *Newsweek*, along with other observers, asked, "Is Keynes Dead?"[3] The *Wall Street Journal* rendered its verdict: a January editorial, titled "Keynes Is Dead," quoted a September 1976 speech by Britain's Labor prime minister James Callaghan, who said, "We used to think that you could spend your way out of a recession and increase unemployment by cutting taxes and boosting government spending. I tell you, in all candor, that that option no longer exists." The *Journal* editorial concluded: "If Lord Keynes were alive today, he would no doubt be back at the drawing boards."[4] A few months later the German Social Democratic chancellor Helmut Schmidt agreed, saying, "The time for Keynesian ideas is past."[5]

In 1983 the Austrian Nobel Laureate in economics F. A. Hayek, no Keynesian, writing in *The Economist* for a centenary on Keynes, said: "It will be for future historians to account for the fact that, for a generation after the untimely death of Maynard Keynes, opinion was so completely under the sway of what was regarded as Keynesianism in a way that no single man had ever before dominated economic policy and development. Nor will it be easy to explain why these ideas rather suddenly went out of fashion."[6] In 1983 "out of fashion" was an understatement.

Meanwhile, economists were advancing ideas to fill the vacuum created by Keynesianism's demise. Two especially influential University of Chicago professors were Milton Friedman, who was mainly interested in monetary policy, revered free markets, and argued against progressive income taxes, and his colleague Robert Mundell, who was breaking new ground in international economics while arguing for keeping the top income tax rate below 25 percent. Friedman and Mundell urged tight monetary policy to curb inflation and tax reductions to increase incentives for savings and investment to reduce unemployment and stimulate economic growth.[7] This combination became known as supply-side economics.

Other economists joined the supply-side revolution. Among the most notable were Paul Craig Roberts, chief economist for Congressman Jack Kemp before becoming President Reagan's assistant treasury secretary for economic affairs, and Norman Ture, who founded the conservative Institute for Research on Taxation in 1977 and became a treasury undersecretary in 1981. Martin Feldstein, a prolific and influential Harvard economics professor and president of the National Bureau of Economic Research (NBER) from 1977 until 2008, served as chairman of President Reagan's Council of Economic Advisers from 1982 to 1984. Of these three, Feldstein (who did not accept all of the supply-siders' claims) had the most influence. The NBER does not take positions on policy, but under Feldstein's leadership, a large group of prominent public finance economists focused on tax barriers to productive investment and produced analyses describing the economic benefits of low or zero taxes on income from capital—an important goal of the antitax movement.[8] These economists, however, did not carry supply-side economics from the backwaters into the mainstream. That crusade was taken up by an unlikely quartet: an unconventional economist, two journalists, and an eager young congressman.

Milton Friedman and Robert Mundell were both awarded the Nobel Prize in economics, but the best-known supply-side economist and the most politically important was Arthur Laffer. Laffer was a Stanford PhD who came to know Mundell during the late 1960s when they were both teaching economics at the University of Chicago.[9] In 1974 Laffer and Mundell brought supply-side economics to the nation's capital in a conference on curbing inflation at the conservative American Enterprise Institute (AEI) where they both argued for tax cuts.

An attendee at the AEI conference was Jude Wanniski, who had worked as a political columnist for the *Las Vegas Review Journal* before becoming a *Wall Street Journal* editorial writer. After dinner following the conference at a Georgetown restaurant with Mundell and Laffer, Wanniski became a passionate supply-sider. He wrote a *Wall Street Journal* editorial called "It's Time to Cut Taxes" based largely on a follow-up interview with Mundell.[10] The following spring Wanniski published a lengthy paper in the *Public Interest* called "The Mundell-Laffer Hypothesis" where he described "the debilitating effect of transfer payments" and explained, "Mundell and Laffer view tax-cutting as a way of augmenting supply when virtually all of their peers see it only as a way to augment demand." Wanniski captured the essence of supply-side thought when he described Mundell and Laffer's economics as going "back to an older style of economic thought in which the incentives and motivations of the individual producer and consumer and merchant are made the keystone of economic policy."[11]

The most consequential consumers of Wanniski's handiwork were a young congressman from Buffalo, Jack Kemp, and Wanniski's *Wall Street Journal* boss, Robert Bartley. The quartet of Laffer, Wanniski, Bartley, and Kemp soon became the most influential proselytizers for supply-side tax cuts. Together they laid the groundwork for the most profound shifts in U.S. tax policy since World War II.

Arthur Laffer Throws a Curve

Arthur Laffer's first opportunity to persuade important policymakers to embrace supply-side economics occurred in a meeting over cocktails Wanniski arranged not long after the AEI conference. On September 13, 1974, about a month after Richard Nixon resigned and Gerald Ford was sworn in as president, Ford's chief of staff Donald Rumsfeld and his deputy Dick Cheney met Laffer and Wanniski at the Two Continents restaurant in the Hotel Washington, a block east of the White House. Rumsfeld and Cheney described the tax increase Ford was considering as a response to stagflation. Laffer then, so the story goes, pulled out a marker and drew his now famous "Laffer Curve" on a napkin.[12] Laffer's drawing became famous as he explained it in

Arthur Laffer and his curve. AP Photo.

numerous speeches, publications, and presentations to powerful politicians and journalists.

Laffer's curve is simple enough: it shows the relationship between income tax rates and government revenue and demonstrates when tax rates are zero, government revenues are zero, and when tax rates are 100 percent, revenues are also zero because no one will produce anything when the government takes all of the proceeds. Somewhere, at the peak of the curve (in the middle in Laffer's drawing) is the tax rate at which taxes are low enough not to inhibit economic growth and high enough to maximize government revenue. The essential claim, which Wanniski labeled supply-side economics, is that when tax rates are too high reducing them will increase work, savings, investment, and economic output, and as a consequence will also increase government revenues.[13]

The mystery, of course, is the revenue-maximizing tax rate. When will reducing the top rate increase or decrease revenues? Laffer put no numbers on his curve, so his drawing fails to answer that question. In the late 1970s, when the top individual tax rate on investment income was 70 percent and the top rate on earned income was 50 percent, Wanniski, Laffer, and others insisted tax rates were on the wrong side of the curve. Republican politicians for nearly a half century since—even after tax rates were reduced substantially—have claimed tax rates are too high, we are on the wrong side of Laffer's curve, and a tax cut will stimulate enough economic growth to pay for itself.

In 1976, two years after his meeting with Cheney and Rumsfeld, Arthur Laffer departed the University of Chicago to become a professor at the University of Southern California School of Business. He moved into a four-bedroom home in Palos Verdes, twenty-seven miles south of Los Angeles, where he raised hundreds of cactus varietals and shared the property with his children and a collection of parrots, turtles, and a pet weasel. By 1978 his home's value was surging.[14] He was a vocal advocate—and beneficiary—of Proposition 13's property tax limits. Laffer erroneously publicly predicted Proposition 13 would pay for itself by stimulating economic growth.[15] This was not the last time he made such a wrong claim. Laffer and proponents of tax cuts have repeated such predictions for more than a generation, no matter the circumstances or contrary experience.

Many economists, including Milton Friedman, criticized Laffer. The conservative Nobel Laureate George Stigler, who had been a colleague of Laffer's at Chicago, called Laffer a "propagandist." In 1978 Alan Greenspan, who served as Gerald Ford's top economist and headed the Federal Reserve from 1987 to 2006, said, "I don't know anyone who seriously believes his argument."[16] Herbert Stein, who chaired the Council of Economic Advisers under Presidents Nixon and Ford, called the Laffer Curve "extreme to the point of bizarre," a "shabby echo of self-serving businessmen's nostrum going back to time immemorial."[17]

But Arthur Laffer never wavered. By 1979 he was delivering nearly one hundred lectures annually to business and political groups, taking long flights from California every week for work with his business and economics consulting firm Laffer Associates, and heading to Washington to meet with policymakers and testify before Congress. In 2006 he moved his business to Nashville and bought a home in the suburb of Belle Meade—he said because of its low business taxes and no state personal income tax.[18]

Supply-Side Economics Finds Its Voice

It is unlikely Arthur Laffer's curve would have become the most renowned symbol of the supply-side revolution without Jude Wanniski's labeling it and the incessant, effective publicity Wanniski and Robert Bartley provided it on the *Wall Street Journal*'s editorial pages.[19] Bartley, a conservative self-confident midwesterner, took control of the *Wall Street Journal* editorial page in 1972 and held that position until the end of 2002. His boss Warren Phillips, CEO of the *Journal's* parent company Dow Jones, instructed Bartley the paper's editorial page was not to be evenhanded but to have a point of view: its guideposts would be free enterprise and individual liberty.

Bartley described his conversion to supply-side economics as stemming from a series of dinners at a Wall Street steakhouse called Michael I. There in comfortable leather armchairs, cutting into thick porterhouse steaks, he and Wanniski met regularly with Laffer and Mundell (and sometimes Lewis Lehrman, who became an investment banker after making his fortune as president and the largest stockholder of the Rite-Aid pharmacies).[20] During Bartley's reign, the *Wall Street Journal* became the most aggressive, consistent, and influential voice for supply-side economics, especially tax cuts to promote savings and investment. The *Journal's* editorial pages, in Bartley's words, "provided a daily bulletin board" for supply-side ideas.[21]

Bartley hired Wanniski for the *Journal's* editorial page in 1972. Wanniski was a passionate, committed, cocksure iconoclast who viewed Laffer's curve as the miracle drug for the nation's ailing economy. He was the son of a Pottsville, Pennsylvania, butcher and had grown up in Brooklyn mediating ongoing arguments between his grandfather, an aggressive communist, and his father, an unwavering free-market devotee. Bartley said Wanniski had "discovered a lost continent of economics." Together they became relentless, zealous advocates for supply-side economics.[22] The *Wall Street Journal* editorial pages offered them the reach of the only genuinely national newspaper of that time with a circulation of over one million readers, including virtually all of America's business and political leaders.

In 1976, writing in the *National Observer* (a Dow Jones weekly newspaper), Wanniski, in an influential article called "Taxes and the Two-Santa Theory," explained the political potential of cutting taxes. He argued Democrats were playing Santa Claus by providing politically popular public spending while Republicans were behaving like Scrooge in insisting on balancing the federal budget. Instead, Wanniski said, the Republicans should be "the Santa Claus of Tax Reduction." The "two-Santa theory," he explained, "holds that the Republicans should concentrate on tax-rate reductions." "As they succeed in expanding incentives to produce," he claimed, "they will move the economy back to full employment and thereby reduce social pressures for public spending." A "cut in tax rates by expanding the private sector will diminish the relative size of the public sector."[23]

In a March 1977 *Wall Street Journal* editorial ironically titled "Tax the Rich," Wanniski summarized the supply-side argument for lowering their taxes:

> Why not tax the rich by lowering the rates they face? They will thus be enticed back from their yachts and once again assemble widget plants in New York City, with tax revenues flowing to Washington, Albany, and City Hall, not only from them, but also from all those who would then be usefully employed in widget-making. By all means tax the rich! But do it right, and in this fashion lift the burdens from those who are not rich.[24]

The *Journal's* editorial pages never wavered from its commitment to tax cuts during the thirty years Robert Bartley served as its editor.[25] Nor has it moderated in its antitax attitudes since. The *Journal's* editorial board apparently believes—no matter the top income or capital gains tax rates—the United States is always on the wrong side of Arthur Laffer's curve.

Jude Wanniski elaborated his arguments for the Laffer Curve and supply-side economics in his modestly titled book, *The Way the World Works*, first published in 1978. This tome became "something of a supply-side bible."[26] The book concluded: "The Republican Party is now in dismal condition. . . . The solutions to domestic and economic problems now require primary commitments to income growth, not redistribution, and the GOP will always win a competition with the Democrats over which is more passionate over growth. The decline and fall of the GOP since 1930 resulted not from its lack of passion, but from its failure to understand the nature of the Laffer Curve."[27]

In his preface to the fourth edition, published in 1998, Wanniski confessed to being "mildly megalomaniacal at the time."[28] When Jude Wanniski died of a heart attack in 2005, the widely read nationally syndicated conservative columnist Robert Novak, a self-described supply-side acolyte, described Wanniski as "an advocate who changed the world." "He fathered supply-side economics," Novak wrote, "which became the doctrine of the Republican Party and enabled it to be the nation's ruling party most of the last half century."[29]

To achieve that success, however, the clout of the *Wall Street Journal's* editorial page, Wanniski's book, and Robert Novak's columns were not enough. Republicans needed to demonstrate that supply-side tax cutting would be an effective force legislatively and in electoral politics. Jack Kemp, a young congressman from Buffalo, took the laboring oar.

Quarterback for the Supply Side

Jack Kemp grew up in Southern California and attended Occidental College, a small private college in Los Angeles, where he played several football positions including quarterback. After the Detroit Lions selected him late in the 1957 draft, he bounced around several professional football teams before becoming a successful, undersized quarterback with the San Diego Chargers and the Buffalo Bills. After seven pro-bowl seasons in Buffalo, Kemp retired from football. In 1970 he was elected as a Republican to the House of Representatives. He set out to improve the economic circumstances of his working-class constituents in Buffalo (and throughout the country) regardless of their race, describing himself as a "bleeding-heart conservative." Given that goal, supply-side tax cuts for wealthy investors were hardly an obvious remedy.

Jude Wanniski met Jack Kemp in an impromptu meeting in January 1976. Wanniski was wandering around the Longworth House Office Building pursuing a story of another congressman's licentiousness when he stopped by Kemp's office unannounced. Wanniski regarded Kemp as just another athlete who had ridden his football fame to Congress, but Robert Bartley and Irving Kristol (an influential neoconservative thinker and the founder and editor of the *Public Interest*) told Wanniski there was "more to Kemp than meets the eye."[30]

Wanniski and Kemp hit it off immediately. Learning Wanniski was there, Kemp rushed out of his office, shouting, "Wanniski! I've just been thinking about how I was going to meet you." They ended up talking for the rest of the day before migrating to Kemp's house for dinner where their conversation continued until midnight. By the end of the evening, Kemp was a supply-side convert. The next day Wanniski told his staff, "He was draining me of everything I know. I've just fallen in love."[31] Later he added, "I had finally found an elected representative of the people who was as fanatical as I was. Kemp would grab people by the lapels."[32]

After that first encounter, Kemp and Wanniski talked at least daily. Bruce Bartlett, then an economic staffer for Kemp, said they were so close that "talking to one was like talking to the other." Arthur Laffer said, "Jack and Jude together were deadly."[33] Wanniski had swayed an important new true believer and cemented a formidable political collaboration. They merged Wanniski's *Wall Street Journal* pulpit with Kemp's political skills and platform.

In 1975, before he met Wanniski, Kemp sponsored the "Fiscal Integrity Act," a bill that would have mandated balanced federal budgets and limited federal taxes as a percentage of GDP. He argued then that tax cuts must be offset with matching spending reductions.[34] After his supply-side conversion, Kemp put his staff to work on what would become the Kemp-Roth tax-reduction legislation, introduced on July 4, 1977, by Kemp in the House and Delaware Republican William Roth in the Senate. The Kemp-Roth bill proposed cutting income tax rates by about 30 percent across-the-board. No spending cuts were included to offset its revenue costs.

Kemp claimed he modeled his tax-cut legislation on John F. Kennedy's rate reductions of the early 1960s. In the spring of 1977, when he told his staff to begin drafting what would become the Kemp-Roth bill, Kemp asked, "Why don't we just replicate [the Kennedy tax cut]?" He said he wanted a "clean, straight duplication."[35] The bill, drafted with the help of supply-siders Arthur Laffer, Paul Craig Roberts, and Norman Ture, proposed reducing the top rate from 70 to 50 percent and the bottom rate from 14 to 8 percent for an overall 30 percent cut in income tax rates. Roth suggested a somewhat smaller cut in the bottom rate and phasing in the rate reductions over three years to reduce somewhat the revenue costs.[36] The bill also proposed reducing the corporate rate by three percentage points over three years. There were three important differences between Kennedy's tax cuts and the Kemp-Roth proposal: Kennedy's tax cuts occurred when the top income tax rate was 91 percent, Kemp's when the top rate on labor income was 50 percent, 70 percent on investment income other than capital gains; Kennedy's cuts were smaller, 18 rather than 30 percent; and Kennedy's reductions were progressive with a tax cut of 36 percent for the lowest-bracket taxpayers, 6 percent for the highest.

Kemp was convinced his tax cuts would pay for themselves through more robust economic growth, frequently citing a Library of Congress study showing revenues had gone up by $54 billion in the five years after Kennedy's 1963 tax cuts.[37] Echoing Arthur Laffer, Kemp claimed his tax cuts would "generate so much additional capital, disposable income, and incentives that the U.S. Treasury will net higher revenues even at lower rates."[38] But the best estimates indicated the federal government recouped only about one-third of the revenue costs of Kennedy's tax cuts through economic growth.[39]

Jack Kemp was the keynote speaker at the Republican National Committee meeting in the fall of 1977. He told the assembled crowd, "Republicans must not be bookkeepers for Democratic deficits" and urged enactment of the Kemp-Roth tax cuts. The committee then voted to approve the Kemp-Roth legislation as the official policy of the Republican Party.[40] It was the first time since 1953 that Republicans supported a large tax cut without calling for a balanced federal budget.[41] Arthur Laffer told the House Ways and Means

Committee, "Kemp-Roth would partially redress the counterproductive structure of current tax rates, leading to a substantial increase in output, and may well, in the course of a very few years, reduce the size of total government deficits from what they otherwise would have been."[42]

Following the June 1978 California vote for Proposition 13, Republican support for the Kemp-Roth tax reductions surged. On July 14, 1978, the Senate Finance Committee held a hearing on the bill where it was supported by Alan Greenspan, among others. Kemp-Roth was ultimately voted down that year by the Democratic House of Representatives, but it garnered the support of thirty-seven Democrats and all but three Republicans.

During the 1978 midterm campaigns, every House Republican candidate supported Kemp-Roth. Jack Kemp traveled the country campaigning, calling Republicans the party of growth and Democrats the party of distribution. Republicans picked up three Senate seats and fifteen in the House. Kemp was reelected with 83.3 percent of the vote in Buffalo, the largest margin of his career. In 1981 he became the third-ranking member of the Republican House leadership.

A Supply-Side Breakthrough

In 1978 the Kemp-Roth tax cut was too radical for the Democratic Congress, but supply-siders still won an important legislative victory. On April 26 the *Wall Street Journal* published an editorial written by Jude Wanniski, titled "Stupendous Steiger," claiming that a "slight, youthful 39-year old Republican has shaken the earth." Wanniski's editorial concluded, "Everyone should know that the Steiger amendment is not one tax provision among many, but the cutting edge of an important intellectual and financial breakthrough."[43]

Who was this "stupendous Steiger"? William Steiger was a young, moderate, six-term congressman from Oshkosh, Wisconsin, whose previous claim to fame was legislation in 1970 establishing the Occupational Safety and Health Administration. The earth-shaking legislation prompting Wanniski's rave was Steiger's proposal to reduce the capital gains tax rate.[44]

Capital gains occur when assets that have increased in value are sold or exchanged for other assets. Increases in assets' values are not taxed as long as their owners hold on to them, and if assets are held until their owner's death, any appreciation that occurred during the owner's lifetime is never subject to capital gains tax. Because wealth is substantially more concentrated at the top than income, the vast majority of capital gains taxes are paid by high-income households. In a typical year, for example, the top 20 percent enjoy 90 percent of the taxable gains; the top 1 percent, about 70 percent of the gains.[45] Capital gains have long been taxed at rates lower than those applicable to wages, interest, rents, and other normal business income. From 1969 through 1977, capital gains were taxed at half the normal rates, producing rates ranging from 7 to 35 percent, but for some high-income taxpayers a "minimum tax" provision sometimes increased the top rate to 49 percent. Steiger's amendment provided for a reduction in the top capital gains rate to 25 percent.

Jimmy Carter's treasury secretary Michael Blumenthal said a capital gains tax cut was the "worst way" to address underinvestment.[46] In addition to insisting the capital gains tax cut would be ineffective, Blumenthal argued against it on fairness grounds, claiming Steiger's amendment would "sharply erode the progressivity of the income tax system" because more than "four-fifths of the benefits would go to persons with incomes over $100,000" ($420,000 in 2021 dollars) and almost "97 percent" of the tax reductions from eliminating capital gains from the minimum tax "would go to those with incomes over $200,000" ($840,000 in 2021 dollars).[47] But low, or even zero, taxation of capital gains was (and remains) an obsessive objective of supply-side conservatives.[48]

Steiger's push for lower capital gains taxes received an important boost from business interests. In the 1970s business groups began forming ad hoc coalitions to support or oppose particular legislation. In the debate over Steiger's efforts to cut capital gains taxes, one of the more effective new organizations was the American Council for Capital Formation (ACCF).

ACCF was founded in 1975 by Charls—without the "e"—Walker, a tall, folksy, gregarious, cigar-chomping, former bomber pilot with an economics PhD from the University of Texas. He had served as chief lobbyist of the American Bankers Association before becoming deputy treasury secretary in the Nixon administration. Charls Walker knew everyone with any power in Washington and nearly everyone liked him. Mark Bloomfield, his successor at ACCF, said, "Charls was the classic caricature of the cigar-smoking super-lobbyist with a limo."[49] The Washington Post called him a lobbying "wunderkind."[50]

Arthur Laffer served on the board of ACCF, along with Democratic presidential whisperer Clark Clifford, liberal Minnesota Democrat Eugene McCarthy, and powerhouses from both parties. Walker insisted it was "fiction" that you cannot "accomplish anything with a Democratic Congress." "That's not true," he said. "You can get things done up there if you know how to do it."[51] In 1978 Walker and ACCF vigorously supported a cut in capital gains taxes, an issue of particular importance to timber and securities businesses that helped finance ACCF.

Charls Walker understood the importance of "scientific" analyses and advocacy in the legislative process long before they became commonplace. In 1978, ACCF commissioned a study from Chase Econometrics claiming a capital gains tax cut would create 440,000 new jobs, boost economic growth, and reduce budget deficits. The study blamed the stock market declines of prior years on increases in capital gains taxes and predicted cutting the capital gains tax rate to 25 percent would raise stock prices by 40 percent by 1982. These predictions were trumpeted by the *Wall Street Journal*.[52] Another widely publicized study, commissioned by the Securities Industries Association, claiming to use "the world's largest computerized bank of economic information," estimated that eliminating capital gains taxes entirely would add nearly $20 billion of economic growth and raise $38 billion of new revenues, making Arthur Laffer's insistence that zero tax rates raise no revenue look cautious. Journalist Robert Kuttner wrote: "Many of these studies later were shown to be based on unverifiable assumptions . . . yet they were presented as scientific fact, and by the time the liberal economists had . . . challenged the methodology . . . the political battle was over and Charlie Walker's capital formation council had moved on to other issues."[53]

After months of convoluted legislative twists and turns and despite threatening to veto the bill, President Carter, on November 6, 1978, signed the Revenue Act of 1978, which contained a version of Steiger's amendment that excluded capital gains from the minimum tax and lowered the top capital gains tax rate to 28 percent.[54] Retiring Wyoming Republican senator Clifford Hansen crowed, "We've turned around the whole thrust of what tax reform was two years ago."[55]

The *Wall Street Journal's* Robert Bartley described Steiger's capital gains victory, along with Proposition 13 and the introduction of the Kemp-Roth tax-cut bill, as crucial turning points in United States economic history. "That was the moment," Bartley wrote, "at which a decade of envy came to its close and the search for a growth formula started in earnest. The year 1978 was a remarkable turning point."[56] Bartley did not care a bit that the capital gains tax cut benefited the rich. "It was entirely appropriate," he wrote, "that the capital gains tax became the fulcrum for tilting from a decade of envy to a decade of 'greed' and growth." "By 1978," Bartley gloated, "fairness was no longer the issue."[57]

An Unlikely Supply-Side Electoral Success

Jeffrey Bell in 1978 became the surprising herald for the electoral clout of supply-side tax cutting. As Steiger's capital gains tax cut was making its way through Congress, Bell was mounting a longshot Senate primary campaign against four-term Republican senator Clifford Case. Case ran successfully for Congress in 1944 and had never lost a New Jersey election.

Bell had been a staffer for Richard Nixon and a speechwriter for Ronald Reagan in his unsuccessful 1976 Republican primary campaign against Gerald Ford. Before the New Hampshire primary, Bell wrote a speech in which Reagan proposed a massive transfer of federal programs to the states.[58] Ford countered by explaining to New Hampshire voters that adding the new responsibilities would require a new state income tax. Reagan lost the New Hampshire primary by less than two thousand votes, and Bell's speech was blamed for Reagan's loss. Bell then became unemployable in Republican politics and moved to New Jersey to mount an improbable primary challenge to Clifford Case.[59]

On June 6, 1978—the same day Howard Jarvis was celebrating his Proposition 13 victory in California—Bell defeated Case by about one percentage point and earned the Republican nomination for the Senate. The key to Bell's campaign was his proposal for an across-the-board income tax cut of 23 percent.[60] Bell lost in November to the Democratic candidate Bill Bradley, a popular former basketball star for Princeton University and the New York Knicks, but Bell showed Republicans the electoral power of large tax cuts.

Bell said his antitax Senate campaign became viable because of successful direct-mail fundraising pioneered by Richard Viguerie. Bell received contributions from Wall Street and from Steve Forbes, the editor-in-chief of *Forbes* magazine, who mounted an antitax campaign for president two decades later. Equally if not more important was support from the preeminent antitax supply-side zealots: Arthur Laffer, Jude Wanniski, and Jack Kemp. All three supplied crucial ideas and political energy to Bell's campaign. Bell met several times weekly with Wanniski, whose firing by the *Wall Street Journal* for partisan political activities occurred after Wanniski handed a Bell campaign leaflet to Ray Shaw, president of the *Journal's* parent company, at the Morristown train station.[61]

Bell's New Jersey primary victory augured well for the electoral power of the antitax issue. As Arthur Laffer told *People* magazine, "Politicians respond to the hoofbeats."[62] Bell ran for a New Jersey Senate seat twice more, to no avail. But in 1980 the Kemp-Roth tax-cut plan and Jeffrey Bell would play an important—some claim decisive—role in Ronald Reagan's successful presidential campaign.

Supply Side's Winners

The essence of the supply-siders' disagreements with Keynesians is that to stimulate a lagging economy Keynesians want the government to give consumers money to spend on goods and services by increasing spending or lowering taxes, while supply-siders, in contrast, want to lower taxes and deregulate the economy to remove barriers for savings and investment.[63] By increasing the supply of capital, supply-siders claim, the productivity of workers and thus their wages will rise. This, they insist, will inspire people to work harder, and the additional capital will ensure they will produce more even if they do not. To supply-siders, giving tax cuts or government spending to people who will spend the money on consumption is worthless at best—and worse if the consumers' additional spending is financed by taxing savers and investors. As Jude Wanniski put it, the "basic belief of supply-side economics is that the individual producer, rather than the consumer, is the dominant actor in the economy."[64]

The crucial supply-side tax changes consist of reducing tax rates on income from capital, or on capital itself. The people with capital, of course, are richer than those without, so supply-side tax breaks concentrate their benefits at the top. No one should be surprised, therefore, that successful supply-side economics makes the rich richer. This is why skeptics call it "trickle-down" economics.

Nevertheless, the supply-side economists along with Arthur Laffer's curve reframed the nation's debates over taxation. Supply-siders claimed that everyone would benefit from reducing taxes at the top, and Laffer's insistence that top tax rates could be reduced without losing revenue offered the elusive promise of a free lunch: tax cuts need not be derailed by debates over the accompanying cuts in popular spending programs necessary to maintain fiscal discipline and stability. Despite ongoing evidence to the contrary, both assertions remained de rigueur for antitax advocates over the following half century—regardless of the level of top tax rates or the economic conditions.

———

By the time the 1980 presidential campaign began in earnest, the building blocks for a supply-side tax-cutting revolution were in place. Creative economists had replaced the Keynesian consensus with an economic rationale for cutting the taxes of savers and investors at the top rather than the taxes of consumers in the middle or bottom. Many mainstream economists who rejected Arthur Laffer's claim that such tax cuts would increase government revenues, nevertheless, became convinced zero was the best tax rate for income from capital. Business leaders and high-income investors saw potential large financial gains from embracing supply-side claims. Almost daily the *Wall Street Journal's* editorial pages told the public that increasing investors' wealth would well serve the nation's economy.

Jack Kemp, an emerging Republican leader often mentioned as a potential 1980 presidential candidate, had produced and marketed a supply-side tax-cut blueprint. Kemp, William Steiger, and Jeffrey Bell, along with Proposition 13's victory, had demonstrated the legislative and electoral appeal of tax cuts. Antitax and antigovernment attitudes were ripe among the populace. Supply-side economists had concentrated on reducing taxes at the top, but Kemp knew to succeed politically such cuts had to be accompanied by tax reductions for people in the middle and the bottom, making the supply-side project much more costly to the fisc—costs he and his small-government Republican allies viewed as a benefit. All the supply-side revolution needed was effective presidential leadership. As the 1970s came to a close, supply-siders lodged their hopes in Ronald Reagan's campaign.

Chapter 5

Reaganomics

The nine most terrifying words in the English language are "I'm from the government and I'm here to help."

—RONALD REAGAN

Ronald Reagan's close, unsuccessful challenge to President Gerald Ford for the 1976 Republican presidential nomination established the former California governor as the front-runner for his party's 1980 nomination. To his admirers, Reagan was larger-than-life, a charismatic, optimistic, anti-communist, political conservative determined to cure America of its malaise by expanding the economy and increasing freedom. To his detractors, he was shallow, uninformed, inattentive, and lazy. Everyone agreed he was an exceptionally gifted communicator. Reagan's prescriptions were straightforward: cut taxes, decrease non-defense domestic spending, deregulate the economy, strengthen the military, and destroy communism. As he entered the presidential race, important potential antitax supporters remained uncertain how committed he was to their tax-cutting agenda.

Reagan had been president of the Screen Actors Guild beginning in 1947 when he was a Democrat acting in low-budget films for Warner Brothers. But by 1964 Reagan was a conservative Republican. That October he gave a powerful televised speech supporting Barry Goldwater called "A Time for Choosing," praising freedom and denouncing communism. Reagan's speech was peppered with folksy anecdotes—reprising successful motivational speeches he had given to workers and civic groups as a spokesman for General Electric. Reagan complained about the nation's tax burden, which he said threatened the country's prosperity; deficits and the size of the national debt; excessive government spending, especially Lyndon Johnson's Great Society programs, Social Security, welfare, and farm programs; and threats from communism and socialism.[1] The widely respected *Washington Post* journalist David Broder called Reagan's speech "the most successful national political debut since William Jennings Bryan electrified the 1896 Democratic convention."[2]

Two years later, Ronald Reagan won 57.5 percent of the votes to defeat two-term Democratic incumbent Edmund G. (Pat) Brown and become governor of California. Reagan inherited the largest budget deficit in California's history. He proposed 10 percent across-the-board spending cuts as a solution. After they failed, he reluctantly proposed record-breaking state tax increases totaling about $1 billion—including large increases in individual and corporate income taxes—to comply with the state's constitutional balanced-budget requirement. As governor, Reagan frequently compromised with Democratic legislators, and in 1970 he easily won reelection for a second term.

When the campaign for the 1980 Republican nomination for president began, Jude Wanniski and some others favored their compatriot Jack Kemp and urged him to run. As the Republican primaries approached, Wanniski, in his typically understated style, told a group of Kemp supporters, "Jack should run for president. The future of Western Civilization depends on it!"[3] But Jack Kemp instead opted for Ronald Reagan.

Kemp became convinced of Reagan's commitment to large tax cuts at a dinner party in the summer of 1979 hosted by Arthur Laffer for Ronald and Nancy Reagan and their close advisors. After the dinner, Kemp described Reagan as supporting "85 percent" of his ideas and told Wanniski and Bell he was going to support Reagan's candidacy. Laffer was also sure of Reagan's supply-side bona fides. "Reagan believed those things long before I was born," Laffer said.[4]

Ronald Reagan had seen Kemp's success rallying Republican candidates behind his proposed tax cuts in the 1978 midterms and Jeff Bell's surprising victory in the New Jersey Republican primary, and he endorsed Kemp's plan. Some supply-siders, however, worried Reagan's embrace of the Kemp-Roth tax cuts was half-hearted and primarily intended to keep Kemp out of the Republican presidential primaries. Wanniski feared Reagan had outmaneuvered Kemp and argued that once Kemp told Reagan he was not running 85 percent support would diminish to "75 percent and then 50 percent and then 5 percent."[5] Concerned about Reagan's California tax increases, Kemp, Laffer, and Wanniski gathered in Los Angeles in January 1980 at the Beverly Wilshire Hotel to convince Reagan of the importance of income tax cuts.

At the Beverly Hills briefing, Reagan regaled his interlocutors with a story he frequently told from his acting days when the top income tax rate was as high as 91 percent. Reagan said, "I came into big money making pictures during World War II." "You could only make four pictures," he complained, "and then you were in the top bracket. So we all quit working after four pictures and went off to the country."[6] Reagan's personal resentment of high tax rates and his conviction they caused less work swayed Wanniski. "We were absolutely thrilled," Wanniski said. "Reagan not only favored the policies, but understood them."[7] Reagan's emphasis on Kemp's income tax rate reductions ebbed and flowed during the campaign, but he never retreated from his commitment to large income tax cuts.

"Voodoo Economics"

Even with Jack Kemp on the sidelines, Ronald Reagan faced seven formidable Republican primary opponents, but by the end of March, he had vanquished all but one. The only candidate left challenging Reagan for the Republican nomination was George Herbert Walker Bush.

George H. W. Bush was an unexciting "moderate conservative" who based his campaign more on a commitment to service than a vision for the country. He emerged as Reagan's principal challenger on January 21, 1980, when Bush, who started 36 points behind Reagan in polling, beat Reagan by 31.6 percent to 29.5 percent in the Iowa caucuses. No one else came close. *Newsweek* put Bush on its cover. The *Boston Globe* reported that after the Iowa vote, Bush was polling nine points ahead of Reagan in the crucial upcoming New Hampshire primary.[8]

Nationally syndicated supply-side enthusiasts Rowland Evans and Robert Novak insisted three television ads were crucial in transferring votes from Bush to Reagan in New Hampshire and decisive for Reagan in securing the Republican nomination. The ads were written by Jeffrey Bell and produced by Elliott Curson, a Philadelphia advertising consultant who produced similar advertisements for Bell's 1978 New Jersey campaign. The commercials accused President Carter of wanting to keep tax rates high. They invoked President Kennedy's tax cuts of the early 1960s, with Reagan saying, "If I become president, we're going to try that again." Promising not to "leave anyone behind," Reagan concluded, "If we make a deep cut in everyone's tax rates, we'll have lower prices, an increase in production, and a lot more peace of mind."[9]

Reagan dominated the New Hampshire primary with 50 percent of the votes to Bush's 23 percent. At his victory party, Ronald Reagan appeared in front of a large red, white, and blue banner with his campaign slogan emblazoned in large capital letters: *"LET'S MAKE AMERICA GREAT AGAIN."*[10] "It is no exaggeration," Evans and Novak insisted, "that those Curson-Bell spots, unpublicized though they were, were indispensable."[11] Tax cuts continued to be a central element of Reagan's campaign throughout the Republican primaries.[12]

The ads got under Bush's skin. Before the Pennsylvania primary, on April 10, 1980, Bush ridiculed supply-side claims that a large tax cut would expand economic growth enough to produce tax revenues sufficient to pay for the cuts. Reagan was also proposing dramatic increases in defense spending and claiming he would balance the federal budget. Bush told an audience at Carnegie-Mellon University, "It just isn't going to work." He added, in one of his few memorable phrases, Reagan's plan is "what I call a voodoo economic plan."[13] Bush overcame a large polling deficit to beat Reagan in Pennsylvania, and he won the Michigan and District of Columbia primaries in May, but Reagan prevailed elsewhere and easily clinched the nomination.

When the Republican convention began in Detroit on July 14, only one mystery remained: Reagan's choice to be his vice president. Bush's campaign manager James Baker signaled to Reagan's team that Bush would readily accept an offer, but Reagan told his advisors he did not want to select Bush. When long-time Republican operative Stuart Spencer listed Bush's advantages, including his important government experience, his indefatigable effort as a campaigner, and his ability to unite the party's moderates and conservatives, Reagan barked, "Why should I? Voodoo economics!"[14]

"Who else is there?" Reagan asked. After a brief flirtation and ultimately ruling out Gerald Ford, the conversation turned to Bush. Reagan finally agreed that if Bush accepted every detail of the platform, including positions he denounced during the primary campaign, Reagan could accept him.[15] At 11:37 that night, after Reagan was nominated, Bush's friends and colleagues heard him answer the nominee, "Why, yes sir. I think you can say I support the platform wholeheartedly."[16]

Are You Better Off?

Tax-cut proposals played a smaller role in the general election campaign than in the Republican primaries, but they remained a key component of Ronald Reagan's policy priorities. Jimmy Carter was stymied by stagflation and his willingness to accept an era of limits. Ronald Reagan, in sharp contrast, epitomized the hero of his favorite story about an optimist faced with a room-ful of manure: "There must be a pony in there somewhere." Denouncing double-digit inflation, high unemployment, and interest rates approaching 20 percent, Reagan frequently proclaimed, "Recession is when your neighbor loses his job; depression is when you lose your job; and recovery is when Jimmy Carter loses his job."[17] Carter's dour outlook—his concern that the country would continue to suffer from ongoing malaise—was no match for Ronald Reagan's sunny optimism and wit.

At the close of the candidates' only presidential debate on October 28 in Cleveland, Reagan posed the question: "Ask yourself," he said, "are you better off than you were four years ago?"[18] Most families believed they were worse off. Ronald Reagan was elected in a landslide, winning nearly 44 million votes to Carter's 35.5 million, carrying 44 states, and dominating the Electoral College by a vote of 489 to 49.

Antitax zealots, naturally, attributed Reagan's electoral success to his embrace of the Kemp-Roth tax cuts. Evans and Novak wrote, "Traveling the nation that last week [after the debate], Reagan won cheers everywhere with his promises of not just one, not just two, not just three years of tax reduction, but three years plus counterinflationary tax indexing after that."[19]

A Wolf in Sheep's Clothing

After Reagan's inauguration, his administration was divided about how bold a tax cut to propose and what shape it should take. Reagan appointed two passionate supply-side economists, Norman Ture and Paul Craig Roberts, to sub-cabinet positions in the Treasury Department, but antitax advocates failed to persuade President Reagan to appoint Lewis Lehrman as treasury secretary. Reagan instead appointed Donald Regan, chairman and CEO of Merrill Lynch, who came into office without any strong tax policy views but became an ardent salesman for President Reagan's tax-cut proposals.

Ronald Reagan appointed only one supply-sider to his cabinet: David Stockman, a smart, young, hardworking, two-term Michigan congressman whom Reagan named director of the Office of Management and Budget. Unlike many antitax enthusiasts, Stockman had not drunk the large-tax-cuts-will-pay-for-themselves Kool-Aid. He believed the federal budget must be balanced and viewed tax cuts as creating an opportunity and necessity to cut spending, especially spending for the elderly and poor, including welfare, Medicaid, Medicare, and Social Security.[20]

Stockman regarded the Kemp-Roth tax cuts as the wedge that would pin "craven politicians" to the wall. "They would have to dismantle . . . bloated, wasteful, and unjust spending enterprises," he wrote, "or risk national ruin." If you stopped inflation, Stockman added, "Professor Laffer's tax cut napkin didn't work. Consequently, only sweeping domestic spending cuts could balance the budget—an action that I believed was desirable but which the other supply siders had denied would be necessary."[21]

Stockman's view—that tax cuts would produce sufficient concern about deficits to create inevitable and irresistible political pressure to cut domestic spending—became known as "starve-the-beast."[22] For Stockman and many other antitax enthusiasts, including Lewis Lehrman and Milton Friedman, starve-the-beast became the justification for supply-side tax cuts: they insisted depriving the government of revenues would necessarily produce large cuts in domestic government spending.[23] Writing about the Kemp-Roth tax-cut proposal in *Newsweek* in 1978, two years after he won the Nobel Prize in economics, Milton Friedman wrote: "I have concluded that the only effective way to restrain government spending is by limiting government's explicit tax revenue—just as a limited income is the only effective restraint on any individual's or family's spending."[24] Irving Kristol agreed in a *Wall Street Journal* editorial a few days later. The "lesson of Proposition 13," Kristol wrote, "is that tax cuts are a prerequisite for cuts in government spending."[25] Ronald Reagan said, "If you've got a kid who is extravagant, you can lecture him all you want about his extravagance or you can cut his allowance and achieve the same end much quicker."[26]

Reagan and Stockman would soon learn, to their great disappointment, Congress is far more willing to cut taxes than spending. Unlike families and state governments, the U.S. government can borrow huge sums from the rest of the world. It is a beast that will not starve. Like the myth that tax cuts will pay for themselves, the starve-the-beast delusion that tax cuts will necessarily produce large reductions in government spending remains an essential, oft-repeated antitax claim—notwithstanding the nation's contrary experience.[27]

Resistance in the Democratic House

On February 18, 1981, less than a month after his inauguration, President Reagan delivered his first speech to a joint session of Congress. He described the national debt of nearly $1 trillion as "out of control" and called for nearly $50 billion in spending reductions, including a ceiling on Medicaid expenditures and cuts in food stamps and welfare. He also requested a $180 billion increase in defense spending over six years. Reagan's headline tax proposal was a three-year, 30 percent across-the-board cut in personal income tax rates modeled after the Kemp-Roth legislation. Reagan described his plan as "an equal reduction in everyone's tax rates," but he tilted his tax cuts toward the rich by making clear the top rate of 70 percent on unearned income would be cut immediately to 50 percent—a deep cut for investment income not applicable to wages.[28]

Business representatives viewed the Kemp-Roth cuts as insufficient: they failed to cut taxes for large corporations. Joined by the Business Roundtable, the U.S. Chamber of Commerce, and the National Association of Manufacturers, Charls Walker's American Council for Capital Formation pushed for a major acceleration of businesses' ability to deduct plant and equipment costs. Even though most of the tax savings from such a change would go to large companies, Walker persuaded the National Federation of Independent Businesses, the most powerful small-business lobby, to join his coalition supporting the business tax cuts.[29] By 1980 Walker had gathered a majority of the House and Senate as cosponsors for his plan. President Reagan endorsed it in February 1981.[30] Reagan claimed the business tax cuts, along with the cut in individual tax rates, would "create millions of new jobs" and "make America competitive once again in the world market."[31]

Because the Constitution requires tax legislation to originate in the House of Representatives, the two most important congressional Democrats for enacting President Reagan's tax proposals were old-style Democratic politicians: Speaker of the House Tip O'Neill, a buoyant, affable, white-haired, Irish Massachusetts liberal, whose politics were as far to the left as Reagan's were to the right, and Dan Rostenkowski, the new chairman of the House Ways and Means Committee.

Reagan's timing was fortuitous. Before 1974 his tax-cut legislation would have faced much rougher sledding. The House Ways and Means Committee was then headed by Wilbur Mills of Arkansas, who had chaired the committee since 1958 and controlled it with an iron fist.[32] One of his colleagues said, "I never vote against God, motherhood, or Wilbur Mills."[33] During the nearly two decades Mills was in charge, an antitax movement would have had little chance of succeeding: Mills was a fiscal conservative who would not allow tax revenues to become insufficient to fund federal spending over any significant period.

Wilbur Mills lost his sway on October 9, 1974, when at 2:00 a.m. U.S. Park Police pulled over a Lincoln Continental speeding erratically near the

Jefferson Memorial. Annabel Battistella, known by her stage name Fanne Foxe, ran from the car and jumped into the cold dark tidal pool nearby. Mills, her companion, exited the car with his face red and adorned with scratches. Mills easily won reelection in November, but on November 30, obviously drunk, he appeared on stage in Boston's Pilgrim Theatre to publicly congratulate Ms. Foxe on a striptease performance he particularly admired. On December 3, 1974, Mills checked into Bethesda Naval Hospital. Mills soon stepped down from his Ways and Means chairmanship and did not run for reelection in 1976.

Mills was succeeded by Oregon's ineffectual Al Ullman, who in 1980 became the first Ways and Means Committee chairman in the twentieth century to be defeated for reelection. After Mills's departure, House Democratic leaders forced the Ways and Means Committee to appoint subcommittees, dispersing power and opening opportunities to reward contributors and constituents with special tax breaks. Because of the tax benefits it provided special interests, the Ways and Means Select Revenue subcommittee became known to Washington lobbyists as "Santa's workshop."[34]

Rostenkowski, Ullman's successor, was a tall, blustery, deal-making politician who earned his chops under Chicago's mayor Richard J. Daley, perhaps the last of the city's Democratic machine bosses. In 1981 Rostenkowski took over as chairman of a demoralized tax committee, skeptical of his ability to lead it. Its Democratic majority was on edge because of poor leadership under Ullman and devastating losses suffered by Democrats in the 1980 elections. Rostenkowski, who had previously shown little interest in the substance of the tax law, was determined to take firm control of the committee. He wanted to work with the new president, but he did not believe Reagan's tax cuts would pay for themselves and feared they would magnify federal deficits.

In mid-March Speaker O'Neill announced, "All factions of the Democratic Party agree they are against Kemp-Roth."[35] Rostenkowski said the president's tax proposals were dead and he would develop an alternative. The House Budget Committee also rejected Reagan's plan, urging a Democratic alternative of one year's tax cuts focused on the middle class and larger reductions in business taxes than Reagan proposed.

Republicans captured the Senate majority in 1980, but the Senate Budget Committee, worried about potential deficits, also rejected the president's proposals with three Republicans joining with Democrats to vote against them. As David Stockman wrote, "The majority of congressional Republicans were nonplussed by the radical and alien premise of the supply-side ideology. When it came to taxes, the GOP's idea of tax reform consisted of opening loopholes in the IRS code."[36]

In late March, Treasury Secretary Don Regan called a press conference and proclaimed the Kemp-Roth tax cuts were "far from dead." President Reagan told Barber Conable, the top Ways and Means Republican, "I can't turn tail and retreat on this. There is a long road ahead. We can't start to back away now." Conable replied unenthusiastically, "I shall do my duty."[37]

The Assassination Attempt

On March 30, 1981, Ronald Reagan delivered an uninspiring twenty-minute speech to the National Conference of the AFL-CIO Building and Construction Trades Unions in the ballroom of the Washington Hilton Hotel. Reagan praised individual freedom and ingenuity, complained about the size of the federal debt, and promised to "cut down the budget deficit," before reviewing his economic plans, including his tax-cut proposals.[38] As Reagan emerged from the hotel, John Hinckley, a mentally ill twenty-five-year-old, fired six shots from a .22-caliber pistol hitting four men: Thomas Delahanty, a D.C. police officer; Timothy McCarthy, a Secret Service agent; James Brady, the president's press secretary; and Ronald Reagan.

Not knowing the president had been hit, the Secret Service pushed him into the back of his limousine. After Reagan began coughing up blood, he was rushed to George Washington University Hospital where doctors quickly discovered a bullet in his lung. Reagan's injuries were far more serious than the public knew. He famously quipped to Nancy Reagan at the hospital before his surgery, "I forgot to duck" and asked his doctors if they were Republicans. After his operation, when his key aides came to his hospital room to assure him that the government was still working well, Reagan asked, "What makes you think I'd be happy about that?"

Ronald Reagan's humor and upbeat attitude generated enormous support, including from Speaker O'Neill, who visited Reagan at the hospital, grabbed Reagan's hands, kissed his forehead, and said, "God bless you, Mr. President." O'Neill then got on his knees and prayed for Reagan's recovery.[39] This began an unlikely, but important, amity.

On April 11 President Reagan returned to the White House with the approval of 66 percent of Americans, up nearly 17 percentage points since Hinckley's assassination attempt.[40] On April 28, less than a month after the shooting, Reagan received thunderous applause when he entered the House chamber to address a joint session of Congress. "Our choice," he said, "is not between a balanced budget and a tax cut." He asked Congress to "work as a team, to join in cooperation," and to "chart a new course."[41]

Let the Bidding Begin

In mid-June, Dan Rostenkowski offered Reagan a 15 percent, two-year tax-rate reduction, rather than the 30 percent, three-year cut the president had proposed. Reagan rejected it as "not good enough."[42] The president was unwilling to accept anything less than a three-year, 25 percent cut in tax rates. "The tax cut was one of the few things Ronald Reagan deeply wanted from his presidency," David Stockman wrote. "It was the only thing behind which he threw the full force of his broad political shoulders."[43]

Other than Stockman, a committed supply-sider, the president's key aides trying to get his tax proposals through Congress—Treasury Secretary Don Regan, Chief of Staff James Baker, and Baker's deputy Dick Darman—did not share the president's passion for tax cuts, but they recognized the political capital Reagan would gain from winning and the political costs of losing. Toward the end of July, when House Democrats were struggling to secure a majority for their smaller, less costly alternative, Darman mused, "I don't know which is worse, winning now and fixing up the budget mess later, or losing now and facing a political mess immediately. . . . It finally has come down to the White House versus the Democrats, to us versus them." After a moment's reflection, he said, "Let's get at it. We win now, we fix it later."[44]

Victory did not come easily. A contest developed between a bill sponsored by House Republicans and the Democrats' alternative. Chairman Rostenkowski did not realize Democrats could never outbid Republicans with tax cuts, and he kept adding new tax breaks in an effort to secure votes. Republicans countered with their own giveaways. A feeding frenzy ensued with Republicans and Democrats competing for votes by offering additional tax breaks.

President Reagan's nationally televised address on Monday, July 27, was the turning point. The president dramatized a chart labeled "our bill and their bill" showing two lines depicting the level of taxes over time. The figures revealed "our bill's" taxes went down and stayed down; "their bill's" taxes went down but soon came back up.[45] Reagan did not mention that "our bill" would reduce federal revenues by more than $2 trillion over the coming decade.[46] His viewers knew instantly which bill they wanted. They responded with telephone

President Reagan Relaxing after signing the 1981 tax cuts.

calls, letters, postcards, and telegrams to Congress. Speaker O'Neill and Chairman Rostenkowski knew they were beaten; Ronald Reagan would get the tax cuts he wanted.

Democrats, nevertheless, decided to give their constituents, supporters, and financial backers additional tax cuts. Richard Rahn, chief economist for the U.S. Chamber of Commerce, said, "If you told me a few years ago that the Democrats would propose this, I would have said you were out of your mind."[47] Although not apparent at the time, the Democrats' decision to respond to President Reagan's proposals by adding even more tax breaks was a precursor to subsequent Democratic surrenders to the antitax movement.

Reflecting on President Reagan's legislative victory, Dick Darman wrote, "Without [Stockman's] continuing to push, drive, organize, negotiate, trade— beyond the point where others would have given in—the full tax bill would undoubtedly have failed to get the necessary votes. A more conventional compromise would have been struck."[48] Taking a bit of the blame for the excesses of the 1981 tax cuts himself, Darman added, "I failed to appreciate soon enough that the times were out of joint. We were dealing with voodoo politics."[49]

Less than a month later, on August 13, 1981, at his ranch in the Santa Ynez Mountains near Santa Barbara, California, surrounded by reporters, photographers, and television cameras, President Reagan signed the Economic Recovery Tax Act of 1981.

Something for Everyone – Especially the Wealthy

The new law contained an immediate reduction in the top tax rate on investment income from 70 to 50 percent and in the capital gains rate from 28 to 20 percent. Other income tax rates for individuals were cut by 5 percent beginning October 1, 1981, another 10 percent in July 1, 1982, and a final 10 percent beginning July 1, 1983. Businesses and real estate investors received massive tax cuts through faster write-offs of new investments in equipment and buildings. Congress also provided special tax rates and deductions to small businesses. There were also new tax benefits for corporate executives' stock options, research and development expenditures, and oil producers. The law was festooned with special tax benefits for utilities, truckers, and peanut growers, to name just three beneficiaries of congressional largesse.

The real estate industry, a particularly lush source of campaign contributions, was so favorably treated that overbuilding became common, producing nearly empty "see-through" office buildings and shopping centers from coast to coast. Financial institutions also left the feast happy. Banks, mutual funds, and upper-income taxpayers all greatly benefited from increases in eligibility and amounts permitted for investments in tax-favored Individual Retirement Accounts (IRAs). The revenues lost from this expansion were nearly three times what was anticipated; Congress's economists greatly underestimated the impact of mass marketing by financial institutions in enticing people to open or expand IRAs.[50]

New tax benefits for business were so generous that corporate tax receipts declined from about 15 percent to less than 9 percent of federal revenues. Many companies did not have enough taxable income to take advantage of the new tax write-offs. Rather than writing checks to them, Congress allowed companies that could not use all of the new tax benefits to sell their tax breaks to companies that could use them. These "buy-a-tax-break" deals simply required documents labeled a "lease," ensuring rewards for the lawyers, accountants, and investment bankers who brought the buyers and sellers together. Ford and Chrysler, for example, each sold more than $100 million of tax reductions to IBM and General Electric. General Electric became the largest purchaser of tax benefits: in 1980 it paid nearly $350 million in taxes, but in 1981 it received a tax refund of about $100 million, despite pretax earnings of $2.67 billion.[51]

The goals and long-term impact of the antitax movement were enhanced immeasurably by another important change. During the 1970s and early 1980s, inflation pushed many households into higher and higher tax brackets and lowered the value of dollar amounts specified in the income tax law. Republican Senate Finance Committee chairman Robert Dole had long favored indexing the income tax brackets, personal exemptions, and the standard deduction to eliminate income tax increases that occurred automatically because of inflation. President Reagan supported the idea but had different priorities and left it out of his proposals because of its large revenue costs. With Dole's encouragement, Colorado Republican Bill Armstrong introduced a Senate amendment to begin indexing tax rate brackets, personal exemptions, and the standard deduction in 1985 after the large rate cuts had been fully phased in. Congress was then using a five-year period to score the revenue effects of tax changes, and, because of its delayed effective date, indexing did not appear to increase substantially the ostensible revenue costs of the legislation. However, by 1990 the inflation adjustments reduced government revenues by nearly $60 billion; over time they became the most costly aspect of the 1981 legislation.[52]

Indexing also changed income tax politics forever. Until 1981, when inflation automatically increased income taxes, Congress routinely enacted tax cuts to offset some or all of inflation's impact. Indexing eliminated these recurring pots of revenue. After the 1981 legislation, whenever Congress or the president wanted to expand or enact a spending program or cut taxes, increasing taxes was necessary to prevent federal deficits and debt from growing. Antitax forces, however, made raising taxes politically costly and often impossible.

Winners and Losers

The 1981 law substantially cut taxes on income generated from wealth, increased opportunities for tax-free savings by upper-income Americans, and greatly expanded tax-shelter opportunities for high-income individuals and corporations. It reduced taxes on transfers of wealth from the richest Americans to their descendants by exempting all but a small fraction of the wealthiest 1 percent of decedents from the estate tax and cutting the top rate on transfers of more than $10 million (nearly $30 million in 2021 dollars) by 20 percentage points.[53] The 1981 law also more than tripled the amounts of wealth that can be transferred annually free from gift taxes. These changes reduced total revenues from the wealth transfer taxes to about one-third of what would have been collected under prior law.[54] The 1981 act was a major victory in an ongoing antitax attack on tax progressivity.

The 1981 tax cuts contributed importantly to rising inequality. *Wall Street Journal* editorial writers, unsurprisingly, disputed this. In an editorial called "Tricklenomics," by looking only at percentages of income taxes paid, the *Journal* claimed the 1981 cuts in income tax rates shifted the tax burden from the poor to the rich by drawing wealthy individuals out of tax shelters and channeling more income into taxable investments.[55] On the contrary, the Congressional Budget Office concluded income tax progressivity declined between 1980 and 1983 and both pretax and after-tax income became more unequal. Instead of dwindling, tax shelters for high-income individuals and corporations multiplied.[56]

In October 1981 Yale's Nobel Laureate in economics, James Tobin, told a New York University audience, "The U.S. budget and tax legislation of 1981 is a historic reversal of direction and purpose. . . . The message is clear enough: inequality of opportunity is no longer a concern of the federal government. . . . The Reagan economic program is advertised to cure inflation and unemployment, to revive productivity, investment, hard work, and thrift. It probably cannot achieve these wonderful results. What it is sure to do is to redistribute wealth, power, and opportunity to the wealthy and powerful and their heirs."[57]

———

In three years, tax policy and politics in the United States were transformed. Beginning with California's Proposition 13, states across the country cut back on property taxes and imposed new political barriers to tax increases. Supply-siders achieved large cuts in individual and business income taxes, especially for the wealthy. Public antitax attitudes and support for tax cuts had expanded and solidified. Federal income tax policy shifted from loophole-closing efforts to tax-rate reductions along with a proliferation of special tax privileges for chosen industries and investors. Replacing Keynesianism with supply-side economics concentrated the largest tax cuts at the top, even though political viability required reductions across-the-board.

The two major claims of the supply-siders were not simply inconsistent: they were fanciful. Arthur Laffer's free lunch never materialized: the 1981 tax cuts failed to pay for themselves. Instead massive deficits occurred. Nor did Congress enact the spending reductions that antitax advocates claimed would inevitably follow the tax cuts.

David Stockman, Dick Darman, and many other top Reagan administration officials were not surprised when federal deficits and debt exploded. In January 1981 the Reagan administration projected the government would enjoy a $28 billion surplus in 1986; in November, three months after President Reagan signed the 1981 tax cuts, the administration estimated that year's deficit would be $320 billion.[58] Supply-siders, including Jack Kemp, Arthur Laffer, Jude Wanniski, Paul Craig Roberts, and Norman Ture, still told the president, "We're still not wrong. Stand pat. It will go away."[59] Treasury Secretary Donald Regan agreed. But large deficits did not disappear despite the insistence of antitax advocates.

Ronald Reagan and his allies transformed what he viewed as an out-of-control tax-and-spend government into one that instead borrowed to spend—with large ongoing deficits and increasing federal debt—not what he intended. As so often happens in American politics, the pendulum swung back for a while: after the 1981 tax cuts, battles over deficits and debt dominated federal fiscal policy and American domestic politics for more than a decade. The following chapters describe the ensuing battles.

Part II

Turbulence

1982–1994

Chapter 6

Resistance

I've been asked if I have any regrets. Well I do. The deficit is one.

—RONALD REAGAN, FAREWELL ADDRESS TO THE NATION,
JANUARY 11, 1989

Ronald Reagan and Jack Kemp got their large tax cuts, but those cuts, along with President Reagan's increases in defense spending, produced unprecedented deficits and increases in the federal debt. Putting the lie to claims that tax cuts would pay for themselves, the 1981 tax reductions were the most important contributor to the rise in federal debt and deficits.

In his inaugural address on January 20, 1981, Ronald Reagan complained, "For decades we have piled deficit upon deficit, mortgaging our future and our children's future for the temporary convenience of the present."[1] Previously he had claimed, "Inflation has one cause and one cause alone: government spending more than government takes in."[2] Influential political leaders from both parties and many prominent economists also feared increases in the federal debt were crowding out private borrowing and inhibiting private investments and agreed that large deficits contributed to inflation.[3] Addressing deficits became the dominant fiscal issue from 1982 into the mid-1990s.

A Deep Hole

Soon after President Reagan signed the largest tax reduction in the nation's history in August 1981, it, along with the spending bill he signed the same day, caused the federal debt to exceed $1 trillion for the first time. Nevertheless,

Reagan claimed his administration would produce a $121 billion surplus by 1983 and begin to reduce the federal debt by then.[4] That did not happen.

Here is how Reagan's budget director David Stockman described the federal budget just before Thanksgiving in 1981:

> I knew we were on the precipice of triple-digit deficits, a national debt in the trillions, and destructive and profound dislocations throughout the entire warp and woof of the American economy. . . . After November 1981, the administration locked the door on its own disastrous fiscal policy. [Defense Secretary] Cap Weinberger hung on for dear life to the $1.45 trillion defense budget. . . . [Key White House advisors] ceaselessly endeavored to keep all the bad news out of the Oval Office and off the tube. The nation's huge fiscal imbalance was never addressed or corrected; it just festered and grew.[5]

Reagan's promises to balance the federal budget and control federal debt were grounded on excessively optimistic economic predictions that Stockman later called "Rosy Scenario." Differences between the administration's unrealistic economic projections and the national economy added $2 trillion to federal deficits between 1982 and 1986.[6]

In 1982 President Reagan's budget projected a $90 billion deficit for the year (about $247 billion in 2021 dollars) with deficits growing steadily after that. A congressional majority was determined to address the fiscal challenge, but how to reduce the burgeoning red ink divided Republicans in both the White House and Congress. Supply-side advocates were adamant that deficits should be restrained entirely by reducing spending, principally benefits for the elderly and the poor.

The president and some of his closest advisors believed a balanced budget could be achieved by cutting administrative inefficiencies and rooting out "fraud, waste, and abuse."[7] As one example, at the first meeting of Reagan's cabinet the morning after his inaugural, the president asked for a report on the efficient operation of the motor pool. Potential savings in those kinds of administrative costs were trivial.

The big money was in defense, health insurance, and spending for the middle class, including Social Security. Without slashing those popular spending programs or raising taxes, ongoing deficits and ballooning federal debt were inevitable.[8] David Stockman's efforts to persuade President Reagan to support deep cuts in Social Security and Medicare ultimately failed, and the president insisted ongoing increases in defense spending were sacrosanct.[9]

Influential *Washington Post* columnist David Broder summarized the difficulties: "Reagan is certain that he did not become President of the United States in order to raise taxes and O'Neill is equally convinced that he did not become Speaker of the House in order to reduce everyone's Social Security."[10]

Despite the deficits, Ronald Reagan was determined not to reverse his 1981 income tax rate cuts. So, the president backed a diversion.

A Balanced-Budget Amendment

The early gambit to eliminate federal deficits was a constitutional charade that would be reenacted repeatedly over the following generation. Politicians began pushing for a constitutional amendment requiring the government to balance the federal budget each year. In 1982 nearly three-fourths of the public supported a balanced-budget amendment. But a constitutional balanced-budget requirement would make recessions harsher and longer than need be and hamstring the nation's ability to respond to wars, pandemics, and financial or other crises.[11] Experience in the states demonstrates such requirements can be eluded through budget gimmicks. Moreover, balanced budgets are not essential to reduce the federal debt: when the economy grows faster than deficits, the debt will diminish. Importantly, neither the public nor its representatives supported the tax increases or spending cuts that would *actually* balance the budget. Only 25 percent favored increasing taxes, and barely 10 percent favored cuts in Social Security or Medicare.[12]

Pushing for a constitutional amendment to balance the budget, however, allowed politicians to look determined to control federal deficits, confident that adding such a requirement to the Constitution—which requires a two-thirds majority in both Houses of Congress and ratification by legislatures of three-fourths of the states—was extremely unlikely, if not impossible.

On Monday July 12, 1982, President Reagan led a rally on the Washington Mall before a crowd of about five thousand demanding Congress approve a balanced-budget amendment. Democratic House Majority Leader Jim Wright of Texas quipped that Reagan's support of a constitutional amendment requiring an annual balanced budget was "like the Saloon Keeper demanding that everyone take a vow of total abstinence."[13]

On August 4, 1982, support for a balanced-budget amendment reached a peak, passing the Senate by 69 to 31, the requisite two-thirds majority, but the amendment fell 16 votes short in the House.[14] Notwithstanding many failures since then to achieve the necessary congressional majorities, proposals for a constitutional balanced-budget mandate have continued to allow politicians to insist on their virtue without addressing the underlying causes of deficits or rising federal debt.

In 1982 tax increases were inevitable, but convincing Ronald Reagan of that and enlisting Republican support in Congress presented difficult obstacles. A Republican congressional leader needed to take charge. That leader—in a contest that triggered a long battle for the soul of the Republican Party—was Bob Dole, who in 1981 became chairman of the Senate Finance Committee.

"The Tax Collector for the Welfare State"

Robert Dole was a Republican senator from Kansas who had been Gerald Ford's 1976 running mate and would later serve for eleven years as the Senate Republican Leader. Dole ran for president in 1980 but dropped out of the race after receiving less than 1 percent of the votes in the New Hampshire primary.[15]

Bob Dole grew up in Russell, Kansas, a small farming, cattle, and oil community nearly three hundred miles west of Kansas City, in a family struggling to stay afloat during the Depression. One year, to cover their expenses, his family moved into the basement of their house and rented out the rest. In 1945, three weeks before World War II ended in Europe, Dole was badly injured while serving with the 10th Mountain Division's topflight skiers and mountain climbers in the Apennine Mountains forty miles south of Bologna, Italy. After three years of hospitalizations and rehabilitation, he had permanently lost the use of his right arm. Depending so long on others, Dole said, "You almost get stubborn the other way. I didn't want anyone to help me."[16] Dole was generous, but his irrepressible sharp wit was frequently mistaken by the press and the public for bitterness and meanness.[17]

Robert Dole was the kind of midwestern Republican senator we used to elect in America, conservative in economic policy but willing to compromise when he regarded it as in the nation's best interests. Senator Dole said he was disappointed with the economic impact of the 1981 tax cuts. By July 1982, he was concerned with the burgeoning federal debt and ongoing deficits and convinced the 1981 tax cuts were excessive.

The power of the Senate Finance Committee depends on its ability to craft legislation that can survive most, if not all, of the potentially unlimited amendments on the Senate floor. Bob Dole came to Washington to get things done and was a brilliant legislative strategist. In 1982 he needed to be.

A Large 1982 Tax Increase

After the balanced-budget amendment failed, persuading Ronald Reagan of the necessity of substantial tax increases fell principally to the president's chief of staff, Jim Baker, who by the spring of 1982 had become Reagan's most powerful White House aide. Once Baker concluded the 1981 tax cuts were greater than the government could afford, he began trying to convince the president's closest allies, including Nancy Reagan, that tax increases were unavoidable. Baker claimed he could get three dollars of spending cuts from Congress for every dollar of tax increases, and President Reagan reluctantly empowered Baker to negotiate with Congress. "All right, goddamn it, I'm going to do it," Reagan grumbled. "But it's wrong."[18]

President Reagan was adamant that opening the door to a tax increase did not allow any flexibility to raise the top income or capital gains rates. Backtracking on indexing for inflation was also out of the question. Nor was Congress willing to curb the most costly tax breaks: benefits for employer-provided health insurance and retirement savings and itemized deductions for home mortgage interest, charitable contributions, and state and local taxes.[19]

Neither President Reagan nor his top aides wanted their imprimatur on any tax-increasing legislation. Treasury Secretary Donald Regan, the cabinet official normally in charge of advocating for tax increases, so relished his 1981 role as a salesman for large tax cuts that he insisted deficits could be controlled by cutting spending—not his bailiwick.[20] In June 1982, as the Reagan administration began seriously to consider tax increases, fervent supply-siders Norman Ture and Paul Craig Roberts resigned their Treasury Department posts.

Ronald Reagan was sure Democrats wanted him to rescind the third year of his tax cuts. He wrote in his diary two days before traveling to Capitol Hill for a "budget summit" with Speaker O'Neill, "Not in a million years."[21] When Democratic Majority Leader Jim Wright suggested the president reduce the final year of the 1981 tax rate cuts by half in exchange for some spending cuts, Reagan responded, "you can get me to crap a pineapple, but you can't get me to crap a cactus."[22]

Tip O'Neill believed President Reagan wanted to trim Social Security benefits and blame Democrats for it.[23] When he learned the president's staff was telling the press Democrats were proposing cuts in Social Security, O'Neill asked the president, "Mr. President, are you putting Social Security on the table or not?"[24] The president responded, "You're not going to trap me on that." "This is [a] proposal that came from the Congress," he added.[25]

Jack Kemp was number three in the House Republican leadership, and no House Republican was willing to push for a tax increase; House Democrats concurred: it was an election year, and they were not going to anger their constituents by raising taxes. Budget negotiations soon collapsed; President Reagan and the House of Representatives were stalemated. By July, only the Senate could address the situation, notwithstanding the House's constitutional prerogative to initiate tax legislation.

In December 1981 the House had passed a twenty-five-page tax bill that would have reduced revenues between 1982 and 1986 by about $1 billion, a trivial amount. On July 23, 1982, by a 50 to 47 vote, Bob Dole and his Senate colleagues deleted its entire substance and substituted six hundred pages of tax increases estimated to raise about $100 billion over the coming three-year period—then the largest tax increase in American history.[26] Reporters on NBC's Sunday news show *Meet the Press* asked Senator Dole whether the Senate's 1982 tax increases represented a reversal of the previous year's supply-side tax cuts. "We're not trying to make a U-turn," Dole responded. "We're just trying to avoid going over a cliff. Maybe we went a bit too far with some of Mr. Kemp's ideas. I never understood all that supply-side business." Dole said he "supported Mr. Kemp last year in some of the things I didn't believe in."[27]

After the Senate passed the tax increases, House Democrats—fearful of the antitax movement and the potential electoral costs of raising taxes—refused to pass any tax legislation of their own. Instead Speaker O'Neill sent Dan Rostenkowski and other Ways and Means Committee members into a conference with the Senate with no House bill to defend. The Senate bill, with a few modifications, soon came to the House for a vote.

O'Neill demanded the president fight for its passage and secure a majority of House Republicans to vote for it. Otherwise, O'Neill said, there would not be a majority of Democrats to support it. Reagan reluctantly agreed and went on television to rally public support for the bill. In the Democrats' response, Tom Foley, a congressman from Spokane, Washington, who would later serve as Speaker of the House, said, "The President says we need this tax bill and the president is right."[28] The next day the stock market surged.

Two days after his prime-time plea, Reagan phoned many House Republicans urging them to support the Senate's tax increases. Speaker O'Neill told House Republicans they owed their positions to Ronald Reagan's election, saying, "You are here because of Reagan. . . . He brought you to the Congress of the United States . . . and he is asking for a change of policy. Are you going to follow the leader that brought you here, or are you going to run?"[29] That evening, August 19, 1982, the bill passed the House with the support of more than half the Democrats and 103 of the 192 Republicans. The law that emerged from this legislative dance was estimated to raise about 1 percent of GDP between 1983 and 1985, offsetting more than a quarter of the costs of the 1981 tax cuts.[30]

Robert Bartley's *Wall Street Journal* editorial page, playing its usual role, claimed the 1982 tax increases would exacerbate the ongoing recession. Bartley, who never approved of tax increases, wrote, "Every school child knows you don't raise taxes in a recession unless you want to make it worse." Newt Gingrich, then a fiery backbench Georgia Republican congressman serving his second term, concurred, "I think it will make the economy sicker." The U.S. Chamber of Commerce said it had "no doubt that [the tax increases] will curb the economic recovery everyone wants."[31] In 1983 and 1984, however, the U.S. economy soared, and unemployment plummeted. Economic growth peaked at nearly 7.25 percent in 1984, and the nation's economy grew from about 3.5 percent to more than 4 percent every year between 1983 and 1989.

The 1983 Social Security Crisis

In 1983 a Social Security crisis demanded attention. During the late 1970s and early 1980s, Social Security benefits increased substantially due to steep inflation, and payroll tax collections were smaller than expected because of stagnant wages—a combination that undermined Social Security's finances. The program's actuaries determined that Social Security could continue to pay full benefits only through June 1983. That July thirty-six million elderly Americans would no longer receive the benefits they were counting on. Talk of Social Security's "bankruptcy" took hold. A financial and political crisis confronted the president and Congress. Notwithstanding the dire predictions, White House officials told the public President Reagan was "adamantly against increasing Social Security taxes."[32]

Despite its unmatched success in reducing poverty among the nation's elderly, Social Security has always had opponents. Many conservative think tanks and economists, including Milton Friedman and Reagan's top economic advisor Martin Feldstein, wanted to substitute voluntary private retirement savings accounts for Social Security.[33] David Stockman described Social Security as "closet socialism" and a "giant Ponzi Scheme." He came to the Reagan White House determined to reduce its benefits. "A frontal assault on the very inner fortress of the American welfare state—the giant Social Security system,

on which one-seventh of the nation's populace depended for its well-being—
was now in order," he wrote.[34]

Ronald Reagan also wanted to substitute voluntary private savings accounts for Social Security. Beginning in the 1950s, as a spokesman for the
General Electric Corporation, Reagan repeatedly gave what he called "the
speech" in which he attacked Social Security and what became Medicare,
describing it as "socialized medicine." In his 1964 nationally televised speech
supporting Barry Goldwater's campaign for the presidency, Reagan asked,
"Why can't we introduce voluntary features [to Social Security] that would
permit a citizen who can do better on his own to be excused upon presentation
of evidence that he had made provisions for the non-earning years?" Reagan
said, "We're against forcing all citizens, regardless of need, into a compulsory
government program."[35] In his 1976 presidential campaign, Reagan said,
"People like me shouldn't get Social Security. My friends at Burning Tree [an
exclusive golf club] don't need Social Security."[36] In January 1983, President
Reagan still hoped to make Social Security voluntary.[37] But that was politically impossible.

In 1981 some congressional Republicans, with support from the Reagan
White House, attempted to reduce Social Security benefits immediately by
almost one-third for recipients who retired at age sixty-two rather than the
standard retirement age of sixty-five and to reduce by about a quarter the inflation adjustments for elderly beneficiaries. These benefit cuts were so large
Reagan suggested postponing some payroll tax increases enacted during the
Carter administration and scheduled to take effect in 1985 and 1990.[38]

Congressional Democrats vigorously attacked these proposals, and they
failed. Speaker O'Neill said Republicans were "willing to balance the budget
on the backs of the elderly."[39] In May 1981, after fending off a harsher Democratic resolution, the Senate, by a 96–0 vote, adopted a resolution proposed
by Bob Dole promising not to "precipitously and unfairly penalize early retirees" or reduce benefits more than "necessary to achieve a financially sound
system and the well-being of all retired Americans."[40] The White House could
not insulate the president from public blowback. The *Washington Post* head-
lined its report: "Senate Unanimously Rebuffs President on Social Security."
The next day President Reagan sent Congress a letter promising to launch "a
bipartisan effort to save Social Security."[41]

Saving Social Security became the Democrats' principal rallying cry during
the 1982 midterm elections. That November, when the unemployment rate
was 10.8 percent, Democrats gained 26 seats in the House, producing an

overwhelming 269 to 166 majority and giving Tip O'Neill firm control. Both parties regarded Social Security as the decisive issue.[42]

The Greenspan Commission

President Reagan wanted to settle the Social Security issue before his 1984 reelection campaign—and he wanted to avoid any blame for necessary tax increases or benefit cuts. In his diary for September 23, 1981, President Reagan wrote, "I'm withdrawing Social Security from consideration and challenging Tip and the Dems to join in a bipartisan effort to solve the fiscal dilemma of S.S. without all the politics they've been playing."[43] On December 16 the president signed an executive order establishing a fifteen-member bipartisan National Commission on Social Security Reform.[44] The president selected five members. Republican Senate Majority Leader Howard Baker picked another five, as did Speaker O'Neill. Eight of the fifteen picks were Republicans; seven were Democrats. Nine commission members were current or recently retired members of Congress. The president instructed the commission to submit its report by December 31, 1982, after the midterm elections. Reagan selected Alan Greenspan, who was running a private economics consulting firm, to chair the commission.

Greenspan—a close friend and admirer of libertarian novelist and philosopher Ayn Rand—had long favored privatization of Social Security. He had endorsed the Republican efforts to cut benefits in 1981, saying it was time to "restore some sanity to the system."[45] Given Reagan's and Greenspan's preferences for a voluntary system, Democrats feared the commission would be a stalking horse for dismantling Social Security. But Reagan's chief of staff Jim Baker told Greenspan fixing Social Security by privatizing accounts, making the program voluntary, or advocating draconian benefit cuts was off the table. As Greenspan's biographer, Sebastian Mallaby wrote, "The Randian scourge of the welfare state had been hired as its repairman."[46] And Ronald Reagan, who had long urged making Social Security voluntary, was working to make the compulsory government program financially secure for a generation.

Speaker O'Neill's surrogate on the commission was Robert M. Ball, Social Security commissioner under three presidents from 1962 to 1973. Massachusetts senator Ted Kennedy described Ball, who had dedicated his professional life to building and protecting Social Security, as the program's "most influential advocate, architect and philosopher."[47] Ball kept O'Neill informed about the commission's deliberations through Jack Lew, then a young staffer in the Speaker's office. Alan Greenspan did the same for President Reagan through Baker and his deputy Dick Darman.

As the commission approached its December 31, 1982, termination date, it had identified the options to address the crisis and put Social Security on a more secure financial footing, but no bipartisan majority agreed on any package of proposals. Greenspan asked for a one-month extension. The White House gave him two weeks.

On January 3, 1983, the first day of the new Congress, Bob Dole, the most influential Republican senator on the commission, published a *New York Times* op-ed titled "Reagan's Faithful Allies" in which he wrote: "With 116 million workers supporting it and 36 million beneficiaries relying on it, Social Security overwhelms every other domestic priority. Through a combination of relatively modest steps, including some acceleration of already scheduled taxes and some reduction in the rate of future benefit increases, the system can be saved."[48] After reading Dole's article, New York's Democratic senator Daniel Patrick Moynihan, also a member of the commission, crossed the Senate floor, tapped Dole on the shoulder, and asked, "Are we going to let this commission die without giving it one more try?"[49]

Two days later, Jim Baker invited a small group of commissioners to his home to see if they could come up with a plan. In addition to Greenspan, Ball, and Senators Dole and Moynihan, he included the ranking Ways and Means Republican Barber Conable. Many other commission members were not even aware of the meetings.[50] Baker and Darman negotiated on the Republicans' behalf, Ball for the Democrats. In Baker's Foxhall Village basement, surrounded by his animal trophies on the walls and a zebra-skin rug on the floor, they hammered out an agreement.[51]

Bob Ball rejected Baker's idea of a three-year delay in cost-of-living increases for benefits, and Baker rebuffed Ball's proposals for new increases in payroll taxes. The breakthrough came when Ball suggested taxing half of Social Security benefits as income to recipients with more than $25,000 of other income, moving income taxation of Social Security benefits closer to that of private retirement savings. Ball's proposal had an unusual advantage: President Reagan and his Republican colleagues could describe such a change as a reduction of benefits, while Speaker O'Neill and the Democrats could label it a progressive tax increase. Because taxing benefits as income reduces the amounts retirees have to spend, its effects are similar to a benefit cut, but the federal budget scores the change as a tax increase. Some Republicans hoped taxing benefits might diminish support for Social Security among higher-income taxpayers and enhance political momentum for privatizing the program.

On Saturday, January 20, 1983, the commission announced an agreement: delaying cost-of-living increases for six months rather than the three years the White House wanted; moving up the 1977 payroll tax rate increases from 12.25 percent to 15.3 percent scheduled to go into effect in 1985 and 1990; increasing payroll tax revenues by bringing employees of nonprofit organizations, new federal civilian employees, and most state and local employees into the Social Security system; requiring self-employed individuals to pay both the employer and employee shares of Social Security taxes; and imposing income taxes on up to half of Social Security benefits of retirees with income exceeding $25,000.

The commission voted by 12–3 to accept the agreement.[52] Saying it "includes elements which each of us could not support if they were not part of a bipartisan compromise," President Reagan promised "to support and work for this bipartisan solution." Speaker O'Neill echoed the president, describing the plan as "acceptable to the President and to me, one which I can support and which I will work for."[53]

The commission's plan solved Social Security's immediate problems. A House amendment slowly phasing in an increase in the full Social Security retirement age from sixty-five to sixty-seven addressed longer-term financing issues.[54] The 1983 legislation was the first time in Social Security's history benefits for retirees were cut, an especially tough vote for Democrats. The tax increases were opposed by some antitax Republicans in the House and Senate, but voting against any and all tax increases had not yet become a common commitment of Republican legislators.

On April 20, 1983, in a large Rose Garden ceremony, Ronald Reagan, flanked by Democrats and Republicans, signed the Social Security changes into law, averting the July crisis. President Reagan said, "This bill demonstrates for all time the nation's ironclad commitment to Social Security. It assures the elderly that America will always keep the promises made in troubled times a half a century ago. Today we reaffirm Franklin Roosevelt's commitment that Social Security must always promise a secure and stable base so that older Americans can live in dignity."[55]

In the short term, the tax increases enacted to make Social Security solvent were greater and took effect earlier than the reductions in benefits.[56] Income taxation of Social Security benefits for recipients with more than $25,000 of other income increased progressivity, but the $25,000 threshold (about

$70,000 in 2021 dollars) was not indexed for inflation, and the amount of ben-efits subject to income tax was subsequently increased to 85 percent for some retirees.[57] In 1984 the income taxation of benefits affected less than 3 percent of income tax returns, taxing about 15 percent of Social Security benefits; thirty-five years later, close to one-half of total Social Security benefits were taxed on nearly 15 percent of income tax returns—burdening many middle-income retirees.[58]

The payroll and income tax increases of the Social Security legislation con-tributed to a shift in tax burdens from taxes on income from wealth to taxes on labor income and to the migration of taxes from the rich onto middle-class workers. Payroll taxes replaced the income tax as the predominant federal taxes paid by families with incomes below the top quarter. But neither supply-siders nor the public squawked about the 1983 tax increases.[59]

The 1983 Social Security legislation preserved the financial strength of So-cial Security into the twenty-first century and fulfilled Ronald Reagan's desire to eliminate Social Security as an issue in the 1984 presidential campaign. When President Reagan, a long-time opponent, confirmed "the nation's iron-clad commitment to Social Security," he took Republican efforts to dismember the program off the agenda, at least temporarily.[60]

Republicans' politically costly failed efforts to cut benefits in 1981, along with the 1983 Social Security legislation, helped confirm the political difficulties of relying on large spending cuts in Social Security, Medicare, Medicaid, or na-tional defense as the way to address the deficit issues. Tax increases became es-sential. That message, however, was resisted by antitax advocates who—against all evidence—continued to insist tax cuts would pay for themselves or, if not, would necessarily produce spending cuts by the government beast.

The "Teflon" President

In addition to the tax increases of 1982 and 1983, Ronald Reagan signed deficit-reducing tax increases in 1984, 1985, and 1987.[61] Together the tax increases from 1982 to 1988 offset about half of the revenue costs of the 1981 tax cuts.[62] Unlike the 1981 tax-cut legislation, when he herded the press and television cameras up to his ranch for a bill-signing production worthy of a Hollywood movie, President Reagan signed the Deficit Reduction Act of 1984 quietly at 10 o'clock in the morning in the Oval Office with only White House staff present. White House spokesman Larry Speakes told the press he "did not know why there was no ceremony for such a significant piece of legislation."[63]

Despite these tax increases, Ronald Reagan failed to redeem his promises to curb federal budget deficits and reduce the federal debt. In the eight years between his first inaugural address in January 1981 and his farewell address in January 1989, the nation's debt rose by more than $1.85 trillion (about $4.5 trillion in 2021 dollars)—from about $1 trillion to $2.86 trillion.[64] President Reagan added nearly twice as much to the federal debt as was accumulated during all of the presidencies that preceded him.[65] The size of debt relative to the economy rose by 15 percentage points, a considerably larger increase than in any previous peacetime decade.[66] Rising federal debt converted the United States from the world's largest creditor nation into its largest debtor. We began borrowing from abroad to finance consumption at home.

No politician wanted credit for the necessary tax increases—least of all Ronald Reagan. He successfully avoided blame from antitax advocates for the tax increases he signed while president, perhaps because of the robust economic growth that occurred. The years 1983 through 1989 were the "seven fat years" that Robert Bartley wrote about in his 1992 paean to supply-side tax cutting.[67] He hardly mentioned the tax increases of 1982–88.[68] Bartley attributed the robust growth of that period to Reagan's 1981 tax cuts.[69] But that view is not universally shared: critics point out the tax cuts failed to produce the promised surges in business investment, workers' productivity, hours worked, or wages promised by the supply-siders. As Princeton historian Sean Wilentz wrote in 2008, "The long-term economic and political effects of Reagan's early triumphs remain hotly debated to this day."[70]

Many supply-siders blamed Jim Baker for the tax increases. After he retired, Baker said he regretted his role in promoting the tax increases. He said he and his colleagues overreacted to concerns about the large deficits and that President Reagan was right to resist tax increases. "I'm a reformed drunk when it comes to supply-side economics," Baker said.[71]

President Reagan's large tax cuts in 1981 and his defense buildup, along with deregulation, became known as "Reaganomics." These policies have long been venerated by antitax and antigovernment advocates. Unlike other presidents, Ronald Reagan avoided criticism for the deep recession of the early 1980s. When ABC's Sam Donaldson asked, "Mr. President, in talking about the continuing recession tonight, you have blamed mistakes in the past. You have blamed the Congress. Does any of the blame belong to you?" Reagan quipped, "Yes, because for many years, I was a Democrat."[72] Reagan's tax increases are forgotten or ignored, ratifying his reputation as a "Teflon president"—who never had bad news stick to him.

Unlike President Reagan, Bob Dole did not escape censure from the antitax forces. Newt Gingrich complained that Dole and other Republicans who supported tax increases had capitulated in the "fight for the soul of the Republican party." Calling Dole the "tax collector for the welfare state," Gingrich protested that the "political establishment in Washington" defeated "ordinary citizens."[73] Dole responded that Gingrich and his fellow insurgents had swallowed supply-siders' claims that the country would simply grow its way out of deficits and were subverting responsible government with their intransigent opposition to any tax increases. Gingrich replied by describing Dole as one of the "first-rate" leaders "running essentially a cheaper and narrower version of the Democratic welfare state." Dole dismissed these attacks, saying he was too busy trying to enact Ronald Reagan's program to engage in Gingrich's civil war.[74] This was not the last time these two Republican leaders would clash over tax increases. Gingrich had fired only an opening volley in his internecine war—a war that would not always be civil.

Gingrich's attacks on Dole foreshadowed a schism within the Republican Party between moderates, who saw the need to narrow the excesses of federal spending over tax revenue as their duty—even if it meant increasing some taxes—and disrupters to their right, who adamantly opposed any tax increase regardless of the nation's economic or budgetary conditions.

———

The excesses of the 1981 tax cuts and battles over the large deficits that followed temporarily halted the momentum of the antitax zealots, but they did not reverse supply-siders' victories in pushing down the top income tax rates. Income tax reform was next. The 1986 reform was hailed as a great achievement by liberals and conservatives alike. It may not have seemed so at the time, but that law was another big accomplishment for Ronald Reagan, Jack Kemp, supply-siders, and the rich, as the next chapter describes.

Chapter 7

An Uneasy
Political Marriage

An historic overhaul of our tax code. . . . The best antipoverty bill, the best profamily measure, and the best job-creation program ever to come out of the Congress of the United States.

—RONALD REAGAN

President Reagan's 1981 tax cut garnered considerable support from Democrats who recognized the antitax advocates' influence with the public and in Congress. In 1982 when tax increases became necessary to address large deficits and rising debt, Democrats faded into the background, becoming invisible in the House and taking a backseat to Robert Dole in the Senate. Democrats also insisted on support from Ronald Reagan, Alan Greenspan, and congressional Republicans for the 1983 tax increases necessary to shore up Social Security's finances. In 1984, however, the Democratic presidential nominee was oblivious to the political sway of the antitax movement.

For the formidable (and ultimately futile) task of challenging Ronald Reagan for the presidency, Democrats chose former Minnesota senator and Jimmy Carter's vice president Walter Mondale. Accepting the Democratic nomination in July 1984, Mondale attacked "President Reagan's deficits" as stunting investment, killing jobs, undermining growth, and limiting Americans' future. Mondale added, "Taxes will go up. And anyone who says they won't isn't telling the truth to the American people. . . . Mr. Reagan will raise taxes and so will I. He won't tell you. I just did."[1]

Mondale badly misread the public's mood. On the convention podium, as the crowd cheered, Dan Rostenkowski whispered to Mondale, "You've got a lot of balls, pal." Rostenkowski said Mondale replied, "We're going to tax their ass off."[2] When Mondale released his economic plan—confronting a deficit of about $300 billion—he called for $105 billion of spending cuts (almost half from lower interest costs on the federal debt) and $85 billion of tax increases. His proposed tax increases mostly would have burdened families with incomes above $100,000 ($261,000 in 2021 dollars), but they also hit families making $25,000 a year ($65,000 in 2021 dollars).[3] One of Ronald Reagan's political advisors said, "I haven't seen even a mayor get elected that way."[4] Instead of receiving the typical post-convention bounce for presidential nominees, Mondale's support declined after the Democratic convention.

In stark contrast to Mondale's gloom, Ronald Reagan promised "morning again in America," running ads showing golden sunrises lighting homes surrounded by white picket fences. The Reagan administration did not announce any plans for cutting the deficit until after the election.[5] Reagan almost (but not quite) pledged not to raise taxes.

The election was a walkover. Reagan beat Mondale by 18 million votes and won the Electoral College 525–13. Mondale carried only his home state of Minnesota and the District of Columbia. Looking back, President Carter's pollster Patrick Caddell said Mondale's candor about increasing taxes was suicidal.[6] Mondale himself later conceded, "While my opponent was handing out rose petals, I was handing out coal."[7]

Democrats took Reagan's rout of Mondale as a clear warning against advocating tax-rate increases to lower deficits. But leading Democrats were concerned about the income tax's deplorable condition. Jimmy Carter ran for president in 1976 calling the income tax "a disgrace to the human race." Carter promised "a complete overhaul of our income tax system," but he barely got an oil change.[8]

Until the early 1970s, most Americans considered the income tax the fairest tax levied by the federal government, but by the 1980s the income tax was viewed as the least fair.[9] Publicity about aggressive tax shelters, which multiplied after the 1981 legislation, convinced most middle-class Americans that wealthy families and large corporations were not paying their fair share.[10] A wide variety of tax breaks produced different tax burdens for families with similar incomes and businesses in different industries. Changing patterns of women's work and marital sorting expanded the number of families facing income tax marriage penalties. Indexing tax brackets, personal exemptions, and the standard deduction for inflation did not take effect until 1985, so inflation continued to increase income taxes when real incomes had not grown. Moreover, the income tax was horrendously complicated, sending increasing numbers of Americans to tax-return preparers, who often were unable to produce correct returns.

In his State of the Union Address on January 25, 1984—after praising the 1981 tax cuts for increasing the take-home pay of American families and spurring economic growth—Ronald Reagan reaffirmed his antitax commitments, saying, "To talk of meeting the present situation by increasing taxes is a Band-Aid solution . . . to say nothing of the fact that it poses a real threat to economic recovery." President Reagan, however, was concerned his Democratic presidential opponent might endorse a popular income tax reform, and he knew large ongoing deficits precluded another round of tax cutting, so he promised a "simplification" of the income tax that he thought might provide him an opportunity to further reduce the top income tax rate.

President Reagan said he wanted "an historic reform for fairness, simplicity, and incentives for growth." He announced he had instructed Treasury Secretary Don Regan to come up with a plan that "could make the base broader so that rates would go down." Reagan added that Treasury's report would be delivered to him by December 1984—after the election.[11] When he said he wanted the report in December, Democrats laughed.[12]

Tax-reform advocates had long argued for taxing all income the same—requiring the elimination of juicy tax breaks, which congressional Republicans and many Democrats were not interested in. However—despite many false starts and long odds against success—in 1986 Democrats ultimately joined with supply-side Republicans to enact tax-reform legislation that curbed many tax benefits, flattened income tax rates, and cut the 50 percent top rate nearly in half—more than Ronald Reagan believed possible. The proliferation of abusive tax shelters provided important impetus for change.

Gimme Shelter

The 1981 tax cuts opened new avenues for tax avoidance by individuals and corporations. For the wealthiest Americans, reducing income taxes was child's play. By transferring assets to children or trusts without relinquishing investment control, wealthy parents or grandparents could shift income to be taxed at lower rates. Few actors, athletes, doctors, lawyers, dentists, or airline pilots believed it was better to pay fifty cents of taxes and keep the rest than to throw their dollars at tax shelters in hopes of keeping it all. Ronald Reagan's campaign manager, CIA director William Casey, claimed to have invented tax-shelter investing.[13]

The growth of tax shelters from the mid-1970s into the mid-1980s produced tax avoidance unprecedented in the history of the income tax. What is a tax shelter? "A deal done by very smart people that absent tax considerations would be very stupid."[14] Capital was chasing after unproductive tax-favored investments: in fruits, flowers, and nuts; bushes and trees; animals of all sorts, including buffaloes, minks, and chinchillas; movies that would never be seen; books that would never be read; and record albums that would never be heard. Martin Ginsburg (a talented tax lawyer and husband of the late Supreme Court Justice Ruth Bader Ginsburg) told the Ways and Means Committee he found it "difficult to believe the United States is in the throes of a rosebush crisis."[15]

The rapid depreciation system enacted in 1981 opened new tax-shelter opportunities for investments that made no money apart from the tax breaks. Tax-driven overinvestment in real estate following the 1981 changes prompted a tax partner at the PWC accounting firm to say the tax-shelter "syndication of real estate has replaced baseball as our national pastime."[16] One real estate tax shelter involved the Manhattan office building leased by the IRS. The tax breaks inspired tax-exempt organizations to try to grab a piece of the extraordinary tax benefits. Bennington College "sold" and leased back $8.5 million of campus dormitories to tax-shelter investors; the city of Atlanta did the same with its Civic Center.[17]

President Reagan's IRS commissioner Roscoe Egger said the government's battle against tax shelters was like Mickey Mouse's clash with multiplying mops in the "Sorcerer's Apprentice" segment of the movie *Fantasia*. Egger said every time the IRS cut a mop in half at least twice as many emerged. He called tax shelters "flaky schemes," saying, "since 1973 every conceivable device, animal, or property has become a candidate for a tax shelter."[18]

The ability under the 1981 law to deduct over a five-year period the costs of equipment that might last thirty years or more, plus tax credits for such investments, led to unprecedented corporate tax-shelter "leasing" transactions. Airlines and other companies without enough income to use these deductions and credits leased their planes and other equipment from corporations that benefited from the tax breaks. By 1982 there had been more than 50,000 transactions involving transfers of tax benefits on more than $37 billion (more than $100 billion in 2021 dollars) of property.[19]

Perhaps the most egregious tax shelter was a "rent-a-navy" scheme between a tax-shelter partnership and the U.S. Navy Department for thirteen ships of the Navy's Rapid Deployment Force. After failing to persuade Congress to provide funds for the ships, the Navy lined up private financiers to provide loans to fund them. Corporate investors, such as Philip Morris and UPS, became "owners" of the ships for tax purposes and deducted their entire costs over five years, along with interest on the loans. The Navy paid "rent" on the ships for twenty-five years to compensate the lenders. For national security reasons, the "owners" were not permitted to board their ships. In 1985 the Navy agreed to indemnify the participants if any anticipated tax benefits were lost and to fund their legal expenses in dealing with the IRS. The IRS subsequently blessed this deal in a 143-page ruling. "Renting" the boats lowered the Defense Department's expenses in the early years, freeing up funds for more equipment and weapons. The gambit added $300 million to taxpayers' costs for the ships, money the Treasury lost from the "owners'" tax breaks.[20]

Corporations came to view their tax departments as potential profit centers: they could sell more goods or services, reduce wasteful costs, or pay less in taxes. Tax savings were often easiest. Individual and corporate tax shelters cost the government billions without producing new productive investments or jobs, except perhaps for tax lawyers, accountants, and investment bankers. The tax-shelter explosion after 1981 debunked supply-siders' claims that lowering income tax rates causes people to focus on their work and make productive investments instead of chasing after tax-avoidance schemes.

The tax reductions achieved by affluent investors were enormous. A 1983 congressional staff study estimated that 40 percent of tax returns with incomes greater than $200,000 (more than $500,000 in 2021 dollars) reported tax-shelter losses reducing their total tax liability by more than 25 percent—a stunning story of tax avoidance at the top.[21] Dick Darman, in an April 15, 1985, speech promoting tax reform, announced that more than a fifth of people with incomes more than $250,000 and a quarter of those with incomes above $1 million (more than $2.5 million in 2021 dollars) paid *10 percent or less* in income taxes.[22]

The expansion of tax shelters among high-income individuals and corporations provided ample reason for reforming the income tax. Eliminating tax shelters would have substantially increased taxes at the top without raising the top tax rate and helped reduce the worrisome deficits. But that did not happen. Ronald Reagan and his antitax allies wanted to use the money from curbing tax shelters and trimming other tax breaks to further reduce the top income tax rate.

Entrenching the massive tax reductions that tax shelters produced for the rich as the touchstone in determining what top tax rate would produce a "distributionally neutral" income tax reform preserved the tax reductions for the wealthy created by tax-shelter opportunities. This, however, was a price that Senator Bill Bradley and his Democratic congressional colleagues were willing to pay—and the siren song that lured Ronald Reagan and congressional supply-siders to support tax reform.

An Unlikely Ally for the Supply Side

On the same day Ronald Reagan carried the 1984 New Jersey presidential contest with 60 percent of the votes, Democratic senator Bill Bradley, who had opposed Reagan's 1981 tax cuts, defeated his Republican opponent by an even greater margin, winning 64 to 36 percent. This was the first time a Democrat won every county in the state.[23]

Bradley was idolized in New Jersey, having attended Princeton University after becoming the most coveted high school basketball player in the country. He led his team to the Final Four in 1965 for the only time in Princeton history—a rare MVP who did not win the national championship. Between basketball and studies, Bradley frequently worked from 6 a.m. to midnight. On Sunday mornings he taught classes at the Presbyterian church. Many teachers, classmates, and his coach predicted Bill Bradley would be governor of Missouri (where he had grown up) when he was forty.[24] After graduation, Bradley delayed his basketball career to earn a degree in political and economic history as a Rhodes Scholar at Oxford University. In 1977 he retired from playing basketball with the New York Knicks to run for the Senate.

Bill Bradley had felt the antitax movement's power in Jeff Bell's 1978 campaign. Although Bradley easily defeated Bell, riding talents and fame from Madison Square Garden into the Senate, the electoral pull of tax cuts astonished him. In 1982 when everyone with power in Washington was focusing on lifting the country out of a deep recession and addressing runaway deficits, Bradley, as a young first-term senator, began crafting a tax-reform plan.[25] He was convinced reforming the income tax would tap into Americans' dissatisfaction with its complexity and concerns that people at the top were not paying their fair share.

Bradley adopted two unusual principles he regarded as crucial for tax reform to succeed. First, his plan would be revenue neutral, neither cutting overall tax revenues nor raising them to address burgeoning federal deficits. Second, his proposal would be essentially "distributionally neutral," not changing overall income tax burdens at different income levels, except for tax relief for low-income families.[26] He believed these constraints were the only way to attract support from President Reagan and congressional Republicans, and he knew Democrats would not support further tax cuts for the wealthy. Bradley's revenue and distributional principles may have enabled tax reform to be enacted, but they meant reform would entrench the tax reductions at the top from shelters and other tax-avoidance techniques, fail to strengthen the government's financial condition, and limit reform's benefits to the economy.[27]

On August 5, 1982, Senator Bradley introduced his tax-reform legislation, "The Fair Tax Act of 1982." He chose Dick Gephardt, a young Democrat from St. Louis who served on the Ways and Means Committee and would later become the House Democratic Leader, to cosponsor the bill. Their bill had three income tax rates: 14, 26, and 30 percent, with about 80 percent of taxpayers subject to the lowest rate. It would have reduced the top rate by 20 percentage points, creating the lowest income tax rates since the 1920s. Bradley financed the rate reductions and increases in personal exemptions and the standard deduction by eliminating many tax breaks and limiting popular itemized deductions to offset the lowest rate rather than the highest. The bill also would have cut the corporate rate from 46 to 30 percent.

Bill Bradley and Dick Gephardt were an unlikely duo to help fulfill supply-siders' goal of further lowering the top income tax rate: they were neither conservative nor supply-siders. Years later, Bradley conceded there was a supply-side component in his tax reform.[28] Bradley and Gephardt tried to convince Walter Mondale to endorse their tax-reform effort in his 1984 presidential campaign, but Mondale wanted to reduce deficits and impose higher tax rates at the top.

In August 1983 about twenty conservative Republican supply-siders, including Irving Kristol, Jude Wanniski, Jeff Bell, Lewis Lehrman (who in 1982 lost in his antitax campaign for New York governor), Paul Craig Roberts, the Chamber of Commerce's chief economist Richard Rahn, and Wanniski's business partner Alan Reynolds, were dining poolside at Jack Kemp's suburban home outside of Washington and discussing how to fashion an antitax plank for the 1984 Republican platform. Kristol, the intellectual leader of the neoconservative movement, suggested endorsing Bradley's bill as the only way to push tax rates further down, given the large deficits. Wanniski and Bell were tempted, but Roberts and Rahn opposed the idea because the Bradley bill proposed eliminating some business tax cuts of the 1981 legislation. Lehrman insisted it would be better politics for Republicans to write their own bill. Ultimately the group concurred.[29]

Jack Kemp produced his tax-reform bill and selected Wisconsin Republican Bob Kasten, who had opposed Bob Dole's 1982 tax increases, as his Senate cosponsor. This bill—"The Fair and Simple Tax Act"—rejected many of Bradley's revenue-raising provisions and advanced even lower tax rates. It proposed a single flat 25 percent rate for individuals and graduated rates from 15 to 30 percent for corporations. Unlike Bradley's bill, Kemp's proposals did not touch the major itemized deductions. Despite eliminating progressive tax rates, Kemp said, "This bill is fair to everyone. But it is especially fair to families with children, to the poor, to working men and women, to homeowners, givers to charity and to those who face discouragingly high rates."[30] His bill would have greatly reduced income taxes of the rich.

The Treasury Department and the Joint Committee on Taxation both concluded that Kemp's plan, unlike Bradley's bill, would add billions to the large federal deficits. Jack Kemp, naturally, countered that the resulting economic growth would make the revenue losses disappear.[31]

Kemp's effort attracted little press attention except for a *Wall Street Journal* editorial, titled "Bradley-Kemp-Reagan?" which speculated Kemp's flat-tax proposal might be "the sleeper of this election year."[32] But neither the Bradley-Gephardt nor Kemp-Kasten bill ever received a vote in Congress.

Tax Reform Takes Shape

Before becoming president, Ronald Reagan, in a speech subtitled "Keep Government Poor and Remain Free," described the progressive income tax as having come "direct from Karl Marx," who "designed it as the prime essential of a socialist state."[33] In his memoir, Reagan asked, "Have we the courage and will to stand up to the immorality and discrimination of the progressive [income tax] and demand a return to traditional proportionate taxation?"[34] President Reagan was enticed by the prospect of further lowering the top income tax rate to 35 percent or less.

In response to Reagan's request for a Treasury Department plan, Treasury Secretary Don Regan and the department's tax experts, without any political input from the White House, began crafting a 262-page tax-reform report that Secretary Regan delivered to President Reagan in a two-hour meeting in the White House Cabinet Room on Monday, November 26, 1984.[35] Treasury proposed slaughtering many previously sacred tax breaks for individuals and businesses to pay for individual income tax rates of 15, 25, and 35 percent, a 33 percent corporate rate, and nearly doubling personal exemptions to $2,000. President Reagan objected only to a recommendation to eliminate deductions for country-club dues. His staff's reaction, however, was chilly: one of the president's top economic advisors, William Niskanen, said "Walter Mondale would be proud."[36]

U.S. News and World Report reported, "Within hours of its unveiling, the Treasury plan drew criticism from big business, big labor, oil, real estate, and many other industries as well as charities, mayors, and a myriad of other groups with stakes in the current tax code." At a press conference in Treasury's ornate marble Cash Room the day the plan was released, Secretary Regan said, "This thing is written on a word processor. It can be changed."[37] And it was.

It was difficult to imagine the leaders of the congressional tax committees producing a major tax reform. In 1985 Oregon's Bob Packwood took the helm of the Senate Finance Committee from Bob Dole, who became the Republican Senate Leader. Packwood, no supply-sider, so frequently praised existing law and urged new loopholes that the *New Republic* dubbed him "Senator Hackwood."[38] When Treasury released its plan, Packwood responded, "I sort of like the tax code the way it is."[39] Dan Rostenkowski, chairing the House Ways and Means Committee, previously had shown little interest in tax reform in 1981 handing out tax favors and staying on the sidelines during Bob Dole's 1982 deficit-reducing tax-increase efforts. Public support for tax reform was tepid and never became a potent force for change. So how was tax reform enacted?

Jim Baker was exhausted after serving as the president's chief of staff for four years. On November 17, 1984, at lunch with Don Regan in the treasury secretary's conference room, Regan said, "You know what we should do Jim? We should swap jobs." Baker replied, "Watch out—I may take you up on that."[40] In January 1985 Ronald Reagan agreed to the swap, and in February Jim Baker was sworn in as secretary of the treasury.[41]

Unlike Don Regan, a feisty, obstinate Wall Street executive without the political suppleness to get tax reform through Congress, Jim Baker was smooth, affable, and a consummate politician. Successful tax-reform legislation became more likely when Baker moved from the White House into the Treasury Department's corner office.

Baker selected Dick Darman as his deputy secretary to serve as Treasury's negotiator with Congress over tax legislation's details. Darman was a Machiavellian player who thought himself an incomparable strategist. Jeffrey Birnbaum and Alan Murray, *Wall Street Journal* reporters who covered the tax-reform saga in their bestselling book *Showdown at Gucci Gulch*, wrote, "In a city full of clever people with large egos, Darman was an extreme. . . . His clever ploys became so well known that Senate Majority Leader Howard Baker created a new word—*Darmanesque*—to describe any maneuver that is too clever by half."[42]

In an attempt to reprise their Social Security success, Baker and Darman began meeting at Jim Baker's home with the chairmen and ranking members of the House and Senate tax committees and the four tax-reform cosponsors, Bradley, Gephardt, Kemp, and Kasten, but Ways and Means chairman Rostenkowski shut down the effort, saying, "Jimmy boy, you're massaging me. I have been handled by better than you, and your hands are cold."[43]

In a televised speech from the Oval Office on the evening of May 28, 1985, President Reagan, with characteristic hyperbole, described his tax-reform proposals as "a great historic effort to give the words 'freedom,' 'fairness,' and 'hope' new meaning for every man and woman in America." The president urged, "Let's not let the prisoners of mediocrity wear us down. Let's not let the special interest raids of the few rob us of all our dreams. . . . We can do it. And if you help, we will do it this year."[44] The president's plan provided greater tax cuts at the top than Treasury's report—a reduction of nearly 11 percent for people earning $200,000 or more ($500,000 in 2021 dollars), compared to only about 7 percent for those making $20,000 to $50,000—and accepted the general principles of a revenue-neutral reform, as Bill Bradley had urged.

Despite an avalanche of economic reports from lobbyists suggesting tax reform would devastate their industries and destroy the nation's economy, at 3:30 a.m. on November 23, 1985, the Ways and Means Committee, led by Dan Rostenkowski, voted for a tax-reform bill providing a top 38 percent rate for individuals, a 22 percent capital gains rate, and a 36 percent corporate rate, paid for by eliminating or curbing numerous tax breaks. "We have not written a perfect law," Rostenkowski said, "but politics is an imperfect process."[45]

Ronald Reagan wondered whether to support the committee's bill because its top rate exceeded his 35 percent ceiling, but the president ultimately decided to support it without publicly announcing his support. On the contrary, Newt Gingrich worked hard to kill the bill, claiming Rostenkowski's bill pitted the president "against the very people who gave him a 49-state victory." Jack Kemp claimed Rostenkowski's bill was anti-family, anti-growth, and anti-investment.

On December 15, 1985, Republicans, with some Democratic votes, achieved a surprise victory in a House vote that threatened to end tax reform. Speaker

O'Neill then told the president that unless he got fifty Republicans to support the committee's bill—fifteen more than Jim Baker's most optimistic prediction—tax reform was dead. The next day President Reagan went to Capitol Hill to muster the necessary Republican votes. He charmed House Republicans, and after the president sent a letter promising he would veto legislation not meeting his requirements for a major increase in personal exemptions and a top rate no higher than 35 percent the bill won a crucial vote with the support of nearly half the House Republicans, including Jack Kemp. At 11 p.m. on December 17, the House of Representatives approved the Ways and Means bill without a recorded vote.[46]

Lifting a glass of champagne after the House passed the bill, Rostenkowski toasted, "To an accomplishment of the House of Representatives and to a bumpy ride in the Senate." Bumpy indeed. Senate Majority Leader Bob Dole was skeptical of tax reform. He said, "To go through the whole process and wind up without a dime's dent in the deficit just doesn't make sense."[47] Most members of the Senate Finance Committee agreed with Dole.[48] The Finance Committee chairman Bob Packwood had little appetite for tax reform, but he knew if he failed to produce a bill, he would be held responsible for killing it. Dick Darman said, "It's like the gallows focusing the mind."[49]

The Senate Finance Committee members began their tax-reform consideration by creating new tax breaks rather than curbing existing ones. Bill Bradley said, "It keeps getting lonelier and lonelier." Wyoming's Republican senator Malcolm Wallop told him, "None of us is committed to tax reform. We've abandoned it a long time ago."[50] On Friday, April 18, Packwood adjourned the committee without taking any more votes. Jim Baker said, "We're in the soup." Daniel Patrick Moynihan described tax reform as "in ruins" and Arkansas senator David Pryor said, "This horse is so lame we can't continue to ride it."[51] Journalists across the country reported tax reform was "down for the count."[52]

Like a Phoenix

After adjourning his committee in despair and fearing his reelection chances were in jeopardy, Bob Packwood invited his staff director and friend Bill Diefenderfer for lunch. They walked a few blocks to their favorite Irish pub for beer and cheeseburgers. Into their second pitcher, they devised a new strategy: eliminate enough income tax credits, deductions, and exclusions to pare the top tax rate down to 25 percent—Jack Kemp's top rate, much lower than the House's 38 percent and even lower than Bill Bradley's 30 percent. Packwood

President Reagan, Senator Packwood, and Bill Diefenderfer meet in the Oval Office.

met with Baker and Darman to explain his new goal. Baker said, "We weren't at all sure that it could be done, but we were certainly willing to give it a try. Anything would be better than the course he was following."[53]

On April 24, Packwood met with his committee in the small private conference room adjacent to the large committee hearing room. He handed out a summary of the Bradley-Gephardt bill, saying, "This is the way Bill did it." He then presented a 25 percent top-rate plan the Joint Committee on Taxation staff had created at his request and asked, "Any interest?" Committee members began to embrace the idea, led by Bradley. George Mitchell, a Maine Democrat who in 1989 would become Senate Majority Leader, objected that the 25 percent top rate was too low and the plan's greatest benefits went to families with the most income. Bradley responded that the existing distribution of the income tax could be maintained with a low top rate. He did not mention how much tax-shelter investments by the affluent had lowered income taxes at the top.

At a Packwood fundraiser after his proposal became public, Jack Kemp compared Packwood's efforts to get the top income tax rate below 30 percent to General Douglas MacArthur's surprise invasion at Inchon, a decisive victory in the Korean War. Antitax champions Rowland Evans and Bob Novak repeated Kemp's analogy in their widely syndicated column. Supply-siders viewed this tax reform as a great victory. On June 24, 1986, the Senate's reform bill was approved by a 97–3 vote.[54] Disappointing many Democrats, Dan

Rostenkowski capitulated, telling a Boston audience that he would abandon the House's 38 percent top rate and shoot instead for the Senate's much lower 27 percent.[55]

When the dust finally settled in late September after a House-Senate conference, tax-reform legislation passed the House by a vote of 292 to 136 and the Senate by 74–23. It was expected to reduce individual income taxes by about $122 billion and increase corporate income taxes by nearly the same amount over the next five years. The Joint Committee on Taxation ignored the corporate tax increases in its tables showing the distribution of the law's changes across income levels, making it look like virtually everyone got a tax cut. The law replaced more than a dozen individual tax brackets ranging from 11 to 50 percent with two rates of 15 and 28 percent.[56] The standard deduction was raised to $5,000 and personal exemptions were nearly doubled to $2,000, protecting low- and moderate-income families from a tax hike. The corporate rate was lowered from 46 to 34 percent. The lower rates were paid for by curtailing or eliminating many tax breaks available under prior law and attacking tax shelters for individuals.[57]

A Triumph for the American People?

On Wednesday, October 22, 1986, basking in sunshine on the crowded South Lawn of the White House, Ronald Reagan signed the Tax Reform Act of 1986. It was the crowning domestic achievement of his second term. He left no doubt the new law was an important supply-side victory: "The steeply progressive nature of the income tax struck at the heart of the economic life of the individual, punishing that special effort and extra hard work that has always been the driving force of our economy. . . . We should not forget, that this nation of ours began in a revolt against oppressive taxation." Calling the new tax law a "revolution," President Reagan claimed it was "the best antipoverty bill, the best profamily measure, and the best job-creation program ever to come out of the Congress of the United States."[58] It was none of those.

Nonetheless, the reform was widely praised by the media and tax experts. The *New York Times* described it as a time to "take unashamed satisfaction in a triumph of the whole over the parts."[59] Tax law experts and public finance economists joined in. The Brookings Institution published an article heralding the legislation with the title, "The Impossible Dream Comes True."[60] Despite discontent with prior law, however, public support for the legislation remained tepid.[61] On the day after the Senate passed tax reform by a 97–3 vote, the

New York Times reported fewer than one-third of Americans believed the Senate bill would create a fairer tax system and only 11 percent thought it would reduce their taxes.[62] A Gallup poll found fewer than one in three participants believed the reform would improve the economy, simplify the tax law, or create a fairer distribution of tax burdens.[63]

The 1986 tax reform was a rearrangement of the income tax law in which lower tax rates and the removal of six million low-income families from the income tax were exchanged for the reduction and elimination of tax breaks. It made the income tax more neutral among businesses and more equal for families with similar incomes. Neither deficits nor the federal debt was reduced. The legislation failed to spur productivity or stimulate robust economic growth. Hundreds of narrowly tailored rules gave special tax breaks to particular companies or individuals in order to secure votes.[64] The new law may have stimulated up to a 1 percent increase in hours worked, a benefit but hardly an economic revolution.[65]

The new law failed as a simplification measure. Compromise is the handmaiden of complexity, and the 1986 law emerged out of hundreds of political compromises. Rather than eliminating many rules of questionable merit, Congress limited their benefits.

Avenues for tax-favored investments remained. Tax lawyers, accountants, and investment bankers joined in the creation and marketing of tax-avoidance schemes, creating "confidential products" that enabled wealthy individuals and large corporations to avoid billions of dollars of income taxes annually.[66] Like assertions that tax cuts will pay for themselves or necessarily curtail government spending, claims that low rates will eliminate tax avoidance are demonstrably false, but that does not diminish antitax advocates' insistence they will.

Reductions in the top individual income tax rate from 70 to 28 percent during Ronald Reagan's presidency along with ongoing increases in payroll taxes and the 1981 reductions in estate taxes advanced antitax advocates' desires to limit the role of progressivity as the guiding principle for fairness in federal taxation. Importantly, most congressional Democrats supported the 1981 tax cuts, and Democrats, most notably Bill Bradley, played leading roles in initiating and abetting the 1986 reform's low top income tax rate.

On the day President Reagan signed the 1986 reform, the *New York Times* acknowledged that Congress would soon feel heavy pressure to undo much of it. Milton Friedman predicted, "As lobbyists get back into action, and as members of Congress try to raise campaign funds, old loopholes will be reintroduced and new ones invented."[67] Brown University political scientist Eric Patashnik treated the 1986 tax reform as a prime example of how reforms erode over time.[68]

The 1986 tax reform was the product of an uneasy marriage of two contrary ideological and political camps: Democratic lawmakers, who favored treating income the same regardless of its source, collaborated with Republican supply-siders principally interested in lowering tax rates. The ink was barely dry on the 1986 tax reform before divorce proceedings started. Democrat Lloyd Bentsen, no tax reformer, took over as head of the Senate Finance Committee. Jim Wright, also of Texas—a fierce partisan with no interest in helping advance Ronald Reagan's domestic agenda who became Speaker of the House in January 1987—began urging increasing the top income tax rate to reduce federal deficits.[69] On the other side, supply-siders began promoting tax incentives for savings and investments. Taxing capital gains at the same rate as ordinary income was a reason some Democrats supported the 28 percent top rate, but that parity came unglued.

The 1986 tax reform significantly reduced tax breaks for specified business investments and individuals' spending and savings, benefits that had nearly doubled in revenue costs between 1967 and 1982.[70] However, the three presidents who followed Ronald Reagan into the White House were all enamored of using the tax law this way: in the two decades after 1986, more than fifteen thousand changes were made to the tax law.[71]

The most enduring aspect of the 1986 reform was a lower top income tax rate. The 50 percent rate President Reagan achieved in 1981 became unacceptably high to antitax Republicans. Democrats began to settle for top income tax rates around 40 percent.

———

In the 1986 midterms Democrats gained eight Senate seats and picked up five in the House. Bob Dole moved from leading a Republican majority to heading the forty-five Republicans senators in the minority.[72] President Reagan's economic revolution stalled during his last two years in office. Over time the 1986 tax reform became a promise failed.[73] A dark cloud hovering above President Reagan's sunny tax-reform celebration was the legislation's failure to address federal deficits. That became his successor's nightmare.

After the 1986 tax reform, three powerful and effective advocates for the antitax movement emerged. Grover Norquist, who claimed he formed his organization, Americans for Tax Reform (ATR), at President Reagan's behest to aid the president's quest for tax reform, was invisible during the reform effort, but the creation of ATR seeded Norquist's antitax crusade. Newt Gingrich, a backbench antitax Republican congressman, began accumulating allies, money, and power. And an obscure radio host in Seattle moved to New York and began spreading the antitax creed to a burgeoning middle-class audience. The nation would reap the whirlwind.

Chapter 8

The Triumvirate

Politics is war without blood.

—NEWT GINGRICH

Despite successes in enacting state property tax cuts and limitations, reducing the top federal income tax rate to 28 percent, and lowering the corporate rate from 46 percent to 34 percent, the antitax movement stalled after the nation's leaders, including most Republicans, became obsessed with reducing deficits after the 1981 tax cuts. This, however, was just an interlude, like the summer quiet before the hurricane season. During this period, three new conspicuous, charismatic, and compelling antitax advocates ascended.

This formidable trio did not reach the pinnacle of their influence in the antigovernment, antitax movement until the 1990s when Democrat Bill Clinton moved into the White House. They had different backgrounds and talents, played different roles, and became three of the most important antitax protagonists. In addition to their antitax commitments, they shared tastes for exaggeration and confrontation; keen appreciation of the power of coalitions, alliances, and the media; and extravagant ambitions for change. Bombastic and detesting compromise, they despised moderate Republicans as much as liberal Democrats. They were known by their first names: Grover, Newt, and Rush. Grover Norquist was a committed libertarian; Newt Gingrich was an ideological shapeshifter, willing to change positions whenever it served his personal ambitions; Rush Limbaugh fomented racial, cultural, and economic grievances and abetted grassroots expansion of the antitax movement. These aggressive, friendly collaborators never abandoned their abhorrence of tax increases or their commitments to tax cuts as the magic elixir for whatever is ailing the economy. During the 1980s, all three began acquiring power that catapulted them into prominence. Grover Norquist became best known for his antitax crusade.

The Enforcer

CBS *60 Minutes* correspondent Steve Kroft described Grover Norquist as "the single most effective conservative activist in the country." He added, "Since creating Americans for Tax Reform at Ronald Reagan's behest back in 1985, Norquist has been responsible more than anyone else for rewriting the dogma of the Republican Party."[1] The *Washington Post* agreed, portraying Norquist as "perhaps the single most important figure" in "shaping the way the Republican party has approached tax policy" for a generation.[2] With his ginger-colored hair, well-trimmed beard, and disheveled attire, Grover, as everyone calls him, looks more like an aging college professor than the man Arianna Huffington designated "the dark wizard of the anti-tax cult." Harry Reid, Democratic Senate Majority Leader, viewed Norquist as Lord Voldemort, saying Republicans in Congress were being "led like puppets" by Norquist.[3] Paul Gigot, who took over the *Wall Street Journal* editorial page after Robert Bartley retired, called Norquist "The V. I. Lenin of the anti-tax movement" in a tribute to his strategic vision and influence.[4]

There is special irony in Gigot's linking Norquist to Lenin. When Grover came to Washington, after helping run the Harvard Libertarian Association while earning his undergraduate and MBA degrees, he led anti-Soviet protests by College Republicans. In 1981 he convinced members to mark the twentieth anniversary of the erection of the Berlin Wall by stacking bricks to block the entrance of the Aeroflot Office in Washington, then watching Russian employees dismantle the wall brick-by-brick.[5] "Get rid of the Soviet government," Grover said, "and I don't really have much use for ours."[6]

Norquist credits his Swiss grandmother with his libertarian outlook and hostility to "leftists" and "big labor."[7] While most libertarians and many of Grover's collaborators in the antitax movement view Ayn Rand's novels and philosophy as their preeminent literary influence, Norquist found his lodestar in Whittaker Chambers's *Witness*, a gripping anti-communist thriller about Chambers's life as a communist spy and his battle to unmask the American diplomat Alger Hiss as a communist operative.[8] As journalist Nina Easton reports, Grover embraced Chambers's "neat divides of history" with "God-fearing freedom fighters on one side" and "Godless communists, socialists, and well-intentioned but easily duped liberals on the other."[9]

Grover's commitment to self-sufficiency originated with his father, a successful Polaroid Corporation executive who moved his family to prosperous Weston, Massachusetts, when Grover was five years old. His father taught Grover about the burdens of taxation: when Warren Norquist took his children to the local Dairy Joy for ice cream, before handing the cone to Grover, his father would take one lick and say, "This is the federal tax," then another, "This is the state tax," and a third, "This is the city tax."[10]

Grover honed his public speaking skills as a child in Weston when his father made him, beginning at age nine, go to the family's encyclopedia, pick a topic, and give a one-minute speech about it—fifteen times or more. His mother sometimes intervened: "This is child abuse. It's time for him to go to bed." Grover practiced public speaking on a ledge overlooking a nearby pig farm, thirty feet below. Speaking of the pigs, Grover said, "They'd come to listen to you. I liked that."[11]

In spring 1978, before matriculating at Harvard Business School, Norquist served briefly as executive director at the National Taxpayers Union (NTU), a conservative antitax, antigovernment organization that has long supported a balanced-budget amendment and state constitutional limits on taxes and spending. Grover says he views constitutional constraints as necessary so that legislators, "slimy sons of guns that they are, cannot drive their Sherman tanks through the loopholes."[12] At the NTU, Norquist connected with leaders of the Republican Right, including Paul Weyrich, Phyllis Schlafly, and antitax advocates across the country.

Norquist traveled to Spokane, Washington, to help Howard Jarvis rally support for that state's version of Proposition 13. He told a Spokane newspaper, "There's no such thing as a just tax—it is a contradiction in terms. We just want the government to steal less of our money."[13]

In June 1981, after graduating from Harvard Business School, Grover and Jack Abramoff, a friend and recent graduate of Brandeis University, took over the national College Republicans. Abramoff, a hard-core conservative from Beverly Hills, spent more than $10,000 on his campaign for chairman, mostly raised from his father's wealthy friends. He appointed Grover as executive director. Abramoff and Norquist began raising money from corporate and individual right-wing funders, such as Joseph Coors.[14]

After taking over the College Republicans, Abramoff and Norquist enlisted Ralph Reed, a college student, as an intern. They were determined to transform the group into a libertarian powerhouse of the Republican Right. Grover spent 1983 as an economist and chief speechwriter for the U.S. Chamber of

Commerce (an important antitax ally). Reed—who was described as Grover's clone—succeeded Norquist as the College Republicans' executive director.

Norquist, Reed, and Abramoff rejected any suggestions for compromise and purged the College Republicans of moderates. They insisted freedom and liberty could be protected only by the far right. Abramoff told the group, "It is not our job to seek peaceful co-existence with the Left. Our job is to remove them from power permanently."[15] They forged close relationships with Jack Kemp and Newt Gingrich, a young backbench congressman who became Grover's friend and collaborator.

Pat Robertson, a prominent televangelist and presidential candidate, subsequently hired Reed, who had become a born-again Christian, as the first executive director of the Christian Coalition, one of the largest conservative political organizations in America. In 1992 the Christian Coalition had 250,000 members and spent $10 million on political campaigns, becoming a potent force for the Religious Right in Republican politics. Reed said evangelical Christians could win political control only if they addressed "the concerns of average voters in the area of taxes," among other issues.[16] Norquist and Reed remained close, providing important links between Christian conservatives and Grover's antitax crusade.

In the mid-1980s, Grover looked abroad, spending much time supporting "freedom fighters," like Angola's Jonas Savimbi in Africa and allies of Afghanistan's Mujahedeen opposing the Soviet invasion.[17] "When the Soviet Union went away it became time to focus even more on keeping the American government to a small size," Grover said.[18] The antitax movement then became his mission.

The Pledge

It was conventional for Republican political operatives who came of age in the 1980s to seek to bask in Ronald Reagan's aura. In a 2012 interview with Jon Stewart, host of Comedy Central's *Daily Show*, Grover Norquist claimed Reagan in 1982 fell for promises by House Speaker O'Neill and the Democrats to cut spending by three dollars for every dollar of tax increases. Grover urged Republicans to "never repeat the debacle of 1982."[19] When Stewart pointed out Reagan raised taxes "seven or eight times," Norquist responded, "George Washington lost the battle of New York. That wasn't on purpose. Reagan didn't want to raise taxes." When Stewart added, "but he did it eight times," Norquist claimed Ronald Reagan told him signing the 1982 tax bill "was the greatest mistake of his presidency." Stewart replied, "But he kept raising them after that."[20]

In September 1986, when the Tax Reform Act was on its way to the House and Senate for a final vote, Americans for Tax Reform, which became Grover's organization, along with a coalition of antitax advocacy groups, including the Chamber of Commerce, the National Taxpayers Union, and the American Conservative Union, began circulating a "Taxpayer Protection Pledge" not to raise taxes to candidates running in the 1986 midterm elections.[21] Grover's innovation was getting Republican legislators, governors, and candidates across the country to sign the pledge promising their "constituents that they would never, ever, vote for anything that would make taxes go up."[22] The no-tax-increase pledge became the hallmark of Grover's antitax crusade.

The pledge is simple, straightforward, and absolute. ATR's website observes that "the pledge has become practically required for Republicans seeking office and . . . for Democrats running in Republican districts." Over time, more than 1,800 elected Republican officials in the White House, Congress, and the states have signed it, including nearly every Republican president, governor, representative, and senator.[23] The pledge, Grover says, is to the taxpayers of their states and to the American people. Its federal signatories promise to "oppose any and all efforts to increase the marginal income tax rates for individuals and for businesses [and] to oppose any net reduction or elimination of deductions and credits, unless matched dollar for dollar by further reducing tax rates." Importantly, closing loopholes without reducing tax rates or adding a new tax break violates the pledge. The pledge by state officeholders is broader: governors and state legislators agree to oppose, vote against, and, if applicable, veto "any and all efforts to increase taxes."[24]

Grover claims he originated the pledge "as part of the effort to protect the lower marginal tax rates of Reagan's Tax Reform Act of 1986." Raising taxes, he says, is "what politicians do when they don't have the strength to actually govern," adding that the pledge "has grown in importance as one of the few black-and-white, yes or no, answers that politicians are forced to give to voters before they ask for their vote."[25] "Our job," he insists, is "to make people free."[26] He certainly has helped free from tax increases the wealthy individuals and corporations who fund his activities.[27]

Grover keeps original signed pledges "in a vault in case D.C. burns down." "When someone takes the pledge," he says, "you don't want it tampered with; you don't want it destroyed."[28] Republicans who will not sign his pledge, he says, are like "rat heads in Coke bottles"; they ruin the brand's reputation.[29]

Grover Norquist at his desk with a Guy Fawkes mask and the Taxpayer Protection Pledge. Photographer/Collection via Getty Images.

The *Wall Street Journal* endorsed Grover's pledge in 1986. Fearing a "coalition of Democrats eager to raise rates and Republicans eager to restore loopholes," Robert Bartley described the pledge as "an effective political pesticide" and praised Norquist for having "signed up some 80 congressmen."[30] By 1998, 101 House Republicans and 2 conservative House Democrats had signed the pledge. Richard Rahn, chief economist for the U.S. Chamber of Commerce, said that the Chamber made the pledge "our top priority."[31]

Grover requests candidates "take the pledge on a Bible."[32] "Traditional Republican business groups can provide the resources," he said, "but [Christian evangelical] groups can provide the votes."[33] Charles Black, a long-time Republican strategist, says, "Grover's got a way of convincing people that they are important and that what they are doing is significant."[34]

Tony Coelho, a California congressman heading the 1986 Democratic congressional campaign, complained to the Federal Election Commission that ATR is a "political committee," attempting to influence elections but failing to register with the commission. "Americans for Tax Reform is nothing but a Republican sham group created to promote GOP candidates," Coelho said.[35] This was not the last time ATR was accused of violating campaign laws to help elect Republicans, but no consequences ever followed.[36]

Cultivating Coalitions

In his second-floor corner office in ATR's headquarters near the corner of Twentieth and L Street in Washington, Grover marches, flitting from topic to topic while holding a large Bowie knife he uses to open his mail and sometimes thumps vaguely toward visitors when he wants to emphasize a point.[37] The *New Yorker*'s John Cassidy describes Grover pacing "back and forth, opening and closing his briefcase, rearranging books on his shelves, moving pens and papers around on his desk, and finally bending down to pick up bits of dust."[38] But it is a big mistake to think Grover is inattentive.

Having turned the College Republicans into a dynamic force pushing the Republican Party to the right, Norquist has been ambitious, creative, and resolute in promoting his antitax pledge and messages. He understands the crucial roles played in legislative politics by financial resources and effective coalitions. He has raised millions of dollars from corporations and business organizations, right-wing billionaires, and the Republican National Committee. He cultivates and maintains close bonds with conservative allies and organizations and Christian evangelical leaders who support his antitax agenda.

Beginning in 1993, Grover started holding off-the-record "Wednesday Meetings" at ATR. The meetings began with only about a dozen attendees but grew to be frequently attended by up to 150 conservative Republican political operatives, think-tank leaders, and others from the Republican Right. These gatherings led political journalist John Fund to call Norquist "the Grand Central Station of conservatism."[39] Urging similar cooperation among diverse Democratic groups, Hillary Clinton said, "Grover Norquist has a weekly meeting where every right-wing wannabe comes and gets their marching orders and then goes out onto the talk shows, writes the columns, holds these endless seminars that C-SPAN covers sponsored by AEI or CATO or whatever, and you know I give them enormous credit because they have done an excellent job of marketing whatever it is they believe in."[40]

Grover is not an advocate for the social issues of the Republican Right, but he welcomes social conservatives into what he calls the "Leave-us-Alone Coalition." According to Grover, his coalition includes taxpayers who do not want higher taxes; representatives of businesses that do not like regulations; advocates for gun rights; and people who want to "transmit their faith to their children without the state throwing prophylactics at their kids in school."[41] "They all want government to go away," Grover says. "That's what holds together the conservative movements."[42]

Grover views being able to live without government interference as essential to freedom. He and his allies in the antitax movement oppose government spending designed to lift Americans out of poverty and reject concepts of freedom that view opportunities for everyone to thrive as essential.[43] Many conservatives in Grover's coalitions, however, urge government coercion to promote their cultural, religious, or political values.

Like Paul Weyrich, who cofounded ALEC (the American Legislative Exchange Council) to press his conservative economic and social agenda in the states, Grover has replicated his Washington Wednesday meetings in forty-eight states to secure support from Republicans and organizations across the country. ATR routinely sponsors and coordinates state and local grassroots antitax efforts.[44]

Grover views Democrats and liberals as "the enemy" and says bipartisanship is "another name for date rape."[45] Echoing Howard Jarvis's distinction between taxpayers and tax recipients, Norquist calls Democrats the "takings coalition," people who view government's function as "taking things from some people and giving them to others."[46] Grover Norquist once compared imposing estate taxes on large transfers of wealth to the Holocaust.[47]

Grover views his antigovernment agenda and antitax pledge as the linchpin for Republican Party success. He repeatedly claims he wants "to get government down to the size where you can drown it in the bathtub."[48] He insists taxation is "the central vote-drawing issue." "You win this issue," he says, "you win—over time—all issues."[49]

The Georgia Firebrand

In 1978, when Grover Norquist was executive director of the antitax National Taxpayers Union and supporting Howard Jarvis's tax-limitation efforts in Seattle, Democrats maintained their large majorities in both chambers of Congress but lost fifteen seats in the House of Representatives. The most fateful Republican gain occurred in Georgia's sixth district, north of Atlanta, where thirty-five-year-old Newt Gingrich defeated Virginia Shepard, a moderate state senator. Few recognized the entry of this former history professor to the Republican backbench as the political earthquake it became. As Yale political scientist David Mayhew wrote, "On Capitol Hill, like it or not, the 1990s was Newt Gingrich's decade."[50]

Newt Gingrich was born in Pennsylvania in 1943 and adopted by an Army lieutenant colonel stationed around the world. He moved to Georgia in high school, graduated from Emory University, and earned a PhD in history from

Tulane University. He began teaching history in 1970 at West Georgia College outside Atlanta. He was a popular teacher but was denied tenure in 1977 because of absences for campaigning and his lack of scholarship.

Gingrich ran for Congress in 1974 and 1976 as a moderate Republican but lost to the conservative segregationist Democratic incumbent. Lee Howell, who became Newt's press secretary, said that in those days Gingrich "never let anybody call him a conservative. You had to use the word moderate."[51] In 1975 Newt attended a campaign training "school" run by Paul Weyrich, who persuaded Gingrich that Republicans needed a consistent message on both economic and social issues to build an effective electoral coalition. Perceiving Gingrich's political talents and extraordinary ambition, Weyrich "made a conscious effort to make Newt a star for the Republican Party."[52]

Abandoning his reputation as a young liberal on the West Georgia campus, his moderation on social issues, and previous enthusiasms for temperate Republicans like Nelson Rockefeller and Richard Nixon, Newt shifted right. Chip Kahn, who ran Gingrich's first two congressional campaigns, said, "By 1978, Newt was rock-hard conservative. . . . He talked about welfare cheaters. . . . On some of the social issues, he moved when he realized how central they were to the Republicans. It took him a while to figure that out. Newt understands waves, and he rides waves."[53]

One wave Newt saw early was the centrality of the antitax movement to Republicans' fortunes. Unlike social issues, which frequently divided Republican business leaders and religious conservatives, opposition to tax increases was becoming the foremost issue unifying diverse components of the Republican coalition. In his 1978 campaign, Newt championed antitax, antigovernment positions, embraced supply-side economics, and pushed for the Kemp-Roth tax cuts, which he insisted would increase government revenue by spurring economic growth.

With the exception of his opposition to tax increases and support for tax cuts, Newt Gingrich was never bound by consistent principles. When balancing the budget became practically impossible without tax increases, his antitax commitments prevailed.[54]

Newt soon became famous for rebellious, confrontational, unprincipled partisanship.[55] He fomented aggressive attacks on Democrats for ethical shortcomings, eliding comparable breaches of his own.[56] As early as 1974 he told friends his goal was to be Speaker of the House. Chip Kahn said, "Newt understands . . . that one should never say you want to be president. . . . But he will be whatever he can be, as high as he can go."[57]

An Antitax Warrior

In 1978 Gingrich allied with Jack Kemp and in 1979 became a cosponsor of the Kemp-Roth tax bill. In October 1979 Kemp hosted a fundraiser in Atlanta that raised more than $20,000 for Newt's reelection campaign. In September 1980 Gingrich returned Kemp's favor by staging a photo on the Capitol steps with Ronald Reagan, George H. W. Bush, 23 Republican senators, 115 Republican representatives, and nearly 150 Republican candidates supporting Kemp's tax cuts.

Although Newt Gingrich's fawning biographer subtitled his book *The Making of a Reagan Conservative*, Newt was perfectly willing to oppose the Reagan administration.[58] Gingrich famously opposed Bob Dole's 1982 tax-increase legislation and called the 1982 law "the dumbest decision of the Reagan Administration."[59] Newt also voted against Reagan's 1982 increase in the gas tax. Presaging battles ahead, Newt said unless the Reagan administration supported large spending cuts and a balanced-budget amendment, he would be "perfectly willing to have the government come to a halt this spring for two, three, four weeks" by voting against any increase in the federal debt ceiling.[60]

In 1982 Newt began rounding up allies for consistent messaging among House conservatives. The *Conservative Digest* put Gingrich on its cover as the Republican "who could one day pick up President Reagan's sword as leader of the conservative cause."[61] In April 1983 Newt held an organizational meeting of what became his Conservative Opportunity Society. The group tried but failed to pass a congressional resolution promising to sustain a presidential veto of any and all tax increases and exhorted all Republicans to support the party's commitment to "no new taxes."[62] Outlining the campaign strategy for 1982 Republican candidates, Newt urged they promise lower taxes and greater take-home pay and emphasize their commitments to tax cuts. He counseled Republicans to describe their opponents as determined to enact "high taxes with less money in your wallet and less take-home pay."[63]

Gingrich (who subsequently advanced proposals to privatize Social Security) opposed the 1983 Social Security tax increases and benefit cuts urged by President Reagan and Speaker O'Neill. Along with Jack Kemp, Newt become one of the key architects of the 1984 Republican platform, which stated, "we . . . oppose any attempts to increase taxes, which would harm the recovery and reverse the trend of restoring control of the economy to individual Americans."[64] In 1985 Gingrich, unlike Jack Kemp, refused to succumb to President

Reagan's pleas to send Dan Rostenkowski's tax-reform bill to the Senate and criticized Kemp for supporting the House Democratic bill. When the 1986 tax-reform legislation came back to the House with a 28 percent income tax rate on the highest earners, however, Newt voted for it. He opposed the 1987 budget legislation, which contained a few tax increases. By the end of Ronald Reagan's presidency, Newt had demonstrated his antitax bona fides even when it required opposing a president he admired.

Money and the Media

In summer 1986, Gingrich revitalized GOPAC, a small, stagnating political action committee founded in 1978 by Delaware governor Pete du Pont to train Republican candidates to run for Congress and state and local offices. Newt used GOPAC as an important financial vehicle to coordinate conservative messaging. He raised funds—$15 million over a decade—from wealthy conservatives, such as textile magnate Roger Milliken and members of the Kohler bathroom fixture family.[65] Weyrich said, "GOPAC was important because it provided an ideological framework for a lot of the candidates."[66]

Newt spread his views and tactics to Republican candidates through audiotapes and videos he produced and narrated. Many successful Republican representatives (including future House Speaker John Boehner) said they were heavily influenced by the tapes. Newt also collaborated with pollster and Republican wordsmith Frank Luntz to produce a pamphlet called *Language: A Key Mechanism of Control*. It recommended repeatedly using words like "corruption," "traitors," "sick," "radical," "steal," "decay," "failure," "hypocrisy," and "lie" to describe Democrats.[67] The Conservative Opportunity Society and GOPAC became key components of interlocking organizations that Newt used to build influence in the Republican Party and spread his antitax message.[68]

By the mid-1980s Newt Gingrich was the leader of a new generation of Republican officeholders. He was a media magnet who created and nurtured organizations to supply resources and opportunities to spread his messages and ideology. In his 1984 campaign, Ronald Reagan echoed Newt, describing his second-term vision as creating a "conservative opportunity society."[69]

Not every Republican was on board with Newt's agenda. Bob Dole called Gingrich a gadfly and the Conservative Opportunity Society "the Young Hypocrites." Dole said, "They think they can peddle the idea that they've taken over the party. Well, they aren't the Republican Party and they aren't going to be."[70]

From the moment he came to Washington as a backbench Georgia congressman, Newt was a master media manipulator who became a media star with aggressive, apocalyptic rhetoric about "a war of civilizations between ['sick'] liberals and true conservatives."[71] Paul Weyrich observed, "Newt started with the premise that in any war whoever controls the means of communication has the upper hand."[72] Newt said, "If you're not in the *Washington Post* every day, you might as well not exist."[73] He claimed, "I'm tough in the House because when I arrived, the Republican Party was a soft institution that lacked the tradition of fighting. You had to have somebody who was willing to fight."[74] "I'm willing to be ineffective in the short run," he added, "if it means that in the long run, we're able to build a majority."[75] Newt was best known for his combative, scorched-earth style. As he said, "you don't get on TV with cars that get home safely."[76] His media attention helped expand the public reach of the antitax movement beyond the editorial reach of the *Wall Street Journal*.[77]

On March 19, 1979, Brian Lamb, a former aide in President Nixon's Office of Telecommunications Policy, launched a new television network called C-SPAN and began providing gavel-to-gavel coverage of the House of Representatives. C-SPAN subsequently expanded to cover the Senate, congressional hearings, and other political events. It initially reached a small audience of about two hundred thousand viewers. Newt distrusted network news, which he viewed as uniformly liberal. So he and his conservative colleagues took advantage of the opportunity C-SPAN offered to communicate nationally "without having [our views] digested or reinterpreted by unfriendlies within the media." Newt predicted C-SPAN's audience would expand if House Republicans engaged in "confrontation rather than capitulation." "Conflict," he said, "equals exposure equals power."[78]

The Man behind the Golden Microphone

In 1987 President Reagan eliminated the "fairness doctrine," a 1949 rule of the Federal Communications Commission (FCC) requiring radio and television stations to present differing views on controversial issues of public importance. On August 4, 1987, the FCC eliminated the doctrine, saying it restricted the journalistic freedom of broadcasters—a change that transformed radio and cable television programming. This change gave Grover Norquist, Newt Gingrich, and their allies opportunities to spread their antitax messages beyond imagining.

Before the fairness doctrine was discarded, the only important national media outlet advocating consistently for the antitax movement was the *Wall Street Journal*, whose positions were sometimes echoed by conservative papers, like the *Washington Times* and the *New York Post*, with local audiences. There were only a handful of relatively small conservative publications, most influentially William Buckley's *National Review*, along with *Commentary*, *American Spectator*, and *Human Events*.[79] There was no Fox News, no Breitbart, no talk radio, no podcasts, no Matt Drudge, no Facebook, no Twitter, no internet. An unknown Sacramento radio host changed that.

Rush Hudson Limbaugh III grew up in Cape Girardeau, Missouri, in a prominent Republican family. His grandfather and namesake was a goodwill ambassador to India during the Eisenhower administration, and the local federal courthouse was named after him. Rush's father, a lawyer, was a Republican activist and Rush's political mentor; his mother was a Republican committeewoman who passed along her sense of humor. She said, Rush "didn't start talking until he was two, and then he didn't stop."[80]

Rush Limbaugh began working for a local radio station during high school, and he became a pop-music radio disc jockey after dropping out of college in 1972. In 1984 he began a successful talk-radio show in Sacramento lambasting California politicians. In 1988, taking advantage of new satellite technology, ABC Radio hired him for a local morning show in New York and a nationally syndicated afternoon program.

From 1988 until Rush's death in 2021, *The Rush Limbaugh Show* was nationally syndicated for three hours a day, five days a week, ultimately reaching a weekly audience of 20 million listeners on 650 radio stations nationwide. For nearly three decades, it was the most popular radio talk show and Rush's platform for remunerative speaking engagements and bestselling books. His newsletter "The Limbaugh Letter" had over 400,000 subscribers. His 1992 book, *The Way Things Ought to Be*, sold more than three million copies. That year he also began a 30-minute weekly television show, produced by Roger Ailes and carried by more than 200 stations. It ended in 1996 when Ailes became the founding CEO of Fox News.[81]

In 1992 Ronald Reagan said Rush Limbaugh was "the number one voice for conservatism in our country."[82] David Remnick of the *New Yorker* described Rush's conservatism as "a mix of the traditional Republicanism of his father and grandfather and the jury of the pro–George Wallace forces that became so popular in his hometown."[83] Limbaugh's show was a precursor to likeminded, successful talk-radio shows by Sean Hannity, Neal Boortz, and others, and in the mid-1990s to shows hosted by Fox News Channel's right-wing hosts, Bill O'Reilly, Glenn Beck, Laura Ingraham, and Tucker Carlson. Rush Limbaugh was the granddaddy of them all, untroubled by factual accuracy, divisive, often bigoted, feasting on outrage. Although better known for pronouncements on other topics, Rush and his acolytes became important opponents of tax increases and proselytizers for tax cuts, reaching huge audiences of middle-class Americans.

A committed antitaxer, Rush Limbaugh used his media platform to motivate Republican activists and voters. He often promoted the canard that cutting taxes would raise revenues. "Charts and graphs," he said, "can prove that tax rate reductions enhance revenue," and "tax cuts" are "the only proven way to raise revenue."[84] "Congressman," he asked, "can you or anyone else show me where any society in human history has taxed itself into prosperity?"[85] Rush and his allies were certain any tax increase portends economic disaster, and "cutting taxes increases revenue for the government."[86]

Rush Limbaugh frequently described himself as a "truth teller," speaking to his audience through his "golden EIB microphone" with "talent on loan from God."[87] His devoted followers, an audience of mostly middle-class white men, called themselves "Dittoheads," signaling their agreement with what he said. By the mid-1990s, about three hundred restaurants around the country provided "Rush rooms" where his fans could listen to Rush's show.[88]

Rush's enterprises made him fabulously wealthy. He earned about $85 million a year and lived in a 24,000-square-foot mansion in Palm Beach, Florida. He owned a $54 million private jet, collected $5,000 bottles of wine, and sometimes tipped waiters as much as $5,000.[89] Rush insisted tax cuts should "benefit the wealthy" because progressive taxation is "an assault on achievement."[90] Rush told his listeners they would make better decisions with their money than the government would. He said, "Never feel guilty for wanting to keep more of [your money] for you and your family. Do not accept the silly notion that there is poverty and suffering in America because you are greedy and aren't paying enough in taxes."[91] He applauded wealthy people who avoided paying taxes and loathed estate and gift taxes on gifts or bequests of large amounts of wealth because they redistribute wealth from the rich.

Rush Limbaugh understood the political potency of antitax messages. Echoing Grover Norquist, he said, "You don't defeat liberals by joining them. You defeat them with taxes, and you defeat them with lower taxes."[92] Like Newt Gingrich, Rush viewed cutting taxes as a signature political issue for the

Republican Party.[93] Newt was among the first politicians to recognize the potential political sway of talk radio. He called Rush's show frequently and described Limbaugh as his friend. Limbaugh reciprocated: during the 1992 campaign, he hosted a fundraiser for Gingrich.

By the end of the 1980s, Grover Norquist's pledge was eliciting promises never to raise taxes from Republican politicians in Washington and across the country. Newt Gingrich was the leader of antitax Republicans in the House. While the *Wall Street Journal* was promoting tax cuts to business elites and politicians, Rush Limbaugh was persuading millions of his middle-class listeners across the country to oppose tax increases and support tax cuts no matter the economic circumstances. The antitax mission, however, continued to face obstacles from ongoing large deficits and new political hurdles due to the end of Ronald Reagan's presidency and turmoil in congressional leadership.

Grover's Pledge in the 1988 Presidential Campaign

During the 1988 Republican presidential nomination campaign, Rush Limbaugh's national radio show was in its infancy, and he did not take sides. Newt Gingrich supported his supply-side House colleague and friend Jack Kemp. Grover Norquist backed the long-shot candidacy of Pierre (Pete) du Pont IV, an antitax conservative heir to the DuPont chemical fortune and two-term Delaware governor. As governor from 1977 through 1985, du Pont promoted and signed into law two cuts in the state's income tax—the first tax cuts in the state's history. Du Pont also promoted a state constitutional amendment requiring a supermajority vote of 60 percent in the legislature to increase "any tax levied or license fee."[94]

Pete du Pont signed Grover's no-tax-increase pledge early in November 1986, becoming the first presidential candidate to do so. On February 14, 1988, in a televised debate in Manchester, New Hampshire, shortly before that state's presidential primary, Du Pont took out a copy of Grover's no-tax pledge. The pledge had been signed by three of the other four contenders there: Jack Kemp, George H. W. Bush, and Pat Robertson. Du Pont urged Bob Dole—the only candidate who had not signed the pledge—to sign it. Dole, who had just won the Iowa vote, quipped, "Give it to George. I have to read it first."[95] Years later Grover described the event: "Remember in 1988, even after Reagan passed tax reform, Dole refused to take the pledge. He won Iowa, but then during a debate in New Hampshire, Pete du Pont handed him the pledge, and he reacted like someone had thrown the cross in the lap of a vampire. George

Bush took the pledge and won."[96] Du Pont dropped out of the race after finishing near the bottom of candidates in Iowa and New Hampshire.

Antitax commitments had become so important to Republican politics that George H. W. Bush doubled down on his refusal to increase taxes when he accepted the Republican presidential nomination in August 1988. Bush won the presidency that November, but when he became president he faced immense economic, political, and legal pressures to reduce federal deficits. He also faced important changes in the House leadership.

Newt Rising

An earthquake in congressional leadership in the late 1980s proved crucial to the fate of George H. W. Bush's presidency and had an enduring impact on the antitax movement and American politics. The first change occurred on the Democratic side. It improved the Republican president's ability to enact legislation, but the more important development occurred among Republicans. Newt Gingrich played conspicuous roles in both.

In January 1987, after serving a decade as Speaker of the House, Tip O'Neill retired. Majority Leader Jim Wright of Fort Worth, Texas, succeeded O'Neill.[97] Once he became Speaker, Wright typically denied House Republicans any role in shaping important legislation, including budget and tax bills—rendering their cooperation irrelevant and intensifying their resentment.[98] Rush Limbaugh sometimes referred to him as "The Sleazer of the House."[99]

As historian Julian Zelizer detailed, Newt Gingrich immediately began planning to attack Wright, setting off an explosive confrontation that "would reshape American politics."[100] At Newt's behest, a House ethics inquiry of Wright began in July 1988, involving sixty-nine charges, most importantly excessive bulk sales of his book to lobbyists and contributors and a controversial job provided to his wife. House Republicans ultimately united in supporting Gingrich's challenge. Wright viewed Gingrich as a "troublemaking, headline-grabbing provocateur" and insisted Newt would find his "destructive" and "seductive promises of achieving a Republican majority by blowing up the House" thwarted.[101] Gingrich, doggedly pursuing a Republican House majority, said, "If you think you are the subordinate wolf, you [spend] a lot of time cultivating the dominant wolf. If you think you are capable of becoming the dominant wolf, you spend a lot of your energy beating the dominant wolf."[102]

George H. W. Bush condemned Wright during his presidential campaign. After his inauguration, however, Bush became skittish about Gingrich's crusade against the Democratic Speaker and had White House aides tell congressional Republicans the new president intended to govern, emphasizing this required bipartisan legislation not partisan confrontation.[103]

In May 1989 the House Ethics Committee, after dismissing most of Gingrich's charges against Wright, announced it would continue to investigate five charges of Wright's misconduct.[104] Three days later, Tony Coehlo, the third-ranking House Democrat, announced he was resigning from Congress due to unrelated financial improprieties. On May 31, 1989, Speaker Jim Wright announced that he would resign from Congress.[105]

In his resignation speech, after defending the charges against him, Wright said that it is "unworthy of our institution" for "vengeance" to become "more desirable than vindication" and urged both parties to "bring this period of mindless cannibalism to an end."[106] *Washington Post* reporter Tom Shales wrote, "It was as if one were watching not just the demise of one politician, but the passing of an entire era of American politics."[107]

On June 6, 1989, Democratic Majority Leader Tom Foley of Spokane, Washington—an outspoken critic of the bitterness and partisanship that Gingrich and his allies fomented—became House Speaker. Foley was more liberal than Wright, but collegial and more conciliatory.[108] He wanted to work with the new Republican president.

In March 1989 the Senate defeated, by a 53–47 vote, President Bush's nomination of his fellow Texan John Tower, a four-term senator, to be secretary of defense. After considering others, Bush nominated Dick Cheney, Wyoming's congressman serving as minority whip, to be his defense secretary.[109] After a bruising contest, Newt Gingrich replaced Cheney in the second-highest position in the Republican House leadership.

Bob Michel, an Illinois representative since 1956, had been House Republican Leader since 1981. He was noted for his ability to negotiate bipartisan deals with Democrats who held the majority during his entire tenure in Congress. Michel insisted Republicans had a "responsibility" to help Democrats govern by supporting "reasonable" compromises.[110] To replace Cheney, Michel selected a well-respected, moderate friend, his fellow Illinois congressman Edward Madigan, who also sought compromises with the Democratic majority.

Although many House Republicans considered Newt Gingrich too polarizing, confrontational, and divisive to be their leader, he entered the race.[111] On March 22, 1989, with a Madigan supporter absent and an uncounted spoiled ballot, House Republicans in an 87–85 vote elected Newt Gingrich to become minority whip.[112] California's Mickey Edwards, chair of the House Republican Policy Committee, said that Michel's defeat by Newt was like "somebody is shoveling dirt on your grave but you're not dead yet."[113]

Democrats held their majorities in the House through George H. W. Bush's presidency, but Newt's elevation into the House Republican leadership guaranteed a combative Republican minority. He consolidated and strengthened his power by expanding and reorganizing the whip's office. He appointed two chief deputy whips: his Pennsylvania ally Bob Walker and Wisconsin moderate Steve Gunderson who had supported him, plus five associate whips, including conservative Texan Dick Armey, a committed antitax, antigovernment enthusiast who would long play a prominent role in the antitax movement.

The most consequential question following Newt's rise was how he would leverage his new power to further his ambition to become Speaker of the House. Beryl Anthony, chairman of the Democratic Congressional Campaign Committee, called Newt a "grenade thrower" and predicted his elevation would make bipartisan appeals much more difficult, an understatement. Anthony said the new number-two House Republican "is probably going to set off a metal detector when he goes into the White House."[114]

———

George H. W. Bush and his aides were relieved that Jim Wright was gone and the Democratic House majority was less truculent. Determined to remain optimistic, President Bush told his diary, "I'm convinced I can work with [Newt] and I want to work with him." Bush could not have been more wrong. Five days later, he added, "I was elected to govern and make things happen, and my . . . view is, you can't do it through confrontation."[115] As Bush's biographer Jon Meacham wrote, "The old politics of the possible was being replaced by the politics of purity."[116] The party of Lincoln had become the party of antitax zealots, with leaders like Grover Norquist, Newt Gingrich, and Rush Limbaugh. President Bush did not immediately realize it, but his obstacles to governing had grown dramatically—principally because of the tax issue. He became the first Republican president to break Grover's antitax pledge—and the last to do so—greatly strengthening the antitax movement.

Chapter 9

A President Undone

My opponent won't rule out raising taxes but I will, and the Congress will push me to raise taxes, and I'll say no, and they'll push again, and I'll say to them, "Read my lips: no new taxes."

—GEORGE HERBERT WALKER BUSH, AUGUST 18, 1988

When George Herbert Walker Bush moved from the vice president's residence to the White House on January 20, 1989, neither Newt Gingrich nor Grover Norquist knew Bush's presidency would catapult them into the vanguard of the nation's Republican leadership. Only a few budget authorities anticipated tax issues might unravel Bush's presidency and help a Democrat unseat him.

Conservative antitax Republicans never took to George H. W. Bush. The son of Connecticut senator Prescott Bush, graduate of Greenwich Country Day School, Phillips Academy Andover, and, like his great-grandfather, Yale University, was a patrician. Having been a decorated hero in World War II before becoming a Texas oilman did not assure Republican conservatives. Nor did Bush's government service as a congressman, ambassador, and head of the CIA. He sinned by calling Reagan's economic revolution "voodoo economics." Serving eight years as Reagan's faithful vice president did not absolve him of that. In his speech accepting the Republican presidential nomination, Bush said "public service is honorable" and called for "a kinder and gentler nation."[1] That was not what right-wing Republican firebrands wanted to hear.

The new president was comfortable with foreign affairs, and the Constitution granted him considerable power to act independently in that realm. But Bush's mastery of foreign policy—his deft handling of the dismantling of the

Soviet Union and Germany's reunification and halting Iraq's Saddam Hussein in his effort to annex Kuwait—generated little clout with Americans facing daunting economic challenges.[2]

On the domestic front, President Bush cared deeply about lowering capital gains taxes and not much else, but he did not want to become a do-nothing president on domestic policy. On December 7, 1988, as he was preparing to take office, Bush wrote in his diary, "If it weren't for the deficit, I'd be feeling pretty good these days."[3] Unfortunately, he faced an economic, political, and legal conundrum. Controlling deficits became a major domestic priority. Like most political leaders of the 1980s and 1990s, he regarded the deficit as more than a nettlesome nuisance: he believed deficits and the mushrooming national debt posed an existential challenge to the nation's economic health and to America's leadership as the world's premier military and economic power.[4]

Alan Greenspan, heading the Federal Reserve, was philosophically opposed to tax increases, but he was convinced the combination of large deficits and low interest rates would induce inflation. He insisted successful bipartisan deficit-reduction legislation was necessary before he would lower interest rates to head off a recession.[5]

President Bush and his economic team confronted an independent and intransigent Federal Reserve chairman with great power over the nation's economy and congressional adversaries on both sides of the aisle.[6] Unfortunately, the president had made his challenges much greater with his only memorable campaign promise.

"Read My Lips, No New Taxes"

When the Republican Convention opened in New Orleans in August 1988, Massachusetts governor Michael Dukakis, the Democratic presidential nominee, led George Bush by about ten points.[7] Bush thought about selecting the charismatic actor Clint Eastwood as his running mate but ultimately picked Dan Quayle, a young conservative Indiana senator. Quayle's halting and awkward introduction to the American people went so badly that Bush considered dumping him. Heading into his Thursday night acceptance speech, Bush wrote in his diary, "I knew what I had to do. The press was building it up and up and up . . . it was the biggest moment of my life."[8]

Peggy Noonan, a former speechwriter for Ronald Reagan, wrote Bush's speech. The read-my-lips line, which begins this chapter, was suggested by Bush's long-time political advisor Roger Ailes. Noonan fashioned the read-my-lips message to mimic Clint Eastwood's movie characters' toughness. Dick Darman, hoping to become Bush's budget director, tried to remove it. He knew George Bush was no Clint Eastwood and feared Bush as president would have to break any no-tax-increase pledge to contain federal deficits.[9] But the "read my lips: no new taxes" line stayed in the speech. Roger Ailes rehearsed Bush until he delivered it perfectly: before a large national television audience, George Bush sounded as powerful and immovable as Eastwood's Dirty Harry urging a robber to "make my day." The Superdome crowd erupted in vigorous, loud, ecstatic applause.

President Bush's pledge added a new political barrier to reducing deficits just when the law required it. During Ronald Reagan's second term Congress enacted a legislative sword to slash spending automatically if specified deficit reductions failed to occur. To produce a deficit-reduction deal, the president needed agreement from Democrats who controlled Congress. Having served on the Ways and Means Committee, Bush enjoyed a cordial relationship with the committee's chairman Dan Rostenkowski. Tom Foley succeeding Jim Wright as Speaker of the House made fruitful negotiations more likely. But George Mitchell, the Senate Democratic Leader, was a shrewd adversary whose thoughtful, judicious demeanor masked his determination to limit the new Republican president to one term.

Congressional Democrats were not about to agree to curtail deficits solely by cutting spending. Liberal Democrats were particularly eager to raise taxes on the rich, anathema to conservative antitax Republicans. Unfortunately for the president, doing nothing was no option.

The Terrible, Not-So-Swift Sword

In 1985 the federal budget deficit hit $212 billion ($536 billion in 2021 dollars), nearly 5 percent of GDP, notwithstanding the deficit-reducing laws of 1982, 1983, and 1984.[10] In October 1985, in order not to default on the nation's debt, Congress raised the federal debt ceiling to more than $2 trillion—an unprecedented level.[11] Two months later, President Reagan signed fateful deficit-reduction legislation: the Balanced Budget and Emergency Deficit Control Act, better known as Gramm-Rudman-Hollings (GRH) after its Senate cosponsors, Republicans Phil Gramm of Texas and Warren Rudman of New Hampshire and South Carolina Democrat Fritz Hollings.[12]

GRH required specific annual reductions in deficits and their complete elimination by October 1, 1990. If Congress failed to meet the deficit targets,

GRH imposed automatic spending cuts called "sequestrations" to meet them. Half the required cuts had to come from non-defense spending, half from defense.[13] Senator Rudman called the law "a bad idea whose time has come."[14]

The original 1985 GRH deficit law required spending cuts and/or tax increases greater than Congress or President Reagan would accept, so in 1987 Congress pushed back the original GRH targets, delaying from 1991 to 1993 the requirement that the federal budget be balanced and tightening GRH's strictures.[15] If the original GRH targets had been met, the 1990 deficit would have been between $36 and $46 billion, and eliminating the deficit by 1991 would have been manageable.[16] Instead the 1990 deficit was more than $220 billion.[17] In January 1989 when George H. W. Bush took office, the deficit for 1993—the year GRH required the budget to be balanced—was estimated to be about $135 billion.[18]

Federal spending was about 21 percent of GDP when Ronald Reagan left office, down less than one percentage point since his inauguration. Even so, with the exception of defense, most politically easy spending cuts had occurred. Deficits had expanded because revenues declined during Reagan's presidency from 19 percent of GDP to around 17.5 percent. In summer 1990, Robert Reischauer, director of the Congressional Budget Office, announced GRH would require a 42 percent cut in defense spending and a 64 percent reduction of non-defense discretionary spending.[19] The defense spending cuts were much larger than the president or congressional Republicans would abide, and non-defense reductions greater than congressional Democrats would tolerate. New budget legislation was unavoidable.

George Bush had handcuffed himself with his assurance to the American people that he would not raise taxes. He confronted an ineluctable dilemma.

1989: Prelude to a Debacle

President Bush eluded the budget conundrum during his campaign by claiming that he would balance the budget through a "flexible freeze" on spending: allowing federal spending to increase at the rate of inflation while being "flexible"—or more accurately, silent—about what spending he would cut. But as president he had to produce a detailed budget blueprint.

Congressional Democrats insisted on a tax increase in exchange for reductions in spending programs. House Republican Leader Bob Michel knew additional taxes would have to be part of any bipartisan budget deal, but a large number of antitax House Republicans opposed any negotiations by the president with the Democrats.[20] Jack Kemp, who joined the Bush administration as secretary of housing and urban development, remained unconcerned about deficits; he urged more tax cuts despite looming GRH sequestrations.[21]

Dick Darman, heading the Office of Management and Budget, and Jim Baker, about to become secretary of the State Department, insisted the president not raise taxes during his first year in office. In December 1988 Dan Rostenkowski said that he would give the president a pass on raising taxes for one year—but only for one year.

On February 9, 1989, George H. W. Bush gave a televised address to a joint session of Congress describing his economic and budgetary priorities. He urged that his proposals become part of a "comprehensive budget agreement" to meet GRH deficit targets without raising taxes. He proposed lowering "the maximum rate on capital gains taxes to increase investments," which he said would "raise revenues, help savings, and create new jobs."[22] Cutting the capital gains rate would raise revenue in the short term by inducing people to sell and pay tax on assets they otherwise would have held, but the great bulk of capital gains tax cuts would benefit people at the top. Although he did not mention it, the president's budget also proposed reducing Medicare costs, which would mainly burden low-income and middle-class retirees.

Foreshadowing larger battles to come, Democrats strongly criticized the president's proposed cuts in capital gains taxes and Medicare. One Democratic congressman said it was "voodoo economics revisited." Dan Rostenkowski said he would "strongly resist" changing the 1986 tax reform and "returning to a preferential rate for capital gains." Leon Panetta, chairman of the House Budget Committee, said Democrats "would have to reject any kind of 'flexible freeze' that would bend with flexibility for the rich and powerful, but freeze out the middle-income families of America."[23]

In late February, Dick Darman and Treasury Secretary Nicholas Brady entered into tortuous budget negotiations with Democratic and Republican congressional leaders. Liberal Democrats wanted to raise the highest income tax rate from 28 to 33 percent, but the president would not agree to that. House Republican Leader Bob Michel complained, "The Democratic leadership believes in redistributing wealth. The Democratic leadership subscribes to the rancid rhetoric of class warfare."[24]

During the negotiations, Dan Rostenkowski advocated a 15-cents-a-gallon increase in the federal gas tax, which enjoyed strong support from environmental groups. The Bush administration was amenable to a gas tax increase but, because of the president's no-new-taxes pledge, wanted to postpone any increase until 1990. Newt Gingrich announced his opposition to any gas tax increase. "No member [of Congress] from the suburbs is going to raise the price of gasoline," he said. "For 90% of working Americans it's nonsense."[25]

The battle lines were clear: Democrats would resist capital gains cuts and spending reductions for the middle class and push for tax increases. Newt Gingrich and his antitax House Republican allies would resist tax increases and insist GRH deficit-reduction targets could be met by cutting spending.

On December 19, 1989, President Bush signed the 1989 budget law—a relatively trivial 800-page hodgepodge of spending cuts and technical tax changes that avoided triggering outrage from either side of the aisle.[26] The law cut the deficit by $14.7 billion, with nearly one-third consisting of automatic spending cuts required by GRH.[27] The White House had muddled through the president's first year in office, but in 1990 the GRH sword was set to fall. *Time* magazine's headline captured the president's predicament: "Wait until Next Year."[28]

Breaking the Pledge

In 1990 the economy was sputtering, but despite pleas from the Bush administration, Alan Greenspan still refused to lower interest rates to stimulate the economy until Congress and the president reached a budget deal. Large GRH sequestrations were approaching. In an Oval Office meeting on March 6, 1990, Dan Rostenkowski told the president that he would soon release a serious, unpopular, deficit-reduction plan. Rostenkowski asked the president not to attack his plan, and Bush agreed.[29] On March 20, knowing a budget agreement with congressional Democrats was impossible without tax increases, Bush told his diary, "I know I'm going to have to bite a major bullet."[30]

On May 9 Senate Democratic Leader George Mitchell insisted the White House release a statement saying budget negotiations with a goal of reducing projected deficits by $500 billion over the coming five years—twice as large as any previous deficit-reducing legislation—would proceed with "no preconditions." The media pushed President Bush to elaborate, but all he said was, "I make this offer to sit down in good faith with no conditions." The next day, the president was more candid to his diary, "The shit," he wrote, has "hit the fan."[31] A few days later, Bush complained, "We're getting pounded, and the right wing is the worst, much more so than the left wing. . . . [W]hen you're attacked by your own, it stings more."[32]

In June the budget negotiations had stalled. Moderate congressional Republicans, including House Republican Leader Bob Michel, were pushing for an agreement even if tax increases had to be an important part of a deal. President Bush was worried about attacks from antitax Republicans on his right and especially wanted to hear from Phil Gramm and Newt Gingrich. Gramm was a conservative antitax Texas Democratic congressman from 1978 until 1982 when he switched to the Republican Party and easily won the same seat. In 1985, after having been elected to the Senate, he cosponsored the GRH deficit-reduction law. Gramm told the president, "If we can get a deal, we ought to take it. If we've got to do a little bit in taxes to get a deal, do it. Just don't break the pledge until there's a deal. . . . I cannot vote to change marginal [income tax] rates. But if the deal includes non-incentive [harming] taxes, I'm willing to take it."[33]

In a meeting with the bipartisan negotiators, Gingrich said, "I can imagine a five-year package where I try to sell taxes." In conversations with former New Hampshire governor John Sununu, President Bush's chief of staff, Newt suggested he was open to a tax increase as long as an agreement with Democrats did not raise marginal income tax rates.[34] He told the president, "There's no way you can deal with income tax rates," appearing to agree with Phil Gramm.[35] A month later, on July 20, the *Washington Post* reported that Newt said "I'm prepared to sponsor and support raising taxes" as part of a deficit-reduction deal.[36]

President Bush and his key advisors reasonably believed two of the most important antitax Republicans in Congress—Phil Gramm and Newt Gingrich—were prepared to accept a budget agreement with the Democrats including tax increases as long as it avoided increasing income tax rates. But the president's advisors underestimated Gingrich's overweening ambition to become Speaker of the House and the support Newt needed from antitax Republicans to secure that office. Many years later Gingrich told George Bush's biographer Jon Meacham, "In my mind, it was a betrayal of his pledge and a betrayal of Reaganism."[37] Newt apparently accepted Oscar Wilde's maxim: "consistency is the last refuge of the unimaginative."[38]

A breakfast meeting on Thursday June 26, 1990, in the White House family dining room revived the negotiations—at great cost to George H. W. Bush. The participants included the president, Darman, Brady, Sununu, and the Democratic and Republican congressional leaders. President Bush asked the Democrats, "What do you propose?" House Speaker Tom Foley, sitting next to the president, said a deal large enough to address the nation's deficits needed an agreed statement that a bipartisan solution requires entitlement reform, defense and discretionary spending reductions, budget process reform, and tax increases.[39] The president who, according to Darman, seemed more focused on the need to be sure all agreed and that blame would be shared than on relinquishing his no-new-taxes pledge, responded, "Okay if I can say you agreed."[40]

Darman, who later described himself as acting out of "some stupid reflex," said the agreement "would be easy to draft." When he wrote Foley's words, "tax increases," Darman anticipated political trouble and handed the draft to Sununu, who was more closely aligned with the Republican Right. Darman subsequently said he thought Sununu might push back on releasing the statement. Instead Sununu only changed "tax increases" to "tax revenue increases" and added "growth incentives," by which he meant to signal a capital gains cut. Sununu hoped to avoid a firestorm of criticism that President Bush had broken his no-new-taxes pledge. But Sununu subsequently admitted, "It was a thin reed, but it was all I could come up with in thirty seconds of editing."[41]

The president circulated the statement to the group, and Republicans and Democrats discussed it separately. George Mitchell proposed adding the words "to me," so the final version released to the press by President Bush read:

> It is clear to me that both the size of the deficit problem and the need for a package that can be enacted require all of the following: entitlement and mandatory program reform, tax revenue increases, growth incentives, discretionary spending reductions, orderly reductions in defense expenditures, and budget process reform to assure that any bipartisan agreement is enforceable and that the deficit problem is brought under responsible control.[42]

Dan Rostenkowski said "read my lips" was history. A *New York Post* headline screamed "Read My Lips—I Lied."[43] The *Washington Post* titled its story, "Bush Abandons Campaign Pledge, Calls for New Taxes," a view echoed by newspapers across the land.[44] Conservative columnist Pat Buchanan titled his complaint, "The End of the Reagan Revolution."[45] When Sununu called Newt Gingrich to try to convince him that "tax revenue increases" meant growth incentives, like a capital gains cut, Newt hung up.

When Vice President Quayle learned the president agreed to a tax increase, he responded, "You're kidding" and called Sununu to tell him that he needed "to roll this damn thing back."[46] Later Quayle, who was in the shower in California when he heard about Bush's statement, wrote, "I probably should have looked at the drain because that's where the Republican Party's best issue—the one that had gotten us elected in 1980, 1984, and 1988, the one that had more than any other made the Reagan revolution possible—was headed."[47]

Dick Darman later claimed the meeting would have accelerated the negotiations without the president releasing any statement and said the president should have waited until there was an agreement before making public any concession on taxes. Darman wrote, "We weakened the president politically. And we reduced our leverage for the negotiations that were to follow."[48]

President Bush believed the nation required substantial deficit reductions, and he and his economic advisors feared GRH sequestrations of defense and other spending were too large and would tank the economy. Democratic Senate Majority Leader George Mitchell made clear he would consider substantial cuts in spending and tighter budget rules only if the president agreed to tax increases. The president violated his "read-my-lips, no-new-taxes" pledge because he thought it was the necessary thing to do for the country. But despite the media blowback and many calls and letters to Republicans in Congress expressing public opposition to any tax increases, the president failed to explain to the public why he broke his pledge.[49]

Conceding the tax issue before the president had an agreement was a mistake. But the no-new-taxes pledge clearly was his original sin. Reflecting later, Bush said, "The problem with the tax pledge was the rhetoric was so hot. Peggy Noonan, you know, 'I'm the man' and that kind of stuff. I felt uncomfortable with some of that. But it was persuasive—the convention loved it. When people ask me . . . 'Did you make any mistakes?' I say, 'Yeah one was to say no more taxes period—I won't raise taxes. It was a mistake.'"[50]

As usual, the president's wife, Barbara, was prescient. She wrote in her diary: "Everyone wants to pile on, but I don't worry. George IS doing the right thing. We just have to get the deficit down. I find myself in the funniest mood. I truly feel that George is doing what is responsible and right for the country and to heck with politics. There is a life after the White House and both of us are looking forward to it."[51]

The Budget Negotiations

Soon after the president released his June 26 statement, Congress left Washington for its Fourth of July recess and dispersed again in August. In mid-July a majority of House Republicans approved a no-taxes resolution, sponsored by Texas Republican Dick Armey, an adamant antitax economist and one of

Newt Gingrich's deputy whips. Ninety House Republicans signed a letter to the president saying a "tax increase is unacceptable."[52] Two dozen Senate Republicans signed a similar letter. George Mitchell was happy letting President Bush roast in his firestorm and watching Republicans split apart.

In September negotiations moved to Andrews Air Force Base (now Joint Base Andrews) in Maryland just outside Washington.[53] There were 26 negotiators, including Democratic and Republican House and Senate leadership, the chairs and ranking members of the relevant congressional committees, and Dick Darman, Nick Brady, and John Sununu representing the president. The group frequently swelled to nearly 125 people with the staffs.

Tensions there felt like taking a shower slowly getting hotter and hotter until it was scalding. Sununu was arrogant and scornful of members of Congress. Robert Byrd, Senate Appropriations Committee chairman and former Democratic Majority Leader, boiled over with rage at Sununu one evening: Byrd said that in forty years in the Senate he had never been treated so rudely by a representative of the president. In private, Senator Bob Dole, the president's ally, called the three negotiators "Nick, Dick, and Prick."

Republicans wanted to cut Medicare and Medicaid spending and adamantly opposed increasing the top income tax rate. Democrats wanted to protect Medicare and Medicaid and raise the top income tax rate. The president wanted to cut the capital gains rate, but George Mitchell was determined to block that.

Notwithstanding personal animosities and large policy differences, fears of unacceptably large GRH sequesters drove both sides to an agreement in less than a month. On September 30, 1990, the last day of the government's fiscal year, President Bush and congressional leaders announced a deal estimated to reduce the deficit by $40 billion in 1991 and by $500 billion through 1995. The agreement reduced projected defense and domestic discretionary spending by a total of $182 billion and cut projected spending on Medicare and other benefits by $119 billion. It increased taxes by $134 billion and saved $65 billion in interest costs on the federal debt. The agreement capped future increases in domestic discretionary spending and introduced a "pay-as-you-go" system requiring new entitlement spending and tax cuts to be offset by spending reductions or tax increases rather than adding to deficits and the federal debt.

Darman estimated the tax increases were less than half as large as those signed by Ronald Reagan in 1982 and spending cuts more than twice as great.[54] Importantly, the budget agreement did not increase individual income tax rates. The agreement contained incentives for investments in new and small businesses, but George Mitchell blocked President Bush's push for a capital gains cut. Two-thirds of the increased revenue came from raising tobacco, alcohol, and gas taxes and a tax on purchases of certain luxury goods. Another 20 percent was from payroll tax increases on high-wage workers to help fund Medicare. Once "tax revenue increases" became inevitable, the agreement largely fulfilled Republican preferences by avoiding any increase in income tax rates and concentrating tax increases on consumption.

Betrayal

Shortly after 1:30 on Sunday afternoon, September 30, 1990, the president, his aides, and members of Congress crowded together in the White House Rose Garden to celebrate the budget agreement. President Bush and Vice President Quayle were there, along with House and Senate Democratic and Republican leaders. Conservative antitax Republican senator Phil Gramm was there. Only one Republican negotiator was missing: Newt Gingrich.

As Dick Darman wrote, Newt "participated cheerfully as a member of the negotiating team in every meeting and preparatory session right through the conclusion of the summit."[55] But given his bombastic style and self-importance, Gingrich was unusually subdued at Andrews. In late August, Alan Greenspan, who wanted a budget deal, spoke with Newt and told Darman, "Gingrich wants to rattle the cage for a while, but he will support a deal in the end."[56] A few days before the agreement, Gingrich sent a memo to Sununu and Darman ending: "With a good agreement and full partnership in the decision process on other items, the Republican leadership will work hard." Darman and Sununu assumed this signaled Newt's support for the deal. Darman later wrote, "He never led people to believe he might bolt."[57] Based on his memo, public statements, and his private conversations with Sununu and Darman, Newt Gingrich appeared willing to support the agreement.[58] He told *Wall Street Journal* reporters he was "absolutely convinced that if offered a bad deal [Phil Gramm] would walk away from it." Gramm supported the agreement.[59]

Gingrich joined the president and the other negotiators in the Cabinet Room before the Rose Garden announcement. There he told the president, "I can't do this. It breaks your word and it's a mistake and I won't do it."[60] Gingrich then left the White House—making sure television cameras captured his exit. After returning to the Capitol, Newt called his friend Bob Walker and said, "I think I just declared war." Then they began mustering House Republican votes against the agreement.[61]

Newt claimed he bolted over the agreement's nickel-a-gallon increase in the gas tax. His more candid colleague Vin Weber told the *Washington Post*, "What is good for the President may well be good for the country, but it is not necessarily good for congressional Republicans. We need wedge issues to beat incumbent Democrats."[62] Newt regarded opposing all tax increases as the best issue separating Republicans from Democrats. He concluded a successful public break with President Bush would improve Republicans' prospects to capture the House majority and advance his desires to become House Speaker. Dan Quayle said House Republicans wanted "to achieve a majority, and the only way they could do that was with a Democrat in the White House." "The truth," he added, "is that minority parties pick up most of their seats during midterm elections that occur while the opposing party holds the other end of Pennsylvania Avenue."[63]

Newt subsequently admitted, "The number one thing we had to prove in the fall of '90 was that, if you explicitly decided to govern from the center, we could make it so unbelievably expensive you couldn't sustain it."[64] If the costs fell on a president of his own party, that was just collateral damage in Newt Gingrich's war.[65]

The Republican and Democratic leaders had promised to supply votes for the agreement from more than half their members in the House and Senate. Newt publicly claimed he would not "whip" opposition to the budget agreement, but he led a rebellion of House Republicans against the deal. On October 3, Tom Foley told the president the deal was in trouble. Dan Rostenkowski warned Bush, "You've got to get to 51 percent, pal."[66] The next morning President Bush met with forty Republican representatives and made twenty phone calls trying to gather support in the House. He wrote in his diary, "Newt is out there, part of the leadership, saying he wasn't elected to support the president . . . and these right-wingers love it. . . . It just makes me furious."[67]

With House Republican votes hemorrhaging, liberal Democrats unhappy about the agreement's spending cuts bolted. On Friday October 5, House Republicans voted 105–71 against the deal; House Democrats opposed it by a 40-vote margin. President Bush, Speaker Foley, and Minority Leader Michel suffered severe political wounds. None would recover.

Following the vote, negotiations resumed among a small group in Speaker Foley's office. President Bush had little leverage to move the bill in his direction, but he got some help from the Senate Finance Committee where Republicans had nine of the twenty votes and the Democratic chairman Lloyd Bentsen and three other Democrats were quite conservative. Despite the president's acceptance of a brief government shutdown in early October to signal his resolve, few in Congress believed he would veto a budget bill and accept a GRH sequestration.[68]

On November 5, President Bush signed the Omnibus Budget Reconciliation Act of 1990, which he described as "the largest deficit reduction package in history." "No one," he said, "got everything he or she wanted, but the end product is a compromise that merits enactment."[69] The legislation was decidedly less appealing substantively to conservative Republicans than the Andrews agreement: its tax increases were greater and spending cuts smaller. Unlike the September agreement, which avoided any income tax rate increase, the top individual tax rate was increased to 31 percent. The top capital gains rate remained unchanged at 28 percent.

The Republican Right's campaign against the budget agreement ratified their enthusiasm for Newt Gingrich's vicious partnership. His revolt weakened President Bush and strengthened Newt's sway over House Republicans. He previously told the *Washington Post*: "I have an enormous personal ambition. I want to shift the entire planet. And I'm doing it. . . . [T]his is just the beginning of a 20- or 30-year movement. I'll get credit for it."[70] Bob Michel survived two more terms as nominal leader of House Republicans, but his desire for bipartisan comity and compromise had become archaic. Opposition to the 1990 budget deal strengthened Newt Gingrich's image as a tax cutter and brought clarity: Republicans would always oppose tax increases and praise and promote tax cuts whatever the economic or fiscal conditions.

The 1990 and 1992 Elections

Newt's strength among House Republicans—the beginning of what historian Julian Zelizer calls "the era of Gingrich"—did not benefit him in his 1990 reelection campaign in Georgia.[71] David Worley, an Atlanta lawyer defeated by Newt with 59 percent of the vote in 1988, was again Newt's opponent. Gingrich outspent Worley 10 to 1, and Worley received little attention from the *Atlanta Journal-Constitution* or local television.[72] Even so, Newt barely survived, winning by only 974 votes, less than 1 percent of the total.[73] As typical in midterm elections, the president's party lost congressional seats. Democrats gained seven seats in the House of Representatives and one in the Senate.

In 1992 Newt's district had changed and was heavily Republican. He prevailed again by less than 1,000 votes against a poorly funded Republican primary challenger.[74] That year the most consequential contest was for the presidency.

In March 1992, 78 percent of the public said the country was on the wrong track: the nation was suffering from a recession. Pat Buchanan, a race-baiting, homophobic, isolationist, right-wing populist media personality, mounted a strong primary challenge to President Bush. Buchanan had been Richard Nixon's speechwriter and liaison to the Republican Right, and he served two years as Ronald Reagan's White House communications director. In 1989 Buchanan returned to writing his syndicated column and starring as a right-wing television commentator. Announcing his campaign in Manchester, New Hampshire, Buchanan asked, "Why am I running? Because we Republicans can no longer say it is all the liberals' fault. It was not some liberal Democrat who declared 'Read my lips! No new taxes!' then broke his word to cut a back-room budget deal with the big spenders."[75]

Buchanan was an early enthusiast of the Kemp-Roth tax cuts. He claimed IRS efforts to deny tax exemptions for segregated Christian schools meant the death of any private school that "does not conform with the social values of secular humanism which is the newly established religion in the United States."[76] Before the New Hampshire primary, Buchanan relentlessly attacked Bush as "King George" for breaking his tax pledge and for his efforts to include Mexico in the North American Free Trade Agreement—tapping into middle-class resentments of trade agreements that many voters believed threatened their livelihoods.[77] He repeatedly asked, "Where is the administration's plan to make America First again by 2000?"[78]

Although he opposed Buchanan's protectionist trade policies, Rush Limbaugh supported Buchanan in the primaries. Buchanan, Limbaugh said, "made it clear that the heart and soul of the Republican Party is conservatism." Among the factors contributing "to the anti-incumbent mood prevalent in America," Rush said, was "George Bush's abandonment of the Ronald Reagan legacy." The *Wall Street Journal* agreed. The "budget deal," the *Journal* editorialized, "will stand as one of the great political mistakes. Before the deal, Mr. Bush stood for something; after the deal, many of his constituents concluded he stood for nothing."[79]

President Bush carried New Hampshire with nearly 55 percent of the vote, but Buchanan's nearly 40 percent was surprisingly strong against an incumbent president. Newt Gingrich liked Buchanan less than he liked President Bush; he told the *New York Times* Buchanan's unexpectedly large vote was a "primal scream" of public anger.[80]

Bill Clinton, who finished second in the Democratic primary, was buoyant as the primary season moved South. He said, "In November, we will win a great victory against Pat Buchanan."[81]

On March 4, the evening before the Georgia Republican primary, George H. W. Bush told the *Atlanta Journal-Constitution* that the 1990 tax increases were his "biggest mistake." He explained to a Baltimore television interviewer, "Anytime you get hammered on something, I guess you want to redo it." Bush previously had defended the agreement as necessary, even if it "tastes like castor oil."[82] The next day, Buchanan pounced. "The reason George Bush is in trouble," Buchanan said, "is not Pat Buchanan. It's because George Bush has said one thing again and again and did another. . . . In 1988 he said, 'Read my lips, no new taxes.' He raised taxes $465 billion. He was then quoted saying . . . 'I never signed any tax pledge.' And then he turned around two days ago and said, 'I may have made a mistake when I broke my pledge.'"[83] Buchanan never won a Republican primary, gaining only 19 delegates, but he refused to drop out and attacked Bush all over the country.[84]

The quixotic, independent populist Ross Perot, a Texas billionaire, entered the 1992 general election campaign as a third-party candidate, emphasizing the need to balance the federal budget. He won 19 percent of the popular vote, more than any third-party presidential candidate since Teddy Roosevelt in 1912, but he failed to carry any state and won no Electoral College votes. Many pundits thought Perot cost Bush reelection, but subsequent analyses showed Perot voters would likely have divided their votes evenly between Bush and Clinton.[85]

George H. W. Bush ran a disorganized and lackluster campaign. He was largely inattentive to domestic policy. His strong suit was foreign policy, but successes in that realm generated little enthusiasm among voters. It subsequently became clear that the recession ended before the election, but it had not felt that way. The weak economy and President Bush's failure to explain how he planned to make it better were the foremost reasons for his defeat. After twelve years of Reagan and Bush in the White House, Americans were ready for someone new.

Bill Clinton relentlessly campaigned emphasizing his plans to revitalize the economy and to enact a middle-class tax cut. Clinton, a Yale Law graduate and Rhodes Scholar, the five-term Democratic governor of Arkansas, and an exceptionally talented campaigner, won the election with 43 percent of the popular vote to Bush's 37 percent, the lowest percentage of the popular vote for any president since Woodrow Wilson in 1912.[86] The Electoral College vote was not close; Clinton won 370 votes to Bush's 168.

Compared to 1988, Bush's share of the vote declined more among independents than Republicans and slightly more among moderates than conservatives. "But after the election," Ron Brownstein wrote, "it was the defections on the right . . . that many Republican leaders remembered most. And it was Bush's budget agreement with congressional Democrats raising taxes that conservatives blamed above all for those defections."[87]

Antitax forces, led by Grover Norquist, Newt Gingrich, and Rush Limbaugh, agreed.[88] A few weeks after the election, Norquist told the *Washington Post*, "George Herbert Walker Bush broke his commitment to the American people. . . . Somehow the American people figured out that he'd broken his commitment to them and he couldn't get 38 percent of the vote when he ran in a general [election]. . . . Without the betrayal on the tax issue, the third party would have been a joke."[89]

Despite all the evidence to the contrary, Grover repeated these claims two decades later in an interview with Jon Stewart of the *Daily Show*, saying, "The pledge allows someone to credibly explain to voters, 'I mean it,' and everybody watched what happened to George H. W. Bush. When he broke his pledge, he threw away a perfectly good presidency."[90] Three years later, Grover sang the same song, claiming, "Had Bush been able to win in 1992, it would have made the pledge meaningless. Bush had a pretty good presidency. He ended the Cold War peacefully. He kicked Saddam Hussein out of Kuwait. But he broke his commitment to the American people. Then he gets thrown out of office by a bum—a nobody from Arkansas. The message was: You can't break the pledge."[91] The view that breaking his no-new-taxes pledge cost Bush the presidency became Republican dogma.

———

Newt Gingrich's successful opposition to President Bush's budget agreement had a more enduring impact on the antitax movement and the subsequent course of American politics than George H. W. Bush's presidency. No Republican president since has broken Grover's antitax pledge—or proposed a tax increase. After Bush lost the presidency, Newt Gingrich was the Republican leader. Dick Darman called the late 1990s the "Clinton-Gingrich Co-Presidency."[92] Bill Clinton's unanticipated tax increases made that happen.

Chapter 10

Showdown and Shutdown

The ticket to admission to American politics is a balanced budget.

—BILL CLINTON, JUNE 1995

In January 1993 Grover Norquist published a self-congratulatory article titled "It's My Party," maintaining that successful Republican presidential candidates would have to exorcise the "stench of betrayal and treason in the air" coming from "the biggest betrayal of all: George Bush's decision in 1990 to tear the heart out of the Republican coalition."[1] Norquist insisted the crucial task of the Republican Party was "to undo the damage of the Bush presidency in losing the tax issue." Quoting Phyllis Schlafly of "Stop-ERA" fame, Grover described opposition to tax increases as the *"unifying principle"* of the Republican Party.[2] He applauded the resurgence of Republican antitax intransigency demonstrated in the defeats of Republican moderates for key House leadership positions by antitax zealots Dick Armey, who helped rally House Republicans' opposition to the 1990 budget agreement, and Tom DeLay, who also fought against the agreement and in 1991 proposed large tax cuts that failed because of opposition from the Bush White House and Democrats. By 1993 the Republican Party was an implacable antitax force.

Having seen the political costs of Walter Mondale's proposed tax increases and George H. W. Bush's accepting them, Bill Clinton ran for president promising tax cuts for the "middle class," whom he defined as families with incomes below $80,000 ($154,000 in 2021 dollars). Clinton said, "The average working family's tax bill will go down about 10 percent, a savings of about $300 a year, and I won't finance it with increasing the deficit."[3] He promised no tax increases for those with incomes between $80,000 and $200,000, but he proposed raising the top rate to 36 percent for Americans with incomes greater than $200,000 ($386,000 in 2021 dollars).[4] Limiting tax increases to the "rich" had become Democrats' strategy in an effort to weaken the political clout of the antitax movement for Republicans.

A Democratic Centrist Takes Charge

Bill Clinton was an early Baby Boomer, born in 1946 to a young widow in Hope, Arkansas, a town of about six thousand residents famous for its large watermelons and talented politicians.[5] Clinton grew up with an abusive and alcoholic stepfather. In a high school essay he described himself as "motivated and influenced by so many diverse forces I sometimes question the sanity of my existence."[6] The conflicts and complexities of his youth were mirrored in his presidency. Historian Sean Wilentz wrote, "He came across as a bundle of contradictions, eternally tangled up in nuance."[7]

Before becoming president, Clinton helped found and lead the Democratic Leadership Council (DLC), formed in 1985 to move the Democratic Party toward the political center. The "New Democrats" looked for a "third way" to refocus the Democratic Party away from its stalwart constituencies of labor, minorities, and anti-establishment progressives toward "Reagan Democrats"—white working-class voters who had defected from the Democratic Party to support Republican candidates—and other swing voters. Clinton said the DLC stood for "the expansion of opportunity, not bureaucracy; choice in public schools and child care; responsibility and empowerment for poor people; and reinventing government . . . to a leaner, more flexible, more innovative model more appropriate for the modern global economy."[8] Liberals such as Reverend Jesse Jackson derided the group as Democrats who "comb their hair to the left like Kennedy and move their policies to the right like Reagan."[9] "Triangulation" became the label for Clinton's approach, defined by his labor secretary Robert Reich as "finding positions equidistant between the Democrat and Republican."[10]

In his presidential campaign, Clinton borrowed heavily from the Republican playbook. He announced he would turn welfare into "workfare"—"a way of temporarily helping people who've fallen on hard times."[11] He emphasized law and order, advancing a proposal to add one hundred thousand more local police officers, and supported the death penalty.[12] He demonstrated his independence from African American supporters, most famously by attacking the Black rap artist Sister Souljah.

Clinton promised to reduce the federal deficit from $400 billion to $146 billion by 1996. His campaign, however, discovered the combination of his promised middle-class tax cuts and spending increases were $100 billion greater than the offsets he had offered. But Clinton never acknowledged that gap. His campaign aide told a *Los Angeles Times* reporter, "You just can't stop a campaign and suddenly revise your platform."[13] Through election day, Clinton insisted he would "absolutely not" delay or abandon a middle-class tax cut.[14]

Once he won, the president-elect, like his predecessor, confronted the challenging realities of deficits and rising federal debt. Despite the political risks, he scrapped his middle-class tax cut and proposed large tax increases. The "bond market" was the villain responsible for his reversal.

Yielding to the Bond Market

More than a decade after Ronald Reagan's claim he would "act today to save tomorrow," federal deficits and debt still dominated the economic agenda. In 1992 the federal debt was over $3 trillion, climbing toward $4 trillion. Interest paid to the public was nearly $300 billion (nearly $600 billion in 2021 dollars), more than 20 percent of total federal spending and about 5 percent of GDP—the third-largest federal expenditure, behind only Social Security and defense.[15]

Clinton's reversal of his tax plans began during a long meeting on December 3, 1992, with Federal Reserve chairman Alan Greenspan at the Governor's Mansion in Little Rock. Greenspan, at the time a deficit hawk, told the newly elected president the crucial impediment to robust economic growth was high long-term interest rates. The Federal Reserve could control short-term interest rates, according to Greenspan, but not long-term rates, which he said turned on expectations of inflation that, in turn, depended on the size of federal deficits. If long-term interest rates came down, Greenspan said, the stock market would rise, businesses would invest more, and reduced interest rates would spur purchases of homes, cars, and perhaps vacations.

Alan Greenspan, a libertarian acolyte and friend of Ayn Rand, ironically became the most important proponent persuading Bill Clinton to raise taxes. If Greenspan's purpose had been to undermine Clinton's efforts to neutralize Republicans' advantages on taxes, he could not have done better. After the meeting, Clinton said that he and Greenspan "could do business."[16]

On January 6, 1993, Dick Darman, leaving office as budget director, announced approximately $60 billion in higher deficits because of reduced tax revenues due to the recession. Clinton regarded the deficits as the "inevitable result of supply-side economics," which he said was "bad arithmetic and lousy economics." Republicans "stayed with it," he said, "because of their ideological aversion to taxes and because, in the short-run, supply-side was good politics." "Spend more, tax less sounded good and felt good," he added, "but it had put our country in a deep hole and left a cloud over our children's future."[17]

The next day Clinton convened a meeting of his economic team in Little Rock to settle his administration's economic priorities. After Alan Blinder, a Princeton economist appointed to Clinton's Council of Economic Advisers, described the economic risks of a tighter budget compared to the economic boost from lower long-term interest rates, Clinton exclaimed, "You mean to tell me that the success of the program and my reelection hinges on the Federal Reserve and a bunch of fucking bond traders?"[18] Clinton regarded "the most important domestic decision" of his presidency as "one big gamble" that depended on the willingness of Congress to enact the changes he proposed.[19] But he decided to take the risks.

On January 28 in the Oval Office, Greenspan told the president that deficit problems were manageable for the next few years but by 1996 the deficit would mushroom and an increase in interest costs would produce instability in the financial system. "That's what financial catastrophe means," Greenspan said.[20] President Clinton assured Greenspan he would propose a major deficit-reduction plan. Dick Morris, a Clinton political advisor, described the administration's economic policy: "You figure out what Greenspan wants and you get it to him."[21] Bob Woodward called Alan Greenspan "the most powerful Republican . . . in Washington."[22] The Federal Reserve chairman orchestrated Clinton's turnabout on taxes without leaving any fingerprints on the president's tax increases.

James Carville, the political wizard of Clinton's presidential campaign, said: "I used to think that if there was reincarnation, I wanted to come back as the President or the Pope, or as a .400 baseball hitter. But now I would like to come back as the bond market. You can intimidate everybody."[23] The bond market, which President Clinton called "the power over the lives of ordinary Americans exercised by thirty-year-old bond traders," became the dominant force guiding the economic policies of the United States.[24]

President Clinton soon learned that you could not achieve serious deficit reduction with tax increases only on the rich and large corporations. He scrapped the middle-class tax cuts he promised during his campaign. Despite his campaign efforts to deprive Republicans of the antitax issue, tax increases across-the-board to reduce deficits became a central feature of Clinton's economic policy.

On January 26 Bob Dole, the Senate Republican Leader, told the president not to expect any Republican votes for his economic plan. If the plan did not work, Dole said, Republicans would blame Clinton.[25] When Ronald Reagan and George H. W. Bush were in the White House, Dole had supported tax increases to reduce deficits, but he was not about to take heat from antitax Republicans for helping a Democratic president. Clinton observed, "Republicans were more antitax than ever" after George H. W. Bush's defeat.[26]

The House was composed of 258 Democrats and 176 Republicans, the Senate 56 Democrats and 44 Republicans. This was the first time Democrats controlled the presidency and Congress since 1979. Despite large Democratic majorities, enacting tax increases was not easy.

An Energy Tax Flames Out

Bill Clinton unveiled his economic plan in his State of the Union Address before a joint session of Congress on February 17, 1993. In the gallery, seated between Hillary Clinton and the vice president's wife, Tipper Gore, was Alan Greenspan.

President Clinton proposed short-term spending increases to create jobs, announced that Hillary Clinton would be heading a task force to expand health-care coverage and control costs, and promised a future plan "to end welfare as we know it." His plan for deficit reduction included raising the top income tax rate from 31 to 36 percent on incomes over $180,000 a year and to 39.6 percent for those making $250,000 ($475,000 in 2021 dollars) or more. He urged Congress to eliminate tax "loopholes," increase Medicare taxes for workers earning more than $125,000, and raise the income tax on Social Security benefits for recipients with significant other income. He also proposed boosting the corporate tax rate from 34 to 36 percent and limiting corporations' ability to move jobs offshore.

In lieu of his promised middle-class tax cuts, President Clinton proposed a new "broad-based tax on energy," measured by its heat content and called "a BTU tax." He described the BTU tax as "the best way to provide us with revenue to lower the deficit because it also combats pollution, promotes energy efficiency" and economic independence, and "does not discriminate against any area."[27] He claimed he would make "real attempts to make sure that no cost is imposed on families with incomes under $30,000" by increasing earned income tax credits (which raise after-tax wages for low-income workers with children). He said his proposed tax increases would be "very modest until you get to the higher income groups where the income taxes trigger in."[28]

President Clinton offset his proposal for a small increase in the corporate tax rate with new tax breaks for equipment investments. Instead, Congress settled for a one-percentage-point increase in the corporate rate to 35 percent without the new investment incentives. Most congressional Democrats agreed with Clinton's view that the "Reagan-Bush" tax cuts for "the rich" had gone too far, but raising income tax rates at the top by nearly nine percentage points to almost 40 percent was not an easy sell. Nevertheless, the Democratic Congress ultimately accepted the president's rate increases.

Clinton's energy tax proposal was especially difficult for congressional Democrats to swallow. A carbon tax is an effective way to curb climate change from carbon dioxide emissions, but taxing carbon would have had a disproportionate impact on West Virginia, an important producer of high-carbon coal. Clinton's congressional liaison told the president that West Virginia senator Robert Byrd, the powerful Democratic chairman of the Appropriations Committee and former Senate Majority Leader, "controls your life."[29] That eliminated the carbon tax. Unlike a carbon tax, Clinton's BTU tax avoided disparate regional impacts.

Fearing failure of his deficit-reduction plan might strike a mortal blow to the Democratic president, the House passed President Clinton's plan, including the BTU tax, by a vote of 219 to 212 in May 1993—after much arm-twisting. Nearly 40 Democrats voted against the bill, worried that supporting the BTU tax risked their reelection. The BTU tax, however, did not survive the Senate, mainly because of fierce opposition from John Breaux of Louisiana and Oklahoma's David Boren, two conservative oil-state Finance Committee Democrats.

After the House and Senate bills were reconciled, Democrats in Congress barely passed most of President Clinton's 1993 tax increases—with a 4.3-cents-per-gallon increase in the gas tax instead of the BTU tax—and no significant cuts in Medicare or Social Security benefits. The House vote was 218 to 216. As Democrats cheered, Republicans shouted "bye-bye" to Marjorie Margolies-Mezvinsky, a first-term Democrat from a Pennsylvania Republican district, one of the last Democrats to vote for the bill.[30] The Senate vote was 50–50 with Vice President Al Gore breaking the tie.[31] Despite his narrow victory with no vote to spare in either chamber, President Clinton told the American public, "What we heard tonight at the other end of Pennsylvania was the sound of gridlock breaking."[32]

Bill Clinton was nonchalant about the failure of his BTU tax. "The bad news," he said, "was that the gas tax would promote less energy conservation than the BTU tax, the good news was that it would cost middle-class Americans less, only about $33 a year."[33]

The energy tax failures in the early 1990s loom large: the BTU tax defeat dissuaded subsequent presidents from advocating a carbon tax to advance environmental goals. Even as the need to address climate change became more urgent, antitax pledges from Republicans and Democratic presidents have continued to bar such a tax.[34]

A Trouncing at the Polls

In 1993 the New Jersey gubernatorial election reconfirmed the popular appeal of the antitax movement. Despite doubling the top income tax rate and raising the sales tax rate by one percentage point, in early October the incumbent Democratic governor Jim Florio led Republican Christine Todd Whitman by as much as 14 percentage points. Whitman's campaign floundered until September 21, when she proposed a three-year, 30 percent across-the-board income tax cut and refocused her campaign on the tax issue.

Grover Norquist secured support for her tax plan by Republican governors from Arizona, Massachusetts, Michigan, New Hampshire, and Wisconsin who sent testimonials describing how tax cuts had spurred economic growth in their states. In late October Jack Kemp published an enthusiastic op-ed in a prominent New Jersey newspaper. The Heritage Foundation and Citizens for a Sound Economy joined in with papers touting the economic success of Ronald Reagan's tax cuts in the 1980s. Whitman ran media ads pushing her tax cuts on three-fourths of the days between announcing her plan and the election. Polls confirmed public approval. Whitman promised in television debates not to run for reelection if she failed to pass her tax cuts, insisting they would create jobs and economic growth in New Jersey. On November 2, 1993, Christine Todd Whitman narrowly defeated Jim Florio, becoming the first woman to serve as governor of New Jersey.[35]

In January 1994 Alan Greenspan informed Bill Clinton that the Federal Reserve was going to increase interest rates because of increasing economic growth and growing inflation expectations. In April 1994, after the Fed's third rate increase that year, long-term interest rates hit a new high of 7.4 percent—despite President Clinton's tax increases.[36] Fortunately for Clinton, those were the highest rates of his presidency. In November a bad year for Bill Clinton got much worse.

Midterm elections commonly produce losses for the president's party, but the Democrats' defeat in 1994 was overwhelming. Bill Clinton said, "On November 8, we got the living daylights beat out of us, losing eight Senate seats and fifty-four House seats, the largest defeat for our party since 1946."[37] Tom Foley became the first Speaker of the House defeated for reelection in more than a century. Dan Rostenkowski, facing an embezzlement scandal, was also defeated.[38] Republicans also added governors in eleven states.

President Clinton ascribed the Democrats' trouncing to low Democratic turnout, the extraordinary energy of Christian evangelicals in the South, and NRA opposition to an assault weapons ban. Clinton also credited Bob Dole, who engineered the Senate defeat of Hillary Clinton's health-care proposals, for the Democrats' disaster at the polls. But President Clinton concluded, "We probably would not have lost either the House or the Senate if I had not included the gas tax and the tax on Social Security recipients in the economic plan."[39] Many House Democrats who voted for the BTU tax were defeated, ushering in a Republican majority in the House for the first time in forty years.[40]

The Contract with America

Newt Gingrich believed nationalizing House elections provided the path to a Republican majority. He tried to unite diverse factions of the Republican Party with similar messages. Along with Grover Norquist, Dick Armey, and others, Gingrich produced a "Contract with America" with ten elements: "Newt wanted there to be ten because ten is a mythical number as in the Ten Commandments."[41] On September 27, 1994, Gingrich unveiled the Contract on the Capitol steps where it was signed by 152 of 157 Republican House incumbents and 185 Republican House candidates. Gingrich vowed Republicans would pass all ten elements of the Contract within the first one hundred days of the next Congress.

With characteristic grandiosity, Newt proclaimed, "If the American people accept this Contract, we will have begun the journey to renew American civilization. Together we can renew America. Together we can help every American fulfill their unalienable right to pursue happiness and seek the American dream. Together we can help every human across the planet seek freedom, prosperity, safety and the rule of law. That is what's at stake."[42] The Contract scarcely fulfilled that billing; it was largely negative, designed to mobilize antitax, antigovernment voters.

The Contract with America called for welfare cuts and tougher work requirements, cuts in social spending and limits on regulations. Tax-cut proposals dominated the Contract: cutting capital gains rates in half, adding new tax breaks for small businesses, increasing estate tax exemptions, repealing income taxes on Social Security recipients, expanding individual retirement accounts, eliminating "marriage penalties," and adding new tax breaks for children, long-term care insurance, adoption expenses, and costs of taking care of a dependent parent or grandparent. The Contract required a 60 percent supermajority vote in the House to pass any tax increase, along with additional changes in House procedures and practices. It also urged a balanced-budget constitutional requirement. To keep the diverse elements of the Republican coalition together, the Contract included only items that polled well and avoided divisive social issues.

Although fewer than one-third of voters heard of the Contract by election day, Republican candidates emphasized the Contract's antigovernment messages and made tax cuts and spending restraint central themes, drawing clear contrasts between Republicans' tax-cutting agenda and the Democratic tax increases.[43] Newt Gingrich claimed the Contract was decisive, but given victories by Republicans in the Senate, governors' races, and state legislatures, along with the relatively small number of voters who said that they had heard of the Contract, he overstated its impact. The Contract did help nationalize the midterms—a strategy the party out of the White House has followed in subsequent midterm elections.

Rush Limbaugh and his talk-radio colleagues were likely more important to the Republicans' success than Newt's Contract. The *New York Times* described Rush as a "kind of national precinct captain for the Republican insurgency of 1994." Rush relentlessly criticized Bill Clinton, called the 1994 elections "Operation Restore Democracy," and pushed for eliminating welfare and cutting capital gains taxes to create jobs.[44] A *Times-Mirror* poll before the vote found that 64 percent of regular listeners to talk radio said they had thought about the elections compared to 35 percent of nonlisteners. After the election, House Republican freshmen presented Rush with a "Majority Makers" pin in gratitude for his influential support. In an aw-shucks response, Limbaugh claimed simply to be reflecting the views of the American people, saying radio hosts like him "only validate what's in people's hearts and minds already."[45]

The *Wall Street Journal* praised Grover Norquist following the Republican House takeover. Describing Norquist as "one of the main power brokers in the new Republican majority," the *Journal* said Grover's "rise helps explain both the power of Newt Gingrich and the ideological makeover of Republicans."[46]

Newt Gingrich's successful incendiary tactics transformed the Republican Party. Comity and conciliation receded. Bipartisanship became a dirty word; Newt's watchword was revolution, accompanied by the rhetoric of a relentless warrior. Voters in 1994 fulfilled Newt Gingrich's ambitions to become Speaker of the House, setting up monumental conflicts between him and Bill Clinton. Newt dominated news coverage through daily press conferences and extraordinary media appearances. His antitax allies Dick Armey and Tom DeLay became Republican House Majority Leader and Majority Whip, respectively.

On the first day of the new Congress, Republicans adopted all of the Contract's changes in House procedures, including its supermajority requirement for tax increases. In Congress's first one hundred days, the House passed all of the Contract's proposals except one limiting representatives to six terms.[47] All but three of the Contract's provisions, however, languished in the Senate; none of the promised tax cuts were enacted.

Showdown over Taxes

On April 5, 1995, the House passed a bill reducing taxes by $189 billion over the following five years, including all the tax cuts proposed in the Contract with America and reducing the capital gains rate from 28 percent to 19.8 percent.[48] Repeating Laffer Curve dogma, new Ways and Means Committee chairman Bill Archer of Texas said, "There are many provisions in this tax package which I am convinced are going to create enough economic activity that they will generate more revenue, which will help us get to a balanced budget."[49] Twenty percent of the House tax cuts would have gone to the top 1 percent of Americans.[50] William Kristol, a Republican strategist and former chief of staff to Vice President Dan Quayle, applauded. "Bush ran on a Reaganesque platform in 1988, reverted to pre-Reagan Republicanism in 1990 and got clobbered in 1992 by a Democrat promising a tax cut," he said. "Call me simple-minded, but I think it's better to cut taxes."[51]

Bill Clinton described the Republican tax cuts as a "fantasy" that "we can't afford." "Let's target a tax cut to the right people and for the right purpose," he said. "We have to choose. Do you want a tax cut for the wealthy or the middle class?"[52] "In the next 100 days and beyond," Clinton added, "the President has to lead the quiet, reasoned forces of both parties in both houses to sift through the rhetoric and decide what is really best for America."[53]

Republicans' tax cuts, of course, meant that achieving a balanced budget required exceptionally large spending cuts. This did not faze Speaker Gingrich, who insisted on balancing the budget by 2002.[54] In May 1995 House Republicans approved a budget proposal to restructure and sharply limit Medicare and deeply cut Medicaid, welfare, job training, student loans, farm subsidies, and a host of other programs. It also proposed eliminating the commerce, education, and energy cabinet departments.[55]

In June 1995 Congress approved a budget resolution calling for the spending cuts, a balanced budget by 2002, and $245 billion in tax cuts—with only one House Republican in opposition and the support of eight conservative Democrats. The Senate agreed by a vote of 54 to 46, with all Republicans voting yes and all Democrats voting no. The spending reductions in the Republicans' budget resolution were far greater than anything Ronald Reagan attempted. Describing the resolution as a "containment strategy" that raised questions about which recipients of federal money would be "thrown off the lifeboat," Grover Norquist said, "All reductions in federal spending weaken the left in America. Defunding government is defunding the left."[56] Journalist Ronald Brownstein wrote, "The Republicans had produced a vision of the federal role in society that polarized the parties in the starkest possible terms."[57]

Looking to "triangulate," President Clinton told his cabinet in June 1995 the "ticket to admission to American politics is a balanced budget."[58] In a brief Oval Office address, the president offered his proposal to balance the budget over ten years without any tax increase and attacked the Republicans' cuts to Medicare, Medicaid, education, and the environment.[59] Congressional Republicans ignored Clinton's intervention.

Grover Norquist—complaining about George H. W. Bush discarding his no-new-taxes pledge and Bill Clinton abandoning his middle-class tax-cut promise—said, "The American people have been lied to in two successive presidential elections. And the Republican Party stood up in 1994 and said 'This is a contract. We know you've been lied to before and that's why we're putting this in writing. And if we don't do what we said, fire us.'"[60] Pennsylvania congressman Bob Walker described the Republican Party's commitment to tax cuts as "a fundamental divide between what Republicans and Democrats believe. Democrats . . . believe all wealth generated in this country is ultimately the Government's to distribute. Republicans believe it belongs to the people and they should be allowed to keep as much of it as possible."[61]

Shutdown

In mid-September, House Republican Whip Tom DeLay told Vice President Gore, "We'll shut down the government if we have to, to balance the budget."[62] Newt repeated the threat to President Clinton, saying, "The problem here is you've got a gun to my head. It's called the veto. But what you don't understand is that I've got a gun to your head and I'm going to use it. I'm going to shut the government down. We are co-equal branches of government, and I'm going to use my veto, which is shutting the government down."[63]

On November 1, 1995—with government funding due to expire in twelve days—President Clinton met with congressional leaders at the White House in an acrimonious session. Newt accused Democrats of playing dirty in ads portraying him and Republicans as robbing old women of their health care to finance tax cuts for the rich. Dick Armey said the Democrats' advertisements had frightened his mother-in-law and her friends. President Clinton complained he compromised on many issues but Republicans compromised on none, and he promised to veto the budget legislation if it were not changed substantially.

The president thought he was in a typical negotiation with Congress. Newt Gingrich believed he was leading a revolution. "One of my key decisions in November of 1994," Newt said, "was to launch a revolutionary rather than a reformist effort." "What we're doing," he added, "is a cultural revolution with societal and political consequences that ultimately change the government."[64] Shutting government down to advance the revolution was fine with Newt and his allies. On November 13, 1995, President Clinton vetoed the Republicans' balanced budget and spending bill. On November 14, the government shut down.

Gingrich and Clinton traveled together the following day to Israeli prime minister Yitzhak Rabin's funeral. On their return, Gingrich whined to the press that no one talked to him on the plane, and when it landed at Andrews Air Force Base, Clinton's staff asked him to exit by the back stairs. Newt asked, "Where is their sense of manners?" In a great mistake, Newt claimed the shabby treatment was one reason that the House budget resolution was designed so that Clinton would have to veto it.[65] Gingrich's resentment was mocked in news reports and political cartoons across the country. Most Americans viewed his behavior as infantile. He and his House allies were blamed for the government shutdown. Newt's popularity dropped with the shutdown, then sunk further. His House colleagues told him, "no more stories about airplanes."[66]

President Clinton and Speaker Gingrich negotiating at the White House.

Bob Dole then initiated a negotiation producing a vague agreement between the White House and Congress to balance the budget in seven years
while protecting Clinton's priorities on Medicare, Medicaid, education, and
the environment. On November 20, 1995, Congress passed and the president
signed a short-term spending bill that reopened the government. But budget
talks again cratered, and the government shut for a second time on December 15. House Republicans believed the only way to get their spending and tax
cuts and balance the budget was to keep the government shut.[67]

Republicans exacerbated their problems with the public when, on December 20, the fifth day of a twenty-one-day shutdown, Tom DeLay announced House Republicans had no intention of reopening the government.
A few hours later, President Clinton walked to the television cameras in the
White House press briefing room and told the American public "the most
extreme members of the House" torpedoed budget negotiations.[68]

Speaker Gingrich considered Bill Clinton to be unprincipled and certain
to cave. But the president did not budge on Republicans' tax cuts or reductions
in Medicare and Medicaid. After meeting with the president on January 2,
1996, Newt realized that Bill Clinton—serving as his own chief negotiator—
was not going to capitulate. The press and the public blamed the Republicans

for the government closures. Newt's control over the House Republican caucus slipped badly as the budget shutdown dragged on. Comedians urged the national parks be reopened and Congress shut down. Americans blamed Republicans: public approval for the Republican House declined from 52 percent in December 1994 to 27 percent in January 1996. Gingrich's popularity tanked: in January 1996 his popularity was as low as Richard Nixon's at the height of the Watergate scandal.[69] George Stephanopoulos later said Gingrich's government shutdown was an important factor leading to Clinton's reelection in 1996. On January 9, 1996, the government reopened without any budget deal. Despite all his bluster and blundering, Newt Gingrich was 1995 Time Magazine's Man of the Year.

Democrats seemed convinced that the 1994 Republican sweep of both Houses of Congress was a temporary interregnum in a natural order that would restore the Democrats to majority control of Congress. The House Democratic leadership did not change until they lost the next four congressional elections. Republicans, in contrast, viewed their 1994 victory as a sea change, not a squall. Hungry for power after decades in the minority, they perceived their 1994 victory as ratification of the Gingrich-led insurgency and his revolutionary odyssey to reshape the Republican Party. With Newt Gingrich leading the front lines, Rush Limbaugh marshaling large audiences across the country, and Grover Norquist enforcing his antitax pledges, Republicans pushed for irreversible changes in American politics and policies.

The Aftermath

Despite the 1993 tax increases, 1994 was a good year economically: investments increased, unemployment declined, the rate of economic growth rose, and inflation declined.[70] By 1995 the United States was on the verge of a burst of economic growth and prosperity unseen for decades. This growth, along with a stock market surge, expanded government revenues.

Bill Clinton's 1993 tax increases concluded more than a decade of efforts to recapture revenues lost from Ronald Reagan's tax cuts. Reagan's 1981 cuts reduced revenues by an average of 2.89 percent of GDP in the four years after enactment, but by 1999 federal taxes relative to the economy had returned to their 1981 level. Notwithstanding vigorous blowback from the antitax forces, tax-increase-and-deficit-reduction legislation from 1982 through 1993, coupled with the burst of economic growth in the late 1990s, eliminated deficits beginning in 1998.

Between 1981 and the late 1990s, however, the distribution of income and wealth changed dramatically. Globalization of trade and capital flows affected the distribution of income around the world and, along with technological changes, began to shift income in the United States away from less-educated to more highly educated workers. The ongoing weakening of private-sector labor unions also contributed to the widening inequality of incomes in the United States.[71] These trends persisted in subsequent decades. Federal taxes remained progressive, but, as wealth and income became more concentrated at the top, the nature of the federal tax system changed.[72]

The tax law in the mid-1990s was quite different than in 1980 before President Reagan took office. The top income tax rate on investment income was reduced from 70 percent to just under 40 percent. The corporate rate was lowered from 46 percent to 35 percent. The only federal taxes on wealth—the estate and gift taxes—were substantially reduced. Tax burdens were shifted from wealth and investment income to labor income. The great majority of Americans paid more in payroll taxes than income taxes. (For many low-wage workers with children, however, increases in the earned income tax credit more than offset their payroll taxes.)

———

The winds of economic change were discernable but their consequences difficult to predict, like a tropical ripple off the African coast that in time turns into hurricane-force winds. By the end of the twentieth century, deficits disappeared and federal budget surpluses emerged. Improvements in the government's financial position, however, did not temper the antitax, antigovernment attitudes of conservative Republicans. After deficits were eliminated in the late 1990s, cutting programs like Medicare, Medicaid, and Social Security began to look punitive rather than necessary for budget discipline. Conservative Republicans wanted to curtail these programs as a matter of principle: budget deficits had just presented opportunities. Any need to raise taxes to eliminate deficits also evaporated, and tax cuts again became politically and fiscally viable.

Reducing or eliminating welfare was the Republicans' top priority. Bill Clinton had signaled his willingness to cut welfare in his 1992 campaign, and joined with Republicans in that effort. President Clinton, however, continued to resist Republican efforts to slash Medicare spending and convert Medicaid into limited grants to the states. He also insisted that the need to preserve Social Security limited the government's ability to cut taxes.

Republicans reinvigorated their efforts to enact tax cuts and remained ada-mant in their opposition to tax increases. More and more Republican politi-cians across the country signed Grover Norquist's pledge never to increase taxes. Antitax resistance was the glue holding the diverse elements of the Re-publican coalition together.

On the Democratic side, stunning defeats in the 1994 election, especially the loss of the House majority for the first time since 1954, led many elected officials and political operatives to blame the losses on the 1993 tax increases.[73] The crucial questions then became: would Democrats resist Republican tax-cut initiatives and would Democrats again support widely distributed tax increases if large deficits and rising federal debt reemerged? As the twentieth century neared its close, tax cuts were back on the table. As the next chapter describes, this was not enough to slake the appetite of the Republican Right: they wanted to abolish the IRS and eliminate progressive income and estate taxes altogether.

Part III

Resurgence

1997–2023

Chapter 11

Moving the Goalposts

The IRS is the most un-American institution this country ever created.
—CONGRESSMAN W. J. "BILLY" TAUZIN, OCTOBER 1997

On a sultry spring Wednesday night, 4,500 people jammed into the Gwinnett Convention Center north of Atlanta to rail against the income tax. A couple of thousand more were turned away. Many drove hundreds of miles to be there. Herman Cain, a successful Black businessman and former Federal Reserve official who failed in a Senate campaign and a run for the Republican presidential nomination on an anti-income-tax platform, brought the crowd to its feet with a diatribe against the IRS and the income tax. Local Republican congressman John Linder and popular nationally syndicated talk-radio host Neal Boortz rallied the crowd to support replacing the income tax with a national sales tax. The *Atlanta Journal-Constitution* likened the affair to the Boston Tea Party, observing this "modern mob" must have made a lot more noise.[1]

This was just one of hundreds of similar rallies that Republicans held over a decade across the country. In October 1997, House Majority Leader Dick Armey and Louisiana congressman Billy Tauzin, along with Speaker of the House Newt Gingrich, rallied a crowd of nearly two thousand at a similar event in the adjacent county at the Cobb Galleria Ballroom—a stop on the Armey-Tauzin "Scrap-the-Code" roadshow, during which the two antitax Republican congressmen in cowboy boots engaged in a friendly, spirited debate about whether the income tax should be replaced with a 15 percent national sales tax or a 17 percent "flat tax." Interspersed with folksy country-music quotes, Armey described the tax law as "so bad that even the people entrusted to enforce it don't understand it." Tauzin claimed the "IRS is the most un-American institution this country ever created."[2] Tauzin asked the audience to remember the Boston Tea Party and shouted to thunderous applause, "This is not just about money. This is much more serious than that. This is about freedom and liberty."[3]

Nothing polled better with the public than attacking the IRS. Republican pollster and focus-group impresario Frank Luntz told Republicans the tax code is "public enemy number one." Polls revealed strong public support for a 25 percent ceiling on income taxes.[4] Once Republicans took over the House and Senate in 1995, polls and focus-group responses convinced them to set their sights on a very ambitious target: eliminating the progressive income tax. When he raised the top income tax rate to nearly 40 percent with only Democratic votes in 1993, Bill Clinton demonstrated that successes in lowering the top income tax rate were unstable.

The Armey-Tauzin debates were financed by Citizens for a Sound Economy (CSE), an antitax group founded and funded by Charles and David Koch with additional funds from major corporations. CSE supported the flat tax. It sponsored the Scrap-the-Code tour because the national sales tax proposal made the flat tax, which would not eliminate the IRS, look moderate. Both the flat tax and the sales tax would shift the tax burden away from the rich. Neither would tax inheritances or capital gains. CSE president Paul Beckner said, "The verdict from the audience in favor of scrapping the code was a unanimous 'yes.'"[5]

The Scrap-the-Code tour, of course, had no one on stage arguing for the progressive income tax. Dick Gephardt, the House Democratic Leader, volunteered for that role but was not invited.

Newt Gingrich, Grover Norquist, and their antitax allies were convinced they could drag President Clinton closer to their goals by enlarging their ambitions. Rush Limbaugh persuaded many of his listeners to support the flat tax, as did other conservative talk-radio hosts.[6] The Scrap-the-Code roadshow and demonizing the IRS helped Republicans shift the antitax movement decisively to the right after Republicans took over Congress in 1995. Jack Kemp played an important supporting role.

The Grand Ambition

In April 1995 Newt Gingrich and Bob Dole announced a new National Commission on Economic Growth and Tax Reform headed by Jack Kemp.[7] Kemp said his fourteen-member commission would "definitely be supply-side."[8] The

Jack Kemp throws the tax law into the trash with Senator
Dole and Speaker Gingrich watching.

Kemp Commission took testimony from economists (mostly supply-siders),
public officials, and business owners in eight cities around the country in 1995.
In January 1996 Kemp's commission issued a report calling the existing tax
system "wildly unjust and excessive." The commission recommended the existing tax law be "repealed in its entirety" and replaced with a single-rate flat
tax that would exempt capital gains, dividends, and interest income from taxation and allow a "generous" personal exemption and payroll tax deduction.
Kemp's commission also recommended abolishing the estate tax, allowing an

immediate deduction for all business expenditures, and requiring a two-thirds supermajority vote in both chambers of Congress to raise taxes.[9] Kemp said a revenue-neutral flat-tax rate would be around 20 percent, but based on optimistic projections of economic growth from the tax changes, his commission claimed a 17 percent flat tax would be revenue neutral.[10] The Treasury Department estimated a 17 percent flat tax would lose revenue of $138 billion a year, about $1.5 trillion over ten years. The liberal organization Citizens for Tax Justice estimated the revenue loss would be more than twice that large.[11] The tax rate necessary to make Kemp's flat tax revenue neutral would have been substantially higher than he claimed, requiring a larger tax increase for millions of middle-income Americans.

Exemptions for capital gains, interest, and dividends would eliminate taxes on income from wealth. Abolishing the estate tax would terminate the only national tax on wealth. The Kemp Commission's report left no doubt Republicans wanted to shift taxes from wealth to wages.

For nearly a century after the adoption of the Sixteenth Amendment, the idea of progressive taxation based on ability to pay seemed as stable and fundamental to American policy as "no taxation without representation." Progressive taxation requires that those who own and earn more contribute a larger share of their resources to support the government. Unlike the early efforts of Republican antitaxers, the Kemp Commission's objectives were not limited to lowering income tax rates at the top and reducing government spending: their goal was to eliminate progressive income tax rates based on ability to pay. The Kemp Commission was no Republican outlier. By the late 1990s, eliminating federal taxes on wealth and income from wealth became a conspicuous objective of conservative antitax Republicans—and a mainstream position of the Republican Party.

On April 15, 1995, Republican House Ways and Means Committee chairman Bill Archer, a Houston conservative, announced, "We intend to pull the income tax out by its roots."[12] Steve Largent, an Oklahoma Republican congressman, who enjoyed much greater success as a college and NFL wide receiver than as a legislator, and Texas Republican senator Kay Bailey Hutchison introduced the Tax Code Termination Act. This legislation proposed ending all taxes except for payroll taxes on December 31, 2001. But it did not say what would replace the current income and estate taxes. The proposed legislation called for "a low rate for all Americans" and "no bias against savings and investment," implying a flat-rate tax on consumption. Jim McCrery, a Louisiana Republican serving on the Ways and Means Committee, summarized the party's dilemma: "If we bash the current system, that's a win," he said. "But when we get out front and talk about how we change it, we run into risks."[13] In June 1998 the Tax Code Termination Act passed the House by a vote of 219 to 209, but it failed in the Senate with a 49 to 49 vote. Almost all Republicans voted for it with nearly all Democrats opposed.[14]

Some Republicans knew what kind of tax they wanted in lieu of the income and estate taxes. Indiana Republican senator Richard Lugar, Ways and Means chairman Bill Archer, and Louisiana congressman Billy Tauzin, to name just three, wanted to replace the progressive income tax and the estate tax with a national sales tax, misleadingly labeled the "Fair Tax."[15] Republican presidential candidate Steve Forbes, the multimillionaire heir and editor-in-chief of *Forbes* magazine, urged replacing income and estate taxes with a 17 percent flat-rate consumption tax. Forbes garnered great applause during his 1996 presidential campaign when he claimed the "IRS would be RIP" if he were elected.[16] Dick Armey, Rush Limbaugh, Grover Norquist, and the Heritage Foundation all endorsed Forbes's flat tax. Jack Kemp also endorsed Forbes's candidacy. Curiously, Kemp's endorsement came the day after Forbes had lost eight state primaries and about a week before he dropped out of the race, despite having spent millions of dollars in television ads promoting the flat tax.[17] Pat Buchanan and Phil Gramm, also candidates for the Republican presidential nomination in 1996, advanced their own versions of flat taxes.[18] Seven of the nine Republican presidential primary candidates urged replacing the income tax with either a national sales tax or a flat tax.[19]

Demonizing the IRS

In 1997 Ways and Means Committee chairman Bill Archer, Senate Republican Leader Trent Lott, and Senate Finance Committee chairman William Roth engaged in an aggressive media campaign alleging IRS abuses of power. Grover Norquist joined in, claiming the IRS performed politically motivated audits of conservative nonprofit organizations, including the Heritage Foundation. Major media, including the *Los Angeles Times, New York Times, Washington Post,* Fox Media, and *60 Minutes,* ran stories depicting IRS abuses of taxpayers' rights—stories promoted by Archer's and Roth's staffs.[20]

Demonizing the IRS was the most popular prong of the Republican attacks on progressive taxation. Polls have long showed Americans prefer a root canal to an IRS audit. Comedian Jerry Seinfeld made the point more colorfully: "An IRS audit is the financial equivalent of a complete rectal examination."[21] If the income tax could not be jettisoned, disabling the infrastructure enforcing it became an attractive alternative for the antitax forces. Attacking the IRS was a surefire winner in electoral politics; hindering the IRS's ability to enforce income tax rules against complex business arrangements and the wealthy also pleased many constituents and contributors.

Attacking the IRS created excellent fundraising opportunities for Republicans. In a fundraising letter for the National Republican Senatorial Committee, Kentucky senator Mitch McConnell wrote, "We can publicly expose the IRS's worst transgressions against honest, responsible taxpayers like you. Armed with your responses and demands, GOP leaders can call for televised hearings on the IRS! I need you to become a charter member of the Senatorial Committee with a contribution of $25, $50 or $100." Senator Lott sent a similar letter on behalf of the Republican National Committee, saying, "I need you to once and for all end the IRS's reign of terror."[22] Republican fundraising successes confirmed Frank Luntz's advice: "Nothing guarantees more applause than the call to abolish the IRS. I urge you in the strongest terms to allocate significant time and attention to this political winner."[23]

In September 1997 Senator Roth's committee held three days of dramatic televised hearings on alleged IRS abuses. Several taxpayers described personal horror stories of IRS malfeasance. One of the complainants, an eighty-two-year-old retired Catholic priest, Lawrence F. Ballweg, said the IRS challenged his signature on a tax document relating to a charitable trust of his deceased mother, claiming that he owed $18,000—a matter not settled until CNN reported on it.[24] Another taxpayer, Katherine Lund Hicks, a California bank employee, described a ten-year saga of IRS computer blunders, liens, levies, audits, and compounding interest and penalties that she said led to her divorce and bankruptcy. "Our lives are now forever altered," she added. "We will pay additional taxes every year as a result. Our confidence in the integrity of the IRS has been completely destroyed, and my husband's credit is seriously damaged. We will suffer the effects of this IRS collection for the rest of our lives."[25]

The most dramatic moments of the Roth hearings came, like a Mafia movie scene, when six IRS agents testified about IRS misconduct hidden behind screens and speaking through voice-altering microphones. The star witness, who testified openly, was Jennifer Long, a career IRS agent from Houston. She claimed the IRS targeted poor people and those who had suffered personal tragedies or financial crises. The IRS, she said, wants to "stick it" to people who "can't fight back."[26] C-SPAN, CNN, MSNBC, and Fox News all carried live portions of the IRS agents' testimony.

Roth's hearings generated front-page headlines across the country. Rush Limbaugh said they demonstrated why Americans "need to be protected against their government" and why it is a problem that the tax laws are interpreted by the IRS.[27] Grover Norquist praised Roth's hearings, saying, "Only when people saw the hearings and Congress started reacting did people realize there was a legitimate reason to be unhappy. . . . There's something wrong with the culture that tolerates this level of abuse."[28]

The IRS did not contest the Republicans' allegations of abuse, even though subsequent investigations showed many were false. Instead, the acting IRS commissioner apologized to the American people and announced a series of reforms intended to make the IRS more responsive and reduce incentives for misconduct in audits and collections. Roth's hearings confirmed people's fears of an out-of-control IRS willing to trample on the rights of ordinary law-abiding Americans.

In 1998, with overwhelming bipartisan majorities, Congress enacted legislation revising the governance and operations of the IRS and strengthening legal protections for taxpayers. This legislation was mostly the result of an effort led by Ohio Republican representative Rob Portman and Nebraska's Democratic senator Bob Kerrey. On signing the bill, President Clinton said the new law would help "create an IRS that respects American taxpayers and respects their values."[29] William Roth credited himself for the IRS reform legislation.[30]

President Clinton's Treasury Department then engaged in an effort to characterize the IRS as a "service" agency rather than an "enforcement" agency and to treat taxpayers as "customers" of the agency. Treasury required the IRS to provide "customer surveys" to people whose returns were audited. But to no avail. People do not view themselves as the tax collector's "customers."

Antitax Republicans and their allies continued to harness public fear and resentment of the IRS and link them to their antitax agenda. They commonly refer to the nation's tax law as the "IRS Code," as if Congress did not produce it. During Roth's hearings, Republican senator Don Nickles of Oklahoma ostentatiously placed the tax law and the Bible side by side on the dais and said, "The tax law is about ten times the size of the Bible, and unlike the Bible contains no good news."[31]

Acquiring New Allies

The Scrap-the-Code debates and Senator Roth's anti-IRS hearings created opportunities to advance the antitax agenda through new media outlets and to spread the anti-IRS, antitax message to new and growing audiences. On

October 7, 1996, conservative media magnate Rupert Murdoch launched the Fox News channel with Republican media strategist Roger Ailes as its chairman and CEO. Initially reaching seventeen million households (not including any in New York City or Los Angeles), Fox News was created as a competitor on the political right to CNN, the then-dominant twenty-four-hour news station which began broadcasting in 1980.

The ground was fertile for a conservative television news network: the audience for Fox News grew much faster than that of MSNBC, which was founded a few months earlier. During its first four years, Fox News reached an audience of about 17 percent of the U.S. population.[32] Within a decade, Fox News had more viewers than its competitors, becoming the most important television news channel in the United States, averaging more than two million viewers in mornings and evenings. Roger Ailes designed the network's mantra "fair and balanced" to distinguish the network from what he believed was the liberal bias of the other television news networks. In 1997 *Television Week* described Fox News as "one of the most important news media in our culture," adding, "Fox News, in combination with a network of conservative talk radio commentators, has changed the way many Americans process news."[33] Richard Viguerie (of conservative direct-mail fame) said conservatives "proudly want to claim Fox as one of their own—it's one of the movement's success stories."[34]

Fox News greatly expanded opportunities for Newt Gingrich, Grover Norquist, Sean Hannity, and their antitax allies to reach more Americans. The Fox News audience was overwhelmingly white, male, and antigovernment. Its viewers wanted taxes reduced and helped elect Republicans.[35] Ways and Means Committee chairman Bill Archer promoted Roth's IRS hearings on Fox News.[36] Sean Hannity said, "I believe in Reagan's economic theory. Economically, we're cutting taxes, and we're reaping the rewards."[37]

In 1995 Matt Drudge started an e-mail newsletter on Hollywood gossip from his home in Los Angeles. Before long the *Drudge Report* became a successful influential web-based news aggregator. It was the first media outlet to report Jack Kemp would be the 1996 Republican nominee for vice president, and in 1998 Drudge broke the story of Bill Clinton's sexual relationship with Monica Lewinsky. Hits on the *Drudge Report* website then multiplied ten times from its previous level of about one million a day. Drudge's first assistant was Andrew Breitbart, who later founded his own right-wing news outlet. In 1998 and 1999 Drudge had a weekly television show on Fox News. Drudge and Breitbart were pioneers who played a major role in producing politically powerful right-wing internet content and expanding how news is disseminated.[38]

While conservative media was transforming and bringing conservative dogma to increasing numbers of Americans outside the Washington beltway, Tom DeLay, Newt Gingrich, Dick Armey, and Grover Norquist in 1995 launched the "K-Street Project," a successful effort to place conservative Republicans (often former senators, representatives, and congressional staff) into positions of power in Washington's communications, lobbying, and influence-peddling businesses. After House Republicans fulfilled their Contract with America's promise to reduce the size of congressional staff, lobbyists played an even greater role—presenting members of Congress their versions of the reasons for and consequences of legislation they favored and sometimes even writing the new laws. By 1998 more than 10,000 registered Washington lobbyists reported spending nearly $1.5 billion a year to advance industry positions.[39] This was the amount required to be reported by law—only the small tip of a much larger concealed iceberg. Business lobbyists, of course, push for tax breaks and tax-reduction legislation and oppose tax increases.

Beginning in the mid-1990s, these developments considerably increased the influence of the antitax movement with the public and lawmakers. The 1996 Republican presidential campaign revealed how much its clout had strengthened.

The 1996 Elections

In June 1996, after twenty-seven years in the Senate and nearly a dozen as the Republican leader, Bob Dole resigned to run for president. When he left Congress, the nation lost a consummate dealmaker and preeminent legislator. Robert Dallek, a presidential historian, described Dole as operating "in a different era, when the idea of bipartisanship was very much in vogue and politicians understood that in a democracy you simply have to work, not just with your fellow party members, but with people from the opposite side. . . . He was masterful at that."[40]

After contentious early primary battles with Pat Buchanan and Steve Forbes, Dole secured the 1996 Republican presidential nomination. He selected Jack Kemp to be his vice-presidential nominee. Years before, Dole had mocked the former quarterback, saying, "There was a certain football player who forgot his helmet and then started talking supply-side theory."[41]

Although he frequently opposed tax increases, Dole had long derided supply-side economics. He refused to sign Grover Norquist's no-tax-increase pledge in his 1988 presidential campaign, but by 1996, Grover's sway among

Republicans had grown exponentially. He had greatly increased the number of federal and state legislators who signed his pledge never to raise taxes under any circumstances. Running as the Republican presidential nominee in 1996 without signing Grover's pledge was unthinkable. In April 1995, Dole signed the pledge quietly in his office. Grover gloated, "Lee didn't say much to Grant when he surrendered at Appomattox."[42] After Dole signed, he announced his presidential campaign with Grover at his side. In a futile effort to repeat Ronald Reagan's success, Dole made a 15 percent across-the-board tax cut the centerpiece of his presidential campaign. He won the Republican nomination but lost in November to Bill Clinton.

Clinton's campaign was bolstered by the strengthening economy and public fears that unified Republican control of government would open the door for Newt Gingrich and his congressional allies to undermine Social Security and Medicare. Despite Clinton's large popular vote and Electoral College margins, Republicans picked up two Senate seats and maintained control of the House. Trent Lott, a conservative Mississippian elected to the Senate in 1988 after serving eight terms in the House, succeeded Bob Dole as Republican Senate Leader. With his habitual hyperbole, Newt Gingrich described Lott as "the smartest legislative politician I've ever met."[43]

When Newt returned to the Speaker's office in January 1997, his party's congressional majorities were too small to override presidential vetoes. This meant, despite his taste for partisan warfare, Newt had to work with the White House to enact any new legislation. President Clinton faced a corresponding constraint: he had to deal with Newt and congressional Republicans to get any legislation through Congress.

The 1997 Budget Law

On January 21, 1997, the House Ethics Committee ordered Newt Gingrich to pay $300,000 for "reckless" or "intentional" use of tax-exempt entities for partisan political purposes and providing misleading information. The committee reprimanded him on 84 other charges. The House voted 395 to 28 to affirm the $300,000 penalty and the reprimands. In June and July 1997, a number of his House colleagues tried but failed to remove Gingrich as Speaker.[44] Newt had been wounded with the public and his House colleagues by the government shutdowns in 1995 and 1996. He described the failed 1995 budget negotiations as "one of the most bitter things I've gone through," and he urgently wanted to avoid a replay of the shutdown debacle.[45]

Senate Majority Leader Trent Lott was also anxious to compromise with President Clinton to enact new tax-cut legislation. Congressional Republicans temporarily shelved their grandiose agenda to eradicate income and estate taxes. But they remained determined to enact tax cuts for the wealthy, which Clinton opposed.

In his State of the Union Address on February 4, 1997, President Clinton announced the federal budget would be balanced within five years, and he advanced proposals for spending increases, including expanded health insurance coverage for uninsured children, tax breaks for higher education, and a new $500-per-child income tax credit.[46] The president believed the budget could be balanced even with new spending and tax cuts.

In April Speaker Gingrich urged repealing the estate tax, which he called the "death" tax, and eliminating the capital gains tax, saying, "We will give the President a chance to veto a tax cut if he wants to. . . . I favor a zero tax on savings and job creation. We're for zero tax on death benefits."[47] These changes would have reduced taxes for the wealthiest Americans over the next decade by more than $400 billion.

Newt also proposed a constitutional amendment requiring a two-thirds congressional majority to increase taxes and continued to keep tax cuts at the forefront of the Republican agenda. He insisted, "There is a moral case for cutting taxes." "Wouldn't it be great," Newt said, "to have the Republican pattern mean that every year we are in power, we will send you a little bit more back in the form of a tax cut and if you had, for example, 10 years of Republican control and you got 10 consecutive annual tax cuts, you are gradually paying less and less of what you earn to the government, so you would keep more and more of what you earn for yourself." He urged Republicans not to be seduced by "the left's efforts" to promote "class warfare, soak the rich, and whatever their revolutionist battle cry is this week."[48]

Economic growth in the first quarter of 1997 was 5.6 percent and remained above 4 percent for the rest of Bill Clinton's presidency. Inflation was stable, and unemployment declined below 5 percent for the first time since 1973. The S&P stock index rose 210 percent during the Clinton administration, and the NASDAQ, where many new technology stocks were traded, grew sevenfold during Clinton's second term (before the bursting of the stock market bubble in March 2000 when half of those gains were lost).[49] Robust economic growth and rising capital gains revenues from large stock market gains paved the way to a budget agreement.

On August 5, 1997, President Clinton signed the Balanced Budget Act of 1997 and the Taxpayer Relief Act of 1997.[50] The tax cuts passed by overwhelming bipartisan majorities in the House and Senate. Concerning the 1997 budget negotiations, Gingrich said, "I made a very conscious decision that it was better for America and better for the Republican Party to prove that we could govern. We decided that four years of incremental achievements in our direction are superior to four years of obstruction while we scream about values."[51]

The 1997 tax legislation lowered estate and gift taxes and provided some estate tax relief for owners of family farms and small businesses, setting the stage for another Republican effort to repeal those taxes in the next administration. The 1997 law reduced capital gains taxes from a top rate of 28 percent to 20 percent, with a 10 percent or zero rate for lower-bracket taxpayers. Up to $500,000 of capital gains on selling a residence became tax-exempt for married couples ($250,000 for single people).

The 1997 Act also expanded the ability of upper-income taxpayers to invest in tax-favored individual retirement accounts and created the Roth IRA, giving taxpayers an option to forgo an immediate deduction for retirement savings in exchange for the ability to withdraw the account's earnings free of any income tax after reaching the age of 59½. Senator William Roth described the new IRA as a way for "hard working middle-class Americans to stow money away tax-free for retirement."[52] The Roth IRA lost very little revenue in the short run and was estimated to cost just over $20 billion over the next ten years—but it cost much more after that.[53] The average Roth IRA had about $40,000 of assets in 2018, but for some rich people, particularly those in private equity firms or successful start-up companies, it became a valuable tax-avoidance vehicle. For example, billionaire investor Peter Thiel—a major funder of antitax politicians—put low-valued stock of new companies into his Roth IRA, which grew to be worth more than $5 billion.[54]

Even with a Democrat in the White House, the tax cuts largely benefited upper-income taxpayers. President Clinton conceded that the tax-reduction legislation gave Republicans about two-thirds of what they initially proposed.[55] In exchange, Clinton got an expansion of health coverage for children, a mélange of tax breaks for higher education, and a $500 tax credit for low- and middle-income families—an idea that enjoyed widespread support from Republicans and Democrats.

The president had made a priority of tax benefits for higher education, estimated to cost $41 billion over five years, the largest increase in federal funding for higher education since the GI Bill. The hodgepodge of tax breaks for higher education, which included two tax credits, three deductions, and three exclusions from income, along with five other provisions promoting saving for college expenses, left unsophisticated middle-income taxpayers bewildered about how to cope with their complexity or maximize their benefits.[56]

Bill Clinton was hardly unique in looking to tax breaks as the way to address an important problem like funding higher education. When the nation has a need, for example, for childcare affordability, adequate retirement savings, health insurance coverage, or access to higher education, an income tax benefit is typically the response. The income tax provides important subsidies for health insurance, homeownership, and retirement income, to name just three of the largest. The 1986 tax-reform law cut back substantially on these kinds of "tax expenditures," but presidents and members of Congress from both parties often turn to an income tax break as the best prescription for virtually any economic or social ill the country faces.[57] As in 1997, Democrats take far less heat from Republicans for offering tax deductions or credits rather than spending increases: antigovernment, antitax advocates often equate any tax reduction with smaller government. Politicians who sign Grover Norquist's pledge agree even not to close "loopholes" except when it funds another tax cut; most Republicans agree with Grover's view that "all tax cuts are good tax cuts."[58]

President Clinton and his Democratic congressional allies believed backing the 1997 tax-cut legislation and the Balanced Budget Act would allow them to shed their reputations as tax-and-spend liberals and become protected from such charges. New York's Charles Rangel, the ranking Democrat on the House Ways and Means Committee, claimed, "We have now shattered the myth that we Democrats are spending Democrats and taxing Democrats."[59] John M. Spratt Jr., a South Carolina Democrat, was more optimistic: "This [higher taxes] is not an issue that'll keep hitting us on the chin."[60] They could hardly have been more wrong. The antitax issue is the centerpiece of Republicans' domestic agenda. The 1997 tax cuts did not slake their antitax zeal. It was simply the first time since 1981 that federal budget deficits were sufficiently controlled to allow for tax cuts. Republicans regarded the 1997 tax cuts as merely as an appetizer for larger cuts to come.

———

The Monica Lewinsky affair and its aftermath dominated the last two years of Bill Clinton's presidency and reenergized a resumption of the aggressive partisanship that had abated briefly during Clinton's second term. Newt Gingrich viewed Clinton's tribulations as creating an opportunity for large Republican gains in the 1998 midterm elections and predicted Republicans would gain thirty seats in the House. Instead, Democrats gained five House seats—the first time since Andrew Jackson's presidency that the president's party gained seats in a president's second midterm elections. The day after the elections, facing opposition from his House Republican colleagues, Newt, who was also having an affair with a younger woman, announced he would resign as Speaker of the House.[61]

In January 1999 Newt Gingrich left Congress, but the poisonous partisanship he pioneered did not depart with him. As Tennessee Republican senator Bill Frist said, "It was not a climate suitable for compromise."[62] Pleasing and appeasing their hard-right constituents deterred Republican compromises with Democrats.[63]

The brief era of bipartisan legislation in 1996 and 1997—which produced welfare reform, a balanced-budget act, and tax-reduction legislation—was an aberration produced by Bill Clinton's policy of "triangulation": giving congressional Republicans much of what they wanted to get some things he wanted. Triangulation can be effective in the short run as long as leaders do not abandon principles in the interest of winning. It undermines one's long-term goals and strategic objectives, however, when the opposition is able to take advantage of a willingness to succeed by moving the goals in their direction—something Newt Gingrich and his allies well understood and helped them shift American politics to the right after the Republican congressional takeover in 1995. Clinton's labor secretary Robert Reich said, "The so-called center has continued to shift to the right because conservative Republicans stay put while Democrats keep meeting them halfway."[64] Garry Wills was harsher: Bill Clinton's "very success," he said, "made Democrats think their only path to success was to concede, cajole and pander. . . . Clinton bequeathed to his party not a clear call to high goals but an omnidirectional proneness to pusillanimity and collapse."[65] The costs of Democratic triangulation and compromise became manifest after the turn of the century with the exceptionally large tax cuts of the George W. Bush administration.

Chapter 12

The Apple Sometimes Falls Far from the Tree

Reagan proved deficits don't matter.

—VICE PRESIDENT DICK CHENEY, NOVEMBER 2002

The 2000 election—one of the closest in American history—was a fateful turning point for antitax advocates. Al Gore, Bill Clinton's vice president and the Democratic nominee, won the popular vote but lost by five votes in the Electoral College after the Supreme Court in a partisan 5–4 vote stopped a recount of Florida votes when George W. Bush, the Texas governor and eldest son of President George H. W. Bush, was ahead by 537 votes.[1]

Rather than endorsing unrealistic Republican efforts to repeal the income tax and replace it with a flat-rate sales or other consumption tax, George W. Bush made large income tax cuts and repeal of the estate tax the centerpiece of his campaign. Bush's ten-year $1.6 trillion tax-cut proposals had four main components: (1) reducing the top income tax rate from 39.6 to 33 percent and the lowest rate from 15 to 10 percent; (2) doubling tax credits for children from $500 to $1,000 and extending them to families with higher incomes; (3) reducing income tax "marriage penalties" for some couples; and (4) repealing the estate tax.

Vice President Gore accused Bush of wanting to spend "more money on tax cuts for the wealthiest one-percent than all of the new spending [Bush] proposed for education, health care, prescription drugs, and national defense."[2] But Bush and his team designed his tax plan to include an across-the-board reduction in income tax rates that provided the greatest benefits to

President Bush at the White House with some "tax-cut" families from his campaign.

the top but also cut income taxes for everyone. Doubling child tax credits allowed him repeatedly to introduce to his audiences middle-class families with two children who would enjoy large income tax reductions under his plan. The prodigious improvement in the government's financial position during the 1990s made 2001 a propitious year to be pushing large tax cuts.

Pushing against an Open Door

When George W. Bush moved into the White House, the federal government expected large budget surpluses to continue for a decade. The Congressional Budget Office (CBO) projected total surpluses of $5.6 trillion over the coming ten years.

On January 25, 2001, at a Senate Budget Committee hearing, Alan Greenspan, reappointed by Bill Clinton to his fourth term as Federal Reserve chairman, testified budget surpluses *might* continue "well past 2030 despite the budgetary pressures the aging of the baby-boom generation" would cause for Social Security, Medicare, and Medicaid. Greenspan admitted the budget surplus projections were "subject to a wide range of error." But—taking a very different tack than he had with President Clinton—he described the "critical long-term fiscal policy issue" as the likelihood the federal government would pay off the entire federal debt before the end of the decade and need to invest ongoing surpluses in "large quantities of private . . . assets." "Short of an extraordinarily rapid and highly undesirable dissipation of . . . surpluses," he said, "it appears difficult to avoid at least some accumulation of private assets by the government."[3] Greenspan feared federal investments in assets like corporate stock because of the potential political pressures on investment choices.

Answering a question from Senator Phil Gramm, Greenspan said lowering marginal income tax rates was the best way to reduce the surplus, claiming it "far exceeds" the benefits of other tax cuts from an economic perspective—echoing the supply-side refrain. Rebutting North Dakota Democratic senator Kent Conrad's plea to wait and see if the federal debt came close to being paid off, Greenspan urged starting tax cuts "sooner rather than later" and essentially endorsed George W. Bush's ten-year, $1.6 trillion cut. Conrad complained a tax cut this large would leave no room to add a prescription drug benefit to Medicare, to strengthen the financing of Social Security, Medicare, or Medicaid, or to increase federal spending on education or defense.[4]

Greenspan's testimony generated front-page headlines around the country, providing an important boost to Bush's tax-cut proposals. In his address to Congress on February 27, 2001, President Bush characterized Alan Greenspan's testimony as a clarion call for congressional action: "We must act quickly," Bush said. "The chairman of the Federal Reserve has testified before Congress that tax cuts often come too late to stimulate economic recovery."[5]

Greenspan's fear that surpluses would be so large to pay off the entire federal debt became laughable: the projected surpluses vanished and the federal debt grew. In 2003 the federal deficit was $375 billion. In January 2004, President Bush announced the deficit would exceed $500 billion—the largest dollar amount in American history. By then, CBO anticipated the federal debt would continue to grow at least for another decade and probably longer.[6] Greenspan confessed later he "was wrong to abandon my skepticism" about the likelihood of ongoing surpluses.[7]

Killing the "Death Tax"

Once the deficit problem was "solved," any new Republican president would have pushed to cut income and capital gains rates. President Bush regarded prompt congressional approval of his tax cuts as crucial to ratify his bona fides as president, and he assembled a talented team to push the legislation through Congress.[8] He enjoyed a Republican majority in the House, but the Senate was split 50–50 and not all its Republicans supported his tax plan. This made securing votes from some Senate Democrats essential.

Unlike his father, President Bush was willing to travel the country selling his plan. He extolled his proposed tax cuts in fourteen states where Democratic senators were up for election in 2002 and where he needed to bolster Republicans' support. He also advocated his cuts in Washington at conferences of state legislators, the National Newspaper Association, and the Hispanic Chamber of Commerce, along with groups of small-business owners, including women and Black business leaders. The boldest part of President Bush's tax plan—and except to a small group of advocates paying close attention, the most surprising—was his proposal to repeal the estate tax.[9]

Since World War II, the estate tax affected only the richest 1 or 2 percent of Americans, encouraged charitable giving, and was ignored by most people. The modern estate tax was enacted in 1916 to help fund World War I. The only serious effort to repeal it had occurred in the 1920s by Treasury Secretary Andrew Mellon, one of the wealthiest Americans.

The estate tax was grounded on opposition to dynastic wealth and the core American value that all people should have equal opportunities to pursue their economic goals. Although the estate tax accounted for nearly 11 percent of federal revenues at its peak in 1936, the tax never produced more than 2.5 percent of federal revenues after World War II ended. The tax, however, had long contributed nearly one-third as much to the progressivity of the U.S. tax structure as income tax rates higher than the average rate.[10] Beginning with the narrowing of the tax in 1982, that role began to decline, and in 2001 the tax produced less than 2 percent of federal revenues, but it still played an important role in enhancing progressivity at the very top.

The effort to kill the "death tax," as its opponents effectively renamed it, began in the mid-1990s far from the Washington beltway with a small, quixotic group of outsiders.[11] The tax's enemies included farmers and cattle ranchers, owners of small businesses, several local newspaper owners, and some of the richest families in America. The early champions for repeal included people like Jim Martin, an intense University of Florida graduate who gave George W. Bush his first political job as a staffer in 1968 and served as president of the "60 Plus Association," a no-frills, shoestring association in Arlington, Virginia; Harold Apolinsky, a bow-tied, Birmingham, Alabama, estate tax attorney who enlisted the Heritage Foundation to join the repeal effort; and Frank Blethen, owner and publisher of the *Seattle Times*, founded by his great-grandfather in 1896, with half a million readers and more than 3,000 workers in 2000 when it was valued at $350 million.

These unlikely repeal advocates engaged in a concerted effort to repeal the tax—including coordination around using the term "death tax" rather than "estate tax." Jim Martin created a "pizza fund" in his office—fining his employees a dollar each time they said "estate" rather than "death" tax. According to Martin, this practice was adopted by the National Federation of Independent Businesses (NFIB), other lobbying shops, and some Republican congressional offices. Rush Limbaugh began decrying the "death tax" in the early 1990s. One key congressional staffer attributed the strategic use of the term to Newt Gingrich, stressing that the phrase sends a specific message: "Estate tax sounds like it only hits the wealthy, but 'death tax' sounds like it hits everyone." The repeal advocates, he said, "focus grouped this" and found "people viewed a 'death tax' as very unfair. You don't have to be really rich to be worried about a death tax"—even if it will never apply to you.[12]

An especially important repeal advocate who provided crucial resources, organizational talent, and the determination and wherewithal to persevere for years was Pat Soldano, a woman in her fifties from Orange County, California, who ran family offices for Frederick Field of the Marshall Field department stores and the California oil and gas industry's Brown family, whose leader died unexpectedly of cancer at age thirty-eight in the mid-1990s. Families such as the Plimpton's of New Jersey, the Mars candy family, the Gallo wine family, the Waltons of Walmart, and heirs to the Campbell soup and Krystal fast-food fortunes all contributed to Soldano's efforts to eliminate the estate tax.[13] In the early 1990s, Soldano was a political novice, but over time she became extraordinarily effective in marshaling support for repeal.

Soldano hired the Patton Boggs law firm of legendary lobbying prowess to help her strategize about repealing the estate tax. Thanks to her wealthy clients, Soldano had financial resources to get attention in Washington, but money buys access—not guaranteed results. In 1992 when Soldano began her lobbying efforts, Patton Boggs's competitors regarded her success as so unlikely they joked the firm was taking Soldano's money for unbelievably expensive guided tours of the nation's capital.

Soldano and her compatriots in the repeal movement understood success depended on divorcing estate tax repeal from other agendas of the Republican Right: it had to appeal to a variety of non-traditionally Republican constituencies. Knowing some first-generation minority business owners would be vulnerable to the tax, Soldano and Blethen began courting their support. She talked to the Black Chamber of Commerce and other minority groups and reached out to gays and lesbians, pointing out how their inability then to take marital deductions increased their potential estate tax liabilities. Soldano's most natural sell was to female business owners. Mobilizing women, minorities, and gays and lesbians required that estate tax repeal not be sullied by association with other controversial conservative political agendas. Popular support could be garnered only if people could empathize with ordinary Americans who had worked hard to build a nest egg about to be destroyed at their death by a voracious federal government. The working rich, not the idle rich, became poster children for the repeal movement, ensuring the public saw the estate tax as an issue confronting small- and medium-sized business owners.

Estate tax repeal advocates chose the public faces of their movement creatively. On the morning of February 1, 1995, in the cavernous hearing room of the House Ways and Means Committee, an elegant, eighty-three-year-old, African American tree farmer from Montrose, Mississippi, moved into the witness chair. Chester Thigpen, a grandchild of slaves, came to Washington to urge lawmakers to exempt family businesses from the estate tax. "Estate taxes matter not just to lawyers, doctors and businessmen, but to people like [my wife] Rosette and me," he said. "We were both born on land that is now part of our tree farm. I can remember plowing behind a mule for my uncle who owned it before me. My dream then was to own land." "Back when I started," he continued, "the estate tax applied to only one estate in 60. Today it applies to one in 20—including mine. I wonder if I would be able to achieve my dream if I were starting out today." His farm, he added, "made it possible for us to leave a legacy that makes me very proud: beautiful forests and ponds that can live on for many, many years after my wife and I pass on."

Thigpen claimed his dream was under threat. "We also want to leave the tree farm in our family. But no matter how hard I work, that depends on you," he said. "Right now, people tell me my tree farm could be worth more than a million dollars." But, he added ominously, "my children might have to break up the tree farm or sell off timber to pay the estate taxes" after he died. Thigpen's family and their tree farm became a symbol of industrious, hardworking, environmentally friendly, minority-owned, family businesses that would benefit from estate tax relief. Before long, his family business became the epitome of the case for estate tax repeal. Thigpen's testimony was cycled and recycled. Opponents of repeal viewed Thigpen as a stalking horse, a front for wealthy white families who were financing the repeal machine. In the end, Chester

Thigpen's estate was not assessed any estate taxes because the value of his assets was below the minimum threshold where the tax applied.[14]

In the mid-1990s repeal seemed a pipe dream. The Republicans' 1994 Contract with America called for gradually increasing the estate tax exemption from $600,000 (the level set by President Reagan's 1981 tax-reduction legislation) to $750,000 over three years, after which it would be indexed for inflation, a relatively modest change. The Clinton-Gingrich budget legislation in 1997 slowly phased in another increase in the estate tax threshold to $1 million ($2 million for married couples) and increased it immediately to $1.3 million for some family businesses. The leaders of NFIB, the most powerful advocate for small businesses, believed repeal was unrealistic. When George W. Bush launched his presidential campaign in June 1999, estate tax reform, rather than repeal, was his goal, but by Labor Day he began urging elimination of the "death tax." Promising to end the death tax garnered him the greatest applause during his campaign speeches. In contrast, Al Gore called for increasing to $5 million the value of a small business or family farm that could be bequeathed free from estate tax—costing less than 10 percent of the revenue lost from repeal.

On October 7, 2000, during the final presidential debate, Jim Lehrer of the Public Broadcasting System asked George Bush what he would do to help America's farmers. Bush said he wanted to get "rid of the death tax," adding it "is a bad tax," one "that taxes people twice" and "penalizes the family farmer." Lehrer then asked the candidates to explain their differences concerning the estate tax, which he called "the inheritance tax." Al Gore went first, claiming he supported "a massive reform of the estate tax or the death tax," falling into the repeal advocates' "death tax" label. Gore said under his proposal "80 percent of all family farms" and "the vast majority of all family businesses" would be "completely exempt" from the tax, but added he "did not favor eliminating the tax for the wealthiest one percent." Repeal of the tax, he said, would produce "an extra heavy burden on middle-class families" who would have to "make up" the lost revenues.

Lehrer then asked Bush, "What's the case for eliminating the tax completely for everybody?" Bush responded, "Because people shouldn't be taxed twice on their assets. It's either unfair for some or unfair for all. . . . I just don't think it's fair to tax people's assets twice regardless of your status. It's a fairness issue. It's an issue of principle, not politics."[15]

In 2001 whenever his aides suggested compromising, Bush held steadfast for repeal, repeatedly returning to his "no double taxation" mantra. Given his background, it is unsurprising that Bush focused on eliminating "double taxa-tion" for the wealthy. But "double taxation" is commonplace and a poor guide to tax fairness. Americans pay state and federal income taxes, taxes on their wages to finance Social Security and Medicare, and sales taxes when they spend what is left. Are two taxes of 10 percent more or less fair than one of 25 percent? The 2001 effort to repeal the estate tax was a crucial feature of an-titax Republicans' attacks on progressive taxation in America.

Creating an Effective Coalition for Repeal

The repeal trailblazers of the early 1990s were easily forgotten, given what the Family Business Estate Tax Coalition later became. By 2001, the coalition in-cluded more than one hundred trade associations and other organizations rep-resenting six million individuals and businesses. It ran one of the most effective legislative campaigns in recent times—a juggernaut for repeal, flawless in its organization and execution, adept at managing internal tensions, professional in its public relations, and formidable in bringing constituency pressure to key leg-islators before critical votes.[16] The *Washington Post* described the group's efforts as "an increasingly sophisticated form of lobbying that coordinates grass-roots work by influential members of local communities with a legislative plan masterminded by Washington strategists representing large associations."[17]

There had been ample time for the Clinton administration to divert the repeal effort by substantially increasing the estate tax exemption and providing genuine tax relief for farmers and small-business owners. Even after the presi-dent learned—to his shock and dismay—that a majority of the Congressional Black Caucus voted for a repeal bill in the House, the Clinton administration ignored or dismissed the estate tax issue. So did others with stakes in opposing repeal. Organized labor was preoccupied with attempting to rebuild unions' diminishing ranks and political prowess. Charities, such as universities and museums, which had as much as 20 percent of their bequests at risk if the tax were repealed, were afraid to speak against repeal because of fear of alienating key donors and board members. Representatives of the life insurance industry, which earns substantial revenues from policies purchased due to the tax, were convinced Al Gore would win the presidency and stayed on the sidelines.

Repeal forces on the other side were well financed, well organized, focused, and sophisticated. Surprising many Democrats, they funded and produced an armful of political polls showing that a large majority of Americans—65 to 70 percent—favored repealing the "death tax." How did this happen?

First, the American public was unrealistically optimistic about their relative and absolute economic circumstances. They underestimated the levels of inequality, overestimated their own wealth compared to others, and exaggerated their likelihood of moving up significantly and getting rich. A *Time*/CNN poll taken in 2000 revealed that 39 percent of Americans believed they either were already in the top 1 percent of wealth or "soon" would be.[18] Pro-repeal forces were clever to design polls simply asking the question: "Do you favor or oppose repeal?"—never giving a hint that repealing the tax might someday cause other taxes to rise or spending on popular programs, such as Social Security, Medicare, or education, to decline. Faced with a stand-alone question about repealing or keeping any tax, a majority of Americans would likely favor repeal. Americans also endorse the ability of decedents to leave their assets to their children and grandchildren, although a majority also says it wants to increase taxes on the "rich."

Second, the repeal forces were enormously successful at creating a compelling narrative against the tax. They effectively marshaled personal stories in support of specific moral principles, conveying the values of asceticism, thrift, and hard work. They merged capitalist economics and Protestant ethics: small-business owners, family farmers, first-generation entrepreneurs—the hardworking folks who comprise the grasstops in local communities—all combined success with virtue. Good narratives including a moral with heroes and villains frequently defeat well-supported analytical arguments in Congress.

Death is the great leveler. Everyone knows they might die tomorrow. By calling this tax on large transfers of wealth the "death tax" and placing the undertaker and the tax collector side by side, the repeal coalition made the IRS the greedy beneficiary of personal tragedies. Travails of the wealthy took on a universal hue.[19]

On the other side, those who fought to retain the tax relied on economic arguments that the tax had little or no detrimental effects on the economy and repeated often that it burdened only the richest 1 or 2 percent of Americans. They made William Gates Sr. the most visible opponent of repeal. As the father of the world's richest man, who in retirement was helping spread his son's largesse around the world, Gates was not a sympathetic figure to whom ordinary Americans could relate. Repeal proponents had no difficulty labeling him a "limousine liberal," most obviously because he had no estate tax problems and everyone knew it.[20] The advocates for wealth transfer taxes failed to understand the political power of storytelling years after Ronald Reagan turned it into an art form.

Preparing to Push the President's Plan
through Congress

Notwithstanding the momentum generated by the estate tax repeal coalition and its appeal to antitax advocates and congressional Republicans, George W. Bush's tax cuts were not a cinch in Congress. The president deliberately left tax reductions for large corporations out of his plan: they win no votes in a presidential campaign. This omission, however, was a liability in Congress where large corporations have sway. Knowing $1.6 trillion in tax reductions might be more than Congress would accept, Bush held firm, rejecting pleas to add corporate cuts to the package after he moved into the White House. But he and his aides feared corporate lobbyists might reshape his priorities for their benefit in Congress, especially because the economy was faltering. The president needed to neutralize corporate America or, better yet, win its support for his plan.

On February 7, the day before he sent his tax proposals to Congress, the president lunched in the White House Cabinet Room with twenty-two business leaders, including Jack Welch of General Electric, Enron's Kenneth Lay, Jerry Jasinowski, president of the National Association of Manufacturers, and Charls Walker. Walker, seventy-seven years old and a long-time friend of the Bush family, had retired, but the prospect of a large tax cut lured him back into the fray. The day before the president's lunch, Walker announced a business coalition supporting an additional $300 billion in tax cuts for large multinational businesses. The Business Roundtable, one of Walker's allies, urged Congress to reduce the corporate tax rate by $1 for every $5 of individual tax cuts—adding 20 percent, $320 billion, to the costs of the president's plan. At lunch President Bush suggested, but did not promise, his support for a second tax cut for corporations if the economy remained weak. He did not need to mention the large personal stakes the corporate leaders had in his proposed reductions of the top income tax and capital gains rates and repeal of the estate tax.

Individual rate reductions and estate tax repeal were especially important to small businesses, which typically operate as partnerships (or "S" corporations) taxed at individual, not corporate, rates. The president's chief political strategist, Karl Rove, recruited the consummate Washington lobbyist and prolific Republican fundraiser Dirk Van Dongen, president of the National Association of Wholesale Distributors, to lead a "Tax Relief Coalition" of businesses supporting the president's plan. Van Dongen was legendary for his political skills: as Grover Norquist said, "Dirk fights outside his weight."[21]

On February 23, 2001, the president welcomed nearly fifty business leaders and lobbyists into the ornate Indian Treaty Room in the Old Executive Office Building next to the White House. This large room, with its French and Italian marble walls, conveys warmth and importance. The president and his colleagues were at one end of the room. Business representatives and lobbyists sat in two large semicircles around the room. Grover Norquist was there, as were representatives from Citizens for a Sound Economy (CSE), the organization of antitax Republicans. Dirk Van Dongen sat at the far end of the room opposite the president.

This well-scripted meeting ended with more than twenty trade associations enthusiastically supporting the president's plan. In addition to Van Dongen's group, three other powerhouse trade associations became leaders of the Tax Relief Coalition: NFIB, the most influential small-business organization; the U.S. Chamber of Commerce, America's largest business organization, representing large and small businesses in every state; and, surprisingly, the National Association of Manufacturers (NAM). NAM, like the Chamber of Commerce, represents both large and small businesses, but its political positions are typically dominated by large Fortune 500 companies. However, Jerry Jasinowski, NAM's leader, hated being on the sidelines and could not resist Van Dongen's plea to help lead the Tax Relief Coalition.

A few days after the meeting, the Business Roundtable joined the Tax Relief Coalition, and Charls Walker postponed his efforts to add corporate tax breaks. The next week the Tax Relief Coalition sent a public letter to all members of Congress urging prompt enactment of President Bush's proposals. The letter was signed by 175 organizations, including many state and national business trade associations. The coalition generated thousands of phone calls, emails, and letters from constituents requesting members of Congress to enact President Bush's plan. It placed supportive editorials in important newspapers and magazines, issued countless press releases, and arranged many radio appearances, some for television, and scores of internet ads. It produced "grassroots action kits" with target lists of key legislators, talking points supporting the president's proposals, and sample letters to Congress and newspaper editors. The coalition also scheduled personal meetings between small-business owners and members of Congress to push for the income and capital gains rate cuts and estate tax repeal.

Business coalitions are common. What made the Tax Relief Coalition unusual was its close relationship with the White House. Van Dongen said members had to be "willing to work on behalf of the president's proposals." "There is an umbilical cord to the White House," he said. "You either support the administration's proposals and only those changes the administration agrees to or you leave the team."[22] The coalition had about five hundred members. That number doubled for a second round of tax cuts in 2003.

Reminiscing about Ronald Reagan's 1981 tax cuts Van Dongen described the "tremendous passion, tremendous human energy on both sides," adding, "That was a battle over the size of government . . . and [we] wanted to cut taxes to cut government—to cut nasty unpleasant things—down." During the George W. Bush years, he said, the country again was engaged in "a quasi-national referendum over the size and method of funding of the government."[23]

Speedy Success in Congress

George W. Bush came into office with a House Republican congressional majority anxious to enact a large tax cut and give the new president an early legislative victory. Dennis Hastert, an evangelical Christian from Illinois, was starting his second term as Speaker of the House.[24] Cooperation with House Democrats was not necessary. Hastert and his deputies, Dick Armey and Tom "the Hammer" DeLay, presided with aggressive partisanship. Over George W. Bush's objections, Hastert shrewdly insisted on breaking the president's tax plan into multiple bills. The Speaker was convinced bringing Bush's package to the House floor in one bite would induce sticker shock among some Republicans who, he feared, might balk at the huge hole it would create in federal revenues. Because each category of Bush's tax cuts was popular with Republicans and some Democrats, Hastert believed he would secure a majority for the income tax rate cuts, expanded tax credits for children, reductions of marriages penalties, and estate tax repeal by voting on them separately.[25] The White House grudgingly agreed. Hastert's strategy worked, but with each vote the tax cuts' costs rose.[26]

On March 29 the Ways and Means Committee voted 24 to 14 to reduce and ultimately repeal the estate tax, effective only in 2011, with one Democrat in support.[27] The committee's bill passed the House in early April by a vote of 274 to 154. Fifty-eight Democrats—more than a quarter of those in the House—voted for repeal. Four members of the Congressional Black Caucus and four Latino Democrats supported repeal; only large-city liberal Democrats consistently voted against repealing the nation's only tax on wealth and the country's most progressive tax. The president's proposals sailed through the House, confirming Hastert's divide-and-conquer strategy, but Senate success was hardly assured.

Unlike the House where the majority has complete control, it takes 60 votes to overcome a Senate filibuster, an impossible hurdle for President Bush's tax proposals. But the "budget reconciliation" process allows Congress to pass budget legislation with only 51 Senate votes. During the first half of 2001, before Republican senator Jim Jeffords of Vermont defected to caucus with the Democrats, the Senate was evenly divided between Republicans and Democrats with Vice President Dick Cheney available to break ties. Every vote was critical.[28] Three Republicans—Jeffords, Lincoln Chafee of Rhode Island, and Arizona's John McCain—expressed concerns over the size of Bush's tax cuts, and only one Democrat, Georgia's Zell Miller, endorsed the president's plan.

President Bush's tax cuts got a boost when House and Senate Democratic leaders decided to propose their own tax cuts costing about half of what the president proposed.[29] That ended debate in Congress over whether to enact a large tax cut; remaining disagreements between Democrats and Republicans were over how large the cuts should be and who should get them.

Two days after the House passed the last component of the president's plan, the Senate adopted a budget resolution calling for a ten-year tax cut of $1.27 trillion, about $330 billion less than President Bush requested. All 50 Republicans and 15 Democrats supported the resolution. Conservative Louisiana Democrat John Breaux secured the Democrats' votes after Republican Senate Majority Leader Trent Lott assured Breaux in writing the ten-year cost would not be raised above $1.25 trillion in negotiations with the House. A happy President Bush said, "I applaud today's action and congratulate the Republicans and Democrats that made it happen."[30] The *Wall Street Journal* described repeal of the estate tax on inherited wealth as the most "contentious tax issue in the budget vote."[31]

Iowa's Chuck Grassley, chairing the Senate Finance Committee, needed to construct a bill that included all the elements necessary to survive numerous amendments on the Senate floor and to fit all the tax-cut ingredients into the $1.3 trillion budget resolution.[32] The crucial artifice was to terminate or "sunset" all of the tax cuts on September 30, 2011, the last day of the government's final fiscal year in the ten-year budget period.[33] Grassley and his colleagues expected a future Congress to extend the large tax cuts, greatly increasing the actual costs of the legislation, but that was irrelevant under Congress's budget rules.

After a few close votes, concerning the top income tax rate and estate tax repeal, on May 23, 2001, the Senate approved the Finance Committee's bill

President Cheney broke the 50–50 tie, casting the deciding vote in favor of the tax reductions. To keep the ostensible revenue costs down, these cuts, like those of 2001, were scheduled to expire in 2010 or sooner.[43]

In December 2003 President Bush signed a law adding prescription drug coverage to Medicare, estimated to cost $534 billion over ten years.[44] This was the largest new entitlement enacted since the 1965 creation of Medicare and Medicaid—the first not paid for with a tax increase.

The 2001 and 2003 Bush tax cuts reduced federal revenues from 20 percent of GDP in 2000 to 15.6 percent in 2004. When all the changes were phased in, they raised the after-tax incomes of people in the top 1 percent by nearly 6.5 percent—$54,000 on average—compared to about 1 percent, or an average of $207, for the bottom 40 percent.[45] Bill Gates, then America's richest person, said the Bush tax cuts would "widen the growing gap in economic and political influence between the wealthy and the rest of America."[46] In 2017 the Center on Budget and Policy Priorities estimated the top 1 percent of households received average tax reductions totaling more than $570,000 between 2004 and 2012.[47] There is meager evidence that these tax cuts stimulated substantial economic growth, although the 2003 cuts did boost the stock market, further increasing economic inequality.[48] They also produced large deficits and expanded the national debt. The historian James Patterson wrote that this "dramatic turn in fiscal policy was the most significant domestic legacy of [Bush's] presidency."[49]

Congress added smaller tax reductions in 2004, 2005, and 2006. With President Bush's blessing, Congress also abandoned the spending limits and "pay-as-you-go rules" of the 1990 budget act signed by his father and continued through the Clinton administration. In 2007, before the financial crisis, the federal debt exceeded $9 trillion, 60 percent of GDP, and was rising. No one needed worry anymore about Alan Greenspan's 2001 concerns that all the federal debt would be paid off and the federal government would have to buy corporate stock. That problem had been solved.

———

As a percentage of the economy the costs of the Bush tax cuts were similar to President Reagan's in 1981. But unlike the period following Reagan's cuts, when the nation's leaders focused on taming deficits, ongoing deficits and rising debt produced no countermovement. Brad DeLong, a Clinton administration economist, predicted the consequences: "The surplus-creating fiscal policies established . . . in the Clinton administration would have been very good for America had the Clinton administration been followed by a normal successor. But what is the right fiscal policy for a future Democratic administration to follow when there is no guarantee that any Republican successors will ever be 'normal' again?"[50]

In 2004 George W. Bush narrowly won a majority of the popular vote and prevailed in the Electoral College. Republicans gained four Senate seats, giving them a majority of 55 to 45, and House Republicans gained five seats, producing a majority of 232 to 202.

In February 2005 President Bush, overreaching his electoral mandate, urged Congress to allow workers to invest part of their Social Security taxes in personal retirement accounts and to cut Social Security benefits.[51] Public disapproval of the president's Social Security proposal, the failures in Iraq, and his poor handling of Katrina, a destructive hurricane that hit New Orleans in August 2005, helped Democrats regain control of both chambers of Congress in the 2006 midterm elections. That ended any possibility of extending or making permanent President Bush's 2001 and 2003 tax cuts before they were all scheduled to expire at the end of 2010.

George W. Bush—determined not to incur the wrath of antitax Republicans who so tormented his father—accepted Vice President Cheney's claim that "deficits don't matter." With nearly universal support from Republicans and crucial help from some Democrats in Congress, Bush proposed and signed large, regressive, budget-busting tax cuts that increased inequality without providing compensatory economic benefits. He refused to ask the American people to pay for the wars he waged following September 11 and, in another major break with historical precedents, enacted an expensive new prescription drug Medicare benefit funded by federal borrowing. George W. Bush squandered the hard-won government surpluses of the 1990s. George Herbert Walker Bush, the forty-first president, never criticized any of his son's decisions. "I'm the father and it's his turn to make the big calls," he said, "and he should know that his father is either going to be quiet or supportive."[52]

Republicans demonstrated they were willing to spend but not tax. George W. Bush showed that sometimes the apple does fall far from the tree. In 2008 Democrats won the presidency and increased their majorities in the House and Senate. The fate of George W. Bush's tax cuts—scheduled to expire in 2010—now depended on Democrats.

Chapter 13

The Nation Splits Apart

The single most important thing we want to achieve is for President Obama to
be a one-term president.

—REPUBLICAN SENATE LEADER MITCH MCCONNELL,
OCTOBER 2010

George W. Bush's aggressive tax cuts reenergized the antitax movement and
confirmed Republicans' long-standing view that reducing taxes is the best
policy, regardless of the nation's economic or fiscal condition. His successor,
Barack Obama, knew Bush's tax cuts were scheduled to expire at the end of
2010. No one knew how the new president would deal with that. The need to
confront more urgent economic concerns came first.

When Barack Obama took office in January 2009, the economy was in free-
fall. The U.S. economy suffered a stunning decline during the summer and fall
of 2008. During spring 2007, financial institutions began suffering heavy losses
due to the collapse of U.S. real estate prices.[1] In 2008 the stock market tum-
bled, defaults on mortgages became common, and auto sales cratered. The U.S.
economy lost 1,500,000 jobs in the last two months of 2008. The stock market
was down nearly 40 percent. Foreclosures were filed on 2.3 million homes.
Household wealth declined by more than after the 1929 stock market crash.[2]
Median households saw their net worth cut by half, from $107,000 to $57,800.
Minorities were hit especially hard: median Latino households lost more than
80 percent of their wealth between 2009 and 2010; median Black households
saw virtually all their wealth disappear. Minority homeownership collapsed.[3]
The government's finances also suffered: the federal deficit was approaching

$1.4 trillion, nearly 10 percent of economic output, and the federal debt was on its way from 39 percent of GDP in 2008 to 70 percent four years later.

President Obama ran his campaign suggesting he would be a transformative president—promising "hope and change" to a divided nation and optimistically insisting "yes we can." He burst into national prominence when, as an obscure Illinois state senator, he gave a seventeen-minute keynote address to the 2004 Democratic National Convention where he famously proclaimed, "Tonight there is not a liberal America and a conservative America; there is the United States of America. There is not a black America and a white America and Latino America and Asian America; there's the United States of America."[4] He ran for president hoping to unite the country. Obama handily defeated the Republican nominee John McCain in the presidential election, becoming the first Black American to become president.

In 2006 Democrats recaptured a large House majority after more than a decade in the minority. In the 2008 election the financial crisis and its attendant economic collapse produced widespread Democratic victories. In 2009 they held a 77-seat House majority. In the Senate, Democrats gained 8 seats producing a 58 to 41 majority. They added a 59th seat in April 2009 when, after 29 years as a Republican, Pennsylvania senator Arlen Specter became a Democrat. The 60th seat—a filibuster-proof majority—came in July when the contested Minnesota election was finally decided in favor of Democrat Al Franken. The 60-vote majority, however, lasted less than a year. On August 25, 2009, Democratic senator Ted Kennedy died. The Massachusetts governor appointed Democrat Paul Kirk to fill Kennedy's seat, but in January 2010 Republican Scott Brown won the contest to finish Kennedy's term.

Despite the large Democratic congressional majorities, Barack Obama never enjoyed a political honeymoon. Republicans in Congress were intransigent. Populist, antitax forces rose from the Republican Right to help thwart his agenda. And the new president faced the greatest economic challenges since the 1930s.

Efforts to Aid Economic Recovery

The economic crisis facing the Obama administration began in the final years of the Bush presidency, but unlike Herbert Hoover, Gerald Ford, or Jimmy Carter, George W. Bush escaped public wrath and political costs for the economic disaster that began on his watch. Public anger, however, bedeviled Barack Obama's presidency.[5]

Herbert Hoover, summarized the Republicans' position: "I don't think the American people are looking for more big spending and bailouts. They're tightening their belts, and they expect us to do the same."[19] It is difficult to imagine a worse time for government austerity. Eric Cantor asked whether a bigger, permanent tax cut would not work better than increasing spending on what he viewed as failed liberal programs, like food stamps.[20] President Obama's inclusion of middle-class tax cuts and postponement of reductions of the Bush tax cuts for the wealthy failed to attract any Republican support.

Republicans never developed genuine alternatives to Obama's plan. South Carolina senator Jim DeMint attacked Obama's plan as a "trillion-dollar social-ist experiment," "a mugging," and "a fraud."[21] His proposal, "The American Option," offered nearly $3 trillion in tax cuts, making the Bush tax cuts perma-nent, cutting corporate and individual income tax rates, and eliminating estate taxes. Only four Republicans—Susan Collins and Olympia Snowe of Maine, Pennsylvania's Arlen Specter, and Ohio's George Voinovich—voted against DeMint's proposal.

After the Recovery Act passed the House on January 28, 2009, with all Re-publicans and 11 Democrats voting against it, Newt Gingrich addressed House Republicans at a Virginia resort and linked Republicans' unified opposition to Obama's plan with their refusal to vote for Bill Clinton's 1993 tax increases as the way to recapture a House majority. Newt said John Boehner would be-come Speaker of the House "at a speed that will shock the Democrats." Cantor, Ryan, and McCarthy described voting against the Recovery Act as a "very defining moment" for House Republicans. "I think that's when we got our mojo back," McCarthy said.[22] Indiana congressman Mike Pence added, "We lost the legislative battle, but we won the argument. Welcome to the beginning of the comeback."[23] Obama lamented later, "It was the opening salvo in a battle plan that McConnell, Boehner, Cantor, and the rest would deploy with im-pressive discipline for the next eight years: a refusal to work with me or mem-bers of my administration, regardless of the circumstances, the issue, or the consequences for the country."[24]

President Obama entrusted Vice President Joe Biden with rounding up the necessary 60 votes in the Senate. With 58 Democrats, the White House needed at least three Republican votes so no single Republican could be tarred with pushing the bill across the finish line.[25] During his efforts to persuade Repub-lican senators, Biden told President Obama that McConnell's view was: "For the next two years we can't let you succeed in anything. That's our ticket to coming back."[26]

On February 10, 2009, the Senate passed the $787 billion Recovery Act by 61 to 37 with all Democrats and three Republicans, Collins, Snowe, and Specter, voting in favor. On February 17, 2009, President Obama signed the legislation in a small ceremony at the Denver Museum of Nature and Science.[27]

Notwithstanding the Recovery Act's help for the crumbling economy, some economists were disappointed the law did not contain more short-term stimulus; others complained about the large increases in federal deficits and debt. Liberal Democrats believed the legislation was too small to successfully address the crisis. The Tax Policy Center graded the effectiveness of the tax provisions: no As, six Bs, seven Cs, and two Ds, grades that will not produce a bumper sticker for an honor student.[28] A poll found that by 52 to 19 percent people believed Obama had increased middle-class taxes even though he had reduced them.[29] Everyone found something to dislike.

President Obama said, "We still had at least three or four big moves to make in order to end the crisis, each one just as urgent, each one just as controversial, each one just as hard to pull off."[30] The unemployment rate hit 10 percent in October 2009; by mid-2010 it was still 9.5 percent and remained high all year.

Republicans remained united. Grover Norquist said Republican legislators learned their voters did not want them to work with a "Euro-socialist president." The Republican base wanted "knife fighters, not 'collaborators,'" he said. "You could make a list of guys who thought their job was to cut the best deal they could," Norquist added. "Then they'd go home and find out their voters wouldn't be pleased. They'd be pissed."[31] Two days after President Obama signed the economic recovery law, Republicans received a major, unexpected boost from a relatively obscure television personality.

The Tea Party and Its Allies

On February 19, 2009, CNBC Business News commentator Rick Santelli, reporting for the show *Squawk Box* from the floor of the Chicago Mercantile Exchange, assailed an Obama administration proposal to spend $75 billion to lower the mortgage principal of homeowners facing foreclosures. In a rant that quickly went viral, Santelli shouted, "The government is rewarding bad behavior! This is America!" He asked the commodities traders there, "How many of you people want to pay for your neighbor's mortgage that has an extra bathroom and can't pay their bills? Raise your hand." This elicited a loud chorus of groans and boos followed by Santelli yelling, "President Obama are you listening?" Santelli concluded by inviting American "capitalists" to a "Chicago Tea Party" to protest measures to "subsidize the losers' mortgages."[32]

Santelli's rant went viral; he later described it as "the best five minutes of his life."[33] Obama's press secretary rebuked Santelli's diatribe, adding gasoline to a media conflagration. Santelli never mentioned the billions taxpayers provided to bail out financial institutions and their executives.

President Obama initially dismissed Santelli's harangue as "mildly entertaining shtick, intended not to inform, but to fill airtime, sell ads, and make the viewers of 'Squawk Box' feel like they were real insiders—not one of the 'losers.' Who, after all, was going to take such half-baked populism seriously?"[34] But Obama underestimated the anger, fear, and resentment simmering across the country. As Harvard sociologist Theda Skocpol and political scientist Vanessa Williamson discovered in their detailed study of the Tea Party, "disgruntled conservatives" found the antitax Tea Party symbolism of American rebels "opposing tyranny by tossing chests of tea into the Boston Harbor" to be the "perfect rallying point" for "people who feel like the United States as they have known it is slipping away."[35]

Reflecting on Santelli's rant in his presidential memoir, Obama described it as having "foreshadowed so many of the political battles I'd face during my presidency." "What Santelli understood, what McConnell and Boehner understood," Obama wrote, "was how easily that anger could be channeled, how useful fear could be in advancing their cause."[36]

Despite the ambitions of the House's "young guns," the Republican Party seemed languid. The Tea Party emerged to fill the vacuum.

Small Tea Party protests in late February attacking the Recovery Act in dozens of cities around the country might have proved insignificant had they not generated disproportionate media attention, especially on conservative websites, talk radio, and Fox News. The Tea Party movement also received organizational support and crucial funding from Americans for Prosperity and FreedomWorks, antigovernment, antitax successors to Citizens for a Sound Economy.

On April 15, 2009, the income tax filing deadline, with President Obama enjoying a 68 percent favorable rating, hundreds of thousands of Tea Party protesters—carrying antigovernment, antitax, and anti-Obama signs—rallied in cities across the country. The *New York Times* data maven Nate Silver estimated the protesters exceeded 300,000 in 346 cities.[37] In Washington protesters hurled tea bags over the White House fence. Posters used the letters TEA to begin "Taxed Enough Already." One Tea Party slogan was "No public money

Tea Party March on Washington.

for private failure."[38] Large Tea Party protests continued through 2009 and 2010. In 2010 about 800 local Tea Party groups with between 160,000 and 200,000 members were meeting weekly or monthly in all 50 states.[39]

Skocpol and Williamson describe Tea Partiers as typically conservative, white, married, economically comfortable, upper-middle-class Americans older than forty-five. The group included many small-business owners and current or former military personnel—all free-market conservatives. About 40 percent were evangelical Protestants (substantially greater than their share of the population), reflecting the long-standing links of evangelical Christians to the antitax movement. They were pessimistic about the country and its economy. Many believed "America's best days are behind us." They viewed Barack Obama's progressive policies as more threatening than the 2007–9 economic crisis. They prioritized economic concerns over social issues and frequently disagreed about matters important to social conservatives. They did not blame businesses or the super-wealthy for any of America's troubles.[40]

Tea Party supporters opposed taxes and government spending and frequently attacked "handouts" to "unworthy categories of people." Echoing long-standing antitax views, the Tea Partiers took a harsh stance toward public assistance for the poor, opposing anything they perceived to be "welfare." About half had a family member on Medicare or Social Security—which cost much more than welfare—but Tea Party members strongly supported both of those programs as "earned." As Skocpol and Williamson observe, there is a pronounced role of racism in this dichotomy.[41]

Tea Party supporters, more than other conservative groups, believed that "Obama is out to destroy the country."[42] They rejected "government policies that give minorities a shot at equality, and prefer to maintain the advantaged status of native born whites more than non–Tea Party supporters."[43] In a 2013 book on the Tea Party, political scientists Christopher Parker and Matt Barreto found that Tea Party supporters viewed President Obama's election as "a clear threat to the social, economic, and political hegemony to which supporters of the Tea Party had become accustomed."[44] They wrote, "Politics, group-based intolerance, and racism cannot *completely* account for the contempt with which Tea Party supporters hold their president."[45] A group of sociologists concluded that "threats to racial status" stimulated support for the Tea Party among white Americans.[46]

More than two-thirds of Tea Party supporters did not believe Barack Obama is Christian. After Obama released his Hawaii birth certificate in April 2011, a majority of Tea Party supporters still refused to believe he was born in the United States—a view Donald Trump famously promoted in 2011. Tea Party supporters held these views to a much greater extent than other conservatives.[47]

Many signs at Tea Party protests were openly racist. Images of President Obama were photoshopped to make him look like an African witch doctor with a bone through his nose. Some protesters carried signs calling Congress slave owners and taxpayers the n-word.[48] Other posters doctored Obama's face to make him look like a more evil version of the Joker from *The Dark Knight*. It was not the first time, nor the last, that racial anxieties, resentments, and antipathy joined with ideology and self-interest to advance antigovernment, antitax activism.

The Tea Party garnered enormous support from the media, especially Fox News and right-wing talk-radio hosts, such as Rush Limbaugh and Michael Savage. Influential rightist blogs, especially the *Drudge Report* with its three million readers, promoted the Tea Party extensively.[49] On April 6, 2009, Glenn Beck, a successful Fox News personality, urged his viewers to attend an upcoming Tea Party tax-day rally and join Fox News hosts Sean Hannity in Atlanta, Neil Cavuto in Sacramento, Greta Van Susteren in Washington, D.C., and Beck himself in San Antonio.[50] Megyn Kelly, another popular Fox News personality, asked her viewers to "join the Tea Party action from your home" by going to the network's website, which directed viewers to nearby events called "FNC Tea Parties."[51]

Fox News owner Rupert Murdoch set the network's tone, insisting, "They're not extremists. They're moderate centrists." Fox described Tea Partiers as "grassroots," "genuine," "organic," "spontaneous," "independent," and, "mainstream." Bill Kristol, Dan Quayle's former chief of staff and a Republican journalist, said the Tea Party was "the best thing that has happened to the Republican Party in recent times." Newt Gingrich told Fox News, "The Tea Party is a direct threat to the elite left, and the elite left is going berserk." Bill O'Reilly, Fox News' most popular personality, told his viewers, "The American media will never embrace the Tea Party. Why? Generally speaking, they look down on the folks, they think you are dumb."[52]

FreedomWorks, headed by the antitax zealot Dick Armey, played a crucial role ensuring the Tea Party's success. The organization was a keystone of Charles and David Koch's political network, dedicated to an extreme antigovernment free-market agenda.[53] FreedomWorks and its sister Koch organization, Americans for Prosperity, began attacking President Obama's economic recovery proposals on talk radio, in television ads, and on the internet two days after his inauguration.

After Santelli's rant, Americans for Prosperity registered a website called TaxPayerTeaParty.com and mobilized its activist network to begin planning rallies across the country. Americans for Prosperity and FreedomWorks, along with the Cato Foundation, also founded by the Kochs, and the Heritage Foundation, which they contributed to, provided local Tea Party groups with speakers, talking points, press releases, organizational support, and transportation.[54] FreedomWorks posted tips about "How to Organize Your Own 'Tea Party' Protest" and offered advice about locations and signs.[55] The liberal political analyst Thomas Frank observed, "It's a major accomplishment for sponsors like the Kochs that they've turned corporate self-interest into a movement among people on the streets."[56]

Dick Armey gave FreedomWorks the lion's share of credit. "When the Tea Party took off," he claimed, "FreedomWorks had as much to do with making it an effective movement as anyone else. We'd been doing this lonely work for years. From our point of view, it was like the cavalry coming."[57] Arthur Laffer congratulated Beck for the Tea Party's success. Frank Luntz, an enthusiastic Tea Party booster, agreed: "That rant from Santelli woke up the upper middle class and the investor class, and then Glenn Beck woke up everyone else. Glenn Beck's show is what created the Tea Party movement. It started on Tax Day 2009, and it exploded at town hall meetings in July. You can create a mass movement within three months."[58]

As journalist Jane Mayer wrote about the right-wing billionaires and their organizations, which helped mobilize the Tea Party: "They gave the nascent Tea Party movement organization and political direction, without which it might have frittered away like the Occupy movements. The protestors in turn gave the billionaire donors something they'd had trouble buying—the numbers needed to lend their agenda the air of legitimacy."[59] The Tea Party repaid its donors with important, visible, right-wing, populist antitax pressure.

Although Tea Party activists were "better off economically" than most Americans, they were "comfortably middle class," not wealthy—"in contrast to many of the professional advocates and media stars who promoted and profited from the Tea Party label on the national stage."[60] Barack Obama, ironically, had promised to protect nearly all Tea Party members from any tax increase. It was the rich conservative funders and advocates and the supportive media personalities who were threatened by potential tax increases under President Obama. He had made that clear in his 2008 campaign.

Another Democratic Surrender on Taxes

Before he moved into the White House, Barack Obama made a major concession, strengthening the power of the antitax movement. On April 16, 2008, in a Philadelphia debate during the campaign for the Democratic presidential nomination, Barack Obama and Hillary Clinton, responding to a general question about taxes, both pledged not to raise taxes on Americans earning less than $250,000 a year—confirming how politically risky a tax increase on anyone but affluent Americans had become. ABC moderator George Stephanopoulos asked both candidates whether this promise was "an absolute, read-my-lips" pledge—harkening back to George H. W. Bush's 1988 antitax vow. Both Democratic candidates insisted it was.[61] Obama repeated this pledge frequently after the debate and once he took office: no tax increase for anyone making less than $250,000.

This pledge was, of course, insufficient to satisfy Grover Norquist, but it confirmed the political power of the antitax movement. When the two progressive Democrats running for president in 2008 ruled out all tax increases except on the "rich," they ratified the potency of the antitax politics that took hold in the United States four decades earlier.

The antitax movement—the linchpin of Republican economic policy—struck fear into liberal Democrats. Republican dogma insists on no tax increases on anyone, anytime. In the 2008 campaign, raising taxes on anyone but the "rich" and large corporations became taboo for liberal Democrats, hardly a sound way to run an effective, fiscally responsible government.[62] President Obama's vow not to increase taxes on anyone earning less than $250,000 constrained him in 2010 when the Bush tax cuts were scheduled to end.

A Midterm Shellacking

In 2009 President Obama proposed legislation to expand health-care coverage and control costs, modeled after a successful 2006 Massachusetts program initiated by Republican governor Mitt Romney. Following advice from Frank Luntz, who tested dozens of messages opposing the legislation, Republicans characterized Obama's proposal, which maintained the important roles played by private health insurers, as a "government takeover" of the health-care system and "socialized" medical care. Republicans made stopping Obama's health-care proposal a priority. South Carolina senator Jim DeMint told conservative activists, "If we're able to stop Obama on this, it will be his Waterloo. It will break him."[63]

Tea Party activists and their supporters made stopping "Obamacare," as it became known, their principal project in the summer of 2009. During what became known as "Tea Party summer," they disrupted town halls of Democratic lawmakers and held rallies to bolster Republican opposition. Referring to the street associated with Washington lobbyists, Grover Norquist said, "K Street is a $3 billion weathervane. When Obama was strong, the Chamber of Commerce said, 'We can work with the Obama administration.' But that changed when thousands of people went into the street and 'terrorized' congressmen. August is what changed it."[64]

Congress enacted Obama's health-care bill with only Democratic votes. At a White House celebration on March 23, 2010, Obama raised a glass to his political director and said, "You know they're gonna kick our asses over this."[65] Republicans introduced legislation to repeal the Affordable Care Act the day after President Obama signed it. Although they never agreed on what should replace it, on Groundhog Day, February 2, 2016, House Republicans voted for the sixty-third time to repeal it.[66]

The Tea Party played an important electoral role in the 2010 midterms, particularly in Republican primaries, moving an antigovernment, antitax

Republican Party further right. Sean Noble, a political operative from Arizona close to the Koch brothers, worked to make President Obama's worries come true. "We made a deliberate recommendation that you gotta focus on the House," he told the *National Review*. "Obamacare clearly was the watershed moment that provided the juice to deliver the majority back to the Republicans in the House."[67] Noble and his group provided $103 million from undisclosed donors to conservative groups active in the 2010 midterms.[68] Grover Norquist's Americans for Tax Reform received more than $4 million.[69]

President Obama handed his opponents an additional fundraising opportunity by persuading House Democrats to vote for legislation eliminating "a carried-interest" loophole that allows hedge fund and private equity managers to have their compensation taxed at the lower capital gains rate rather than the top rate on wages.[70] Blackstone's Stephen Schwarzman (whose compensation was estimated to be $1.1 billion in 2021) said Obama's effort started a "war," adding, "It's like when Hitler invaded Poland in 1939."[71] Schwarzman later described this as an "inappropriate analogy." Private equity moguls mobilized a campaign against Obama's proposal and the House Democrats who voted for it. Republicans and their supporters spent at least $200 million on the 2010 midterm elections, an amount that stunned President Obama.[72] The carried-interest tax break was retained.

Attempting to replay Newt Gingrich's 1994 Contract with America, the Tea Party released a "Contract from America" at its second tax-day rally on the Washington Mall on April 15, 2010. It called for a single-rate tax system governed by a tax law no longer than the original Constitution, permanent extension of all the Bush tax cuts, and a two-thirds majority to enact any tax increases.[73] Not to be outdone, House Republicans five months later released a twenty-one-page "Pledge to America," a lengthy update to the 1994 "Contract with America." There was substantial overlap with the Tea Party's contract, including making the Bush tax cuts permanent and repealing Obamacare. In a harbinger of future tax cuts, the pledge called for a new tax deduction for 20 percent of small businesses' income.[74]

In 2010 Republicans gained 63 House seats—the largest increase since 1948—producing a Republican House majority of 224 seats to Democrats' 193. Republicans also gained 6 Senate seats, leaving Democrats with a 51-seat majority, plus two independents who caucused with the Democrats. Republicans picked up 675 seats in state legislatures across the country. "It feels bad," Obama said, calling the midterm elections a "shellacking."[75]

Going into 2011, President Obama faced a Republican House determined not to compromise with him on any legislation. The 2010 post-election session of Congress—the last time Democrats controlled the House during his presidency—offered him a brief window of opportunity.

The 2010 Fiscal Cliff

President Obama in the lame-duck session after the 2010 midterms had an opportunity to address the nation's tax system. Obama had long opposed the Bush tax cuts of 2001 and 2003, scheduled to expire at the end of 2010. Ben Bernanke, Federal Reserve chairman, labeled the expirations of the tax cuts a "fiscal cliff."[76] Their termination gave unusual power to the president. Contrary to the normal legislative process, President Obama did not need help from Congress to repeal the Bush tax cuts; he could stand aside and let them expire on December 31, 2010.

Fulfilling his 2008 campaign promise, however, Barack Obama concluded "that the Bush tax cuts [should] be repealed selectively, affecting only those people with annual incomes greater than $250,000 a year."[77] Notwithstanding his limited leverage, Republican Senate Leader Mitch McConnell threatened to block any legislation other than a full extension of the Bush tax cuts. Some Democrats urged the president to let the tax cuts expire, then propose extending all the cuts except those reducing taxes for families earning more than $250,000 in January, daring the House Republican majority to oppose that. But President Obama worried a tax increase might throw the "still fragile economy" back into recession and feared many Democrats might vote with a Republican proposal to make all the Bush tax cuts permanent.[78] He also had other priorities requiring congressional action during the lame-duck session: ratification of a nuclear non-proliferation treaty with Russia which required 67 Senate votes; repeal of the "Don't Ask, Don't Tell" law that barred gays, lesbians, and bisexuals from serving openly in the military; the DREAM Act to establish a path to citizenship for children of undocumented immigrants; and a child nutrition bill, which was Michelle Obama's priority.[79]

The president tasked Joe Biden with negotiating with McConnell over these issues, along with an extension of unemployment benefits and additional tax credits for low-income workers, in exchange for a two-year extension of all the Bush tax cuts. Ultimately Biden struck a deal, and President Obama got additional stimulus spending, a two-year, two-percentage-point reduction in the payroll tax (instead of tax credits for low-wage workers),

Michelle's child nutrition bill, repeal of the Don't-Ask-Don't-Tell legislation, and ratification of the new nuclear arms treaty. The DREAM Act fell five votes short.[80]

This was a reasonable bargain in exchange for extending President Bush's tax cuts at the top for two more years—the only tax reductions that President Obama wanted to eliminate. Obama wrote later, "I was betting that in November 2012 [before the tax cuts expired again], I'd be coming off a successful reelection campaign, allowing me to end the tax cuts for the wealthy from a position of strength."[81]

One consequence of Obama's deal was that 2010 became an advantageous year for very wealthy people to die, the year as Paul Krugman predicted "to throw mama from the train"—or at least from her private jet.[82] The billionaires who died that year free from the estate tax included Mary Janet Cargill, an heir of the Cargill multinational agricultural business; Houston energy tycoon Dan Duncan; California real estate baron Walter Shorenstein; John Kluge, a media magnate who once was America's richest person; and George Steinbrenner, owner of the New York Yankees. Steinbrenner bought the Yankees for about $10 million in 1973, and the team, worth about $1.6 billion in 2010, passed to his heirs free of estate tax. When George's son Hank died in 2020, the team's value was more than $5 billion. Hank's share was worth over $1 billion, but his gains were never subject to capital gains or income tax.

The 2010 Act also created a new opportunity for multimillionaires and billionaires to transfer assets into trusts, enabling them to avoid estate taxes for many generations, in some cases forever. For example, two New York City lawyers in late 2010 each arranged more than $1 billion of tax-free transfers before year's end. Many wealthy people took advantage of this temporary new loophole. In a further blow to progressivity at the very top, Obama's 2010 deal with Congress restored the estate tax in 2011 and 2012 with a $5 million exemption and a 35 percent top rate, leaving common, widespread techniques for avoiding the tax untouched.

The 112th Congress, which began on January 3, 2011, and ended on January 3, 2013, was extremely unproductive: it considered very few bills and enacted very few laws.[83] This inaction was hardly surprising given the political and policy gulfs between the Obama administration and House Republicans.

In 2011 House Republicans refused to raise the federal debt ceiling unless President Obama and Senate Democrats agreed to substantial spending cuts and a balanced-budget constitutional amendment. Congress had raised the debt ceiling—a statutory limit on federal borrowing—eighteen times under President Reagan and seven times under George W. Bush. If the federal government is prohibited from borrowing additional funds to pay for spending previously voted, that could trigger a default on the national debt or delay or eliminate government payments, such as for Social Security, Medicare, or national defense. A default would likely produce catastrophic economic and financial consequences. Republican senator John McCain called holding the debt ceiling hostage for spending cuts "worse than foolish." Adam Posen, president of the Peterson Institute for International Economics, said this was the first time a solvent democracy flirted with default simply out of political stubbornness.[84]

In a victory for the Tea Party, House Republicans, Senate Democrats, and President Obama, on July 31, 2011, agreed to curtail current and future spending in exchange for a debt-ceiling increase. Two days later, on the day the government faced an economic catastrophe by exhausting its ability to borrow, President Obama signed the Budget Control Act of 2011. Matt Kibbe, president of FreedomWorks, said, "When Obama is talking about trillions of dollars in spending cuts, we've changed the conversation."[85] This would not be the last time congressional Republicans held the debt ceiling hostage when a Democrat was in the White House, risking a potentially disastrous default on U.S. debt as a political bargaining chip.

A Second Fiscal Cliff

In November 2012 Barack Obama won reelection, defeating Mitt Romney with 51.1 percent of the popular vote and a 332 to 206 majority in the Electoral College. Democrats gained eight seats, but Republicans retained a large House majority, 234 to 201. Democrats gained two Senate seats and kept the majority with 55 votes. President Obama's second term, like the last two years of his first, was dominated by ongoing conflict with congressional Republicans.

In December 2012 President Obama again enjoyed extraordinary leverage over the tax law. The 2010 extension of the 2001 and 2003 Bush tax cuts expired on December 31, 2012, along with the two-percentage-point reduction in payroll taxes and the extension of unemployment benefits enacted in 2010. More than $500 billion of tax increases and automatic across-the-board spending cuts were scheduled to take effect in 2013, absent new legislation. The economy was stronger than in 2010, but the Congressional Budget Office predicted a short recession if no agreement occurred. Polls showed most Americans would blame Republicans if negotiations with the president failed.[86]

President Obama again sent Joe Biden to negotiate with Mitch McConnell. On January 1, 2013, just before the new Congress was seated, Congress, after acrimonious negotiations, passed the American Taxpayer Relief Act of 2012, which President Obama signed the next day. The new law extended all the Bush tax cuts permanently for all but the top 1 percent, fulfilling President Obama's campaign promise not to raise taxes for people with incomes below $250,000.[87] The legislation raised the top income tax rate from 35 percent to 39.6 percent (the top rate under President Clinton) for married couples with income in excess of $450,000 ($400,000 for singles).[88] The maximum 15 percent capital gains and dividend rate was made permanent except for taxpayers in the top bracket with at least $400,000 of income, who faced a 20 percent rate. The estate tax was preserved for decedents with more than $5.25 million in wealth in 2013 ($10.5 million for married couples), and the estate tax rate was increased from 35 to 40 percent. The two-percentage-point reduction in payroll taxes enacted in 2010 expired, reducing the take-home pay of more than 75 percent of American workers.[89]

The expiration of the Bush tax cuts on December 31, 2012, as scheduled, would have raised $4 trillion over the decade from 2013 to 2022. The new law lost $3.6 trillion of that, making a bad joke of Democrats' efforts in 2001 to limit the costs of President Bush's tax plan to $1.35 trillion rather than the $1.6 trillion President Bush proposed. Even Glenn Hubbard, former chairman of George W. Bush's Council of Economic Advisers, was disappointed. He conceded the 2001 and 2003 tax cuts were not the "best anchoring point." "We need a tax system that can promote economic growth and raise the revenue the American people want to devote to government," he said.[90] But neither party would raise sufficient taxes to pay for the government's spending.

The *Wall Street Journal*, nevertheless, described the 2013 legislation as "the largest tax increase in the past two decades."[91] Newt Gingrich said he would have voted against the bill. Republican Ways and Means chairman Dave Camp of Michigan, in contrast, described the measure as the "largest tax cut in American history." Many progressive Democrats expressed disappointment with President Obama's deal. Paul Krugman, writing in the *New York Times*, said he was "despondent."[92] Bill Kristol blogged, "President Obama has gotten relatively little at his moment of greatest strength."[93]

Grover Norquist, maintaining his status as the arbiter of permissible Republican votes on tax issues, told CNN's Anderson Cooper that voting for the American Taxpayer Relief Act "technically" did not violate his no-tax-increase pledge. Grover said the Bush tax cuts legally expired on December 31, 2012, so Republicans were free to vote for the bill in January.[94] After the vote Grover told NBC's Andrea Mitchell, "No Republican voted for a tax increase"—a surprise to taxpayers at the top who saw their income taxes increase.[95] They, however, blamed Barack Obama and Democrats, not the Republicans.

Why hadn't President Obama played hardball when the Bush tax cuts expired in 2012? He was in his last term, never to face voters again. Having watched Republicans increase deficits by enacting large tax cuts while complaining vigorously about federal debt and deficits, the president may have wondered why a Democratic president should spend his political capital trying to stop the antitax waves. Obama knew what happened after Bill Clinton raised taxes in 1993, ushering in a Republican House majority for the first time in forty years, and no doubt feared allowing a widespread tax increase would greatly enhance the likelihood he would be succeeded by a Republican president. Having extended the vast majority of the Bush tax cuts, he was.

———

Despite Republicans' moaning, they had won the war over taxes. Republicans remained steadfast against tax increases at any time. Democrats had acquiesced, except for tax increases on the "rich," which President Obama defined as families with incomes of at least $250,000 and large corporations. After the 2013 fiscal-cliff agreement, Democrats' minimum threshold for tax increases moved up to $400,000 of income.

During Barack Obama's presidency, the Tea Party, and its allies in the media and organizations funded by rich, antitax conservatives, moved the Republican Party further right. As Christopher Parker and Matt Barreto wrote, "People are driven to support the Tea Party from the anxiety they feel as they perceive the America they know, the country they love, slipping away, threatened by the rapidly changing face of what they believe is the 'real' America: a heterosexual, Christian, middle-class, (mostly) male, white country."[96] The Tea Party's antitax protests were inextricably linked with cultural concerns. During the 2016 presidential election, Tea Party sympathizers obtained more popular support than they anticipated, catapulting their unlikely standard-bearer Donald Trump, a xenophobic and racist "populist," into the White House.

Chapter 14

Tax Cuts Are Trump

Call it the "Cut, Cut, Cut Bill."

—DONALD TRUMP, OCTOBER 2017

Donald J. Trump became a well-known personality in New York first in the gossip columns then on television. He emerged as a national political figure and Tea Party favorite in spring 2011 leading the "birther" movement and insisting Barack Obama was born in Kenya, even after Obama released his birth certificate confirming he was born in Hawaii.[1] To say Trump ran an unconventional campaign for the Republican presidential nomination is understatement. Trump relentlessly assailed alleged villains at home and abroad: Muslim terrorists, brown-skinned immigrants crossing the southern border, and low-wage Asian workers. Contrary to Republican economic orthodoxy, he attacked globalization and free trade. He rejected long-standing Republican efforts to cut social insurance, promising to "save Medicare, Medicaid, and Social Security without cuts."[2] Republican senator Ben Sasse of Nebraska said Trump "waged an effective war on almost every plank of the Republican Party's platform."[3] Trump, however, borrowed the headline pitch for his campaign from Ronald Reagan: "Make America Great Again," implying he planned to restore something taken away from millions of Americans, fueling the politics of victimization, anger, and resentment.[4] His xenophobic and racist messages rallied voters fearful of cultural changes and losing out to others they thought were "cutting in line."[5]

After overpowering 17 contenders for the Republican presidential nomination, Donald Trump pulled off a great upset by defeating Hillary Clinton for the presidency. He lost the popular vote by nearly 3 million votes, but won nearly 63 million votes, the most ever for a Republican candidate, winning the Electoral College 304 to 227. Counties Trump won tended to be suffering from recession or sluggish economic growth.[6] Donald Trump never focused on the nation's income and wealth gaps: instead he gloated about being rich and boasted about paying little or no taxes. Embracing Republican antitax orthodoxy and the Tea Party's rallying cry, Trump promised huge tax cuts. He also claimed he would raise taxes on the rich, including himself—a pose that polled well—although his tax proposals would cut taxes on the wealthy.

Trump's Antithesis

When Donald Trump became president in January 2017, Republicans held a 52 to 48 majority in the Senate and a large House majority. Senate Republican Leader Mitch McConnell said when he learned Trump won the 2016 election, "the first thing that came to my mind was the Supreme Court."[7] Speaker of the House Paul Ryan's Faustian bargain with Donald Trump was about cutting taxes, not appointing right-wing judges. Ryan was the most important member of Congress for advancing President Trump's tax agenda.

Paul Ryan was Donald Trump's antithesis—born and raised in Janesville, Wisconsin, a small town where his great-great-grandfather James Ryan settled after fleeing Ireland in 1851 to escape the potato famine. Ryan still lived on the block where he grew up. When he was a teenager, sixty-seven of his cousins lived nearby. "Our town shaped my values and my worldview," Ryan said. "For me, Janesville was—and is—the embodiment of the American Idea."[8] Nearly every week, after his first election to Congress in 1998 at age twenty-eight, Ryan flew to Washington, sleeping on a cot in his office before returning home.

In high school Ryan worked at McDonald's, washed hearses for a local funeral director, and repaired signs for local dairy farmers. His father, who had a "weakness for drink," died when Paul Ryan was a high school sophomore. After that his family received essential financial help from Social Security survivor benefits.[9]

Before his election to Congress, Ryan worked for Wisconsin senator Bob Kasten, an avid supply-sider, and served as legislative director for the antitax Kansas senator Sam Brownback. During the Clinton administration, Ryan worked closely with Jack Kemp, whom Ryan described as a "huge influence."[10] After Mitt Romney selected Ryan as his vice-presidential running mate in 2012, Nate Silver said Paul Ryan was "the most conservative Republican member of Congress to be picked for the vice-presidential slot since at least 1900."[11] The midwesterner Paul Ryan was a conservative star of the Washington swamp Donald Trump promised to drain.

Paul Ryan wanted to enact large tax cuts and drastically cut government spending on Social Security, Medicare, and Medicaid. In 2005 Ryan said, "The reason I got involved in public service, by and large, if I had to credit one thinker, one person, it would be Ayn Rand." In a 2009 interview, his brother Tobin added, "Paul can still quote every verse out of Ayn Rand."[12]

Speaker Ryan struggled whether to support Trump for president.[13] When Trump accused a judge of bias because of his Mexican heritage, Ryan disavowed Trump's comments as "the textbook definition of a racist comment."[14] In September Ryan disinvited Trump to a joint appearance in Wisconsin after release of Trump's graphic sexist comments and suggestions of sexual assault in a 2005 conversation with the television host Billy Bush.[15] Ryan said he was "sickened by what I heard today." Trump said he apologized, "if anyone was offended."[16]

Paul Ryan never again campaigned with Trump, nor did he rescind his endorsement or pledge to vote for Trump. Ryan knew he needed a Republican president to support the large tax cuts he yearned for; Donald Trump was his only choice.

A President Who Hates Paying Taxes

For more than a half century, presidents released their tax returns, but Donald Trump never did. During their first presidential debate on September 26, 2016, Hillary Clinton attacked Trump, saying, "The only years that anybody's ever seen were a couple of years when he had to turn them over to state authorities when he was trying to get a casino license, and they showed he didn't pay any federal tax." Trump retorted, "that makes me smart."[17] Rush Limbaugh celebrated Trump as "a master of using the tax code legally," claiming naively if Trump had "done all of this illegal stuff . . . it would have caught up with him by now."[18]

Donald Trump claimed to be a self-made billionaire. He said his father gave him an initial loan of $1 million, which he paid back, and he built a real estate empire producing a net wealth of over $10 billion.[19] This was fantasy: after reviewing more than 100,000 pages of confidential records, including more than 200 tax returns filed by his father, Fred Trump, the *New York Times* estimated his father had transferred at least $413 million (adjusted for inflation) to Donald Trump over his lifetime.[20] According to the *Times*, many of these wealth transfers occurred through shell corporations and "dubious tax schemes during the 1990s, including instances of outright fraud" that Donald Trump "participated in."[21]

A pivotal lesson Donald Trump learned is that the IRS is a paper tiger when auditing transactions involving complex legal arrangements and large mis-valuations. When the IRS audited his father's tax returns containing large un-derstatements, the agency increased the taxes due, by $100,000 and $5 million in two cases—tiny adjustments relative to the amounts saved. IRS audits of Donald Trump were similarly ineffectual. Donald Trump and the Trump organizations view their tax returns as opening bids, requiring the IRS to ferret out—if it can—how much their taxes were understated.

The *New York Times* obtained many of President Trump's tax returns. They showed in 10 of the 15 years after 2000, Donald Trump paid no federal income taxes. In 2016 and 2017 he paid only $750.[22] Trump reported $14,222 as his salary for *The Apprentice*, less than the wages of a full-time, minimum-wage employee, and no salary from the more than 200 corporations he ran with mil-lions of income and losses. This gambit allowed him to avoid paying millions in Medicare taxes.[23]

The House Ways and Means Committee in 2019 requested six years of Presi-dent's Trump's returns, which the tax law allows it to obtain. Trump's treasury secretary Steven Mnuchin refused, however, leading to years of litigation fi-nally resolved by the Supreme Court in November 2022.[24] During the last weeks of a Democratic House majority, the committee released Trump's re-turns. In combination with his returns obtained by the *New York Times*, they showed that in 2018, when he had $22 million of gains on properties or invest-ments he sold, he paid $999,466 in taxes (4.5 percent of the gains) because deductions for business losses ran out.[25] (Trump, for example, had claimed a questionable $916 million loss on his 1995 and subsequent tax returns—an amount he never lost.)[26]

The law requires all presidents' tax returns to be audited, but the IRS did not begin auditing President Trump's returns until 2019. The one revenue agent assigned to his complex returns failed to request help from any IRS specialists. Supporting his position that only a cursory examination was neces-sary, the agent "noted that the taxpayer hires a professional accounting firm and counsel to prepare and file his tax returns, and those parties perform the necessary activities to ensure that the taxpayer reports all income and deduc-tion items correctly."[27] This is absurd. Trump's tax returns showed income and deductions from four hundred different entities. Complex returns of wealthy individuals are prepared by professional accountants and lawyers. If the IRS were to accept that as a Good Housekeeping Seal of Approval, it might as well stop auditing these kinds of returns at all, making taxes essentially voluntary for wealthy business owners.[28]

The staff of the Joint Committee on Taxation uncovered numerous issues in Trump's returns that the IRS failed to investigate. These included large "loans" to his children that may have been taxable gifts, a variety of dubious "business" expenses, unreported income from discharges of debt, questionable business losses, and overstated charitable contribution deductions.[29]

The *Washington Post* uncovered federal tax and state law violations in Trump's charitable deductions and illegalities by the Donald J. Trump Foundation.[30] The acting New York State attorney general said Trump's foundation was "functioning as little more than a checkbook to serve Mr. Trump's business and political interests" and engaged in "a shocking pattern of illegality."[31] Donald Trump admitted to nineteen illegal acts and was ordered to pay $2 million, distributed with the foundation's remaining assets to eight charities chosen by a New York state judge.[32] The Trump Foundation was shut down in 2019.

In February 2022 Mazars, Trump's accounting firm, withdrew from representing Donald Trump and his organizations, announcing the financial statements it prepared for him from 2011 to 2020 should not be relied on.[33]

On July 1, 2021, New York indicted the Trump Organization, the Trump Payroll Corporation, and Trump's long-time chief financial officer Allen Weisselberg for defrauding taxes on $1.7 million of compensation received by Weisselberg and his family. These payments included about $360,000 for private school tuition for his grandchildren, more than $100,000 annually in rents for New York City apartments for Weisselberg and family members, and nearly $200,000 in leases for Mercedes-Benz cars. The Trump Organization maintained two sets of books to conceal Mr. Weisselberg's compensation. Daniel Hemel, a University of Chicago Law School tax law professor, described the conduct alleged in the indictment as "blatant tax evasion," "out-and-out tax fraud," and "the type of conduct that puts other people behind bars."[34] In August 2022 Weisselberg pled guilty to crimes of tax fraud and conspiracy in exchange for a lenient sentence of no more than 100 days in prison, a $2 million fine, and agreeing to testify against the Trump Organization.[35] The Trump Organization was convicted of 17 counts of tax fraud, a scheme to defraud, conspiracy, and falsifying business records. It received a $1.6 million penalty, the maximum allowed by New York law. The prosecutor argued at trial that Donald Trump knew of this fifteen-year tax fraud, but he was not charged.

Weisselberg was required to pay nearly $2 million in taxes, penalties, and interest and was sentenced to five months imprisonment on Rikers Island. He steadfastly refused to testify against Donald Trump.[36]

In January 2023 Donald Trump eliminated any lingering doubts about his willingness to evade taxes. Writing on his internet platform Truth Social, Trump questioned whether the agreements that allowed the Trump Organization and Weisselberg to evade taxes on his compensation was "even a crime."[37]

In January 2016 Donald Trump said, "I try to pay as little tax as possible, because I hate what they do with my tax money." "I hate the way they spend *our money*, the way they give it to Iraq, the way they give it to Iran," he added.[38] But precious little tax money came from Donald Trump. The sentiment attributed to Oliver Wendell Holmes, "I like to pay taxes. Taxes are what we pay for civilized society," seems a minority view.[39]

During his campaign, Trump advanced two kinds of tax proposals: (1) cutting corporate and individual income taxes and repealing the estate tax, which would lower taxes for most Americans, especially wealthy people like him; and (2) increasing tariffs—taxes on imported goods. Tax cuts came first.

Trump and Ryan Propose Large Tax Cuts

Donald Trump's calls for tax cuts were common for a Republican president but were exceptionally large for a growing economy facing large deficits. Singing from the classic antitax songbook, Trump insisted his tax cuts would not add to federal deficits or debt. He said they would be paid for by eliminating unspecified loopholes "for special interests and the very rich" and by cutting spending "without losing anything." Those claims were as farfetched as Trump's assertions that "it's going to cost me a fortune."[40] Newt Gingrich, a close Trump campaign advisor, and Grover Norquist applauded Trump's plan.

In an August 2016 speech Trump modified his tax plan to conform more closely to House Republicans' proposals, including a top individual income tax rate of 33 percent—a move bolstering the support of Speaker Ryan and his colleagues.[41] The conservative Tax Foundation estimated these changes reduced the costs of Trump's plan over the following decade from $10 trillion to between $2.6 trillion and $3.9 trillion, taking into account the substantial additional economic growth the Tax Foundation predicted.[42]

Paul Ryan long insisted large deficits and rising federal debt were the country's most serious economic problems, and he proposed offsetting his massive tax-cut proposals by slashing federal spending on health care, including Medicare and Medicaid, and Social Security.[43] The nonpartisan Tax Policy Center concluded Ryan's tax proposals would still produce huge deficits, a result Ryan denied.[44] "For too long," Ryan said, "policymakers in Washington have traveled the path of least resistance . . . of relentless spending and constant borrowing. This path has left us on the brink of a national bankruptcy, and continuing down it will push our nation into a debt crisis characterized by uncontrollable interest rates . . . unsustainable taxes . . . and an unprecedented economic collapse."[45] Despite increasing debt and deficits, House Republicans voted for Ryan's proposals every year from 2011 to 2016.[46]

Unlike Ryan and his Republican House colleagues, Trump insisted he would not cut Medicaid, Medicare, or Social Security benefits. The only major spending cut Trump and Ryan agreed on was to "repeal and replace" President Obama's Affordable Care Act—although neither offered any replacement. Their efforts to repeal Obamacare collapsed when three Republican senators, Susan Collins, Lisa Murkowski, and John McCain, voted "no." Tax cuts became Republicans' sole opportunity for legislative success.

In June 2016 Ryan and Kevin Brady, the conservative Texas Republican Ryan chose to head the Ways and Means Committee, released wide-ranging tax proposals supported by House Republicans called *A Better Way: A Pro-Growth Tax Code for All Americans*.[47] Their "Better Way" proposed replacing the corporate income tax with a 20 percent tax on goods and services consumed in the United States. The press labeled the proposal, which resembled a sales or value-added tax with a deduction for wages, a "border-adjustment tax (BAT)."[48] Like value-added taxes around the world, the BAT would have taxed imports and exempted exports. Because the United States imports hundreds of billions of dollars more than it exports every year, the BAT would have produced more than $1 trillion over the coming decade to help pay for other tax cuts.[49]

Ryan and Brady, of course, claimed their large tax cuts would generate economic growth sufficient to balance the federal budget. The Tax Policy Center, to the contrary, estimated the Ryan-Brady plan would increase the federal debt by $3 trillion in its first decade and another $3.6 trillion over the following ten years. The Tax Policy Center also estimated 99.6 percent of their tax cuts would go to the top 1 percent.[50] Republicans who claimed reducing deficits was their top priority were again willing to sacrifice fiscal responsibility to cut taxes for wealthy individuals and businesses. Large importers, the Treasury, and Republican senators ultimately opposed the BAT, and it died a quiet death.[51] When the BAT officially died, Lloyd Doggett, a Texas Democrat, observed, "Republicans have created a trillion-dollar hole in their plan."[52]

On April 26, 2017, President Trump released one page with bullet points describing his tax plan, titled: "The Biggest Individual and Business Tax Cut in American History."[53] Trump proposed changing individual tax rates to three brackets with a top rate of 35 percent, doubling the standard deduction, eliminating deductions for state and local taxes, reducing corporate and partnership tax rates to 15 percent, revising international taxation of multinational corporations, and repealing the estate tax. Trump also suggested eliminating tax "breaks for special interests," without specifying any. He said the Trump administration would "continue working with the House and Senate to develop the details of a plan that provides massive tax relief, creates jobs and makes America more competitive—and can pass both chambers."[54]

Trump's one-pager was a sharp departure from previous presidents who detailed their tax proposals in annual budgets, supplemented by many pages of Treasury Department explanations. In 1985, for instance, Ronald Reagan released nearly five hundred pages describing his tax-reform proposals.

President Trump dispatched his two key economic advisors, Treasury Secretary Steven Mnuchin and White House chief economic advisor Gary Cohn, to explain his tax plan to reporters. Mnuchin and Cohn had been executives at Goldman Sachs. Mnuchin, who served as the firm's chief information officer, left after seventeen years in 2002 with nearly $60 million in stock and cash compensation. In 2016 he became national finance chairman for Trump's campaign. Cohn, a smart, arrogant Democrat, was president and chief operating officer of Goldman Sachs before coming to the White House after the firm provided him a $285 million severance package. At their press briefing, Mnuchin claimed Trump's plan would "pay for itself with growth and with . . . reduction of different deductions and closing loopholes."[55] That did not happen.

Gary Cohn soon learned President Trump had little interest in the tax bill's details so long as Trump's financial interests were protected and he "could call it a win." Trump told Cohn, "I'll take the top personal rate to 44 percent [from its 39.6 percent level] if I can get the corporate rate to 15 percent." "Sir," Cohn responded, "you can't take the top rate up. You just can't." Trump asked why not. Cohn explained, "You're a Republican."[56] What Cohn did not say was that the congressional Republican debt and deficit scaremongers preferred larger deficits and growing debt to raising rates at the top.

On July 27, 2017, the self-styled "Big Six"—Mnuchin, Cohn, Ryan, Brady, Senate Finance Committee chairman Hatch, and Republican Majority Leader

McConnell—released a statement describing their goals for tax legislation: to increase economic growth through lower tax rates on businesses and individuals, reform international tax rules, achieve greater fairness (principally through lower taxes on families with children), and reduce complexity.[57] Forty-five of the forty-eight Senate Democrats sent McConnell a letter containing three principles for tax reform, two of which were that it neither "benefit the wealthiest individuals" nor "increase the deficit."[58] McConnell rejected those constraints in a Kentucky minute.

Two months later the Big Six released nine pages listing their proposed changes, called a "Unified Framework for Fixing Our Broken Tax Code."[59] One large New York law firm told its clients the Sixers handed us a frame without a picture.[60] Less than three months after that, with no public hearings and input almost exclusively from businesses, high-income constituents, and their lobbyists, Republicans filled in the picture with more than five hundred pages of far-reaching tax changes officially estimated to reduce government revenues by $1.5 trillion during the next decade—a gross understatement facilitated by ploys, such as terminating large middle-class cuts at the end of 2025 to comply with congressional budget scorekeeping.

On November 29, 2017, President Trump gave a long speech in Missouri emphasizing the tax cuts would benefit the middle class. He falsely insisted the new law would increase his taxes and those of his wealthy friends. "I think my accountants are going crazy right now," he claimed, adding, "It's all right. Hey look I'm President. I don't care. I don't care anymore. Some of my wealthy friends care. Me, I don't care. This is a higher calling."[61] His gullible audience cheered, even though the bill preserved massive tax benefits for real estate and lowered taxes for partnerships—the way Donald Trump's business empire is organized.[62] Trump added, "we're going to try our best" to repeal the estate tax.[63]

On December 22, 2017, President Trump signed the tax-cut legislation—the first time in modern history that Republicans enacted major tax cuts without any Democratic votes. Having been frozen out, Democrats howled. Nancy Pelosi, the House Democratic Leader, called the law "Armageddon," saying a "dark cloud hangs over our negotiations on keeping the government open."[64]

Paul Ryan was happy. But he was done. He got the tax cuts he pushed for but, like David Stockman in the 1980s, not the large spending cuts he wanted. On April 11, 2018, he announced he would not seek reelection, saying he wanted to spend more time with his family.[65] The *Washington Post* wrote that Ryan left "a legacy of . . . immense deficits, a GOP president unchecked . . .

Speaker Ryan, President Trump, and Vice President Pence celebrate passing the 2017 tax cuts.

and a party that's fast abandoning the free trade principles that he himself championed."[66] Donald Trump tweeted Ryan "is a truly good man," adding "we are with you Paul."[67]

The Cut, Cut, Cut Act

The budget resolution allowing the Senate to pass tax cuts with 51 votes permitted the bill to lose $1.5 trillion in revenue over the ten-year budget period. Reprising George W. Bush's gambit of stuffing trillions of dollars of tax cuts into ten-year budget-constrained tax legislation, Republicans terminated popular individual tax cuts at the end of 2025. They assumed any president would extend the cuts for middle-income individuals, like Barack Obama did in 2010 and 2013. The less-popular corporate cuts were made permanent. Republicans also enacted some delayed tax increases unlikely ever to take effect. The Committee for a Responsible Federal Budget estimated the 2017 tax bill would cost at least $3 trillion through 2029 if its expiring provisions were extended.[68] The 2017 tax law introduced large new differences in income taxes depending on how a business is organized, what kind of business is being conducted, and where people invest, live, and work. President Trump urged Paul Ryan to call the 2017 law the "Cut, Cut, Cut Bill." House Republicans labeled it the "Tax Cuts and Jobs Act."[69]

President Trump claimed the tax cuts would provide "rocket fuel for the economy" and help "the folks who work in the mailrooms and the machine shops of America—the plumbers, the carpenters, the cops, the teachers, the pipe-fitters, the people that like me best."[70] The Tax Policy Center, to the contrary, found that in 2018 taxpayers in the middle (with incomes between about $49,000 and $86,000) received a tax cut around $900 or 1.6 percent of their after-tax income. In contrast, taxpayers in the top 5 percent (with incomes between about $308,000 and $733,000) received a cut of about 4.1 percent, and those in the top 1 percent (with income greater than $733,000) got an average cut of $51,000 or 3.4 percent of their after-tax income.[71] This may explain why few Americans believed they got a tax reduction, even though nearly two-thirds did. One Associated Press poll revealed nearly two of every three people said their taxes went up in 2018.[72]

The 2017 law doubled the estate tax exemption from $5.5 million to $11 million ($22 million for a married couple, which rose to nearly $26 million by 2023 because of increases for inflation). The increased exemption was estimated to cost $83 billion by 2025 when it, like the other provisions affecting individuals, is scheduled to expire. The number of wealthy people subject to the estate tax dropped from more than 50,000 in 2001 to about 1,800 in 2019, and the 2017 changes saved the one-in-a-thousand decedents rich enough to be taxable about $4.4 million each.[73]

Wealthy real estate investors, like Donald Trump and his children, did quite well. In addition to the estate tax changes, they got lower income tax rates for partnerships—about 70 percent of which benefited the top 1 percent.[74] A unique capital gains tax break was preserved only for real estate.[75] As David Wessel, a former *Wall Street Journal* journalist, details in his book *Only the Rich Can Play*, the 2017 law also allows real estate investors to avoid capital gains taxes through an innovative, trickle-down, tax break enacted at the behest of Napster and Facebook billionaire Sean Parker.[76] Capital gains taxes are reduced when proceeds are reinvested in designated "opportunity zones" and held for seven years and eliminated entirely when the investments are held for a decade or more. Proponents claimed this tax break would raise up collapsed and collapsing neighborhoods. However, as Wessel shows, it produced "an archipelago of tax havens" in 8,764 "opportunity zones" across the country.[77]

Congressional scorekeepers estimated the opportunity-zone tax break would cost $1.6 billion over ten years, but this is a gross understatement: the provision pushed its largest revenue costs beyond the ten-year congressional budget window. Congress also underestimated opportunities for tax-avoidance investments in gentrifying communities. Governors select eligible "opportunity zones" without meaningful constraints. Florida's governor Rick Scott picked a marina harboring 300-foot yachts in West Palm Beach. Chris Sununu, New Hampshire's governor, chose a 300-square-mile tract that includes his family's ski resort. Nevada's governor selected an area around the Las Vegas football stadium and another where Tesla had built a Gigafactory for making batteries and motors. New York's Andrew Cuomo picked a Brooklyn neighborhood with median home values of about $1 million. California's Democratic governor chose gentrifying tracts in Berkeley, Oakland, and San Francisco. With virtually no oversight, millions of dollars are flowing to places that need no tax breaks; some money nonetheless will go to disadvantaged communities.[78]

The most important change for middle-class Americans was doubling the standard deduction, which simplified tax-return filing for many Americans. President Trump and Paul Ryan claimed most taxpayers could file tax returns on a simple postcard. On June 25, 2018, the Internal Revenue Service unveiled the new postcard form. Treasury Secretary Mnuchin hailed it, saying, "The new postcard-size Form 1040 is designed to simplify and expedite filing tax returns, providing much-needed tax relief to hardworking taxpayers."[79] The new form added six new schedules to Form 1040, making the total more than thirty. Forbes magazine said, "You . . . might flashback to those college assignments where you spent hours shrinking the font, rather than editing your work, to make the text fit."[80]

Congress also limited deductions for state and local income and property taxes to $10,000, raising more than $1 trillion over a decade and targeted by congressional Republicans at voters in high-tax Democratic states. Several northeastern states challenged the limit as unconstitutional, but their lawsuits failed. In another effort to increase taxes of political opponents, the 2017 Act imposed a low-rate tax on the investment income of nearly forty university endowments: Harvard, Stanford, and Yale paid the most. Amherst, Swarthmore, and Williams were also hit. So was Notre Dame, which was not targeted.[81]

Tariff Man

After signing huge tax cuts, his major domestic legislative achievement, Donald Trump departed from Republican antitax and economic orthodoxy by imposing large tariffs.[82] Congress would not have approved Trump's efforts to increase prices on imported goods by enacting tariffs, but the law allowed President Trump to impose tariffs unilaterally when he claimed to be responding to national security threats.[83] From the nation's founding to the Civil War, tariffs were the most important source of U.S. revenues and were again from the late nineteenth century until World War I.[84] After World War II, both parties supported agreements to liberalize international trade and reduce tariffs. In 1988 President Reagan said, "One of the key factors behind our nation's great prosperity is the open trade policy that allows the American people to freely exchange goods and services with free people around the world."[85] Reagan's embrace of international trade and reducing or eliminating tariffs confirmed Republican commitments to free markets and limited government.

Most economists agree that freer trade has enriched the United States. Gary C. Hufbauer and Lucy Lu estimated that from 1950 to 2016 trade liberalization, along with cheaper communication and transportation costs, increased total U.S. GDP by $2.1 trillion.[86] But not everyone wins from freer trade. Consumers benefit through greater choice and lower prices, but some workers see their wages diminished or lose jobs.[87]

In March 2018 President Trump announced a 25 percent tariff on steel imports, reprising a long history of ineffectual presidential efforts to protect the U.S. steel industry by taxing imports. In 2018 the United States had fewer steelworkers than manicurists.[88] Trump added a 10 percent tariff on aluminum. He initially exempted imports from allies, including Canada, the European Union, Japan, and Mexico, but in June he ended the exemptions, prompting widespread retaliation, with those countries raising tariffs on U.S. agricultural and other products. *Washington Post* columnist Catherine Rampell quipped, "So you're telling me my Subaru is a national security threat."[89]

Trump also imposed tariffs up to 25 percent on $234 billion of Chinese imports and threatened tariffs on $300 billion more. Attacking China was good politics: Trump's strategist Steve Bannon crowed, "the politics now drive the economics."[90] China responded with tariffs on U.S. goods, initially focusing on agricultural products such as soybeans, corn, pork, and poultry. U.S. farm income dropped by about half, from $123.4 billion in 2013 to $63 billion in 2018. In 2019 Trump transferred $16 billion to help offset farmers' losses.[91] President Trump erroneously insisted his tariffs produced job increases and claimed falsely that China paid for his tariffs, not American consumers.[92] He insisted his trade war with China was highly popular with his political base and would help him win reelection in 2020 despite the immediate economic pain. Trump called himself "tariff man."[93]

Grover Norquist objected. "Tariffs are taxes," he said. "It's a weapon, tariffs, that raise the costs of goods and services on Americans. Tariffs on Chinese goods are paid by American consumers. You're shooting your own team."[94]

Trump's tariffs failed to improve the nation's trade balance with China. In 2016 the U.S. imported $462.4 billion of goods from China and exported $115.6 billion, for a trade deficit of $346.8 billion. In 2021, the U.S. exported goods totaling $151.4 billion and imported $504.3 billion, for a $352.9 billion trade deficit.[95] Nor did Trump's tariffs change China's state-run mercantilist economy.

Trump's tariffs were the most extensive since the harmful Smoot-Hawley tariffs of the early 1930s. In 2019 they were expected to raise $72 billion of revenue, one of the largest tax increases as a percentage of GDP since 1993.[96] These revenues, however, were small compared to the 2017 tax cuts. Wages rose a bit for workers in sectors protected by the tariffs, but price increases were substantially larger; American consumers' and producers' disposable income was reduced by nearly $69 billion.[97] Federal Reserve economists reported that Trump's tariffs reduced U.S. manufacturing jobs overall.[98] Trade experts estimated the steel and aluminum tariffs cost American consumers and businesses about $900,000 for every job they saved or created.[99] In August 2023 Trump indicated, if reelected, he would impose 10 percent tariffs on all imports, raising prices by more than $300 billion a year before any retaliations.

Massive Increases in the Federal Debt

Republican deficit hawks, like Speaker Ryan and Republican senator Bob Corker of Tennessee who insisted he would not vote for any tax legislation if it "added one penny to the deficit," became hummingbirds in voting for the 2017 tax cuts. Corker confessed, "If [the tax bill] ends up costing what has been laid out, it could well be one of the worst votes I've made."[100] It will cost much more than those estimates.

Secretary Mnuchin continued to repeat the discredited claim that "this tax law will not only pay for itself but in fact create additional revenue for the government."[101] The Congressional Budget Office estimated the 2017 tax law would add nearly $2 trillion to federal deficits over the next decade—after accounting for increased economic growth and assuming fancifully that all of the individual tax cuts scheduled to expire in 2025 will not be extended.[102]

In July 2018 Trump told Fox News, "We have $21 trillion in debt. When [the 2017 tax cut] really kicks in, we'll start paying off that debt like water."[103] A week later, he credited his tariffs with reducing the debt. Trump's tariffs raised an additional $71 billion in 2019, enough to pay for about six weeks' interest on the federal debt if Trump had not sent nearly half that revenue to compensate farmers for their lost exports.[104] In 2019, when the nation's economy was strong, federal revenues were 16.3 percent of GDP, a percentage point below the average for the previous 50 years. Spending was 21 percent of GDP, above the 50-year average of 20.4 percent. The deficit was $984 billion.[105]

A detailed analysis by the conservative Manhattan Institute concluded (based on ten-year estimates) that President Trump enacted $7.8 trillion of new initiatives (assuming the 2017 tax cuts actually expire at the end of 2025) offset by nearly $3.9 trillion in better economic growth and lower interest rates than expected. During his four years in office, he added more in federal spending and tax cuts than President George W. Bush ($6.9 trillion) or President Obama ($5.0 trillion) in their eight years.[106] During the decade from 2010 to 2019, federal spending averaged 21.3 percent of GDP while revenues averaged 16.4 percent. When Donald Trump—the self-proclaimed "king of debt"—left office in January 2021 after the Covid pandemic hit, the national debt was 39 percent higher than when he took office.[107] The total federal debt exceeded 100 percent of the size of the economy for the first time since World War II, rapidly approaching the highest amount in the nation's history.[108] CBO director Phillip Swagel said, "Not since World War II has the country seen deficits during times of low unemployment that are as large as we project—nor, in the past century, has it experienced large deficits for as long as we project."[109]

In August 2020, responding to the Covid pandemic, President Trump signed an order allowing workers to postpone paying their payroll taxes until 2021, but few workers or employers other than in the federal government accepted that invitation. Trump also promised, if reelected in November, to terminate payroll taxes.[110] It was difficult to know what such a drastic action would mean for Social Security and Medicare's hospital insurance, which are funded by these taxes, or for deficits and the federal debt. Trump did not clarify that: at a press conference, he said, "And now, at the end of the year, on the assumption that I win, I'm going to terminate the payroll tax, which is another thing that some of the great economists would like to see done. We'll be paying into Social Security through the General Fund. And it works out very nicely."[111] Trump failed to win reelection in 2020, and that proposal quietly disappeared.

———

The nation did not need and could not afford tax cuts of the magnitude the Republicans enacted in 2017. A few years earlier, the Republican chairman of the Ways and Means Committee demonstrated how economic and simplification benefits comparable to the 2017 legislation could be achieved without losing revenue or cutting taxes at the top, but he attracted no support from his colleagues.[112] Since California adopted Proposition 13 in 1978, antipathy to taxes is one thing that Trumpers, never-Trumpers, businesses large and small, social conservatives, and Christian evangelicals agree about. Republicans always embrace tax cuts. Democrats are willing to raise taxes only on wealthy people and large corporations—and many are reluctant even to do that. Democratic votes from 1981 through 2016 helped enact the large tax cuts of that period. In 2017 Republicans were able to pass massive tax cuts without any votes from Democrats. After the 2017 cuts, federal taxes were low in the United States compared to our nation's historical experience, but the antitax movement has erected very high hurdles for raising taxes.

In November 2020 Joe Biden defeated Donald Trump. Unlike presidential candidates who preceded him, President Trump refused to accept his loss, trying to reverse the vote and claiming he won reelection. On January 6, 2021, President Trump's supporters attacked and ransacked the Capitol building in an unsuccessful effort to halt congressional certification of Biden's victory. During his campaign, President Biden urged rolling back Trump's tax cuts for corporations and wealthy Americans, but it would not be easy to convince the slim Democratic congressional majority to do that.

Chapter 15

Tax the Rich?

Nobody making less than $400,000 will pay a penny more in taxes.

—PRESIDENT JOE BIDEN

Economists debate the exact numbers, but no one doubts the rich have become much richer since the late 1970s. According to Federal Reserve economists, in 2019 the wealthiest 10 percent of U.S. households owned about 70 percent of the country's wealth; the top 1 percent nearly one-third.[1] As Vermont senator Bernie Sanders has complained, the richest 400 Americans own more assets than the bottom half of the population—more than 150 million people—and the 25 highest-earning hedge fund managers make more income than the total wages of 425,000 public school teachers.[2] The Democrats challenging for the 2020 presidential nomination urged increasing taxes on the rich, a prospect popular with a majority of the American people.

Pew Research concluded: "far more Americans continue to say they are bothered 'a lot' by the feeling that some corporations and wealthy people do not pay their fair share of taxes than by the complexity of the system or even the amount they pay in taxes."[3] Numerous polls agree, but as a Gallup researcher cautioned, and the temporary repeal and shrinking of the estate tax demonstrated, reducing wealth and income inequality is a high priority for only a small slice of Americans and rarely makes the top half in rankings of issue priorities.[4] Americans want to become rich themselves.

During the 2020 presidential campaign, Joe Biden took a less aggressive stance on taxing the rich than the Democratic competitors to his left, shunning proposals by Senators Elizabeth Warren and Sanders to impose annual taxes on the wealth of the "extremely" rich. Biden's signature tax promise was not to raise taxes on Americans with less than $400,000 of income. "Nobody," he said, "making under $400,000 bucks would have their taxes raised, period, bingo."[5] The $400,000 threshold was the level for increasing the top income tax rates Biden had negotiated during the Obama administration. According to the Penn-Wharton Budget Model, ignoring corporate tax increases, Biden's proposals implied no tax increase for the bottom 90 percent and an average $5.00 tax increase for households between 90 and 95 percent. Almost 97 percent of his proposed tax increases would be paid by the top 1 percent.[6] Biden promised to cut taxes for the middle class, boost manufacturing in the United States, and "help working families immediately by making the super-rich" and large corporations "finally pay their fair share."[7]

In a campaign ad, Biden contrasted the taxes paid by firefighters, teachers, and nurses with those paid by Donald Trump, who became Biden's archetype of a wealthy American who did not pay his fair share. Biden's campaign sold bumper stickers saying, "I Paid More in Taxes than Donald Trump."[8]

Antitax Republicans, like Grover Norquist, attacked Biden's proposals, focusing especially on Biden's proposals to raise taxes on large businesses. Grover said corporate tax increases would likely raise prices to consumers, clearly so for regulated utilities, reduce the value of Americans' retirement accounts, and, over time reduce workers' wages.[9]

As Donald Trump grudgingly moved out of the White House in January 2021 and Joe Biden moved in, the Senate was evenly divided with Vice President Kamala Harris holding the tie-breaking vote. Democrats held a narrow nine-vote majority in the House, so they could not lose more than four votes on any partisan issue. Of course, no Republican in Congress would vote for any of President Biden's tax-increase proposals. The question for President Biden was whether the Democrats in Congress would.

More Massive Spending

In 2020, soon after the coronavirus pandemic hit, Congress added about $3 trillion in spending and tax breaks to address the public health and economic challenges.[10] Subsequent legislation was smaller and more contentious, but legislation reluctantly signed by Donald Trump on December 27, 2020, added another $900 billion in Covid relief spending and funded the government through September 2021, averting a potential government shutdown.

The American Rescue Act, signed by President Biden on March 11, 2021, added an additional $1.9 trillion in spending and tax cuts to address ongoing difficulties from Covid and fulfill some Democratic policy priorities, such as paid family leave and expanded tax credits for children and childcare. This legislation passed the House by a vote of 220–211, with all but one Democrat voting for it and all the Republicans voting against. The Senate vote was 50–49, also on strictly partisan lines. According to the Tax Policy Center, 70 percent of the tax cuts in the Rescue Act went to families with less than $91,000 of income, providing $3,000 on average, more than $6,000 to families with children. About 80 percent of these tax benefits expired at the end of 2021.[11]

The most important assistance in the Rescue Act was the expansion of tax credits for children under age seventeen from $2,000 to $3,000 and to $3,600, for children under six years old, paid monthly. According to Columbia University's Center on Poverty and Social Policy, the enhanced credits for children benefited sixty million families and lifted three to four million children out of poverty without causing any significant reduction in whether their parents worked.[12] Nonetheless, public polls revealed lukewarm support for the expanded child credits, and they expired at the end of 2021, returning to their 2020 level of $2,000 and applying to many fewer low-income families.[13] Absent new legislation, child credits will revert to $1,000 for eligible families in 2025 when the 2017 tax cuts are scheduled to expire.

One unintentional consequence of the Rescue Act was enabling states to cut taxes in 2022. The legislation provided states and localities $500 billion in additional grants to relieve Covid costs and bolster education, public transportation, and other state and local programs. Previous federal spending to address the pandemic also boosted state and local tax revenues through generous grants, tax credits, and loans to keep businesses operating; expansions of unemployment benefits to help keep jobless workers afloat; and stimulus checks to most Americans. As a consequence, total state and local revenues were greater in 2021 than in 2019 before the pandemic hit when the economy was strong.[14] Numerous states enacted tax cuts in 2022, including some led by Democrats. Republican governors in Iowa, Missouri, South Carolina, and Utah, to name four, proposed large income tax cuts, and in the nation's poorest state, Mississippi, the Republican governor (with encouragement from Grover Norquist) proposed eliminating the state income tax and cutting sales and car taxes—not what the Democrats in Congress and the White House intended for federal money borrowed to finance the Rescue Act.[15]

In 2021 inflation reemerged, hitting levels unseen since the 1980s. Coupled with resistance to large spending and tax increases from moderate Democrats, this hampered efforts by President Biden and liberal Democrats to enact large spending proposals for what Democratic House Speaker Nancy Pelosi called "human infrastructure."[16] President Biden's "Build Back Better" proposals, announced in April, called for more than $2 trillion in additional spending.[17] They were too large for moderate Senate Democrats, notably West Virginia's Joe Manchin and Kyrsten Sinema of Arizona, and too small for liberals, such as Bernie Sanders, who introduced a $6 trillion plan. Manchin and Sinema were also reluctant to support tax increases to pay for additional spending.

Ultimately in 2021 and 2022 the Biden administration and Democratic Congress spent large sums to aid middle-class and low-income workers by attempting to preserve and create jobs, expand and extend health-care subsidies, and increase and expand tax credits for children, adding nearly $5 trillion in new spending, financed mostly by borrowing.[18] Despite President Biden's promises to tax only affluent Americans, some polls showed more than 60 percent of voters believed he would raise taxes on the middle class.[19] Many middle-class Republicans undoubtedly heard from Republican media, including Fox News and talk radio, how Biden's proposed corporate tax increases would hurt consumers and workers. Others simply did not believe the president's claims that his proposals would not hurt them. Even with Biden's $400,000 threshold for any tax increases, wresting antitax voters from the GOP remained a difficult hurdle for Democrats.

Difficulties of Taxing the Rich

Democrats across the country ran for office in 2020 claiming they would repeal President Trump's 2017 tax cuts and raise tax rates on rich individuals and large corporations, but with only 50 Democrats in the Senate and universal opposition from Republicans, one Democratic defection could block a tax increase. Undaunted, President Biden proposed large tax increases on high-income individuals. In March 2021 he recommended raising the top 37 percent individual income tax rate (then applicable to single people with $523,600 of income, married couples with $628,300) to the 39.6 percent rate enacted during the Clinton administration. He also urged taxing capital gains at ordinary income rates for people with income over $1 million, treating gifts and bequests of appreciated property as taxable sales, and eliminating the ability to escape taxation on capital gains by holding assets until death (for gains greater than $1 million per person with exceptions for family-owned-and-operated businesses). He proposed closing loopholes enabling individuals to avoid the 3.8 percent tax on investment income and other Medicare taxes through partnerships and companies not subject to the corporate tax. In addition, he urged Congress to eliminate the ability of private equity and hedge fund partners to be taxed at capital gains rates on fees for their services rather than at the ordinary rates applicable to other compensation—a tax advantage for "carried interests"—renewing a decades-long effort to eliminate this tax break.[20]

In June 2021 the Biden administration received a boost for its tax efforts when a group of investigative *ProPublica* journalists published a series of articles based on a trove of IRS data revealing the income, taxes, investments, stock trades, gambling winnings, and results of IRS audits of thousands of the wealthiest Americans—information which the IRS is required by law to keep private.[21] The first was a blockbuster article revealing that Jeff Bezos and Elon Musk, the world's two richest men, along with billionaires Michael Bloomberg, Carl Icahn, and George Soros, had paid no income taxes in some of the prior fifteen years, and Warren Buffett, among others, paid remarkably little.[22] The *ProPublica* exposés received widespread coverage by newspapers, radio, and television and on the internet. *ProPublica* journalists estimated that the 25 richest Americans, worth a combined $1.1 trillion, paid 3.4 percent in taxes from 2014 through 2018 on total wealth increases of over $400 billion—compared to the 14 percent paid on average by median households with about $70,000 in earnings. The writers claimed it would take 14.3 million "ordinary American wage earners" to equal the wealth of the top 25.

The technique detailed in the first article is simple: "buy, borrow, and die," a phrase coined years ago by University of Southern California law professor Edward McCaffery. Rich Americans borrow cheaply against their stock and bond portfolios to fund their lifestyles without paying any income taxes.[23] Increases in the values of assets are not taxed as income until the assets are sold, and the tax law forgives any income tax on a lifetime of gains if assets are held until death. Nor does the law tax borrowed funds even when the amounts borrowed exceed the original costs of assets used to justify or secure the amounts borrowed. So, the appreciation in asset values can be cashed out and spent free from any income tax whenever assets are held until death.

As the *ProPublica* article put it, "The IRS records show that the wealthiest can—perfectly legally—pay income taxes that are only a tiny fraction of the hundreds of millions, if not billions, their fortunes grow each year." *ProPublica*'s journalists reported Elon Musk pledged 92 million Tesla shares worth more than $57 billion as collateral for personal loans; Larry Ellison, CEO of Oracle, used a line of credit secured by about $10 billion of his shares; and the investor Carl Icahn, the fortieth-wealthiest American according to *Forbes*, had

		Wealth Growth	Total Income Reported		Total Taxes Paid		True Tax Rate
	Warren Buffett *Berkshire Hathaway Inc.*	$24.3B	$125M	▊▁▁▪▪	$23.7M	▊▁▁▪▫	0.10%
	Jeff Bezos *Amazon.com Inc.*	$99.0B	$4.22B	▪▪▊▊▪	$973M	▫▪▊▊▫	0.98%
	Michael Bloomberg *Bloomberg LP*	$22.5B	$10.0B	▊▊▊▊▊	$292M	▊▊▫▪▊	1.30%
	Elon Musk *Tesla Inc.*	$13.9B	$1.52B	▫▪▊	$455M	▫▊	3.27%

Wealth, income, and taxes for four of the richest people in the United States, 2014–18. Source: Jesse Eisinger, Jeff Ernsthausen, and Paul Kiel, "The Secret IRS Files: Trove of Never-Before-Seen Records Reveal How the Wealthiest Avoid Income Tax," *ProPublica*, June 8, 2021.

an outstanding $1.2 billion line of credit with Bank of America. Not all billionaires borrowed large sums; some sold some of their shares. Others lived off dividends or other income and used other tax-avoidance techniques, which *ProPublica* journalists described in subsequent articles. For example, Peter Thiel, a billionaire technology investor and one of the largest contributors to Republican candidates, legally accumulated $5 billion in a Roth retirement account, which *ProPublica* called a "tax-free piggy bank."[24]

Republican senators and representatives responded to the *ProPublica* reports by attacking the IRS. "This is an astonishing breach of trust that should make taxpayers very concerned," said Kevin Brady, the top Ways and Means Committee Republican. Senate Finance Committee Republicans, who opposed President Biden's requests for more IRS funding, regarded the *ProPublica* story as proving no additional IRS funding should be enacted. Grover Norquist said, "I think this kills the effort." One Republican Pennsylvania congressman claimed the release of the information was "political," being used "to advance the Democrats' narrative that the wealthy individuals don't pay enough of their taxes." A Republican political strategist added, "If the goal is to fire up the base before 2022 [midterm elections], just uttering the letters I-R-S will do that." The *ProPublica* journalists insisted, "We do not know the identity of our source. We did not solicit the information they sent us."[25]

In September 2021, Senator Sinema told her Senate colleagues she would not accept any corporate or individual income tax rate increases.[26] In October *Business Week* published a detailed analysis of how Nike founder Phil Knight and other wealthy families, including the Waltons of Walmart and Zoom founder Eric Yuan, used tax strategies to transfer large amounts of wealth to their heirs free from estate taxes.[27]

On November 19, 2021, House Democrats (with all but one Democrat in favor and all Republicans opposed) passed their version of Build Back Better, a $1.75 trillion package of spending and taxes, including a one-year extension of the 2021 refundable tax credits for children.[28] Roughly 90 percent of the spending increases were paid for by tax increases and additional funding for the IRS. Republican House Leader Kevin McCarthy of California spoke against the legislation for 8 hours and 42 minutes, calling the legislation "the single most irresponsible spending bill in our nation's history."[29]

The House Democrats' tax provisions were divided nearly evenly between increased taxes on wealthy individuals and large corporations. They included a five-percentage-point tax increase on individuals' income above $10 million, and eight more percentage points on income above $25 million (for a 50 percent top rate at that level), restrictions on Individual Retirement Accounts (IRAs) worth more than $10 million, and some corporate tax increases, notably a 15 percent minimum tax on income reported to shareholders applicable to corporations with profits over $1 billion, and a 1 percent tax on stock buybacks.

Early drafts of the House legislation would have eliminated many of the well-publicized estate tax-avoidance techniques and curbed others, but those provisions quietly disappeared from the House Democrats' bill. When he was trying to convince Senate Democrats to support repealing the estate tax in 2017, President Trump's multimillionaire chief economic advisor Gary Cohn said, "Only morons pay the estate tax." Later explanations claimed he meant "rich people with really bad tax planning."[30] In 2021, House Democrats apparently decided to keep it that way.

Negotiations in the Senate were stalled. Undeterred, the Biden administration in March 2022 advanced numerous proposals to close tax-avoidance avenues and to raise billions in taxes from the wealthy and large corporations over the next ten years.[31] Spurred by the extensive public attention generated by *ProPublica* and other exposés, President Biden, for example, proposed a minimum tax of 20 percent on total income, including the annual appreciation of assets not sold during the year, applicable only to people with more than

$100 million of wealth.[32] Treasury estimated this proposal would raise more than $360 billion over the decade beginning in 2023.[33]

By the summer of 2022, investigative journalists, House Democrats, and the Biden administration had produced a menu of techniques used by extremely wealthy people to avoid paying income and estate taxes. The table was set. The question was whether a Congress narrowly controlled by Democrats would enact legislation to block any of them—or otherwise raise taxes on wealthy individuals.

The Inflation Reduction Act

On July 27, 2022—after Senator Manchin "pulled the plug" on the Build Back Better legislation, seemingly refusing to support any of the spending and tax bills Democrats were trying to enact—the Senate passed the "CHIPS Act" with a bipartisan 64 to 33 vote.[34] This legislation provided more than $50 billion in subsidies for new semiconductor manufacturing facilities, including new tax credits and other incentives totaling $170 billion for scientific research and development to improve the nation's ability to compete with China. Senate Republican Leader Mitch McConnell and his Republican Senate colleagues had refused to support the CHIPS legislation as long as Democrats were pursuing a budget reconciliation bill increasing spending and taxes, but seventeen Republican senators, including Leader McConnell, voted for the CHIPS Act believing Senator Manchin had doomed the Democrats' budget reconciliation efforts.[35] The day after the CHIPS legislation passed the Senate, Senator Manchin and Democratic Majority Leader Schumer announced they had reached agreement on a $740 billion, ten-year tax and spending bill, providing $369 billion in energy tax credits and other subsidies, designed principally to reduce carbon emissions by about 40 percent by 2030; $64 billion to lower health-care costs and maintain insurance coverage for low- and moderate-income families; and an effort to curb inflation by reducing deficits by roughly $300 billion.

Close to $300 billion in financing their agreement came from government savings in health-care costs by allowing Medicare to negotiate with pharmaceutical companies over prescription drug prices. The remainder was due to tax increases: over $300 billion from a 15 percent corporate minimum tax, $14 billion from a relatively minor limitation on the carried-interest loophole, and $124 billion from increased IRS funding to allow the agency to improve its ability to collect taxes due under existing law.[36]

President Biden promptly announced support for the deal. The carried-interest change was the only item in Manchin and Schumer's agreement increasing taxes on rich individuals. All the tax-avoidance techniques identified by *ProPublica* and urged to be changed by President Biden were retained: there were no income tax or capital gains rate increases; no minimum tax on the extremely wealthy; no wealth tax; no closing of estate tax–avoidance techniques, no limits on billion-dollar tax-free individual retirement accounts; no limits on Medicare tax-avoidance strategies; no income taxes on gains from borrowing in excess of the costs of unsold assets; no capital gains taxes on gains in assets held until death.

Senator Sinema, who had not participated in the Manchin-Schumer negotiations, insisted on dropping the carried-interest provision, which would have required hedge fund and private equity managers to hold investments for five rather than three years to get the capital gains tax break, raising less than a quarter of the revenue from taxing carried-interest compensation as ordinary labor income.[37] Senator Sinema also successfully removed companies owned by private equity firms from the 15 percent corporate minimum tax, added provisions to help capital-intensive manufacturing firms and utilities and wireless internet companies avoid the minimum tax, and obtained drought relief for Arizona.[38] The Senate replaced the revenues lost from Sinema's changes by adding a 1 percent tax on stock buybacks, a provision from the House version of the Build Back Better bill.

Once Sinema's vote was secured, all 50 Democratic senators voted for the Inflation Reduction Act. With the 50 Republicans opposed, the tie was broken by Vice President Kamala Harris on Sunday, August 7, 2022. The House passed the Senate bill five days later by 220 to 207, also on a strict party-line vote. President Biden signed the legislation a few days later in a White House ceremony.

Republicans, of course, maintained their long-standing refusal to raise taxes on anyone. Despite strong urging to do so by the Biden administration and Democratic control of both chambers of Congress, all of Biden's proposals to increase the taxes of wealthy individuals failed. The tax increases for funding the Inflation Reduction Act came from taxing large corporations and increasing IRS funding. That proved politically easier for Democrats than taxing billionaires.[39]

Although large corporations bore the brunt of the tax increases in the 2022 legislation, their extensive lobbying was quite successful; they might have fared much worse.[40] The Biden administration had proposed raising the corporate tax rate to 28 percent, and many Democrats in Congress were coalescing around a 25 percent rate. The additional revenues expected from the 15 percent minimum tax—limited to companies reporting at least $1 billion in book profits and paying taxes of less than 15 percent of that—are roughly equivalent to those of an increase of two percentage points in the corporate rate, to 23 percent. Since the 1980s, much of the public has viewed the ability of large profitable corporations to pay little or no income tax as unfair.[41] The book minimum tax is complex and challenging for the IRS to administer, but if the problem Congress needed to address was companies reporting large profits to the public and paying low taxes, the only way to align those is to base their tax liability on book profits, at least to some extent.[42]

The new 1 percent excise tax on corporate stock buybacks is likely to raise revenue without changing behavior. Corporations with more cash than attractive investment opportunities prefer stock repurchases to increasing their dividends, which entail ongoing outflows of corporate cash to shareholders. Share repurchases also enjoy a tax advantage over dividends. Some members of Congress object to stock buybacks, which sometimes occur after tax cuts are enacted intended to stimulate investments and increase jobs. Senator Schumer praised the excise tax on buybacks as reducing the likelihood that corporate managers would pursue buybacks to boost their companies' share values, but the 1 percent tax is unlikely to curb buybacks.

Republicans insisted the corporate tax increases broke President Biden's campaign pledge not to raise taxes on people with incomes below $400,000, even though Biden had consistently urged raising taxes on large corporations. Republicans pointed to tables published by the Joint Committee on Taxation showing the corporate increases would raise taxes in nearly all income categories. Economists generally assume roughly 80 percent of corporate tax increases will lower returns to stockholders and other investors, while about 20 percent will lower wages over time. These economic assumptions are not without controversy, however. Recent work by the Brookings Institution's Bill Gale suggests the top 20 percent of workers will bear a disproportionate share of any potential wage impact while workers in the bottom 60 percent will bear less than the standard assumptions imply.[43] In any event, workers do not seem to worry that collecting more taxes from large profitable corporations will reduce their wages. Republicans were poised to enjoy greater political success with their antitax complaints about the IRS.

Attacking the IRS – Again

The Inflation Reduction Act provided $80 billion in additional funding over the following decade to allow the IRS to modernize its archaic technology, improve its services to taxpayers, and beef up its ability to collect taxes owed under the law, especially from wealthy individuals, large corporations, and complex partnerships. In 2022 the IRS had the same number of employees it had in 1970, when many fewer tax returns were filed. The agency's enforcement staff was down 30 percent since 2010, and its audits of millionaires' tax returns fell more than 70 percent since then. The IRS commissioner told Congress the agency collects $1 trillion a year less in taxes than what the government is legally owed.[44] Republicans successfully shrank the IRS budget over decades and opposed increasing it. Echoing a long-standing anti-IRS refrain, Texas Republican senator Ted Cruz said, "Instead of increasing funding for the IRS we should abolish the damn place."[45]

Millions of taxpayers experienced long delays in getting refunds because of the agency's inability to promptly process tax returns.[46] To anyone who has tried to reach the IRS on the phone to determine when a long-awaited refund is coming, clear up a collection mistake, or verify their identity, the additional IRS funding should be welcome news. A *Wall Street Journal* reporter described waiting five and a half hours in line, along with about a hundred other people, on a Saturday to meet with an IRS agent to verify her identity so the IRS would release her refund. She and the others in line had tried to reach the IRS by phone, but they were among the 80 percent of callers who could not reach anyone.[47] In August 2022, when President Biden signed the Inflation Reduction Act, the IRS had about 17 million paper tax returns of individuals and businesses it had not yet processed plus untold amounts of unanswered correspondence.[48]

According to the Treasury Department, the new funding will be used to hire 87,000 new workers to replace 50,000 who have left or expect to leave, doubling the number of enforcement personnel from about 6,500 to 13,000 over the decade. The IRS maintains it takes three to five years to train a new agent. On August 10, 2022, Treasury Secretary Janet Yellen wrote the IRS commissioner mandating that the new funding "shall not be used to increase the share of small businesses or households below the $400,000 threshold that are audited relative to historical levels." Another Treasury official added, "for honest taxpayers earning less than $400,000, the chances of being audited are going down."[49] In September 2022 Secretary Yellen pledged to add 5,000 new IRS workers to answer phones and respond more quickly to taxpayers' questions.[50]

Former Senate Finance Committee chairman and Iowa Republican Chuck Grassley told Fox News that new IRS agents might be coming with "loaded AK-15s" and "ready to shoot some small-business person in Iowa." Florida

Republican senator Rick Scott, head of the Republican senatorial campaign committee, claimed the new law would create "an IRS super-police force," "willing to kill" people. Republican National Committee chairwoman Ronna McDaniel warned of an "IRS SWAT team" attacking "your kids' lemonade stands."[51] Steven Moore, a conservative advocate who cofounded the antitax Club for Growth, described additional IRS funding as "the lightning rod issue that has really aggravated and activated conservative activists around the country." On a Republican fundraising call, billionaire donor Steve Wynn, owner of several Las Vegas casinos, urged Republican candidates to run aggressive TV ads describing Democrats as hurting lower-income wage earners and small businesses. "Hard-hitting . . . spots with a man's voice, no soft pedal," he said. "They're coming after you if you're a waiter, if you're a bartender, if you're anybody with a cash business . . . they're coming after you."[52]

Fox News spread fear and loathing of the IRS: Brian Kilmeade, co-host of the *Fox and Friends* morning show, said IRS agents would "hunt down and kill middle-class taxpayers that don't pay enough."[53] The *Wall Street Journal* published an editorial warning its readers, "The IRS Is About to Go Beast Mode."[54] Claims of heavily armed IRS agents spread on social media. Thousands of Twitter users asked why the IRS needed "a massive stock pile of guns and ammo" and accused Democrats of "weaponizing" the agency with agents "trained to kill Americans." On TikTok, people suggested the IRS, "armed to the teeth, was coming to seize their guns" and threatened to retaliate.[55] Other online websites compared IRS employees to Nazi SS officers and urged taxpayers to have a "tea party" and "tar and feather" IRS employees.[56]

IRS employees said they were fearful about being targeted at work or in public. One said, "This terrifies me. This is the reason that I don't tell people that I work for the IRS." The president of the Chicago area union advised IRS employees not to wear their identification badges outside their offices. The IRS commissioner said, "Our workforce is concerned about its safety."[57]

For a generation, attacking the Internal Revenue Service has been a recurring theme of the antitax movement. New in 2022, however, were widespread characterizations of the tax-collection agency as armed and dangerous to the American people—claims coming from important elected Republican officials and conservative media along with violent threats of retaliation from many of their supporters.

Cutting the IRS budget has been a common Republican tactic since the Reagan administration. Republicans responded to the new funding provided to the IRS in 2022 by reducing the annual IRS appropriation, which was about

$13 billion in 2022. They will continue to seek further cuts and endeavor to shift the IRS budget away from enforcement. An IRS unable to challenge tax avoidance by high-income individuals and businesses is as central to the antitax playbook as tax cuts at the top.

Republicans Recapture a House Majority

In the 2022 midterm elections, a widely predicted Republican "wave" failed to materialize, and Republicans fared worse than usual in the midterms for the party out of the White House. Democrats did better than predicted, gaining one Senate seat, giving them a 51–49 majority. (In December, however, Kyrsten Sinema announced that she was leaving the Democratic Party to become an independent, but she said she intended to continue voting the way she always had and kept her Democratic committee assignments.) Democrats also gained two governors and control of four state legislatures. Republicans picked up nine House seats, giving them a narrow majority. In the most contentious House election in more than a century, after fifteen ballots and days of negotiations with some of his most right-wing colleagues, Republican representatives elected California's Kevin McCarthy Speaker of the House—the last of the "young guns" left in Congress. The new congressional mixture was unlikely to produce important legislation before 2025, after the next presidential election when the Trump tax cuts for individuals are scheduled to expire. But Congress needed to keep the government up and running and ensure that the Treasury could pay its obligations.

The first legislation passed by the new Republican House, on January 9, 2023, was the cunningly named Family and Small Business Protection Act, a one-sentence bill to repeal the additional funds appropriated to the IRS by the (misnamed) Inflation Reduction Act, based on Republicans' ongoing claims of protecting middle-class Americans from 87,000 new revenue agents. Grover Norquist's (also misnamed) Americans for Tax Reform applauded the action. Ron Wyden, the Democratic chair of the Senate Finance Committee, described the House bill as a "handout to wealthy tax cheats," adding, "Senate Democrats will not entertain it."[58] The Congressional Budget Office estimated the bill would increase the federal debt by $115 billion over ten years. The repeal bill was going nowhere. In his opening statement as the new chairman of the House Ways and Means Committee, Jason Smith, a Republican representing the district in southwestern Missouri where Rush Limbaugh grew up, made clear that he would hold hearings "asking the tough questions about how the Biden Administration wishes to use [the IRS] to snoop on Americans' finances or why that agency has repeatedly betrayed the trust of American taxpayers."[59]

To secure enough votes to become Speaker of the House, Kevin McCarthy promised his Georgia Republican colleague Buddy Carter to allow a vote by the House on Carter's reintroduced "FairTax" bill, which claims to "promote freedom, fairness, and economic opportunity." Like its forerunners in the 1990s, Carter's bill proposes replacing income, payroll, and estate and gift taxes in 2025 with a national sales tax of 30 percent (23 percent on a tax-inclusive basis). Rebates based on poverty levels by family size would be provided to all U.S. citizens and the national sales tax would be collected by the states. The IRS would be abolished and unfunded beginning in 2027.[60] A Brookings economist estimated the proposal would add at least $1 trillion a year to federal deficits, and it would increase taxes for low- and middle-income families while substantially cutting taxes at the top.[61] Grover Norquist criticized the bill as "a free gift to Democrats," and Democrats agreed. Democratic congressional leaders blasted it, claiming it would increase taxes for almost every American, create particular burdens for the elderly, and "detonate" Social Security.[62] The *Wall Street Journal* published an op-ed praising it.[63] A number of Republicans opposed the idea, Speaker McCarthy among them. The bill was referred to the Ways and Means Committee from which it may never emerge. It had no chance with the Senate Democratic majority.

Republicans also passed House rules requiring that any new mandatory spending be paid for by cutting other spending, not tax increases, and mandating a two-thirds majority of all House members to pass any tax increase. They made clear that passing a permanent extension of all the individual income and estate tax cuts enacted in 2017 and scheduled to expire in 2025 was a priority. The Tax Policy Center estimated that extending the individual tax cuts would lower tax revenues and increase federal deficits by about $3.1 trillion over ten years, or about 0.9 percent of GDP, and that more than 60 percent of the benefits would go to the 20 percent of households with the highest incomes, with more than 40 percent going to those in the top 5 percent.[64]

Despite their willingness to increase deficits by extending the 2017 tax cuts, some Republicans in 2023 renewed calls for a constitutional balanced-budget amendment, which would obviously die in the Senate in the unlikely event it could muster the necessary two-thirds vote in the House—an ongoing political charade that continues without end.[65] House Republicans also made clear their intentions to insist on spending cuts as a condition of raising the federal debt ceiling, which limits the amount the United States can legally borrow to pay for spending *previously* enacted.

A Debt-Ceiling Drama

The United States is exceptional in having a legal limitation on the amount of debt it can issue. If the debt ceiling is not raised allowing new debt to be issued, the consequences would be dire. For example, the United States might have to stop making legally required payments, such as for military or civilian salaries, veterans' benefits, Social Security, or health care. If the U.S. government becomes unable to pay required interest on its existing debt or to refinance debt as it comes due, calamitous results would follow.[66] The chief economist at Standard and Poor's predicted a default on the national debt would devastate "markets and the economy." Treasury Secretary and former Federal Reserve chair Janet Yellen concurred, saying that failure to raise the debt ceiling would be a "catastrophe," causing a financial crisis and likely a recession.[67] Since the 1980s, threats to block debt-ceiling increases have often been political posturing, but as the Republican Party has moved further to the right, the risks of a catastrophic default have increased. When the lame-duck session of the Democratic Congress met in December 2022 after the November midterm elections, it was obvious the nation would hit the debt limit when Republicans controlled the House and they would not want to raise the debt ceiling without exacting concessions. But Democrats had other priorities and seemed to believe that Republican intransigence would benefit them politically—a high-risk strategy. Democratic leader Schumer told *Politico*, "The plan is to get our Republican colleagues in the House to understand they're flirting with disaster and hurting the American people. And to let the American people understand that as well. And I think we'll win."[68] President Biden insisted he would not negotiate over spending cuts to raise or suspend the debt ceiling. Republicans were sure he would.

In January 2023 Secretary Yellen announced the government had hit the statutory debt limit of $31.4 trillion and that she would begin using "extraordinary measures," such as delaying contributions to federal employees' retirement funds, to provide the government with enough cash to meet its financial obligations—extending the date when the debt ceiling must be raised until June 2023.[69] In March 2023 President Biden released his budget proposals for fiscal year 2024, claiming they would produce almost $3 trillion in deficit reductions.[70] The president's budget was a political document, not a blueprint for realistic change. It included spending totaling nearly 25 percent of

GDP (greater than before the Covid pandemic hit) and taxes approaching 20 percent of GDP. The budget proposed more than $3 trillion in tax increases over the coming decade, reprising many recommendations, such as a minimum tax on billionaires and rate increases at the top, that Democrats failed to enact in 2022 and would not be considered by the House Republican majority. His budget, however, allowed the president to claim that he had proposed substantially reducing the anticipated growth in the federal debt by increasing taxes on corporations and high earners rather than cutting politically popular programs.[71]

The question what spending cuts Republicans would demand was unsettled. Some claimed they wanted to legislate a ten-year path to a balanced budget by cutting spending without raising any taxes. In January 2023 the Committee for a Responsible Federal Budget estimated that balancing the federal budget by 2032 would require $14.6 trillion of deficit reductions, a 26 percent cut in spending if taxes were off the table, rising to 33 percent if defense and veterans affairs were excluded, 85 percent if Medicare and Social Security were also protected from benefit cuts.[72] That obviously was not going to happen.

On April 19, 2023, Speaker McCarthy released a 320-page bill containing the House Republicans' demands. McCarthy's bill would extend the debt ceiling until no later than March 31, 2024—providing Republicans another opportunity for a debt-ceiling crisis before the 2024 elections. In exchange, the proposed legislation included a demand that non-defense discretionary spending not exceed its 2022 fiscal year level, requiring a reduction in anticipated federal spending of $130 billion, without specifying what programs would be cut, and a limit of future growth of federal spending to 1 percent a year; new work requirements for eligibility for government assistance, such as Medicaid and food stamps; elimination of many of the green energy tax credits enacted in 2022; and a repeal of the additional IRS funding, which Speaker McCarthy described as "repeal of Biden's army of 87,000 IRS agents."[73] Speaker McCarthy said his legislation would reduce deficits by $4.5 trillion over the coming decade. More than $3 trillion of that amount was attributable to the large, deliberately unspecified cuts in non-defense discretionary spending—which includes federal spending for things like education, energy, transportation, some income security programs, veterans' health care, NASA, NIH, the national parks, and homeland security that total less than 15 percent of total federal spending and historically have amounted to 3 to 4 percent of GDP. Cuts this large were unlikely to occur even in the implausible event that McCarthy's bill were enacted.[74] On

April 26, after some last-minute changes to appease some colleagues to his right and midwesterners who insisted on maintaining subsidies for ethanol, Speaker McCarthy's bill passed the House by the narrowest possible 217–215 party-line vote.

Shortly before Speaker McCarthy's bill passed the House, the White House tried to derail it by pointing out that it violated Grover Norquist's "Taxpayer Protection Pledge," raising taxes by more than $300 billion over the coming decade by repealing the clean-energy tax breaks added by the Democrats' 2022 Inflation Reduction Act. A White House spokesman told the conservative *Washington Examiner*, "Months after promising not to raise taxes, House Republicans are voting for a middle-class tax increase. . . . [They are] voting to raise taxes on working families when they buy efficient appliances, electric vehicles, and other products that would lower utility bills, even as they continue to push for massive tax giveaways for the super-wealthy and special interests."[75] The Tax Foundation agreed that although the tax credits "largely skewed" to higher earners, repealing the credits would reduce benefits for the "bottom 20% of earners."[76] Jason Smith, the Republican Ways and Means Committee chairman, countered that those tax credits should be treated as cutting spending and a spokesman for Norquist's Americans for Tax Reform agreed.[77] But believing that the debt-ceiling vote marked a breakthrough—reversing decades of Republican refusals to repeal tax breaks targeted to specific industries without offsetting tax cuts—was foolish. Republicans made clear their votes were limited to reversing President Biden's green-energy efforts, and House Republican leaders marshalling votes for the debt-ceiling bill assured their colleagues that any final legislation would not raise taxes.

Speaker McCarthy believed passing his bill in the House would require the president and congressional Democrats to negotiate with him over a debt-ceiling increase. President Biden claimed Republicans wanted "massive cuts in programs you count on," adding that Republicans are threatening default "unless I agree to all these wacko notions they have."[78] He emphasized that President Reagan had warned about brinksmanship over the debt ceiling, and he urged Republicans to take default "off the table" and "have a real serious detailed conversation about how to grow the economy, lower costs and reduce the deficit."[79] Making clear that the Republican bill would not get any Democratic votes in the House, Ways and Means Committee ranking member Richard Neal said, "This proposal is not serious and . . .

shows that if it isn't a tax cut for the wealthy, Republicans can't govern."[80] Democratic Majority Leader Chuck Schumer said it had "no chance of moving forward in the Senate."[81] Treasury Secretary Yellen subsequently clarified that the government would require borrowing in excess of the debt limit by June 5.

Speaker McCarthy's success in passing debt-ceiling legislation—unrealistic as it was—forced President Biden to the negotiating table. After a month of contentious negotiations, on Saturday, May 27, 2023, McCarthy and Biden announced an agreement to suspend the debt ceiling through January 1, 2025, and on January 2, 2025, to raise the debt ceiling to the amount of debt incurred. This would allow the government to borrow the money needed to pay for its obligations until after the 2024 elections and require another debt-ceiling increase in 2025. In exchange, McCarthy got caps limiting the growth of non-defense discretionary spending for 2024 and 2025 to less than the rate of inflation; nonbinding limits on such spending for subsequent years through 2029; increases in spending for defense and veterans' benefits similar to President Biden's budget requests; new work requirements for food stamps for some Americans at ages fifty through fifty-four; new rules to allow faster approvals for energy projects; a clawback of about $30 billion of unspent Covid relief money; and a transfer to other spending of $21.4 billion of the $80 billion of IRS funding.

The agreement did not include any of the House Republicans' cancellations of the green energy tax incentives or proposals by President Biden to further reduce Medicare spending on prescription drugs. Republicans, unsurprisingly, rejected the president's suggestions to raise taxes on corporations and high-income individuals and his recommendations for closing some tax loopholes. Speaker McCarthy crowed that the agreement raised no taxes. In fact, it would reduce revenues by cutting back on IRS funding.

On Wednesday, May 31, the House passed the debt-ceiling agreement by a vote of 317 to 117, with 149 Republicans and 165 Democrats voting for the bill. The 46 Democrats who opposed the bill were mostly liberals who opposed the spending cuts and representatives who rejected the idea of attaching spending reductions to a debt-ceiling increase. Republican opponents were mostly far-right members of the Freedom Caucus disappointed that Speaker McCarthy had compromised with the White House. The Senate passed the legislation the next night by a vote of 63–36. Thirty-one Republican senators voted against the bill.

In his first Oval Office speech to the nation on Friday evening June 2, President Biden told the American people that "an economic crisis and an economic collapse" had been averted. "The stakes could not have been higher," he said. The president criticized Republicans' refusal to support closing "special interest tax loopholes," but he praised congressional leaders of both parties for enacting the bipartisan legislation, commending especially Speaker McCarthy for his "good faith" and "honest" negotiations. On Saturday, June 3, the president signed the legislation.[82]

Speaker McCarthy repeatedly called the debt-ceiling bill the largest spending cut in history, claiming the legislation would save $2.1 trillion over the next ten years, about 0.6 percent of GDP (assuming the legislation's suggested spending limitations will actually occur through 2029). If, however, the spending caps hold only for 2024 and 2025, the total ten-year savings could be as low as about $250 billion or as much as $1.8 trillion. At best, the federal debt in 2023 of $31.4 trillion (97 percent of GDP) is expected to rise to about $45 trillion (115 percent instead of 119 percent of GDP) by 2023.[83]

Neither Republicans nor Democrats were willing to risk the political costs or potential consequences of proposing cuts in Social Security, Medicare, or veterans' benefits. Both parties wanted to increase defense expenditures. Republicans were determined to repeal, or at least reduce, IRS funding even if it would increase deficits. They continued to claim they could curb the federal debt and deficits while extending the large 2017 tax cuts, which would more than undo the largest potential debt and deficit reductions from the debt-ceiling legislation. Republicans adamantly refused to abandon their long-standing resistance to any tax increases. Indeed, less than two weeks after the debt-ceiling crisis was resolved, the House Republicans introduced additional tax-cut legislation for individuals and businesses that the Committee for a Responsible Federal Budget estimated would cost more than $1 trillion over the following decade if these "temporary" tax cuts were made permanent.

Democrats relaxed and rejoiced that the debt-ceiling negotiations avoided a major economic calamity, viewing the deal as roughly comparable to what the House Republican majority could have accomplished later in the year through the budget process. The media spilled much ink and time debating whether Speaker McCarthy or President Biden won the negotiations. The good news was that the White House and Congress found a way to raise the debt limit without catastrophic economic dislocations. But such an outcome was hardly guaranteed. Going forward, the debt ceiling remains a tinderbox, allowing the full faith and credit of the United States to be held hostage in fiscal negotiations.

Successful resolution of the 2023 impasse neither deterred subsequent conflicts nor addressed the ongoing imbalances between federal spending and taxes that produced the unprecedented levels of debt facing the nation.

———

For nearly a half century Democrats supplied important support to antitax advocates by voting for income tax cuts and to repeal or emasculate the estate tax, long-standing Republican goals. By the third decade of the twenty-first century, Democrats essentially surrendered to the antitax movement by limiting any tax increases to large corporations and the top 1 to 2 percent of income taxpayers while advancing large increases in taxes applicable only to the top .01 or even .001 percent. In 2021 and 2022, those dogs didn't hunt: billionaires and multimillionaires successfully avoided numerous presidential proposals to raise their taxes and to close well-publicized tax-avoidance avenues. Emphasizing these failures does not imply that any and all tax increases should apply only to the very top. Rather, it exposes the extraordinary challenges in paying for the spending, including through tax breaks, both parties have enacted. Genuine crises no longer produce an increased willingness to tax—even after the crisis passes. Threats to stop paying the government's debts under these circumstances are folly beyond imagination.

During the same period, the American people—and their political representatives—have demonstrated an unwillingness to limit government spending and tax expenditures to anywhere near the levels the public funds with taxes. Matching tax revenues to spending, a goal of leaders of both parties through the end of the twentieth century, became archaic: neither Democrats nor Republicans are willing to enact tax laws producing sufficient revenues to fund the expenditures they view as essential. The remaining questions, naturally, are: How long can this go on? And if and when it becomes necessary, how will it stop?

Chapter 16

The End of American Exceptionalism?

Insanity is doing the same thing over and over again and expecting different results.

—RITA MAE BROWN (OFTEN ATTRIBUTED TO ALBERT EINSTEIN)

Previous chapters showed how a fringe movement to cut taxes moved into the mainstream and transformed opposition to taxes into the cornerstone of U.S. fiscal and economic policy. Rejecting any and all tax increases became Republican Party dogma—the glue that has held its disparate coalitions together. Republicans have relied on large tax cuts as their universal remedy regardless of the country's economic circumstances. Democrats supplied essential support for tax cuts, beginning in 1978 with capital gains cuts, continuing during Ronald Reagan's tax-cut revolution, and in enacting and making permanent nearly all of George W. Bush's 2001 and 2003 tax reductions. Since 2008 Democrats have been willing to raise taxes only on a top slice of high-income earners, extraordinarily wealthy people, and large corporations. Numerous spending programs, including for research and development, infrastructure, education, Social Security, health-care coverage, unemployment insurance, and work adjustment assistance, along with refundable earned income and child tax credits, help protect and lift up Americans in the middle class and below.[1] Measures like these require resources. For nearly a half century, the antitax movement has endured and strengthened, requiring the United States to borrow trillions of dollars from abroad to fund critical needs and provide adequate public services.

A stunningly large number of Republican legislators have pledged never to raise taxes, even to close glaring loopholes, finance a war, or respond to any other crisis.[2] By cutting taxes for the wealthy, the antitax movement has supported rising inequalities of income and wealth at the top. Antitax attitudes, conspicuous among the rich, have aided and abetted tax avoidance and evasion. The antitax movement also contributed to dysfunctional partisanship, beginning when Republicans captured a House majority and elevated Newt Gingrich to Speaker in 1995. It is a movement grounded in fantasies.

Clinging to False Beliefs

From 1978 into the 2020s, the antitax movement has clung to its foundational myths, despite their inherent inconsistency and compelling evidence discrediting them. It is surprising that a social movement built on a foundation of long-disproven economic claims never stopped asserting those claims as reasons for tax cuts. Three have been fundamental for the antitax movement: (1) cutting taxes will increase government revenues, or, at the extreme, cutting taxes is the only way to raise government revenues; (2) lowering taxes will necessarily "starve the beast" by cutting government spending; and (3) reducing taxes at the top is the best way to grow the nation's economy no matter the circumstances. These claims have been repeatedly debunked, but for more than four decades they have never disappeared from antitax advocates' playbook.

First, Arthur Laffer's curve—which was drawn cleverly without any numbers illustrating the revenue-maximizing tax rates—is advanced to justify cutting taxes regardless of the current rates. While it may have been plausible in 1980 that the United States was on the wrong side of the curve, with a top individual income tax rate as high as 70 percent, claims that cutting top income tax rates will raise revenue have been implausible at least since the mid-1980s when the top federal income tax rate dropped to 28 percent. Since then, it ranged between 35 percent and 39.6 percent for decades. Nevertheless, antitax advocates continue to insist the U.S. income tax is on the wrong side of Laffer's curve. Likewise, capital gains rates, maintained at no more than 15 to 28 percent since 1978, are below the revenue-maximizing rate of around 30 percent estimated by the Joint Committee on Taxation and the Tax Policy Center.

Oft-repeated antitax claims that lowering tax rates will necessarily lower federal government spending are risible. Federal spending as a share of the economy was as high when Ronald Reagan left the presidency as when he entered it. Nor did government expenditures decrease after the large tax cuts of the George W. Bush and Donald Trump presidencies. Federal spending has increased under both Republican and Democratic presidents.[3] Tax and spend was replaced by borrow and spend.

Antitax proselytizers often insist the period during Ronald Reagan's administration from 1983 to 1990 demonstrates the power of tax cuts to stimulate economic growth, even though the most robust economic growth since 1978 occurred during years following Bill Clinton's 1993 tax increases. Tax reductions at the top have spurred neither great increases in domestic investment nor bursts of increased productivity. This held true after cuts in the top income tax rate in 1981, 1986, 2001, and 2017. Supply-side economics became the lodestar for Republican economic policies in the late 1970s and early 1980s before capital began moving freely around the world and investments became global. It might have been reasonable then to believe job-creating investments depended solely on the level of domestic savings.[4] But investments by foreigners into the United States became much more important subsequently as the United States changed from the world's largest capital exporter into the largest capital importer. Federal Reserve actions during the global financial crisis in 2007–9 and the Covid pandemic of 2020–22 demonstrated the potential for expanding credit to fund private investments is far greater than the original supply-siders and other antitaxers imagined.

Economist William Gale of the Brookings Institution describes the large tax cuts enacted in 2012 and 2013 by Kansas governor Sam Brownback and the Republican legislature as "one of the cleanest experiments the country has ever had in measuring the effects of tax cuts on economic growth." Gale points out that after the state's large tax cuts, Kansas lagged behind the nation and neighboring states in economic growth, causing significant reductions in vital programs, including funding for courts, public education, and infrastructure. The state's bond rating was downgraded, raising interest costs. The reduction in business taxes from 5 percent to zero generated tax-sheltering activity by individuals who recharacterized themselves as self-employed independent contractors rather than employees and from businesses in neighboring states who reallocated income to Kansas without increasing business activity there. After the elections of 2016, the Republican legislature rolled back the tax cuts over Governor Brownback's veto. Gale concludes that "people are more willing to pay higher taxes when they see the link between tax revenues and the societal benefits that government provides."[5]

A Circumscribed View of Freedom

In addition to relying on discredited economic claims, antitax advocates frequently insist that any and all tax cuts serve to guarantee freedom for individuals from government interference. Many leading antitax advocates have accepted the controversial, constricted view of freedom reflected in Ayn Rand's extreme claims for self-reliance and unfettered market outcomes. Putting aside important and controversial questions whether U.S. labor markets and markets for goods and services are always free and competitive bastions of voluntary exchanges, maintaining that freedom from taxes is essential for liberty—or as Harvard philosopher Robert Nozick put it more forcefully, taxes are equivalent to slavery—ignores the necessity of paying for the physical, intangible, and legal protections that enable the market to function. It dismisses philosophical arguments, such as those of John Rawls and Amartya Sen, which emphasize the role and potential of insisting on equality in political and sometimes economic arrangements. It abandons the durable American creed favoring equality of opportunity. The antitax conception of liberty insists market outcomes always and inevitably reflect rewards to diligence, hard work, and entrepreneurial risk-taking, ignoring the impacts of technological changes and globalization in producing "winner-take-all" markets.[6] As Columbia law professor Katharina Pistor has detailed, many legal protections for capital ownership create important financial advantages for the wealthy, which "freedom" does not demand and governments should not ignore.[7]

Insisting market rewards are always and inevitably "fair" also fails to take into account how market rewards reflect tastes of others. The enormous demand for Taylor Swift's music has made her an extraordinarily wealthy person, but if tastes change and demand for her music decreases, no matter how diligently or hard she works, her income will fall. The widespread displacement of manufacturing workers in the United States by lower-wage workers abroad and by technology does not mean they should not receive a hand-up from government in transitioning to other work.[8] Many antitax advocates and political leaders who insist Americans' liberty requires freedom from taxes want to have the government limit core values such as whom people can marry, what schools can teach, and who makes decisions concerning control over people's bodies, to name just a few. Antitax proponents often endorse bizarre and unrealistic conceptions of freedom.

The Role of Racial Resentment

Previous chapters identified important links of racial resentment and racially freighted language to the antitax movement. Some of these connections occurred in the 1970s and 1980s as the antitax movement gained early momentum, but they continued with the Tea Party's overtly racist actions in its antitax demonstrations during Barack Obama's presidency. As previous chapters describe, the nation's history of racial antipathy, including slavery's link to the tax provisions of the Constitution and poll taxes to deter African Americans from voting, affirms connections between taxation and race.

Political scientists have found racial issues are salient when white Americans fear being displaced in the workplace or schools by people of color, when expanding government benefits for minorities are conspicuous, and when Black leaders hold important political offices.[9] The oldest state supermajority voting rule for tax increases was enacted in Mississippi in 1890 when Black voters were disenfranchised following the end of Reconstruction.[10] Recent predictions of an imminent United States majority of people of color heightened the anxieties of many white voters who embrace antigovernment and antitax policies. Racial dog whistles have been common in antitax efforts, except when, as with Donald Trump, they are in a register everyone can hear. The tax literature connects the history of taxation in the United States to the nation's history of racial discrimination and demonstrates ways the tax law has disadvantaged people of color.[11]

The modern antitax movement rose and gained strength within the Republican Party alongside the party's "Southern Strategy," an electoral effort explicitly linked to racial division. Spending cuts following large tax cuts tended disproportionately to affect people of color. Disputing the link between racial resentment and antitax politics is not plausible: the overlap between racial aversion and the antitax movement is unmistakable. Taxation is commonly viewed as solely an economic issue by the public, but the tax law is inextricably intertwined with the culture and inevitably political. As antitax guru Grover Norquist insists, "when you win the tax issue, you win everything."

Framing Public Attitudes

The antitax movement has been adroit in framing how the public receives tax policy debates. Transforming estate and inheritance taxes—taxes on large intergenerational transfers of wealth limited to a small slice of the wealthiest

Americans—into "death taxes" and bringing overbearing IRS revenue agents to the funerals of average families offer a prime example. Making a Black tree-farming descendant of slaves the face of the movement was the crowning metamorphosis. Vilifying the IRS has stimulated antigovernment and antitax sentiments and provided political benefits in a variety of contexts over decades.

It used to be said that opponents of tax increases hide behind selected widows; they now hide behind Americans' esteem for family farms and small businesses. The emergence of private equity and sovereign wealth funds, along with business investments by big charitable and educational institutions, makes it possible to amass substantial amounts of capital without going to the public capital markets and allows many large businesses to operate without being subject to the corporate income tax. Tax legislation enacted during the Trump administration added a large and unprecedented tax cut for most partnerships, costing $60 billion annually and reducing the top income tax rate from 37 percent to 29.6 percent.[12] About 70 percent of the tax savings from this provision went to business owners in the top 1 percent, but Congress described the cut as if the only beneficiaries were small businesses. Congress has long resisted taxing very large partnerships and similar entities as corporations.

To take just one more example, antitax supporters from Howard Jarvis to the Tea Party have mislabeled any redistributive spending, especially for the poor, as "socialism" and linked tax cuts to potential reductions in "unearned" government spending, such as for food stamps and welfare, and to foreign aid and waste, fraud, and abuse. In his 2012 presidential campaign, Republican nominee Mitt Romney took the divisive effort a step further by trying to separate the "makers" from the "takers." He was caught on video telling his donors and supporters there were "47 percent of the people who will vote for [President Obama] no matter what" because they are "dependent upon government . . . believe they are victims . . . believe the government has a responsibility to care for them . . . these are people who pay no income tax."[13]

Romney was in error when he said people in the bottom half of the income distribution do not vote Republican: in fact, nine of the ten states with the highest percentage of people who pay no income tax are Republican strongholds.[14] In 2020 the income tax threshold for a married couple with two children was $61,425; in 2021, with the additional $1,000 tax credit for children, the level was $78,092, higher than median income. In 2021, 57 percent of Americans paid no income tax. According to the Tax Policy Center, about half the people who pay no income tax are off the rolls because they have low incomes, and at least three-fourths of the rest pay no income tax because of provisions

benefiting the elderly or families with children. Romney was wrong in describing these people as "dependent on government"; they pay federal payroll taxes
to fund Social Security and Medicare, excise taxes on gasoline, tobacco, and
alcohol, state and local property and sales taxes, and, in some cases, state income taxes.[15] Nevertheless, these characterizations, often with racial over-
tones, are a recurring feature of the antitax playbook.

Eliminating a Valuable Policy Instrument

Aside from monetary policy, governments generally employ four techniques
for implementing policies: taxing, spending, regulating, and sometimes purchasing goods or services. The antitax movement inhibits government's flexibility in choosing among these alternatives. Antitax barriers—including both
Republicans' intransigence about raising any taxes and Democrats' insistence
that tax increases be limited to the highest earners—make it inconceivable
politically to impose taxes in response to situations where market transactions
impose costs on people other than the buyers and sellers.

An important example of such effective taxes are tobacco taxes, directed at
the most important cause of preventable deaths in countries around the world.
Tobacco taxes have significantly reduced tobacco consumption. They have long
been considered regressive because lower-income people in the United States
smoke more cigarettes, but lower-income consumers are more responsive to the
disincentives of substantial tobacco taxes and benefit more by stopping smoking.
MIT economist Jonathan Gruber and his colleagues have concluded that in the
United States at least, tobacco taxes are mildly progressive.[16]

Another instance where a tax can be an appropriate policy instrument is
when the market price for products fails to reflect the costs of attendant pollution. Taxes on gasoline and other transportation fuels and carbon taxes are
examples: the market price of gasoline fails to reflect the costs of building or
maintaining roads and bridges or of the harmful emissions of carbon dioxide
or other pollutants by motor vehicles. Such taxes incentivize producers and
consumers to take such costs into account—even when the revenues from
these taxes are returned to the public per capita or by reducing other taxes
on desirable activities, such as wage taxes. But, as has been discussed, the
federal gasoline tax has not been increased since 1993 and the failures of
broad-based energy taxes in the 1990s, coupled with ongoing political obstacles to any broad-based tax increase, have eliminated a carbon tax as a
viable option.[17]

Using Tax Breaks in Lieu of Spending

The United States has long used income tax deductions and credits as if they are the best prescription for virtually any economic or social problem the nation faces. As a result, the frequently reviled and persistently underfunded IRS is the administrator of many of the nation's most important spending programs. These include tax benefits for childcare, health care, homeownership, education, low-income housing, dirty and clean energy, semiconductor manufacturing, personal retirement accounts, and tax credits for children. The Joint Committee on Taxation lists such "federal tax expenditures" for individuals and business entities and estimates their costs.[18] Some provisions, such as refundable earned income and child tax credits, help low- and moderate-income families, but others, like the home mortgage interest deduction and tax breaks for retirement savings, concentrate their benefits in the top half of the income distribution.[19] Many bestow greater benefits as income rises. Numerous tax breaks favor particular industries.

The 1986 tax-reform law decreased the costs of many such provisions in exchange for lower rates. The top individual rates have risen since then, but they remain more than ten percentage points lower than before that legislation. The number and costs of tax expenditures have grown substantially. Tax expenditures dropped from 8.5 percent of GDP in 1985 to 6 percent in 1988, but after 1993 they grew back to around 7 percent by 2020.[20] The Joint Committee on Taxation estimated that they would total more than $8 trillion from 2020 through 2024, not counting the large new tax breaks added in 2022.[21]

Republicans view such tax benefits as advancing their tax-reduction mission and, somehow, as making government smaller. Legislators who sign Grover Norquist's pledge bind themselves not to eliminate any tax breaks without providing an offsetting tax cut. It is as if they nonsensically pledged to accompany all spending cuts with tax cuts. Nor are tax breaks included in Republican efforts to curb "entitlement spending," even though, like other entitlements, they require no annual congressional appropriations and routinely endure long past appropriate termination dates. Democrats frequently prefer targeted tax cuts over spending programs in an effort to divert charges that they are big spenders. Tax cuts are not counted on the ledgers of government spending. No matter how wasteful or inequitable tax breaks may be, they rarely produce public moral outrage of the sort that erupts for government spending on the poor. Tax expenditures reduce taxes as a percentage of GDP, a common metric for measuring the size of government. Tax breaks are often the only way to get policies enacted.

Creating Risks and Sending Americans'
Money Abroad

Tax reductions, of course, are not exclusively responsible for the unparalleled increases in the federal debt since 1980, but they have produced many trillions of additional national debt. Although supply-side economics demanded tax cuts for the affluent and businesses, securing votes necessary for such cuts required income tax cuts across-the-board. Even when tax-cut legislation has primarily benefited people at the top, tax reductions have been spread down the income scale. For much of the nation's history, taxes were increased to fund wars and new entitlement spending, such as for Social Security and Medicare. In the twenty-first century, however, commitments not to raise taxes meant that massive spending to fund the wars following the terrorist attacks on September 11, 2001, to add prescription drug coverage to Medicare, to keep the economy afloat during the global financial crisis, and to respond to the Covid pandemic all went unfunded.[22]

In 2022 federal government spending (not counting tax expenditures) totaled $5.8 trillion, about 24 percent of GDP. Because of strong economic growth, revenues that year reached $4.8 trillion, 20 percent of GDP, the highest level relative to the size of the economy in more than two decades. During the half century leading up to 2021, revenues averaged 17.3 percent of GDP, while spending averaged close to 21 percent. Deficits from the excesses of spending over revenues have resulted in nearly $25 trillion of U.S. debt to the public in January 2023, about 100 percent the size of the national economy, the highest level since the end of World War II. The ongoing gap between spending and revenues implies the federal government will accumulate nearly another $15.7 trillion of debt by 2032, according to the Congressional Budget Office (CBO)—plus another $3 trillion if Congress extends the Trump tax cuts scheduled to expire in 2025.[23] The nation's debt has reached unprecedented heights in peacetime.[24]

CBO's estimates of federal debt increasing to more than $40 trillion by the end of 2032 assumes no disruption in the U.S. government's ability to borrow at reasonably low interest rates. Republicans, however, in 1995, 2011, and 2023 threatened to block increases in the debt ceiling, which could cause the United States to default on its debt obligations. Failing to raise the debt ceiling and halting the nation's ability to borrow jeopardize Americans' economic well-being and the stability of the global economy. Threats to block debt-ceiling increases have sometimes been political posturing, but as the Republican Party has moved further to the right and elected representatives who call themselves populists but behave more like nihilists, the risks increase.[25] In August 2023 one of the three private credit-rating firms downgraded its rating for US debt, noting a deterioration in the nation's standards of governance.

The United States has been fortunate that interest rates on the accumulated federal debt have been abnormally low. Even so, borrowing has not been costless. The onset of inflation in 2021 and 2022 at levels not seen since the early 1980s ended the period of extraordinarily low interest rates, at least for some time. Interest on the federal debt cost $400 billion in 2022, 1.6 percent of GDP. The Congressional Budget Office estimates interest costs will triple to $1.2 trillion by 2032, 3.3 percent of GDP (even if the 2017 tax cuts are all allowed to expire). CBO's estimates of interest rates assume interest on three-month Treasury bills will never exceed 3.8 percent, a level they exceeded in 2023.[26] Even so, interest on the federal debt will still be the most rapidly rising government expense, devouring an ever-increasing share of the federal budget. By 2052 the CBO estimates interest costs will be an unprecedented, unthinkable 7.2 percent of GDP.[27] The markets and the Federal Reserve, not the Congress, control interest costs. Neither the politicians nor the public sees it this way, but the costs of the nation's debt are similar to a large tax increase on the American people. Importantly, this is a somewhat optimistic scenario: it assumes interest rates are relatively low, the Trump tax cuts are not extended, and the United States can continue to borrow unlimited funds without sparking any economic crisis. What if these rather sunny predictions prove wrong?

When the federal debt was previously so high after World War II, the United States economy was poised to grow for decades at an unprecedented pace: Europe and Japan were in postwar shambles, and China was entering into a dark Communist era. The U.S. government owed 98 percent of the money it borrowed to finance the war to Americans. At the end of 2022, nearly a third of the nation's debt was owed to foreigners, not all of whom are friends. More than 30 cents of every dollar in interest costs is money transferred abroad.[28]

When liberals claimed Ronald Reagan's 1981 tax cuts were "a free lunch for the rich," Arthur Laffer responded, "Damn right it's a free lunch."[29] But, as rising interest costs on growing federal debt demonstrate, tax cuts are not free for the American people. The increasing public debt runs risks of higher interest rates and perhaps another financial crisis. Over time, it may undermine the dollar's exceptional role as the world's reserve currency and threaten the living standards of the American people.

Abetting Rising Inequality

Globalization of trade in goods and services and of capital flows, innovations in technology, and the decline of labor unions have contributed to growing inequality across the industrialized world, with the United States leading the pack. Just how much more income and wealth than everyone else the top 1 percent or even the much smaller 0.1 percent at the very top are accumulating is controversial, but a substantial shift to the top is incontrovertible. A crucial supply-side tenet maintains reducing tax rates on the wealthy is the best mechanism for stimulating economic growth. But there is evidence that rising inequality decreases economic growth: an OECD analysis, for example, estimated rising inequality in the United States between 1990 and 2010 reduced cumulative per capita GDP by about five percentage points.[30] Beginning in 1981, the antitax movement succeeded in nearly halving the highest federal income tax rates, reducing capital gains taxes, and emasculating the estate tax. The antitax movement has successfully targeted property taxes, individual and business income taxes, and taxes on large transfers of wealth to descendants, enhancing inequality at the top, even as political necessity required tax cuts for people in the middle and below.

Federal taxes remain progressive and some observers, such as the *Wall Street Journal*, claim that progressivity has increased, often by looking only at the share of income taxes paid by the top 1 percent relative to their incomes.[31] The Congressional Budget Office, however, concluded that average federal tax rates for the top 1 percent declined from 35.1 percent in 1979 to 30 percent in 2019 and dropped for the top .01 percent from 39.7 percent to 30.2 percent during the same period.[32] The CBO's calculations ignore changes in estate and gift taxes, omitting the large decline in those taxes achieved by the antitax movement during this period, even as wealth has become more highly concentrated at the top.[33]

Cutting spending for large popular programs for the middle class, such as Social Security and Medicare, would increase inequality and economic insecurity and has proved politically difficult, often impossible. As the population has aged and Baby Boomers retired, the costs for these programs (and for Medicaid) have increased.[34] The antitax movement, however, has thwarted any increase in the ceiling on payroll taxes to fund Social Security since 1983 (other than automatic annual inflation adjustments). When Social Security taxes were first collected in 1937, about 92 percent of earnings from the covered jobs were taxed. After falling in some decades, the amount of covered taxable earnings reached 90 percent in 1983. As more labor income has become concentrated at the top and earnings for the highest-paid workers have grown faster than average earnings, however, the Social Security payroll tax, now the largest federal tax paid by three-quarters of Americans, applied in 2020 only to about 83 percent of earnings, making the tax more regressive. The Congressional Budget Office estimated that restoring the taxable share of earnings from jobs covered by Social Security to 90 percent (and providing a corresponding increase in benefits) would reduce deficits by $670 billion between 2023 and 2032.[35]

Even closing well-publicized loopholes in payroll taxes, the estate tax, and income taxes at the top, such as for carried interests of private equity and hedge fund managers, has become extremely challenging. Large contributions and expenditures for legislative advocacy play crucial roles in blocking tax increases and advancing tax cuts. The debilitating role of money in U.S. politics has been well documented elsewhere.[36] The Supreme Court exacerbated the role of money in the nation's politics when it determined that political contributions are the equivalent of speech protected under the First Amendment. But money has many more uses in politics than making contributions. Financial support from wealthy families during efforts to repeal the estate tax financed organizational meetings and efforts, well-designed polls, grassroots advertising, research by supportive think tanks and other organizations, and advocates' travel to meet with members of Congress and testify before congressional committees. Funding by FreedomWorks and others sustained the Tea Party and kept it active during primary campaigns and numerous legislative events. Even if the constitutional protections for campaign contributions were somehow rolled back—a reversal certainly not foreseeable—large and perhaps decisive sums of money will be available for antitax efforts.

———

The United States is a low-tax country compared to other developed nations. In 2021, counting state as well as federal taxes, U.S. taxes as a share of the economy were 7.5 percentage points lower than the average of the 38 OECD member countries, 20 percentage points lower than the highest (Denmark); only six countries—Costa Rica, Turkey, Chile, Ireland, Colombia, and Mexico—were lower.[37] The difficulties of increasing taxes—even when limited to rich Americans—and the continuing potential for further reductions, coupled with the ongoing exemption of almost half the population from the income tax, which funds most of the federal government's expenditures, are not sustainable. Because of an aging population, economic and fiscal challenges are increasing while taxes to fund spending the public demands fall short. The antitax movement has ensured no politically viable remedy is in sight.

Government fell into disrepute with the American people during the 1970s, and public approval has declined since: Americans' trust in government was lower in 2022 than during the late 1970s and early 1980s, when the modern antitax movement took off.[38] Everyone seems to believe the taxes necessary to fund government should be paid by someone else. As Senate Finance Committee chairman Russell Long quipped, "Don't tax you, Don't tax me. Tax the fellow behind the tree."

When politics functions well, people with different views compromise for the common good. The nation's founders created a government with separations of powers at the national level and federalism to ensure such compromises were necessary. Rigidly partisan politics makes compromising much more difficult, sometimes impossible. Absolute pledges, such as Grover Norquist's not ever to raise taxes no matter the circumstances, prohibit compromising over taxes. Assembling coalitions to block tax increases is not a high hurdle. Creating coalitions to cut taxes by trillions in the face of mounting debt even when the economy is strong, as in 2017, has been no problem. By the early 2020s, other important twentieth-century American social movements had suffered major setbacks: the civil rights movement in its voting protections and affirmative action, the women's movement with abortion rights. But the antitax movement seems to prevail inexorably. Herb Stein, chairman of the Council of Economic Advisers under Presidents Nixon and Ford, concerned about the rising levels of debt relative to the size of the economy in 1986, told Congress: "if something cannot go on forever, it will stop."[39] The question is: will the antitax movement disprove Stein's Law?

In the late 1970s and early 1980s, with the country facing high unemployment and raging inflation causing increasing income and property taxes, enacting tax cuts and curbing inflation's impact on those taxes was appropriate, probably necessary. In the twenty-first century with significant inequalities of wealth and income, a growing economy, and unprecedented levels of national debt and interest costs, large tax cuts are irresponsible. Disguising their real costs to fit into ten-year congressional budget constraints by terminating politically popular tax reductions for the middle class that will surely be extended is legislative malpractice. Continuing down the antitax path poses risks to Americans' standards of living and the nation's claims to be a land of responsibility, hope, and opportunity. In an 1819 Supreme Court case, Chief Justice John Marshall wrote, "The power to tax involves the power to destroy; the power to destroy may defeat and render useless the power to create."[40] So, it turns out, does the power not to tax.

Acknowledgments

Writing a book always involves a mixture of collaboration and solitude—never more so than in this case. I started shaping the proposal for this book after the Covid pandemic hit in 2020 at the urging and with the typical careful scrutiny of my friend and agent Wendy Strothman. In the fall I began teaching a seminar based on material referenced here for Yale law students, an endeavor I repeated in 2021 and 2022. Their questions, comments, and insights contributed more to shape and sharpen this book than they realize. Thanks to Zoom, we benefited in those seminars from the experiences and insights shared by Bruce Bartlett, David Brockway, Ken Kies, Janice Mays, Pam Olson, David Wessel, and Vanessa Williamson, all of whom participated in or closely observed many of the events that comprise this story.

Participants in workshops at Columbia and Loyola law schools also offered useful insights on early drafts of some chapters. My Yale friends and colleagues Anne Alstott and Daniel Markovits, along with the Washington journalist Al Hunt, provided helpful comments on an early draft of the entire manuscript. Len Burman, Bill Gale, David Mayhew, and Emmett Witkovsky-Eldred offered invaluable, detailed comments, as did anonymous reviewers for Princeton University Press. My talented editor Bridget Flannery-McCoy was enthusiastic about this project from its inception and edited the manuscript with extraordinary care, skill, and insights. Jenn Backer copyedited the manuscript carefully and perceptively, sparing me many mistakes.

Numerous students provided essential research assistance, including Leila Halley-Wright and Julia Zrihen at Yale and Claire Park, Lina Pan, and Marta Poplawski at Columbia. I owe special debts of gratitude to Zachary Dulabon, who labored mightily and effectively on this project through all three of his years at Columbia Law School, and Emily Caputo, who provided crucial analysis, support, and assistance during her third year at Yale Law School and helped shepherd this book through the production process after she graduated.

This book also benefited greatly from the dedicated assistance of Patricia Page and Miriam Benson at Yale and John Christian White, Harry Edwin

Whomersley, and Santiago Mendoza at Columbia. Working from my hand-written drafts and edits no doubt drove several of them to change jobs or retire. I am also grateful to Mariana J. Newman and Maryellen Larkin of the Columbia and Yale law libraries, respectfully, who tracked down and provided me an ever-growing list of research materials. My deans, Gillian Lester at the Columbia Law School, and Heather Gerken of Yale provided important en-couragement and research support, as did the Grace P. Tomei Endowment Fund at Columbia Law School. My friends and colleagues Jed Britton-Purdy and Ian Shapiro made suggestions for what became this book's title.

Listing the people who contributed to a project like this risks overlooking someone important, so I offer an apology to those I inadvertently left out. This book, of course, inevitably draws on work and conversations over many years with people and groups necessarily omitted here.

Finally, and most importantly, I thank my family—my children, grandchil-dren, and especially my spouse Brett Dignam—for humoring and supporting me through another book. You are everything to me.

Notes

Chapter 1

1. Russell Baker, "Observer," *New York Times*, September 19, 1971.

2. Romain D. Huret, *American Tax Resisters* (Cambridge, MA: Harvard University Press, 2014).

3. Sidney Ratner, *American Taxation: Its History as a Social Force in Democracy* (New York: W. W. Norton, 1942), 18. For a more recent analysis of the debates over taxation during the founding, see Max M. Edling, *A Revolution in Favor of Government: Origins of the U.S. Constitution and the Making of the American State* (Oxford: Oxford University Press, 2008).

4. For a good short explanation of the Boston Tea Party, see Joseph J. Thorndike, "Four Things You Should Know about the Boston Tea Party," *Tax Notes*, April 12, 2010, 141–43.

5. Adam Gopnik, "Finding the Founders," *New Yorker*, October 31, 2022, 63.

6. For further discussion of Fries's Rebellion, see Paul Douglas Newman, *Fries's Rebellion: The Enduring Struggle for the American Revolution* (Philadelphia: University of Pennsylvania Press, 2005). This "direct tax" was apportioned among the states, as the Constitution requires. U.S. Constitution, Article I, Section 9.

7. Pollock v. Farmers' Loan & Trust Company, 157 U.S. 429 (1895), *affirmed on rehearing*, 158 U.S. 601 (1895).

8. "Sources of Revenue for the Federal Government," *DataLab*, 2021, https://datalab .usaspending.gov/americas-finance-guide/revenue/categories.

9. See, e.g., Thomas Byrne Edsall, *The New Politics of Inequality* (New York: W. W. Norton, 1985), 213.

10. Dominic Sandbrook, *Mad as Hell: The Crisis of the 1970s and the Rise of the Populist Right* (New York: Knopf, 2011), xiii.

11. Ruth Rosen, *The World Split Open: How the Modern Women's Movement Changed America*, rev. ed. (New York: Penguin Books, 2006).

12. Lyndon B. Johnson, "Commencement Address at Howard University: 'To Fulfill These Rights'" (speech, Washington, DC, June 4, 1965), The American Presidency Project, https:// www.presidency.ucsb.edu/documents/commencement-address-howard-university-fulfill -these-rights.

13. Robert D. Putnam, *Bowling Alone: The Collapse and Revival of American Community* (New York: Simon and Schuster, 2000).

14. The literature on the 1970s is now vast. A few examples include: James T. Patterson, *Restless Giant: The United States from Watergate to Bush v. Gore* (New York: Oxford University Press, 2005); David Frum, *How We Got Here: The 70's, The Decade That Brought You Modern Life—For Better or Worse* (New York: Basic Books, 2000); Jefferson Cowie, *Stayin' Alive: The 1970s and the Last Days of the Working Class* (New York: New Press, 2010); Laura Kalman, *Right Star Rising: A New Politics, 1974–1980* (New York: W. W. Norton, 2010); Sandbrook, *Mad as Hell*; Michael J. Graetz, *The End of Energy: The Unmaking of America's Environment, Security, and Independence* (Cambridge, MA: MIT Press, 2011); Michael J. Graetz and Linda Greenhouse, *The Burger Court and the Rise of the Judicial Right* (New York: Simon and Schuster, 2016).

15. Daniel T. Rodgers, *Age of Fracture* (Cambridge, MA: Harvard University Press, 2011).

16. Ibid., 10–12.

17. Steven A. Bank, Kirk J. Stark, and Joseph J. Thorndike, *War and Taxes* (Washington, DC: Urban Institute Press, 2008); Walter Scheidel, *The Great Leveler: Violence and the History of Inequality from the Stone Age to the Twenty-First Century* (Princeton: Princeton University Press, 2017).

18. Gerald R. Ford, "Address before a Joint Session of the Congress Reporting on the State of the Union," January 19, 1976, https://www.presidency.ucsb.edu/documents/address-before -joint-session-the-congress-reporting-the-state-the-union; Eileen Shanahan, "Ford May Consider Tax Cuts in 1976," *New York Times*, June 26, 1975.

19. Graetz, *The End of Energy*, 37.

20. See, e.g., Edsall, *The New Politics of Inequality*, 13, 213–14.

21. Lester C. Thurow, *The Zero-Sum Society: Distribution and the Possibilities for Economic Change* (New York: Basic Books, 1980), 1–25.

22. Gunnar Myrdal, Richard Sterner, and Arnold M. Rose, *An American Dilemma: The Negro Problem and Modern Democracy* (New York: Harper & Brothers, 1944).

23. Ibid., xlvi–xlvii, lii.

24. Articles of Confederation, Articles II and VIII (1781).

25. U.S. Constitution, Article I, Section 8.

26. U.S. Constitution, Article I, Section 9.

27. The first time the Supreme Court interpreted the scope of the phrase "other direct tax" was in Hylton v. United States, 3 U.S. 171 (1796), holding that a federal tax on carriages was not a direct tax and did not need to be apportioned to the states.

28. See, e.g., Robin L. Einhorn, *American Taxation, American Slavery* (Chicago: University of Chicago Press, 2006), 157–60; Bruce Ackerman, "Taxation and the Constitution," *Columbia Law Review* 99, no. 1 (1999): 1–58. For a detailed discussion of how the struggle over taxation, including the apportionment of capitation or other direct taxes, was a critical aspect of the struggle between nationalists and states-righters, see Edling, *A Revolution in Favor of Government*.

29. Eric Foner, *Reconstruction: America's Unfinished Revolution* (New York: HarperCollins, 1988), 346–411.

30. Harper v. Virginia Board of Elections, 383 U.S. 663 (1966).

31. Alberto Alesina, Edward Glaeser, and Bruce Sacerdote, "Why Doesn't the US Have a European-Style Welfare System?" (National Bureau of Economic Research, working paper 8524, 2001).

32. J. Harvie Wilkinson III, *From Brown to Bakke: The Supreme Court and School Integration: 1954–1978* (New York: Oxford University Press, 1979), 6.

33. Green v. County School Board of New Kent County, 391 U.S. 430, 438 (1968).

34. Swann v. Charlotte-Mecklenburg Board of Education, 402 U.S. 1 (1971). In 1974 the Court decided mandatory busing for desegregation stopped at the school district's boundary. Milliken v. Bradley, 418 U.S. 717 (1974). That decision halted desegregation across city lines, prompting flight to suburbs and exurbs by many white families who could afford to move.

35. Betty K. Koed, "The Politics of Reform: Policymakers and the Immigration Act of 1965" (PhD diss., University of California, Santa Barbara, 1999), 171–72.

36. Hugh Davis Graham, *Collision Course: The Strange Convergence of Affirmative Action and Immigration Policy in America* (New York: Oxford University Press, 2002). For the immigration numbers in the text, see table 5.1, 95.

37. In 1974 the Supreme Court decided that school systems must provide English-language instruction and the failure to do so violates the Civil Rights Act of 1964. Lau v. Nichols, 414 U.S. 563 (1974). In 1982 the Supreme Court required free K–12 education for undocumented immigrant children. Plyler v. Doe, 457 U.S. 202 (1982).

38. Arlie Russell Hochschild, *Strangers in Their Own Land: Anger and Mourning on the American Right* (New York: New Press, 2016); Desmond S. King and Rogers M. Smith, *Still a House Divided: Race and Politics in Obama's America* (Princeton: Princeton University Press, 2011).

39. Edsall, *The New Politics of Inequality*, 39.

40. "'Welfare Queen' Becomes Issue in Reagan Campaign," *New York Times*, February 15, 1976; Josh Levin, "The Real Story of Linda Taylor, America's Original Welfare Queen," *Slate*, December 19, 2013; Gillian Brockell, "She Was Stereotyped as 'The Welfare Queen'; The Truth Was More Disturbing, a New Book Says," *Washington Post*, May 21, 2019.

41. Kevin P. Phillips, *The Emerging Republican Majority* (New York: Arlington House, 1969); James Boyd, "Nixon's Southern Strategy—It's All in the Charts," *New York Times*, May 17, 1970.

42. Rick Perlstein, "Exclusive: Lee Atwater's Infamous 1981 Interview on the Southern Strategy," *The Nation*, November 13, 2012.

43. Frum, *How We Got Here*, 90–98.

44. E.g., Reva B. Siegel, "Constitutional Culture, Social Movement Conflict and Constitutional Change: The Case of the De Facto ERA," *California Law Review* 94, no. 5 (2006): 1323–1420; see also Donald T. Critchlow, *Phyllis Schlafly and Grassroots Conservatism: A Woman's Crusade* (Princeton: Princeton University Press, 2005); Jane J. Mansbridge, *Why We Lost the ERA*, 2nd ed. (Chicago: University of Chicago Press, 1986); and Graetz and Greenhouse, *The Burger Court and the Rise of the Judicial Right*, 162–91.

45. It is impossible in a progressive rate income tax to tax equally all married couples with the same total income and keep an individual's tax liability unchanged by marriage. Boris I. Bittker, "Federal Income Taxation and the Family," *Stanford Law Review* 27, no. 6 (July 1975): 1395–96, 1429–431.

46. E.g., Druker v. Commissioner, 697 F.2d 46 (2d Cir. 1982); Boyter v. Commissioner, 688 F.2d 1382 (4th Cir. 1981).

47. Michael J. Graetz, *The Decline (and Fall?) of the Income Tax* (New York: W. W. Norton, 1997), 32–39.

48. Obergefell v. Hodges, 576 U.S. 644 (2015); William N. Eskridge Jr. and Christopher R. Riano, *Marriage Equality: From Outlaws to In-Laws* (New Haven: Yale University Press, 2020).

49. Thomas Sewall Adams, "Ideas and Idealism in Taxation," *American Economic Review* 18, no. 1 (1928): 1–8.

50. E.g., Michael J. Graetz and Ian Shapiro, *The Wolf at the Door: The Menace of Economic Insecurity and How to Fight It* (Cambridge, MA: Harvard University Press, 2020), 58–60.

51. See Larry M. Bartels, *Unequal Democracy: The Political Economy of the New Gilded Age* (Princeton: Princeton University Press, 2017).

52. Federal Election Commission v. Cruz, U.S. Supreme Court, No. 21-12, Slip Opinion, May 16, 2022, 13–23; Graetz and Greenhouse, *The Burger Court and the Rise of the Judicial Right*, 243–65.

53. Jeffrey H. Birnbaum and Alan S. Murray, *Showdown at Gucci Gulch: Lawmakers, Lobbyists, and the Unlikely Triumph of Tax Reform* (New York: Random House, 1987).

54. In the 1972 elections, corporate and business trade association political action committees (PACs) contributed $2.7 million to congressional candidates. In 1976, they gave $10 million, outspending labor unions for the first time. In 1980, they contributed $19.2 million.

55. Mark S. Mizruchi, *The Fracturing of the American Corporate Elite* (Cambridge, MA: Harvard University Press, 2013), 265.

56. Louis Eisenstein, *The Ideologies of Taxation* (New York: Ronald Press, 1961), 12, 49.

57. Steven R. Weisman, *The Great Tax Wars: Lincoln to Wilson—The Fierce Battles over Money and Power That Transformed the Nation* (New York: Simon and Schuster, 2002), 349.

58. Jennifer Burns, *Goddess of the Market: Ayn Rand and the American Right* (Oxford: Oxford University Press, 2009), 2, 4, 254–78.

59. Robert Nozick, *Anarchy, State, and Utopia* (New York: Basic Books, 1974); John Rawls, *A Theory of Justice* (Cambridge, MA: Harvard University Press, 1971).

60. Nozick, *Anarchy, State, and Utopia*, 149.

61. Ibid., 169.

62. "The Hundred Most Influential Books since the Second World War," *Times Literary Supplement*, October 6, 1995, https://www.goodreads.com/list/show/38381.TLS_The _Hundred_Most_Influential_Books_Since_the_Second_World_War.

63. Michael J. Graetz and Ian Shapiro, *Death by a Thousand Cuts: The Fight over Taxing Inherited Wealth* (Princeton: Princeton University Press, 2005), 85.

64. Ibid., 89.

65. Ana Hernández Kent and Lowell R. Ricketts, "Has Wealth Inequality in America Changed over Time? Here Are Key Statistics," Federal Reserve Bank of St. Louis, December 2, 2020, https://www.stlouisfed.org/open-vault/2020/December/has-wealth-inequality-changed -over-time-key-statistics; Congressional Budget Office, *Trends in the Distribution of Family Wealth, 1989 to 2019*, September 2022, https://www.cbo.gov/publication/58533#:~:text=By%20 the%20end%20of%20the,the%20first%20quarter%20of%202022.

Chapter 2

1. Robert Lindsey, "Howard Jarvis, 82, Tax Rebel Is Dead," *New York Times*, August 14, 1986. Typically, opponents of California's referendums outspend the proponents and usually defeat the proposals, but Proposition 13 was unusual because the campaign favoring it was exceptionally well financed. The proponents spent an amount slightly greater than that of the opposition: $2,152,874 versus $2,000,204. Most financial support for 13 was raised through sophisticated direct-mail fundraising efforts that produced thousands of relatively small donations and from larger amounts supplied by apartment owners and their associations. Small businesses and other real estate interests also strongly favored 13 and contributed to support it. Daniel A. Smith, "Howard, Jarvis, Populist Entrepreneur: Reevaluating the Causes of Proposition 13," *Social Science History* 23, no. 2 (Summer 1999): 195–201.

2. Peter Schrag, *Paradise Lost: California's Experience, America's Future* (New York: New Press, 1998), 151.

3. Ibid., 141; Robert Kuttner, *Revolt of the Haves: Tax Rebellions and Hard Times* (New York: Simon and Schuster, 1980), 83.

4. Evelyn Danforth, "Proposition 13, Revisited," *Stanford Law Review* 73, no. 2 (February 2021): 513.

5. Although rents were not reduced, some tenants may have paid lower rents over time than they would have if property taxes had risen faster than they did under Proposition 13. Nada Wasi and Michelle White, "Property Tax Limitations and Mobility: The Lock-In Effect of California's Proposition 13" (National Bureau of Economic Research, working paper, no. 11108, February 2005), https://www.nber.org/system/files/working_papers/w11108/w11108.pdf.

6. Kuttner, *Revolt of the Haves*, 20.

7. Dominic Sandbrook, *Mad as Hell: The Crisis of the 1970s and the Rise of the Populist Right* (New York: Knopf, 2011), 286.

8. Jack Anderson, "The Prop. 13 Man and Some Scams," *Washington Post*, July 25, 1978.

9. Howard Jarvis, *I'm Mad as Hell* (New York: Times Company, 1979), 22.

10. Jarvis reports the facts of his life in ibid., 193–280.

11. Ibid., 210.

12. Ibid., 258.

13. In 1970, Jarvis lost in a statewide contest for the state Board of Equalization, and in 1977 he lost in the Republican primary for mayor of Los Angeles. Jarvis insisted these campaigns were intended to serve his tax-limitation efforts. Ibid., 33–44.

14. Anderson, "The Prop 13 Man and Some Scams"; Schrag, *Paradise Lost*, 130–35.

15. Jarvis, *I'm Mad as Hell*, 25.

16. Ronald Reagan, "Reflections on the Failure of Proposition #1," *National Review*, December 7, 1973.

17. "Maniac or Messiah," *Time*, July 19, 1978. Proposition 13 was known as the Jarvis-Gann initiative, but Paul Gann, a former automobile and real estate salesman, barely merited the co-authorship. Having just missed the ballot with his 1976 tax-limitation effort, Jarvis had enlisted the Northern Californian Gann to collect signatures from the area near Sacramento. Gann managed to collect 150,000 signatures, but they were unnecessary surplus. Proposition 13 got 1,264,690 signatories, the most ever for a California initiative.

18. Ibid.

19. Kuttner, *Revolt of the Haves*, 51.

20. Martin Gilens, *Why Americans Hate Welfare* (Chicago: University of Chicago Press, 1999), 41.

21. Kuttner, *Revolt of the Haves*, 31–33.

22. In San Francisco, for example, the convicted property tax assessors had valued business property at just under half its market value but had valued homes at 10 to 20 percent of their market value. Ibid., 35.

23. Schrag, *Paradise Lost*, 135. Shortly before the vote, the Los Angeles property tax assessor released new information describing additional property tax increases in Los Angeles, which further prompted votes for Proposition 13. Kuttner, *Revolt of the Haves*, 75–77.

24. Schrag, *Paradise Lost*, 173–74.

25. Danforth, "Proposition 13, Revisited," 522.

26. "Maniac or Messiah."

27. Danforth, "Proposition 13, Revisited," 513, 549.

28. Nordlinger v. Hahn, 505 U.S. 1, 6 (1992).

29. Schrag, *Paradise Lost*, 177.

30. Serrano v. Priest, 96 Cal. Rep. 3d 584 (1971); see William A. Fischel, "Did *Serrano* Cause Proposition 13?" *National Tax Journal* 42, no. 4 (1989): 465–73.

31. San Antonio Independent School District v. Rodriguez, 411 U.S. 1 (1973).

32. Serrano v. Priest, 18 Cal. Rep. 3d 728 (1976). In affirming the trial court's remedy, the Court did not insist on the $100 differential as the only remedy, but it soon became a crucial decisive test. Alan Post, "Effects of Proposition 13 on the State of California," *National Tax Journal* 32, no. 2 (June 1979): 384. (The $100 limit was indexed for inflation.)

33. Fischel, "Did *Serrano* Cause Proposition 13?" 465.

34. Ibid., 472. The New York case was Board of Education v. Nyquist, 453 New York State 2d 643 (1982).

35. Kuttner, *Revolt of the Haves*, 23.

36. Howard Jarvis, "Illegal Aliens Take Free Ride on Gravy Train," *Sacramento Bee*, September 17, 1978.

37. Lew Cannon, "Californians to Vote on Busing Issue," *Washington Post*, October 26, 1979; Pamela G. Hollie, "Foes of Busing Hail Los Angeles Victory," *New York Times*, March 13, 1981.

38. Regents of the University of California v. Bakke, 438 U.S. 2651 (1978). A crucial opinion by Justice Lewis Powell, however, permitted special admissions consideration of "blacks and Chicanos and other minority students" to achieve racial diversity in the student body, thwarting the ambitions of white complainants of "reverse discrimination" to eliminate affirmative action in college admissions. Twenty-five years later, in a case involving the University of Michigan Law School, a 5–4 majority of the Court held that, with individualized evaluation of each applicant, "student body diversity . . . can justify the use of race in university admissions." Grutter v. Bollinger, 539 U.S. 306, 323–25 (2003). In June 2023 the Court barred taking race into account

in college admissions in cases challenging the admissions practices of Harvard and the University of North Carolina. Students for Fair Admissions, Inc. v. President and Fellows of Harvard College, No. 20-1199, Slip Op. June 29, 2023.

39. Jarvis, *I'm Mad as Hell*, 125 (emphasis original).

40. Terry Schwadron, ed., *California and the American Tax Revolt: Proposition 13 Five Years Later* (Berkeley: University of California Press, 1984), 150.

41. Margaret A. Kilgore, "Jarvis Criticizes Affirmative Job Training Programs," *Los Angeles Times*, May 24, 1978

42. Ronald L. Soble, "Minorities' Leaders Expect Setback If Prop. 13 Wins," *Los Angeles Times*, June 5, 1978.

43. Ibid.

44. George Skelton, "Voters Didn't Believe Warnings," *Los Angeles Times*, June 7, 1978.

45. Arnold Sawislack, "The Limits of Proposition 13," *Press Democrat*, July 19, 1978; Timur Akman-Duffy, "The Hidden Values in Tax Reform: Examining Coded Language and Racial Bias during the Proposition 13 Campaign" (manuscript, August 2020, Yale Law School).

46. Jimmy Breslin, "Why Don't These People Get the Message of Prop. 13 and Just Disappear," *Los Angeles Times*, June 25, 1978.

47. Earl Raab, "The Message of Proposition 13," *Commentary*, September 1978.

48. Austin Scott, "Prop. 13, Bakke Decision Poses Serious Problems for Blacks, NAACP Believes," *Los Angeles Times*, July 5, 1978.

49. Compare Swann v. Charlotte-Mecklenburg County Board of Education, 402 U.S. 1 (1971) with Parents Involved in Community Schools v. Seattle School District No. 1, 551 U.S. 701 (2007) (school desegregation) and Griggs v. Duke Power Co., 401 U.S. 424 (1971) with Washington v. Davis, 426 U.S. 229 (1926) (employment discrimination).

50. The night before the vote for 13, David Brinkley on *NBC Nightly News* used the phrase "sticking it to the man" to describe some of the enthusiasm for Proposition 13.

51. Smith, "Howard Jarvis, Populist Entrepreneur," 183–84.

52. Eric Smith and Jack Citrin, "The Building of a Majority for Tax Limitation in California, 1968–1978" (University of California State Data Program research paper, 1979), quoted in Smith, "Howard Jarvis, Populist Entrepreneur," 183.

53. Schwadron, *California and the American Tax Revolt*, 132–40.

54. Janet L. Yellen, "Perspectives on Inequality and Opportunity from the Survey of Consumer Finance" (speech, Boston, October 17, 2014), https://www.federalreserve.gov/newsevents/speech/yellen20141017a.pdf.

55. Danforth, "Proposition 13, Revisited," 524.

56. For discussions of referendums as "direct democracy" and the relationship of supermajority rules to majority rules, see, e.g., Leah Trueblood, "Are Referendums Directly Democratic?" *Oxford Journal of Legal Studies* 40 (2020): 425–48; John Charles Bradbury and Joseph M. Johnson, "Do Supermajority Rules Limit or Enhance Majority Tyranny? Evidence from the United States, 1960–1997," *Public Choice* 127, no. 3 (June 2006): 429–41.

57. Kuttner, *Revolt of the Haves*, 26, 55. Kuttner notes that the people of California were not as agitated by the income tax or by income tax increases due to inflation as much as by property taxes, a phenomenon he explains because withholding income taxes from wages makes the income tax far less visible than property taxes, which need to be paid in one or two installments. But, beginning in 1978, antitaxers targeted income taxes at the federal level. See chapters 4 and 5.

58. Danforth, "Proposition 13, Revisited," 521.

59. Daniel R. Mullins and Bruce A. Wallin, "Tax and Expenditure Limitations: Introduction and Overview," *Public Budgeting and Finance* 24 (2004): 1–15; Ariel Jurow Kleiman, "Tax Limits and the Future of Local Democracy," *Harvard Law Review* 133, no. 6 (April 2020): appendix.

60. Bethany P. Paquin, "Chronicle of the 165-Year History of State-Imposed Property Tax Limitations" (Lincoln Institute of Land Policy, working paper WP15BP1, April 2015); Biing

Yuan, Joseph Cordes, David Brunneri, and Michael Bell, "Tax Expenditure Limitations and Their Effects on Local Public Finances" (George Washington Institute of Public Policy, August 30, 2007), http://www.gwu.edu/ngwipp/lincoln/yeean/condes/Brunore_Bell .pdf.

61. California Proposition 58, Tax Assessments on Real Estate Transfers Within Families Amendment (1986); California Proposition 193, Property Appraisal Exception for Grandparent-Grandchild Property Transfers Amendment (1996).

62. California Proposition 60, Replacement Property Valuation Amendment (1986).

63. Scott Schafer, "10% of Landowners Will Pay 92% of New Property Tax Revenue, Prop. 15 Supporters Say," KQED, July 15, 2020, https://www.kqed.org/news/11829012/10-of -landowners-will-pay-92-of-new-property-tax-revenue-prop-15-supporters-say.

64. Alex Padilla, *Statement of Vote: General Election November 3, 2020* (Sacramento: California Secretary of State, 2020), https://elections.cdn.sos.ca.gov/sov/2020-general/sov /complete-sov.pdf.

65. David Brinkley, *NBC Nightly News*, June 5, 1978.

66. Schrag, *Paradise Lost*, 9.

67. "Howard Jarvis," *People*, December 25, 1978, https://people.com/archive/howard-jarvis -vol-10-no-26/.

68. Sandbrook, *Mad as Hell*, 290.

Chapter 3

1. Kristin Green, *Something Must Be Done about Prince Edward County* (New York: Harper-Collins, 2015), 42. See also Katy June-Frieson, "Massive Resistance in a Small Town," *Humanities* 34, no. 5 (September–October 2013), https://www.neh.gov/humanities/2013/septemberoctober /feature/massive-resistance-in-small-town.

2. After oral argument in December 1952, the Court was split with only four justices clearly viewing segregated public schools as unconstitutional; two disagreed and the remaining three were undecided. Then, in September 1953, Chief Justice Fred Vinson died from a sudden heart attack, and President Eisenhower—in a decision he would come to regret—chose Earl Warren, the three-term California governor, to replace Vinson. Michael Klarman, *From Jim Crow to Civil Rights: The Supreme Court and the Struggle for Racial Equality* (New York: Oxford University Press, 2004), 293–300, 302 (citing papers of Justice William Douglas); see also Richard Kluger, *Simple Justice: The History of Brown v. Board of Education and Black America's Struggle for Equality* (New York: Knopf, 1976).

3. Klarman, *Jim Crow*, 313; Mark V. Tushnet, *Making Civil Rights Law: Thurgood Marshall and the Supreme Court, 1936–1961* (New York: Oxford University Press, 1994), 217–18.

4. Brown v. Board of Education of Topeka, Kansas, 349 U.S. 294, 300–301 (1955).

5. Klarman, *Jim Crow*, 315.

6. The most famous confrontation came on September 25, 1957, when a reluctant President Eisenhower sent the 101st Airborne to Little Rock, Arkansas, to enforce a federal court desegregation order to admit nine Black children to Little Rock's all-white Central High School. In a 1958 opinion, signed by all nine justices, the Supreme Court ordered integration to proceed. The Arkansas governor and legislature responded by closing all Little Rock high schools for a year. Cooper v. Aaron, 358 U.S. 1 (1958).

7. Green, *Something Must Be Done*, 75.

8. Ibid., 80–82.

9. Ibid., 168.

10. Griffin v. County School Board of Prince Edward County, 377 U.S. 218 (1964). In January 1963, celebrating the centennial of the Emancipation Proclamation, Robert Kennedy described Prince Edward County as a "disgrace to our country." He added, "We may observe, with

as much sadness as irony, that outside of Africa, South of the Sahara, where education is still a difficult challenge, the only places on earth known not to provide free public education are Communist China, North Vietnam, Sarawak, Singapore, British Honduras—and Prince Edward County, Virginia"; "The Story of Prince Edward County Schools," Public Broadcasting System, https://www.pbs.org/newshour/classroom/app/uploads/2014/04/Prince-Edward -County-School-Handout.pdf.

11. Green, *Something Must Be Done*, 144–45, 196.

12. David Nevin and Robert E. Bills, *The Schools That Fear Built: Segregationist Academies in the South* (Washington, DC: Acropolis Books, 1976); Green, *Something Must Be Done*, 97. In Memphis alone the public schools lost 25,000 white students to private all-white schools. Nevin and Bills, *The Schools That Fear Built*, 12.

13. Coffey v. State Educational Finance Commission, 296 F. Supp. 1389 (S.D. Miss. 1969).

14. Ibid., n7.

15. Green v. Kennedy, 309 F. Supp. 1127, 1135 (D.D.C. 1970).

16. Ibid., 1140.

17. Green v. Connally, 330 F. Supp 1150, 1174 (D.D.C. 1971). John Connally had replaced David Kennedy as secretary of the treasury and as defendant in the lawsuit.

18. Coit v. Green, 400 U.S. 997 (1971).

19. Internal Revenue Service, *IRS News Releases*, July 10 and 19, 1970.

20. Internal Revenue Service, Revenue Ruling 71-447, 1971–2, *Cumulative Bulletin* 230 (1971).

21. "Statement of Randolph W. Thrower before the Ways and Means Committee on the Tax Exempt Status of Racially Discriminatory Private Schools," *Tax Lawyer* 35, no. 3 (Spring 1982): 701–13, 709; see also Norwood v. Harrison, 413 U.S. 455 (1973), holding that the Constitution barred state provision of textbooks to segregated private schools. In that case, the federal district court judge observed that "the ultimate issue . . . is not whether black students are actually enrolled, but whether their absence is because the school has restrictively denied their access." Norwood v. Harrison, 382 F. Supp. 921, 926 (N.D. Miss. 1974).

22. Olatunde C. A. Johnson, "The Story of *Bob Jones University v. United States*: Race, Religion, and Congress' Extraordinary Acquiescence," in *Statutory Interpretation Stories*, ed. William Eskridge, Phillip P. Frickey, and Elizabeth Garrett (St. Paul: Foundation Press, 2010), quoting the complaint in Goldsboro Christian Schools v. United States, 461 U.S. 574 (1983).

23. Internal Revenue Service, Revenue Procedure 75-50, 1975-2, *Cumulative Bulletin*, 587; Internal Revenue Service, Revenue Ruling 75-231, 1975-1, *Cumulative Bulletin*, 158.

24. Wright v. Regan 656 F.2d 820, 825 (D.C. Cir. 1981). Originally filed as Wright v. Simon, No. 76-1426 (D.D.C. 1476).

25. Ibid.

26. Internal Revenue Service, Proposed Revenue Procedure, 43 Fed. Reg. 37296 (1978).

27. Sidney M. Milkis and Daniel Tichenor, *Rivalry and Reform: Presidents, Social Movements, and the Transformation of American Politics* (Chicago: University of Chicago Press, 2019), 210 (emphasis added).

28. Rick Perlstein, *Reaganland: America's Right Turn, 1976–1980* (New York: Simon and Schuster, 2020), 468.

29. Matthew Avery Sutton, *Jerry Falwell and the Rise of the Religious Right* (Boston: Bedford/ St. Martin's, 2013), 12. In March 1965, just after the Selma to Montgomery marches in Alabama, Falwell gave a famous sermon called "Ministers and Marchers" to a crowd of about 1,000 people packed into the Thomas Road Baptist Church—a sermon he published and distributed widely in evangelical churches. Falwell began by questioning "the sincerity and non-violent intentions of some civil rights leaders, such as Dr. Martin Luther King, Jr., Mr. James Farmer and others, who are known to have left-wing associations," adding, "It is very obvious that the Communists . . . are taking advantage." "Believing in the Bible, as I do," Falwell said, "I would find it

impossible to stop preaching the pure saving gospel of Jesus Christ, and begin doing anything else—including fighting Communism or participating in civil rights reforms. . . . Preachers are not called to be politicians, but to be soul winners." Ibid., 57–60. In 1980, when he was vigorously supporting Ronald Reagan's presidential campaign, Falwell repudiated his "Ministers and Marchers" sermon as "false prophesy." Frances FitzGerald, *The Evangelicals: The Struggle to Shape America* (New York: Simon and Schuster, 2017), 286–87.

30. Milkis and Tichenor, *Rivalry and Reform*, 205.

31. Perlstein, *Reaganland*, 468.

32. FitzGerald, *The Evangelicals*, 277–88; Milkis and Tichenor, *Rivalry and Reform*, 199–202.

33. Perlstein, *Reaganland*, 476.

34. Ibid., 473.

35. Ibid., 472.

36. Internal Revenue Service, Proposed Revenue Procedure on Private Tax-Exempt Schools, 44, no. 31 Fed. Reg. (February 13, 1979): 9451. For vivid description of the contentious IRS hearings, see Perlstein, *Reaganland*, 475–85.

37. Green v. Miller, No. 1355–69 (D.D.C. May 5, 1980) (amended June 2, 1980). G. William Miller was then secretary of the treasury.

38. "Statement of Randolph W. Thrower," 711.

39. Kenneth Bredemieir, "Pr. Edward School Tax-Exempt Status Is Revoked by the IRS," *Washington Post*, October 14, 1978.

40. Prince Edward School Foundation v. Commissioner, 487 F. Supp. 107 (D.D.C. 1979) affirmed, No. 79-1622 (D.C. Cir. 1980), cert. denied, 450 U.S. 944 (1981).

41. William Martin, *With God on Our Side: The Rise of the Religious Right in America* (New York: Broadway Books, 2005), 170.

42. Rachel Weiner, "How ALEC Became a Political Liability," *Washington Post*, April 24, 2012. In 1974 Weyrich founded the Committee for the Survival of a Free Congress, an organization to train and mobilize conservative activists, raise funds for conservative causes, and recruit conservative candidates. Ruth Murray Brown, *For a "Christian America": A History of the Religious Right* (New York: Prometheus Books, 2002), 131–35. In 1981 Weyrich cofounded the Council for National Policy, an organization focused on political strategy for social conservatives.

43. Linda Greenhouse and Reva B. Siegel, "Before (and After) *Roe v. Wade*: New Questions about Backlash," *Yale Law Journal* 120 (2022): 2028–87, 2063.

44. Milkis and Tichenor, *Rivalry and Reform*, 202.

45. FitzGerald, *The Evangelicals*, 302.

46. Ibid., 303. Francis Schaeffer—an anti-abortion activist who had influentially attacked "secular humanism" as anti-Christian in twenty books that sold three million copies—also urged Falwell to bring evangelicals into the political arena. In 1965 Falwell had given a widely publicized sermon in which he declared, "Preachers are not called to be politicians, but to be soul savers." Sutton, *Jerry Falwell and the Rise of the Religious Right*, 57–60.

47. Sutton, *Jerry Falwell and the Rise of the Religious Right*, 32.

48. Martin, *With God on Our Side*, 173; FitzGerald, *The Evangelicals*, 303–4.

49. Martin, *With God on Our Side*, 200. In June 1979, the Moral Majority was formally organized with its headquarters in Washington, D.C. Ibid.

50. Perlstein, *Reaganland*, 491. Perlstein regards the account in the text as one of several alternatives and dates the newsletter quotation as from February 23, 1979. Ibid., 491, 498.

51. Jerry Falwell, *Listen America!* (New York: W. W. Norton, 1980).

52. Ibid. (Bantam edition, 1981), 191–92. Falwell quoted North Carolina senator Jesse Helms, "I shed no tears over clipping the wings of the Internal Revenue Service. They have asked for it. By heavy-handedness, by arbitrariness, by harassment of Christian schools, the Internal Revenue Service has asked for [congressional action]."

53. Ibid., 227–28.

54. Jerry Falwell frequently invoked opposition to abortion as the genesis of the Moral Majority, saying that when he first learned of the Supreme Court's ruling in *Roe v. Wade*, "I could not believe that seven justices on the nation's highest court could have so little regard for the value of human life." "I began to preach against abortion," he claimed, "calling it 'America's national sin.'" When "it soon became apparent that preaching was not enough," he said, the new Christian Right movement was born. Milkis and Tichenor, *Rivalry and Reform*, 201–2, 211. In its ascension to political prominence in the 1980s, Jerry Falwell's Moral Majority and his Christian evangelical allies constructed what Randall Balmer, a Columbia University professor of American religious history, calls "the abortion myth." Christian evangelicals have been quite successful in inculcating this version of their entry into politics. The political historian Jon Meacham, for example, wrote in 2015: "In the wake of the Roe v. Wade Supreme Court decision in 1973, religious conservatives were also becoming more politically active, calling for constitutional amendments banning abortion and allowing prayer in public schools." Jon Meacham, *Destiny and Power: The American Odyssey of George Herbert Walker Bush* (New York: Random House, 2015), 211. Ballmer disagrees: "Leaders of the Religious Right would have us believe that their movement began in direct response to the U.S. Supreme Court's 1973 Roe v. Wade decision." "It isn't true," he writes, describing how the battle over tax exemptions for racially discriminatory private schools was the generative event; Randall Balmer, *Thy Kingdom Come: How the Religious Right Distorts the Faith and Threatens America* (New York: Basic Books, 2006), 11–17. In 1990, years after the segregated school tax controversy had receded into the background, at a meeting of an Evangelical Right organization, the Ethics and Public Policy Center, Paul Weyrich reminded two dozen movement leaders of its origins. "Let's remember," he said, "that the Religious Right did not come together in response to the Roe decision." Instead, Weyrich insisted, what got this group going as a political movement was the attempt by the IRS to rescind the tax exemption of Bob Jones University because of its racially discriminatory policies; Balmer, *Thy Kingdom Come*, 14–15. Randall Balmer, who was at the meeting, says that Weyrich viewed the evangelical discontent over the tax-exemption issue as the "opening he was looking for to start a conservative movement using evangelicals as foot soldiers." "I had discussions with all the leading lights of the movement in the late 1970s and early 1980s, post–Roe v. Wade," Weyrich said, "and they were all arguing that the decision on segregated schools enraged the Christian community and drove them into action. It was not the other things," Weyrich concluded. Robert Billings agreed. Ibid., 15–16.

55. Thomas Byrne Edsall and Mary D. Edsall, *Chain Reaction: The Impact of Race, Rights, and Taxes on American Politics* (New York: W. W. Norton, 1991), 133.

56. C. Vann Woodward, *The Burden of Southern History* (Baton Rouge: Louisiana State University Press, 1960 and 1968), 12.

57. In *Listen America!* race is mentioned only once, when Falwell asks (in question 20), "Do you favor busing schoolchildren out of their neighborhood to achieve racial segregation?" (228). Falwell insists that "parents have the primary right and responsibility to educate their children according to the philosophy of their choice without government interference or financial penalty." Ibid., 117.

58. Robert Freedman, "The Religious Right and the Carter Administration," *Historical Journal* 48, no. 1 (March 2005): 237.

59. Ibid., 238.

60. Kiron Skinner, Annelise Anderson, and Martin Anderson, *Reagan in His Own Hand: The Writings of Ronald Reagan That Reveal His Revolutionary Vision for America* (New York: Simon and Schuster, 2001), 355.

61. Joseph Crespino, "Civil Rights and the Religious Right," in *Rightward Bound: Making America Conservative in the 1970s*, ed. Bruce Schulman and Julian E. Zelizer (Cambridge MA: Harvard University Press, 2008), 104.

62. Kathy Sawyer, "Linking Religion and Politics," *Washington Post*, August 24, 1980; Perlstein, *Reaganland*, 845.

63. Ronald Reagan, "National Affairs Campaign Address on Religious Liberty" (speech, Dallas, August 22, 1980), American Rhetoric, https://www.americanrhetoric.com/speeches/ronaldreaganreligiousliberty.htm.

64. Ibid.

65. E.g., Melton Wright, *Fortress of Faith: The Story of Bob Jones University* (Grand Rapids, MI: Eerdmans, 1960).

66. Johnson, "The Story of *Bob Jones University*," 11–12.

67. Ibid., 12–13.

68. Goldsboro Christian Schools v. United States, 436 F. Supp. 1314 (E.D.N.C. 1977). The school had never received an IRS determination that it was tax-exempt but operated as tax-exempt.

69. Bob Jones University v. United States, 468 F. Supp. 890 (D.S.C. 1978).

70. Bob Jones University v. United States, 639 F.2d 147 (4th Cir. 1980); Goldsboro Christian Schools v. United States, 644 F.2d. 879 (4th Cir. 1981).

71. For a detailed description of the internal analyses and disputes within the Reagan administration, see David Whitman, *Ronald Reagan and Tax Exemptions for Racist Schools* (Cambridge, MA: Kennedy School, Harvard University, 1984).

72. Government attorneys divided over the Reagan administration's policy change. The strongest advocate for change was Assistant Attorney General for Civil Rights William Bradford Reynolds, a DuPont family heir and corporate lawyer who had criticized many Supreme Court civil rights decisions. Some other Reagan appointees in the Justice Department and the White House and some high-ranking lawyers at the Treasury Department also supported the change. It was opposed by Deputy Solicitor General Lawrence Wallace, who had urged the Supreme Court to take the case. Treasury's top tax official and the IRS commissioner and chief counsel also wanted to defend the denial of tax benefits for segregated private schools. Wallace said he could not remember "another occasion during my 14 years in office when we've changed our position in a case after taking a position with the Supreme Court." Ibid., 49.

73. Ibid., 67.

74. Ibid., 62.

75. Ibid., 65.

76. Aaron Haberman, "Into the Wilderness: Ronald Reagan, Bob Jones University, and the Political Education of the Christian Right," *The Historian* 67, no. 2 (Summer 2005): 244.

77. Ronald Reagan, "Statement on Tax Exemptions for Private Nonprofit Educational Institutions," Reagan Library, January 12, 1982, https://www.reaganlibrary.gov/archives/speech/statement-tax-exemptions-private-nonprofit-educational-institutions-january-12-1982. See also Haberman, "Into the Wilderness," 283.

78. Whitman, *Ronald Reagan and Tax Exemptions for Racist Schools*, 106.

79. The order was issued in *Wright v. Regan*, a companion case to *Green* by parents of Black schoolchildren urging the courts to order enforcement of the IRS nondiscrimination requirement nationally. Wright v. Regan, Order No. 17-142 (D.C. Cir., February 18, 1982).

80. Johnson, "The Story of *Bob Jones University*," 18.

81. Bob Jones University v. United States, 461 U.S. 574 (1983).

82. "Tax-Exempt Hate Undone," *New York Times*, May 25, 1983, quoted in Johnson, "The Story of *Bob Jones University*," 23.

83. Haberman, "Into the Wilderness," 250.

84. Johnson, "The Story of *Bob Jones University*," 25.

85. Ibid., 26.

86. Sandra Sugawara, "Prince Edward Academy Regains Tax-Exempt Status," *Washington Post*, October 10, 1985.

87. In 1993 J. B. Fuqua, a wealthy businessman, made a large contribution to the school, which was then renamed Fuqua School, and the school instituted an open admissions policy, although it never attracted a substantial cohort of Black students. Donald P. Baker, "A $10 Million Gift of Inclusion," *Washington Post*, August 24, 1993.

88. E.g., Balmer, *Thy Kingdom Come*, 180; Cathleen Falsani, "The Prosperity Gospel," *Washington Post*, December 20, 2009, https://www.washingtonpost.com/wp-srv/special/opinions/outlook/worst-ideas/prosperity-gospel.html.

89. Perlstein, *Reaganland*, 469.

Chapter 4

1. "We Are All Keynesians Now," *Time*, December 31, 1965; "Nixon Reportedly Says He Is Now a Keynesian," *New York Times*, January 7, 1971.

2. E.g., Michael J. Graetz, *The End of Energy: The Unmaking of America's Environment, Security, and Independence* (Cambridge, MA: MIT Press, 2011), 9–20.

3. "Is Keynes Dead?" *Newsweek*, June 20, 1977; James Tobin, "How Dead Is Keynes?" *Economic Inquiry* 15, no. 4 (October 1977): 459–68; Thomas Balogh, "Is Keynes Dead?" *New Republic*, June 7, 1980.

4. "Keynes Is Dead," *Wall Street Journal*, January 31, 1977; Robert Bartley, *The Seven Fat Years and How to Do It Again* (New York: Free Press, 1992), 45–47.

5. Bruce Bartlett, *The New American Economy: The Failure of Reaganomics and a New Way Forward* (New York: Palgrave Macmillan, 2009), 103.

6. F. A. Hayek, "The Keynes Centenary: The Austrian Critique," *The Economist*, June 11, 1983, 39.

7. E.g., Milton Friedman, *Capitalism and Freedom* (Chicago: University of Chicago Press, 1962); Robert A. Mundell, "The Dollar and the Policy Mix: 1971," *Essays in International Finance*, no. 85 (May 1971): 24–28, https://ies.princeton.edu/pdf/E85.pdf; Tom Redburn, "Robert A. Mundell, a Father of the Euro and Reaganomics, Dies at 88," *New York Times*, April 5, 2021; Bruce Bartlett, "Robert Mundell's Theories Spawned Decades of Economic Debate and Still Matter to the Big Ideas of Today," *New Republic*, April 7, 2021.

8. Thomas Edsall was an exception in recognizing the importance and influence of Feldstein and the NBER in the antitax movement. Thomas Byrne Edsall, *The New Politics of Inequality* (New York: W. W. Norton, 1985), 118, 219–21.

9. Arthur Laffer, "Economist of the Century," *Wall Street Journal*, October 15, 1999.

10. Jude Wanniski, "It's Time to Cut Taxes," *Wall Street Journal*, December 11, 1974; see also Jude Wanniski, "It's Time to Cut Taxes," *Polyconomics*, June 13, 1997, http://www.polyconomics.com/ssu/ssu-970613.htm.

11. Jude Wanniski, "The Mundell-Laffer Hypothesis: A New View of the World Economy," *Public Interest* (Spring 1975): 49–51, https://www.nationalaffairs.com/public_interest/detail/the-mundell-laffer-hypothesis-a-new-view-of-the-world-economy.

12. There has long been doubt whether this story—promoted vigorously by Wanniski, who christened the drawing the "Laffer Curve"—is true. Laffer often denied it happened, but in 2015 Peter Leibhold, a curator at the Smithsonian's National Museum of American History, obtained the cloth napkin from Wanniski's widow and concluded the story was real. Naysayers still insist that Wanniski probably created this napkin long after the restaurant meeting. But the curve is certainly real. For an example of Laffer saying that he had no memory of the event, see Arthur Laffer, "The Laffer Curve: Past, Present and Future," Heritage Foundation, June 1, 2004, https://www.heritage.org/taxes/report/the-laffer-curve-past-present-and-future. Sidney Blumenthal,

among others, claims the meeting occurred in December 1974 after the November midterms. Sidney Blumenthal, *The Rise of the Counter-Establishment: The Conservative Ascent to Political Power* (New York: Harper and Row, 1988), 183–84. For a reenactment of the 1974 events by Laffer, Cheney, and Rumsfeld, see Brandon Lisy, "Dick Cheney, Donald Rumsfeld and Arthur Laffer on the Dinner Napkin That Changed the Economy," Bloomberg Businessweek, December 3, 2014, YouTube video, 7:18, https://www.youtube.com/watch?v=4yBgTN5JT-Y.

13. The phrase was derived by Wanniski from the label "supply-side fiscalism" that economist Herbert Stein adopted to distinguish the ideas from demand-side Keynesianism. James Tobin, *Policies for Prosperity: Essays in a Keynesian Mode* (Cambridge, MA: MIT Press, 1989), 73.

14. Sue Ellen Jares, "Arthur Laffer Is a Man with All the Reasons for a Big Tax Cut," *People*, April 9, 1979.

15. Jude Wanniski, *The Way the World Works*, 4th ed. (Washington, DC: Regnery Publishing, 1998), 347. (The first edition was published in 1978. All cites here are to the twentieth anniversary fourth edition.)

16. Rick Perlstein, *Reaganland: America's Right Turn, 1976–1980* (New York: Simon and Schuster, 2020), 292, citing Seymour Zucker, "Massive Tax Cuts Won't Work," *Newsday*, August 9, 1978.

17. Ibid.

18. Jim Stinson, "Laffer's Curve Lands in Nashville," *Nashville Business Journal*, January 27, 2008, https://www.bizjournals.com/nashville/stories/2008/01/28/small62.htmlr.

19. In addition to his energetic efforts to secure supply-side tax cuts, Wanniski, following Robert Mundell's lead, was an obsessive advocate for relinking the dollar to gold and reversing the changes in monetary policy wrought in 1971–73 by Richard Nixon, John Connally, and Paul Volcker. Robert D. Hershey Jr., "Notion of Reviving Gold Standard Debated Seriously in Washington," *New York Times*, September 18, 1981. In this endeavor, unlike supply-side tax cuts, Wanniski was unsuccessful.

20. Bartley, *Seven Fat Years*, 43–54.

21. Robert Bartley, "Introduction to the Third Edition," in *The Way the World Works*, ed. Jude Wanniski (Morristown, NJ: Polyconomics, 1989), 368.

22. Jude Wanniski, "Introduction to the Second Edition," in *The Way the World Works*, ed. Jude Wanniski (New York: Simon and Schuster, 1983), ix.

23. Jude Wanniski, "Taxes and the Two-Santa Theory," *National Observer*, March 6, 1976, https://wallstreetpit.com/26546-jude-wanniski-taxes-and-a-two-santa-theory.

24. "Tax the Rich!" *Wall Street Journal*, March 8, 1977, quoted in Rowland Evans and Robert Novak, *The Reagan Revolution* (New York: E. P. Dutton, 1981), 89.

25. Robert Bartley published his paean to supply-side economics in 1992 in *Seven Fat Years*.

26. John Brooks, "The Supply Side," *New Yorker*, April 11, 1982, 99.

27. Wanniski, *The Way the World Works* (1989), 326.

28. Ibid., xv.

29. Robert Novak, "Father of Supply-Side," CNN, September 1, 2005, https://cnn.com/2005/POLITICS/09/01/supply.side/index.htm.

30. Blumenthal, *The Rise of the Counter-Establishment*, 184.

31. Morton Kondracke and Fred Barnes, *Jack Kemp: The Bleeding Heart Conservative Who Changed America* (New York: Sentinel, 2015), 38.

32. Blumenthal, *The Rise of the Counter-Establishment*, 186; Perlstein *Reaganland*, 289.

33. Kondracke and Barnes, *Jack Kemp*, 38–39.

34. Statement of Jack Kemp, December 18, 1975, 94th Cong., 1st sess., 121 Cong. Rec., pt. 32:41702.

35. Kondracke and Barnes, *Jack Kemp*, 45, quoting Kemp staffer Bruce Bartlett.

36. Ibid., 45–46.

37. Ibid., 43.

38. Richard Booth et al., "Starring for the GOP," *Newsweek*, February 20, 1978.

39. Perlstein, *Reaganland*, 289.

40. Ibid., 291.

41. Booth et al., "Starring for the GOP."

42. Bartlett, *The New American Economy*, 114.

43. Jude Wanniski, "Stupendous Steiger," *Wall Street Journal*, April 26, 1978; Bartley, *Seven Fat Years*, 65.

44. A week earlier, the *Journal* cheered Steiger's claim "to be close to the 19 votes" he needed to get his capital gains tax cut approved by the 27 members of the House Ways and Means Committee. With only 12 Republicans on the committee, Steiger needed 7 Democrats to get a majority. John Pierson, "President's Tax Measures May Soon Die at Hands of Democrats on House Panel," *Wall Street Journal*, April 20, 1978; Bartley, *Seven Fat Years*, 61.

45. "Distribution of Long-Term Capital Gains and Qualified Dividends by Expanded Cash Income Percentile, 2018," Tax Policy Center, November 16, 2018, https://www.taxpolicycenter .org/model-estimates/distribution-individual-income-tax-long-term-capital-gains-and -qualified-30.

46. Perlstein, *Reaganland*, 279.

47. Department of Treasury News, "Secretary Blumenthal Opposes Ad Hoc Changes in Tax Rules for Capital Gains," May 15, 1978, quoted in Bartley, *Seven Fat Years*, 69–70.

48. E.g., Bartley, *Seven Fat Years*, 64–71; Bruce Bartlett, "The Case for Ending the Capital Gains Tax," *Financial Analysts Journal* 41, no. 3 (June–July 1985): 23–30. Proponents of low capital gains taxes claim that: (1) much capital gain is due to inflation; (2) taxing gains on corporate stock is "double" taxation; (3) taxing capital gains inhibits investment, capital formation, and capital mobility; (4) capital gains taxes deter risky entrepreneurial investments; and (5) taxing capital gains reduces the standard of living of all Americans. Some of these claims are true, but not all.

49. "Charls Walker," *Wikipedia*, last modified April 8, 2022, https://en.m.wikipedia.org/wiki /Charls_Walker. ACCF was originally known as the American Council on Capital Gains and Estate Taxation.

50. Bart Barnes, "Charls E. Walker, Tax Lobbyist for GOP and Big Business, Dies at 91," *Washington Post*, June 29, 2015.

51. Perlstein, *Reaganland*, 278.

52. Ibid., 275; Charles Elia, "Economist Says Capital Gains Tax Reduction Would Benefit Economy More than a Tax Cut," *Wall Street Journal*, May 5, 1978.

53. Robert Kuttner, *Revolt of the Haves: Tax Rebellions and Hard Times* (New York: Simon and Schuster, 1980), 248.

54. The Revenue Act of 1978, Pub. L. No. 95-600, §§ 401, 402, 421, and 515, amending Internal Revenue Code, §§ 55, 1201, and 1202 (1978). In addition to lowering capital gains rates, these changes also repealed a provision that would have taxed unrealized capital gains on property transferred at death when sold by the heir.

55. Bartley, *Seven Fat Years*, 70–71.

56. Ibid., 61.

57. Ibid., 64–65, 70.

58. Evans and Novak, *The Reagan Revolution*, 41–43.

59. David Wildstein, "The Life and Times of Jeff Bell," *New Jersey Globe*, February 12, 2018; Emily Langer, "Jeffrey Bell, GOP Senate Candidate and Architect of Reaganomics, Dies at 74," *Washington Post*, February 22, 2018.

60. Jeffrey Bell, interview by Bill Kristol, *Conversations with Bill Kristol*, November 21, 2014, audio, 1:30:47, https://conversationswithbillkristol.org/transcript/jeff-bell-transcript/.

61. Ibid.; Bartley, *Seven Fat Years*, 149.

62. Jares, "Arthur Laffer Is a Man with All the Reasons for a Big Tax Cut." In 1982, Jeffrey Bell lost in the Republican primary to Millicent Fenwick, a congresswoman. Fenwick then was beaten in the general election by Frank Lautenberg. In 2014, Bell narrowly won a four-person Republican primary, but he was defeated in the general election by Cory Booker. Langer, "Jeffrey Bell Dies at 74."

63. See Garry Wills, *Reagan's America: Innocents at Home* (New York: Doubleday, 1987), 364.

64. Brooks, "The Supply Side," 127.

Chapter 5

1. Ronald Reagan, "A Time for Choosing Speech" (National Television Broadcast, October 27, 1964), Reagan Library, https://www.reaganlibrary.gov/reagans/ronald-reagan/time-choosing-speech-october-27-1964. Background on Reagan before his presidency can be found in Lou Cannon, *President Reagan: The Role of a Lifetime* (New York: Simon and Schuster, 1991). For a brief summary, see Lou Cannon, "Ronald Reagan: Life before the Presidency," University of Virginia Miller Center, https://www.millercenter.org/president/reagan/life-before-the-presidency.

2. E.g., William Kristol, "In His Heart, He Knew He Was Right," *New York Times*, April 1, 2001.

3. Morton Kondracke and Fred Barnes, *Jack Kemp: The Bleeding Heart Conservative Who Changed America* (New York: Sentinel, 2015), 55. Irving Kristol also thought Kemp likely to be the best candidate. Jeffrey Bell, interview by Bill Kristol, *Conversations with Bill Kristol*, November 21, 2014, https://conversationswithbillkristol.org/transcript/jeff-bell-transcript/.

4. Sidney Blumenthal, *The Rise of the Counter-Establishment: The Conservative Ascent to Political Power* (New York: Harper and Row, 1988), 202.

5. Ibid., 166, 201.

6. E.g., David A. Stockman, *The Triumph of Politics: Why the Reagan Revolution Failed* (New York: Harper & Row, 1986), 10.

7. Blumenthal, *The Rise of the Counter-Establishment*, 202.

8. Jon Meacham, *Destiny and Power: The American Odyssey of George Herbert Walker Bush* (New York: Random House, 2015), 216–28.

9. Rowland Evans and Robert Novak, *The Reagan Revolution* (Boston: E. P. Dalton, 1981), 60–62; Blumenthal, *The Rise of the Counter-Establishment*, 202–3; Rick Perlstein, *Reaganland: America's Right Turn, 1976–1980* (New York: Simon and Schuster, 2020), 729–31.

10. Perlstein, *Reaganland*, 739.

11. Evans and Novak, *The Reagan Revolution*, 62.

12. Craig Shirley, *Rendezvous with Destiny: Ronald Reagan and the Campaign That Changed America* (Wilmington, DE: Intercollegiate Studies Institute, 2009), 259–64; Blumenthal, *The Rise of the Counter-Establishment*, 203.

13. Peter Baker and Susan Glasser, *The Man Who Ran Washington: The Life and Times of James A. Baker III* (New York: Doubleday, 2020), 116. Bush also described Reagan's plan as "economic madness." Meacham, *Destiny and Power*, 235.

14. Perlstein, *Reaganland*, 799.

15. Reagan considered asking former president Gerald Ford to run as vice president. Former Ford cabinet officials Henry Kissinger and Alan Greenspan urged Reagan to try to enlist Ford, as did some of Reagan's other advisors. Negotiations ensued between the Reagan and Ford camps with Ford laying down important conditions, such as choosing the secretaries of state and treasury. The idea died a quiet death, however, on Wednesday, July 18, 1980, when Ford in an interview with CBS's Walter Cronkite, America's most revered news anchor, described his conditions for serving as Reagan's vice president. Cronkite summed up their conversation

saying that it sounded "something like a co-presidency," a term Ford embraced. Ibid., 802–6; Baker and Glasser, *The Man Who Ran Washington*, 120–23.

16. Baker and Glasser, *The Man Who Ran Washington*, 121, 122.

17. Peggy Noonan, *When Character Was King: A Story of Ronald Reagan* (New York: Viking, 2001), 131.

18. "Presidential Debate with Ronald Reagan and President Carter in Cleveland, Ohio on October 28, 1980," Reagan Library, recorded on October 28, 1980, YouTube video, 1:34:21, https://www.youtube.com/watch?v=tWEm6g0iQNI&ab_channel=ReaganLibrary.

19. Evans and Novak, *The Reagan Revolution*, 83.

20. E.g., Stockman, *The Triumph of Politics*, 125.

21. Ibid., 65–68.

22. Bruce Bartlett traces the history of the "starve the beast" phrase and claims that the first time it was used in connection with Reagan's economic policy was when a *Wall Street Journal* reporter quoted an unnamed White House official (who sounds very much like David Stockman), saying, "We didn't starve the beast. It's still eating quite well by feeding off future generations." Bruce Bartlett, *The New American Economy: The Failure of Reaganomics and a New Way Forward* (New York: Palgrave Macmillan, 2009), 143–45.

23. The claim that tax cuts will cause reductions in federal spending was urged by many distinguished economists, including not only Milton Friedman but also Harvard's Robert Barro, the University of Chicago Nobel Laureate Gary Becker, and Stanford's Edward Lazear. See Christina D. Romer and David H. Romer, "Do Tax Cuts Starve the Beast? The Effect of Tax Changes on Government Spending," *Brookings Papers on Economic Activity*, no. 1 (Spring 2009): 140.

24. Milton Friedman, "The Kemp-Roth Free Lunch," *Newsweek*, August 7, 1978.

25. Irving Kristol, "Populist Remedy for Populist Abuses," *Wall Street Journal*, August 10, 1978; Bartlett, *The New American Economy*, 149.

26. "Presidential Debate with Ronald Reagan and President Carter in Baltimore, Maryland on September 21, 1980," Reagan Foundation, recorded on September 21, 1980, YouTube video, 1:01:04, https://www.youtube.com/watch?v=wiAf2Ch9QbM&ab_channel=ReaganFoundation.

27. Romer and Romer, "Do Tax Cuts Starve the Beast?"; William G. Gale and Peter R. Orszag, "Bush Administration Tax Policy: Starving the Beast?" *Tax Notes*, November 15, 2004, 999–1002.

28. To limit the costs of his tax cut to $500 billion, Reagan said, to his disappointment, the tax cuts would not begin until July 1, 1981, as a way of reducing their first-year costs by half. Ronald Reagan, "Address before a Joint Session of the Congress on the Program for Economic Recovery," February 18, 1981, https://www.presidency.ucsb.edu/documents/address-before -joint-session-the-congress-the-program-for-economic-recovery.

29. Thomas B. Edsall, "How a Lobbyist Group Won Business Tax Cut," *Washington Post*, January 17, 1982.

30. Perlstein, *Reaganland*, 601.

31. Reagan, "Address before a Joint Session of the Congress on the Program for Economic Recovery."

32. Julian E. Zelizer, *Taxing America: Wilbur D. Mills, Congress, and the State, 1945–1975* (New York: Cambridge University Press, 1998).

33. Adam Bernstein, "Fanne Foxe, 'Argentine Firecracker' at Center of D.C. Sex Scandal, Dies at 84," *Washington Post*, February 24, 2021.

34. Elizabeth Drew, *Politics and Money: The New Road to Corruption* (New York: Macmillan, 1983), 66.

35. Kondracke and Barnes, *Jack Kemp*, 92; Stockman, *The Triumph of Politics*, 232.

36. Stockman, *The Triumph of Politics*, 231. Like many antitax Republicans, David Stockman liked to call the tax law enacted by Congress the "IRS code."

37. Ibid., 233.

38. Ronald Reagan, "Remarks at the National Conference of the Building and Construction Trades Department, AFL-CIO" (speech, Washington, DC, March 30, 1981), Reagan Library, https://www.reaganlibrary.gov/archives/speech/remarks-national-conference-building-and -construction-trades-department-afl-cio.

39. Baker and Glasser, *The Man Who Ran Washington*, 157.

40. Ibid., 159 (66 percent); Monica Prasad, *Starving the Beast: Ronald Reagan and the Tax Cut Revolution* (New York: Russell Sage Foundation, 2018), 111 (73 percent).

41. Reagan, "Address before a Joint Session of the Congress on the Program for Economic Recovery" (speech, Washington, DC, April 28, 1981, Reagan Library), https://www.reaganlibrary .gov/archives/speech/address-joint-session-congress-program-economic-recovery-april-1981.

42. Stockman, *The Triumph of Politics*, 246.

43. Ibid., 239.

44. Ibid., 263.

45. Ronald Reagan, "Address to the Nation on Federal Tax Reduction Legislation," Reagan Library, recorded on July 27, 1981, YouTube video, 22:40, https://www.youtube.com/watch?v =gfq_1tJ3K18&ab_channel=ReaganLibrary.

46. Stockman, *The Triumph of Politics*, 264.

47. Jeffrey H. Birnbaum and Alan S. Murray, *Showdown at Gucci Gulch: Lawmakers, Lobbyists, and the Unlikely Triumph of Tax Reform* (New York: Random House, 1987), 21.

48. Richard Darman, *Who's in Control? Polar Politics and the Sensible Center* (New York: Simon and Schuster, 1996), 83.

49. Ibid., 85.

50. Emil M. Sunley and Randall D. Weiss, "The Revenue Estimating Process," *American Journal of Tax Policy* 11, no. 6 (Fall 1992): 283–84.

51. Michael J. Graetz, *The Decline (and Fall?) of the Income Tax* (New York: W. W. Norton, 1997), 124–28. For additional discussion, see chapter 7.

52. C. Eugene Steuerle, *The Tax Decade: How Taxes Came to Dominate the Public Agenda* (Washington, DC: Urban Institute Press, 1992), 43–44; Stockman, *The Triumph of Politics*, 254–55, 267–68; Prasad, *Starving the Beast*, 114.

53. Michael J. Graetz, "To Praise the Estate Tax, Not to Bury It," *Yale Law Journal* 93, no. 2 (December 1983): 262; Harry Gutman, "Federal Wealth Transfer Taxes after the Economic Recovery Tax Act of 1981," *National Tax Journal* 35, no. 3 (September 1982): 254

54. Graetz, "To Praise the Estate Tax," 262.

55. Editorial, "Tricklenomics," *Wall Street Journal*, April 11, 1984.

56. Congressional Budget Office, *Effects of the 1981 Tax Act on the Distribution of Income and Taxes Paid*, August 1986, A. 59, https://www.cbo.gov/sites/default/files/99th-congress-1985 -1986/reports/doc20a-entire.pdf.

57. John Brooks, "The Supply Side," *New Yorker*, April 19, 1982, 150.

58. Stockman, *The Triumph of Politics*, 397.

59. Ibid.

Chapter 6

1. Ronald Reagan, "Inaugural Address 1981," January 20, 1981, https://www.reaganlibrary.gov /archives/speech/inaugural-address-1981.

2. Edward Nelson and Jason J. Buol, "Budget Deficits and Interest Rates: What Is the Link?" *Central Banker: News and Views for Eighth District Bankers* (July 2004): 5, https://fraser .stlouisfed.org/title/central-banker-6284/summer-2004-603083/budget-deficits-interest -rates-586375.

3. E.g., Thomas Sargent and Neil Wallace, "Some Unpleasant Monetarist Arithmetic," *Federal Reserve Bank of Minneapolis Quarterly Review* 5, no. 3 (Fall 1981): 1–17.

4. James M. Poterba, "Federal Budget Policy in the 1980s," in *American Economic Policy in the 1980s*, ed. Martin Feldstein (Chicago: University of Chicago Press, 1994), 245. The Federal Reserve, led by Paul Volcker, was determined to arrest inflation. The fight against inflation was successful, but costly. Increases in consumer prices dropped from 14 percent in 1980 to less than 3 percent by 1983. Several factors played a role in this decline, including falling oil prices and cheaper imports, but the most important was tightening of the money supply, which is why Volcker, who chaired the Federal Reserve from August 1979 until August 1987, was given the lion's share of credit for curbing inflation. The Federal Reserve's tight money policies, however, produced a sharp recession that cost average American households $3,300 ($5,415 in 2021 dollars) in lost income. Isabel V. Sawhill and Charles F. Stone, "The Economy," in *The Reagan Record: An Assessment of America's Changing Domestic Priorities*, ed. John L. Palmer and Isabel V. Sawhill (Washington, DC: Urban Institute, 1984), 79, 82–84. The jobless rate rose from 7.5 percent when Reagan took office to 10.8 percent in November 1982. Martin Feldstein, "American Economic Policy in the 1980s: A Personal View," in *American Economic Policy in the 1980s*, 7; Peter Baker and Susan Glasser, *The Man Who Ran Washington: The Life and Times of James A. Baker III* (New York: Doubleday, 2020), 189. The recession formally ended in November 1982, but that was not apparent by the time of the midterm elections that month or early in 1983. Feldstein, "American Economic Policy in the 1980s." During the period from 1981 to 1984, families at the top of the income distribution enjoyed a substantial increase in their incomes, while families in the bottom 40 percent lost the gains they had made during the preceding two decades. Marilyn Moon and Isabel V. Sawhill, "Family Incomes," in *The Reagan Record*, 32.

5. David A. Stockman, *The Triumph of Politics: Why the Reagan Revolution Failed* (New York: Harper & Row, 1986), 13.

6. Ibid., 399. Even with Rosy Scenario's help, David Stockman was unable to make the costs of President Reagan's planned increases in spending for national defense and his tax reductions balance in any year without substantial deficits. So Stockman "invented a 'magic asterisk.'" The magic asterisk, which in the president's first budget was labeled "Future savings to be identified," was a plugged number that permitted the president to claim that the budget would be balanced by 1984. Ibid., 124–25.

7. Richard Darman, *Who's in Control? Polar Politics and the Sensible Center* (New York: Simon and Schuster, 1996), 43–45.

8. Ibid.; Stockman, *The Triumph of Politics*, 125, 395–411.

9. As David Stockman pointed out (to his chagrin) more than a decade later, what he called "the old people's budget"—Social Security, Medicare, and other retirement programs—and "the poor people's budget"—Aid to Families With Dependent Children ("welfare") food stamps, Medicaid, and an assortment of other means-tested transfer programs—accounted for 10 percent of the national economy in 1980 and the same percentage in 1986. He lamented, "The Reagan Revolution was all over except for the shouting." David Stockman, "Commentary," in *American Economic Policy in the 1980s*, 271–72.

10. Chris Matthews, *Tip and the Gipper: When Politics Worked* (New York: Simon and Schuster, 2013), 199, quoting David Broder, "45 Years In," *Washington Post*, April 22, 1982.

11. These exigencies inevitably produce deficits and require debt finance, although for much of the nation's history they were followed by tax increases to curb the growth of the federal debt.

12. Poterba, "Federal Budget Policy in the 1980s," 262–63.

13. Matthews, *Tip and the Gipper*, 212–13. Claude Pepper, an eighty-one-year-old Miami congressman famous for protecting benefits for the elderly, held a smaller counterrally of about one hundred people at the Capitol where he described the amendment as a "sneak attack on Social Security."

14. Congressional Budget Office, Balancing the Federal Budget and Limiting Federal Spending: Constitutional and Statutory Approaches, September 1982, 1–8, https://www.cbo.gov/sites/default/files/97th-congress-1981-1982/reports/doc28-entire_0_0.pdf. The vote in the House was opposed by Speaker O'Neill and failed by a vote of 236 to 187. In 1995 Oregon's Republican senator Mark Hatfield cast the decisive vote against a balanced-budget amendment that had passed the House—the only Republican to do so. The 1982 and 1995 votes were as close as a balanced-budget requirement came to achieving the constitutionally required congressional majorities. Ernest Istook, "Considering a Balanced Budget Amendment: Lessons from History," Heritage Foundation, July 14, 2021, https://www.heritage.org/budget-and-spending/report/considering-balanced-budget-amendment-lessons-history.

15. Dole ran for president again in 1988 and became the Republican Party's 1996 presidential nominee but lost to Bill Clinton. See chapter 11.

16. Martin Tolchin and Jeff Gerth, "The Contradictions of Bob Dole," *New York Times*, November 8, 1987.

17. Ibid.

18. Baker and Glasser, *The Man Who Ran Washington*, 186.

19. See U.S. Congress, Joint Committee on Taxation, *Estimates of Federal Tax Expenditures for Fiscal Years 1982–1987*, 97th Cong., 2nd sess., JCS-4-82, https://www.jct.gov/CMSPages/GetFile.aspx?guid=2dcd81a9-f240-4d6c-ba24-dafdc3610d9c.

20. Donald T. Regan, *For the Record: From Wall Street to Washington* (New York: Harcourt Bruce Jovanovich, 1988), 173–75.

21. Matthews, *Tip and the Gipper*, 200.

22. Ibid., 203.

23. Ibid., 193–203.

24. Stockman, *The Triumph of Politics*, 354.

25. Ibid.; Matthews, *Tip and the Gipper*, 202.

26. Edward Cowan, "A Tax Increase of $99 Billion Voted in Senate," *New York Times*, July 24, 1982. Dole had important support from many Republican and Democratic Senate colleagues. There were moderates, including, for example, Republicans Jack Danforth, John Chafee and John Heinz and Democrats Lloyd Bentsen, Daniel Patrick Moynihan, and Bill Bradley on the Senate Finance Committee and deficit hawks like Republican Pete Domenici in the Senate.

27. David Hoffman, "Baker: 1981 Tax Cuts Have Failed in Impact," *Washington Post*, August 16, 1982.

28. Matthews, *Tip and the Gipper*, 215–19.

29. Ibid., 223.

30. Thomas B. Edsall, "Congress Passes $98.3 Billion Tax Bill," *Washington Post*, August 20, 1982. The tax increases largely consisted of cutting back on the 1981 tax benefits for equipment purchases; limiting tax breaks for certain industries, including oil and gas, construction, insurance, and pharmaceuticals; increasing excise taxes on cigarettes, telephone calls, and airline tickets; and enhancing penalties for tax noncompliance. Tax Equity and Fiscal Responsibility Act of 1982, Pub. L. No. 97-34, 96 Stat. 324. Because the House bill would have reduced taxes and the Senate version raised them, eighteen members of the House of Representatives filed a lawsuit challenging the law as violating the Constitution's requirement that "All bills for raising revenue shall originate in the House of Representatives, but the Senate may propose or concur with Amendments and on other Bills." U.S. Constitution, Article I, Section 7, Clause 1. Disgruntled taxpayers also filed more than fifty lawsuits challenging the legislation on the same ground. The courts of appeals that heard these lawsuits found them without merit, and the Supreme Court refused to consider the issue. As Yale law professor Boris Bittker observed, both the House and Senate must approve legislation before it goes to the president for signature "so it hardly matters which chamber acts first. Since it takes two to tango, what difference does it

make whose foot first touches the ballroom floor?" Boris I. Bittker, "Constitutional Limits on the Taxing Power of the Federal Government," *Tax Lawyer* 45, no. 1 (Fall 1987): 5. Not everyone agrees; see, e.g., Thomas L. Jipping, "TEFRA and the Origination Clause: Taking the Oath Seriously," *Buffalo Law Review* 35, no. 2 (1986): 636. President Reagan also signed the Highway Revenue Act in 1982, more than doubling federal gasoline taxes to raise an additional $3.3 billion.

31. Bruce Bartlett, "Higher Taxes: Will the Republicans Cry Wolf Again?" *Forbes*, February 27, 2009.

32. Edward Cowan, "Pension Trust Set to Borrow Money to Meet Payments," *New York Times*, October 18, 1982.

33. E.g., Martin Feldstein, "Toward a Reform of Social Security," *Public Interest* (Summer 1975): 88; Michael J. Boskin, *The Crisis in Social Security* (San Francisco: Institute for Contemporary Studies, 1977).

34. Stockman, *The Triumph of Politics*, 181–82.

35. Ronald Reagan, "A Time for Choosing Speech" (National Television Broadcast, October 27, 1964), Reagan Library, https://www.reaganlibrary.gov/reagans/ronald-reagan/time-choosing-speech-october-27-1964.

36. Sebastian Mallaby, *The Man Who Knew: The Life and Times of Alan Greenspan* (New York: Penguin, 2016), 272.

37. Robert M. Ball, *The Greenspan Commission: What Really Happened?* (New York: Century Foundation Press, 2010), 40.

38. R. Douglas Arnold, *Fixing Social Security: The Politics of Reform in a Polarized Age* (Princeton: Princeton University Press, 2022), 35–36.

39. Ibid., 36. "I've been warning since 1964 that Social Security was heading for bankruptcy," Reagan said, "and this is one of the reasons why." Stockman, *The Triumph of Politics*, 187. See also Martha Derthick and Steven M. Teles, "Riding the Third Rail—Social Security Reform," in *The Reagan Presidency: Pragmatic Conservatism and Its Legacies*, ed. W. Elliot Brownlee and Hugh Davis Graham (Lawrence: University of Kansas Press, 2003), 182–208.

40. Helen Dewar, "Senate Unanimously Rebuffs President on Social Security," *Washington Post*, May 21, 1981.

41. Ibid.; "Reagan Letter on Social Security," *New York Times*, May 21, 1981.

42. Matthews, *Tip and the Gipper*, 240, 252. Republicans fared better in the Senate, adding one seat to their majority. Howell Raines, "Reagan Facing Demands for Compromise on Economy after 26-Seat Loss in House," *New York Times*, November 4, 1982.

43. Matthews, *Tip and the Gipper*, 169.

44. Executive Order 12335: National Commission on Social Security Reform, December 16, 1981.

45. Mallaby, *The Man Who Knew*, 272, 273, 719n42; Peter J. Ferrara, *Social Security: The Inherent Contradictions* (Washington, DC: Cato Institute, 1980).

46. Mallaby, *The Man Who Knew*, 273.

47. Thomas N. Bethel, Editor's Note to *The Greenspan Commission—What Really Happened?* by Robert Ball (New York: Century Foundation Press, 2010), vii. Ball's biographer Edward Berkowitz said Ball was "the major non-congressional player in the history of Social Security in the period between 1950 and the present." Carolyn Puckett, "Robert M. Ball: A Life Dedicated to Social Security," *Social Security Bulletin* 68, no. 3 (2008): 67, https://www.ssa.gov/policy/docs/ssb/v68n3/v68n3p67.pdf.

48. Bob Dole, "Reagan's Faithful Allies," *New York Times*, January 3, 1983.

49. Matthews, *Tip and the Gipper*, 247.

50. Ball, *The Greenspan Commission*, 41.

51. Journalists reported that the meetings were taking place, but they did not know where, so some of them staked out Bob Ball's house, thinking the meetings were being held there. After

a charade by Ball's wife puttering around in casual clothes outdoors failed to throw the press off, Ball called Dick Darman and asked that he send a car down the hill behind Ball's house to take him to Baker's home. After sneaking out the back door and stumbling down a snow-covered hill, Ball skidded down to the White House car and headed to the meeting, having eluded the press. Ball, *The Greenspan Commission*, 42–43. On January 6, knowing his Ways and Means Committee would need to act first on the commission's recommendations, Dan Rostenkowski said, "I'm not discouraging the President and Tip O'Neill from getting together, but I've got to move. I've got to have a bill through the House by the end of next March. If I don't, the system goes belly-up next June." Hedrick Smith, "A Hand Reaches for Hot Potato of Social Security," *New York Times*, January 6, 1983. As the January 15 deadline approached, President Reagan became anxious—even about reducing benefits. He said that if he did, "the same old political football would be seen going up in the air like a punt on third down." His key legislative aide Ken Duberstein summed up the dilemma: "We weren't going to put our head back in that noose, and the speaker wasn't going to come forward unless the President did, and so we just danced around and around." Matthews, *Tip and the Gipper*, 248.

52. The three holdouts were conservative former Democratic Louisiana congressman Joe Waggonner, Republican senator Bill Armstrong, and Houston's fervent Republican antitax congressman Bill Archer (who in 1995 became chairman of the House Ways and Means Committee). All three opposed the agreement because of its tax increases. For more detail, see Derthick and Teles, "Riding the Third Rail," 199–200.

53. Matthews, *Tip and the Gipper*, 248–49.

54. Legislation in 1977 had reduced future benefits and increased payroll tax rates and the amount of earnings subject to taxation, changes that over time were then expected to put Social Security on a sound financial footing for the following fifty years. See John Snee and Mary Ross, "Social Security Amendments of 1977, Legislative History and Summary of Provisions," *Social Security Bulletin* 41, no. 3 (March 1978): 3–20.

55. Ronald Reagan, "Remarks on Signing the Social Security Amendments of 1983," The American Presidency Project, https://www.presidency.ucsb.edu/documents/remarks-signing -the-social-security-amendments-1983. Conservative Democratic congressman J. J. "Jake" Pickle from a safe Texas district, who chaired the Social Security subcommittee of the Ways and Means Committee, with a bipartisan vote of 278 to 202, added a provision that slowly raised the normal retirement age from sixty-five to sixty-seven beginning seventeen years later in 2000 and ending in 2027. This was the first effort to take increases in the longevity of elderly beneficiaries into account and did more to improve the long-term financial well-being of Social Security than any of the commission's recommendations. Rudolph G. Penner, "The Greenspan Commission and the Social Security Reforms of 1983," Urban Institute, March 23, 2000, https://www .urban.org/sites/default/files/publication/65126/2000323-Myth-and-Reality-of-the-Safety -Net-The-1983-Social-Security-Reforms.pdf.

56. Arnold, *Fixing Social Security*, 37–38. Counting the income taxes on Social Security benefits, which accounted for 29 percent of the long-term solution, as a benefit cut, Arnold estimates that tax increases were only 10 percent of the long-term solution. Ibid., table 2-1.

57. Social Security Administration, *Research Note #12: Taxation of Social Security Benefits*, by Larry Dewitt (Washington, DC, 2001), https://www.ssa.gov/history/taxationofbenefits.html. An increase from 50 percent to 85 percent of Social Security benefits subject to income taxes occurred in 1993 for single people with incomes above $34,000 and married couples above $44,000 (with neither level indexed to inflation).

58. Internal Revenue Service, *Statistics of Income 1984: Individual Income Tax Returns* (Washington, DC: General Printing Office, 1986), table 1.4; Internal Revenue Service, *Statistics of Income 2019: Individual Income Tax Returns* (Washington, DC: General Printing Office, 2021), section 2, figure A, https://www.irs.gov/pub/irs-prior/p1304--2021.pdf#page=21. Subsequent tax-cut

legislation, such as the doubling of standard deductions in 2017, offset some of the impact of the taxation of Social Security benefits for many middle-income recipients.

59. Andrea Louise Campbell, "Participatory Reactions to Policy Threats: Senior Citizens and the Defense of Social Security and Medicare," *Political Behavior* 25, no. 1 (March 2003): 33. The Greenspan Commission entered political legend as a model for bipartisan cooperation and still is advanced as demonstrating how presidents and Congress can hand off difficult fiscal issues requiring tax increases to an independent commission. *Washington Post* editor and bestselling author Bob Woodward wrote, "One of Greenspan's finest moments [came] as head of the nonpartisan National Commission on Social Security that restored the Social Security system to temporary financial solvency. It had been a masterstroke of consensus building." Bob Woodward, *Maestro: Greenspan's Fed and the American Boom* (New York: Simon and Schuster, 2000), 20. This is fantasy. Although he was charged with explaining the agreement to the public, Alan Greenspan was mostly a passive player in the final negotiations between Jim Baker and Bob Ball; on Greenspan's role, including a scolding he received from Ayn Rand shortly before her death, see Mallaby, *The Man Who Knew*, 272–81. The commission was stalemated by its expiration date. Only after Baker (on behalf of President Reagan) entered into negotiations with Ball (on behalf of Speaker O'Neill) did an agreement emerge. Both Ball and Greenspan gave much of the credit for the commission's success to Jim Baker. "The commission he built was a virtuoso demonstration of how to get things done in Washington," Greenspan said; Baker and Glasser, *The Man Who Ran Washington*, 195. Bob Ball was more candid. "The commission," he said, "became primarily a cover for the negotiations between the leaders of the two parties, Reagan and O'Neill"; Ball, *The Greenspan Commission*, 68. With an exception for the military base closing commission created in 1988, the Greenspan Commission's success has not been repeated.

60. For discussions of challenges to Social Security after 1983, see, e.g., Eric Laursen, *The People's Pension: The Struggle to Defend Social Security since Reagan* (Oakland: AK Press, 2012); Arnold, *Fixing Social Security*, 197–223. The metaphor describing Social Security as the dangerous "third rail of American politics" was suggested by Speaker O'Neill's aide Kirk O'Donnell, although it is often attributed to O'Neill himself. E.g., Derthick and Teles, "Riding the Third Rail," 184, citing George Hager and Eric Pienin, *Mirage* (New York: Times Books, 1997), 142. Tom Oliphant of the *Boston Globe* wrote that "few lines have been ripped off more." William Safire, "Third Rail," *New York Times*, February 18, 2007.

61. The Tax Reform Act of 1986 also temporarily raised taxes.

62. Bruce Bartlett, *The New American Economy: The Failure of Reaganomics and a New Way Forward* (New York: Palgrave Macmillan, 2009), 153, table 1; U.S. Department of the Treasury, Office of Tax Analysis, *Revenue Effects of Major Tax Bills*, by Jerry Tempalski, working paper 81 (Washington, DC, 2006), https://home.treasury.gov/system/files/131/WP-81.pdf.

63. Jonathan Fuerbringer, "Reagan Signs Bill to Cut Spending, Raise Taxes," *New York Times*, July 19, 1984.

64. Kimberly Amadeo, "U.S. Debt by President by Dollar and Percentage," *The Balance*, https://www.thebalancemoney.com/us-debt-by-president-by-dollar-and-percent-3306296.

65. In 1945 at the end of World War II the federal debt was 118 percent of the size of the economy. During the presidencies of Harry Truman and Dwight Eisenhower, the debt declined to 46 percent, and then under Presidents Kennedy and Johnson to 25 percent. Russell B. Long, "Commentary," in *American Economic Policy in the 1980s*, ed. Martin Feldstein (Chicago: University of Chicago Press, 1994), 221.

66. Poterba, "Federal Budget Policy in the 1980s," 240–41.

67. Robert Bartley, *Seven Fat Years and How to Do It Again* (New York: The Free Press, 1992).

68. Ibid. The tax increases Reagan signed are also glossed over in Dick Darman's memoir of his time in the Reagan White House. See Darman, *Who's in Control?*

69. Bartley, *Seven Fat Years.*

70. Sean Wilentz, *The Age of Reagan: A History, 1974–2008* (New York: HarperCollins, 2008), 145.

71. Baker and Glasser, *The Man Who Ran Washington*, 188.

72. David McGrath, "What Trump Shares with Reagan, the Teflon President," *Chicago Tribune*, March 22, 2017.

73. Julian E. Zelizer, *Burning Down the House: Newt Gingrich, the Fall of a Speaker, and the Rise of the New Republican Party* (New York: Penguin, 2020), 54.

74. Helen Dewar, "Republicans Wage Verbal Civil War," *Washington Post*, November 19, 1984.

Chapter 7

1. "Transcript of Mondale Address Accepting Party Nomination," *New York Times*, July 20, 1984.

2. Jeffrey H. Birnbaum and Alan S. Murray, *Showdown at Gucci Gulch: Lawmakers, Lobbyists, and the Unlikely Triumph of Tax Reform* (New York: Random House, 1987), 35.

3. Fay S. Joyce, "Mondale Program Would Raise Taxes $85 Billion by '89," *New York Times*, September 11, 1984.

4. David Hoffman and John M. Berry, "Reagan, Mondale Tax Brawl Defies Political Convention," *Washington Post*, July 29, 1984.

5. Ibid.; Michael Beschloss, "The Ad That Helped Reagan Sell Good Times to an Uncertain Nation," *New York Times*, May 7, 2016.

6. Jane Mayer, "Remembering Walter Mondale," *New Yorker*, April 19, 2021.

7. Dan Balz, "Mondale Lost the Presidency but Permanently Changed the Office of Vice Presidency," *Washington Post*, April 19, 2021.

8. Edward R. Kantowicz, "The Limits of Incrementalism: Carter's Efforts at Tax Reform," *Journal of Policy Analysis and Management* 4, no. 2 (Winter 1985): 221.

9. Birnbaum and Murray, *Showdown at Gucci Gulch*, 9–11; Advisory Commission on Intergovernmental Relations, "Changing Public Attitudes on Taxes, 1980," https://library.unt.edu/gpo/acir/Reports/survey/S-9.pdf and "Changing Public Attitudes on Government and Taxes, 1991," https://library.unt.edu/gpo/acir/Reports/survey/S-20.pdf. Since the late 1980s, the public has consistently ranked the federal income tax as the first or second worst major tax (the local property tax has edged out the income tax for bottom billing in some surveys—unsurprising given the rapid increase in property values). For survey data, see John Kincaid and Richard L. Cole, "Changing Public Attitudes on Power and Taxation in the American Federal Tax System," *Publius* 31, no. 3 (Summer 2001): 205–14.

10. For details on these problems with the income tax, see Michael J. Graetz, *The Decline (and Fall?) of the Income Tax* (New York: W. W. Norton, 1997), chaps. 2–6.

11. Ronald Reagan, "Address before a Joint Session of the Congress on the State of the Union" (speech, Washington, DC, January 25, 1984), The American Presidency Project, https://www.presidency.ucsb.edu/documents/address-before-joint-session-the-congress-the-state-the-union-4.

12. Donald T. Regan, *For the Record: From Wall Street to Washington* (New York: Harcourt Brace Jovanovich, 1988), 202–3; Birnbaum and Murray, *Showdown at Gucci Gulch*, 41. President Reagan's interest in tax reform had been piqued during a golf outing when Secretary of State George Shultz described a "flat tax," designed by two of his former colleagues at Stanford University. Soon thereafter, the president sent a note praising the idea to Treasury Secretary Don Regan. Birnbaum and Murray, *Showdown at Gucci Gulch*; Timothy J. Conlan, Margaret J. Wrightson, and David R. Beam, *Taxing Choices: The Politics of Tax Reform* (Washington, DC: CQ Press, 1990), 47.

13. Graetz, *The Decline (and Fall?) of the Income Tax*, 42–51.

14. U.S. Department of the Treasury, *The Problem of Corporate Tax Shelters: Discussion, Analysis and Legislative Proposals* (July 1999), v, https://home.treasury.gov/system/files/131/Report-Corporate-Tax-Shelters-1999.pdf.

15. Graetz, *The Decline (and Fall?) of the Income Tax*, 45.

16. Susan Dentzer, "How Americans Beat the Tax Man," *Newsweek*, April 6, 1984, 56.

17. There were many others. "A Tax-Leasing Twist That Is in Trouble," *Business Week*, July 18, 1983, 57; Shirley Hobbs Scherbla, "Leasing City Hall: That's the Latest Twist in Municipal Financing," *Barron's*, May 16, 1983, 39; William Harris, "Wanna Buy the Brooklyn Bridge?" *Forbes*, March 15, 1982, 59. Congress limited tax-shelter deals involving tax-exempt entities in 1984.

18. Graetz, *The Decline (and Fall?) of the Income Tax*, 42; Jim Powell, "The Pleasures and Perils of Tax Loopholes," *Forbes*, March 7, 2012, https://www.forbes.com/sites/jimpowell/2012/03/07/the-pleasures-and-perils-of-tax-loopholes/?sh=4df5de176bca.

19. Margaret Riley, "Safe-Harbor Leasing, 1981 and 1982," https://www.irs.gov/pub/irs-soi/81-82sahale.pdf.

20. Graetz, *The Decline (and Fall?) of the Income Tax*, 46–48; Jonathan Barry Forman, "Tax Considerations in Renting a Navy," *Tax Notes*, March 25, 1985.

21. Graetz, *The Decline (and Fall?) of the Income Tax*, 47.

22. Richard Darman, *Who's in Control? Polar Politics and the Sensible Center* (New York: Simon and Schuster, 1996), 155.

23. Joseph F. Sullivan, "Bradley Wins Handily in New Jersey Despite Strong Vote for Reagan," *New York Times*, November 7, 1984; "Reagan Is Key for GOP in Senate Race in New Jersey," *New York Times*, September 24, 1984.

24. John McPhee, "A Sense of Where You Are," *New Yorker*, January 23, 1965.

25. See also Conlan, Wrightson, and Beam, *Taxing Choices*.

26. Birnbaum and Murray, *Showdown at Gucci Gulch*, 35.

27. Michael J. Graetz, "Tax Reform Unraveling," *Journal of Economic Perspectives* 21, no. 1 (Winter 2007): 69–72.

28. Morton Kondracke and Fred Barnes, *Jack Kemp: The Bleeding Heart Conservative Who Changed America* (New York: Sentinel, 2015), 156.

29. Kemp said later, "We came to the conclusion that Kristol was right, that Reagan and Kemp should endorse Bradley-Gephardt. That would have thrown the Democratic party into a state of real confusion." Birnbaum and Murray, *Showdown at Gucci Gulch*, 36–38; Kondracke and Barnes, *Jack Kemp*, 150, 152–53.

30. Kondracke and Barnes, *Jack Kemp*, 133; Introduction of the Kemp-Kasten "Fair and Simple Tax" (FAST), April 26, 1984, 98th Cong., 2nd sess., 130 Cong. Rec., pt. 8:10227.

31. Kondracke and Barnes, *Jack Kemp*, 154.

32. "Bradley-Kemp-Reagan?" *Wall Street Journal*, March 5, 1984.

33. Ronald Reagan, "Encroaching Control: Keep Government Poor and Remain Free," *Vital Speeches of the Day* 27 (July 28, 1961): 677, quoted in Michael J. Graetz, "The Truth about Tax Reform," *University of Florida Law Review* 40, no. 4 (September 1988): 621.

34. Ronald Reagan, "A Time for Choosing Speech" (National Television Broadcast, October 27, 1964), Reagan Library, https://www.reaganlibrary.gov/reagans/ronald-reagan/time-choosing-speech-october-27-1964.

35. U.S. Department of the Treasury, *Tax Reform for Fairness, Simplicity and Economic Growth: The Treasury Department Report to the President* (November 1984), vols. 1–3 (including two supplemental volumes of an additional 536 pages). For descriptions of the development of these proposals, see Birnbaum and Murray, *Showdown at Gucci Gulch*, 42–64; Conlan, Wrightson, and Beam, *Taxing Choices*, 48–72.

36. Birnbaum and Murray, *Showdown at Gucci Gulch*, 63.

37. Ibid., 64.

38. Graetz, "The Truth about Tax Reform," 621.

39. Quoted in Regan, *For the Record*, 214.

40. Peter Baker and Susan Glasser, *The Man Who Ran Washington: The Life and Times of James A. Baker III* (New York: Doubleday, 2020), 210–21, 246–47; Regan, *For the Record*, 219–20.

41. In his State of the Union Address on February 6, 1985, observing that he had to get used to saying "Treasury Secretary James Baker," President Reagan described his principles for "an historic reform of tax simplification for fairness and growth," including "a top rate of 35 percent and possibly lower, reducing corporate rates" and "increasing significantly the personal exemption" so that "individuals living at or near the poverty line will be totally exempt from Federal income tax." Ronald Reagan, "Address before a Joint Session of Congress on the State of the Union" (speech, Washington, DC, February 6, 1985), The American Presidency Project, https://www.presidency.ucsb.edu/documents/address-before-joint-session-the-congress-the-state-the-union-5.

42. Birnbaum and Murray, *Showdown at Gucci Gulch*, 69.

43. Ibid., 77.

44. Ronald Reagan, "Address to the Nation on Tax Reform" (speech, Washington, DC, May 28, 1985), The American Presidency Project, https://www.presidency.ucsb.edu/documents/address-the-nation-tax-reform.

45. Birnbaum and Murray, *Showdown at Gucci Gulch*, 148–51.

46. The lack of a recorded vote on the House tax-reform legislation was surprising. Witnesses say that the Republicans who under their rules could insist on a recorded vote were out of the House chamber when O'Neill called for a voice vote. Despite the louder "nays," Speaker O'Neill smiled and announced, "in the opinion of the Chair, the 'ayes have it,'" and pounded his gavel, allowing the legislation to move to the Senate.

47. Birnbaum and Murray, *Showdown at Gucci Gulch*, 175, 193–94.

48. Darman, *Who's in Control?* 150.

49. Birnbaum and Murray, *Showdown at Gucci Gulch*, 189. Lobbyists were confident they could stop any adverse legislation in the Senate. Packwood alone collected more than $1 million in contributions from special interests, inspiring a friend of his to quip, "Raising money for Bob Packwood is like making love to a 700-pound gorilla. It doesn't matter when you get tired." Ibid., 183.

50. Ibid., 200.

51. Ibid., 202–3.

52. A list of similar headlines can be found in Darman, *Who's in Control?* 162. The one in the text is from the *Chicago Tribune*.

53. Birnbaum and Murray, *Showdown at Gucci Gulch*, 209.

54. On the Senate floor the biggest issue was the committee's elimination of the IRA tax break. Delaware Republican William Roth was the strongest advocate for IRA restoration, but Bill Bradley, who had rounded up Democratic support for the committee bill, convinced Packwood to organize a coalition to oppose all amendments, a strategy that Jim Baker convinced President Reagan to support. Roth's amendment was defeated by a 51–48 vote after Packwood had made some deals. George Mitchell offered an amendment to raise the top individual tax rate to 35 percent, but it was also defeated. Ibid., 224, 243–53.

55. Ibid., 258. After a series of long, contentious meetings, on Saturday, August 17 at 8:30 p.m. with help from Bradley, Baker, and Darman, the House and Senate tax writers reached an agreement. The top rate would be 28 percent with a bubble rate of 33 percent. Personal exemptions and the standard deduction would be raised to remove families at or below the poverty level from the income tax. Capital gains would be taxed at the same rate as ordinary income. The

corporate rate would be 34 percent but still would produce $120 billion of additional corporate taxes to pay for the individual tax cuts. The conferees approved the agreement at a public meeting that began an hour later. The next day President Reagan issued a statement saying, "This is a triumph for the American people and the American system." Ibid., 283.

56. The 15 percent rate phased out for high-income taxpayers and a 5 percent surtax applied in the phaseout range, making the marginal rate for some taxpayers 33 percent, but no one faced an average tax rate greater than 28 percent.

57. For details, see U.S. Congress, Joint Committee on Taxation, *General Explanation of the Tax Reform Act of 1986*, 100th Cong., 1st sess., JCS-10-87, https://www.jct.gov/publications/1987/jcs-10-87; Alan J. Auerbach and Joel Slemrod, "The Economic Effects of the Tax Reform Act of 1986," *Journal of Economic Literature* 35, no. 2 (June 1997): 595–98.

58. Ronald Reagan, "Remarks on Signing the Tax Reform Act of 1986" (speech, Washington, DC, October 22, 1986), Reagan Library, https://www.reaganlibrary.gov/archives/speech/remarks-signing-tax-reform-act-1986.

59. Editorial, "A Tax Law to Hail, Yes a Tax Law," *New York Times*, October 22, 1986.

60. Henry J. Aaron, "The Impossible Dream Comes True: The New Tax Reform Act," *Brookings Review* 5, no. 1 (Winter 1987): 3–10.

61. Moral Majority Republicans strongly supported the large increase in personal exemptions because they wanted the tax law to be more "family friendly" to parents with large numbers of children. Kondracke and Barnes, *Jack Kemp*, 161.

62. Adam Clymer, "Doubt Found on Fairness and Cuts," *New York Times*, June 25, 1986.

63. Eric M. Patashnik, *Reforms at Risk: What Happens after Major Policy Changes Are Enacted* (Princeton: Princeton University Press, 2004), 47.

64. For a partial list, see Birnbaum and Murray, *Showdown at Gucci Gulch*, 240–41. The Senate Finance Committee rewarded 174 recipients.

65. Auerbach and Slemrod, "The Economic Effects of the Tax Reform Act of 1986," 602–3.

66. Some tax-shelter efforts crossed the line into fraud. The most notorious case involved the Enron Corporation, an energy company whose tax-shelter and financial accounting misconduct not only brought down the company, which had once been the seventh-largest corporation in the United States, but also caused the dissolution of Arthur Andersen, then one of the "Big Five" accounting firms. The Joint Committee on Taxation produced a three-volume, 2,700-page report on this debacle. U.S. Congress, Senate, Committee on Finance, *Enron: The Joint Committee on Taxation's Investigative Report: Hearings before the Committee on Finance*, 108th Cong., 2nd sess., February 13, 2003. A few years later, after an investigation by the Senate's Permanent Subcommittee on Investigations shined a light on the practices, additional criminal investigations followed. U.S. Congress, Senate, Permanent Subcommittee on Investigations of the Senate Committee on Governmental Affairs, *U.S. Tax Shelter Industry: The Role of Accountants, Lawyers, and Financial Professionals: Hearings before the Permanent Subcommittee on Investigations of the Committee on Governmental Affairs*, 108th Cong., 2nd sess., November 18 and 20, 2003. The accounting firm KPMG avoided criminal prosecution by paying a $456 million fine, agreeing to terminate tax-shelter practice areas, cease its production of "pre-packaged tax products," and replace many of its managers. Nine members of the firm were charged with crimes. U.S. Department of Justice, "KPMG to Pay $456 Million for Criminal Violations in Relation to Largest Ever Tax-Shelter Fraud," press release, August 29, 2005, https://www.justice.gov/archive/opa/pr/2005/August/05_ag_433.html; Tanina Rostain and Milton C. Regan, *Confidence Games: Lawyers, Accountants, and the Tax Shelter Industry* (Cambridge, MA: MIT Press, 2014).

67. Patashnik, *Reforms at Risk*, 54.

68. Ibid., chaps. 1 and 3.

69. President Reagan's domestic policy agenda essentially stalled after the 1986 tax reform. Two weeks after he signed the tax-reform legislation, President Reagan confronted an existential crisis. His administration had sent proceeds from a secret arms sale to Iran's revolutionary leaders to Nicaragua to help fund rebel Contras' efforts to overthrow the government despite a congressional ban on funding the Contras. The Iran-Contra affair, as it became known, dragged on and ultimately led to criminal convictions of nearly a dozen administration officials, including Defense Secretary Caspar Weinberger. Lawrence E. Walsh, *Firewall: The Iran-Contra Conspiracy and Cover-Up* (New York: W. W. Norton, 1997).

70. Tax expenditures are defined as "revenue losses attributable to provisions of the federal tax laws which allow a special exclusion, exemption, or deduction from gross income or which provide a special credit, a preferential rate of tax or a deferral of tax liability." They include "any reductions in income tax liabilities that result from special tax provisions or regulations that provide tax benefits to particular taxpayers." Joint Committee on Taxation, "Estimates of Federal Tax Expenditures for Fiscal Years 2020–2024," JCX-23-20, November 5, 2020. In 1982 tax expenditures totaled 8.2 percent of GDP compared to 4.4 percent in 1967. Patashnik, *Reforms at Risk*, 37. There has been considerable debate over the concept and lists of tax expenditures.

71. Patashnik, *Reforms at Risk*, 53.

72. E. J. Dionne Jr., "Elections; Democrats Gain Control of Senate, Drawing Votes of Reagan's Backers; Cuomo and D'Amatio Are Easy Victors; What Awaits Congress; Broad GOP Losses," *New York Times*, November 5, 1986; R. W. Apple Jr., "The Elections: Issues and Interest Groups; Democrat Wins a Close Contest for House Seat," *New York Times*, November 7, 1986.

73. See Graetz, "Tax Reform Unraveling"; Michael J. Graetz, "Tax Reform 1986: A Silver Anniversary, Not a Jubilee," *Tax Notes*, October 21, 2011.

Chapter 8

1. Grover Norquist, interview by Steve Kroft, *60 Minutes*, CBS, November 20, 2011, https://www.cbsnews.com/news/the-pledge-grover-norquist-hold-on-the-gops-26-08-2012.

2. Jackie Alemany, "Transcript: A Conversation with Grover Norquist, President of Americans for Tax Reform," *Washington Post*, April 9, 2021.

3. Molly Ball, "Grover Norquist, the Happiest Man in Washington," *The Atlantic*, April 18, 2017.

4. Paul A. Gigot, "Dole Bows to GOP's New Powers: Potomac Watch," *Wall Street Journal*, April 14, 1995.

5. Report, "Soviets Needled," September 15, 1981, box 4, folder: College Republicans National Committee (2 of 4), Blackwell, Morton C.: Files 1981–1984, Ronald Reagan Library, Simi Valley, CA, https://www.reaganlibrary.gov/public/digitallibrary/smof/publicliaison/blackwell/box-004/40_047_7006969_004_021_2017.pdf.

6. Nina J. Easton, *Gang of Five* (New York: Simon and Schuster, 2000), 74.

7. Ibid., 75.

8. Grover said anyone who viewed Hiss as innocent was "either a liar or an idiot." Ibid., 79.

9. Ibid., 80.

10. Ibid., 77. Other versions of the story have the licks of the ice cream as representing the income tax and the property tax. Neil Swidey, "Grover Norquist, Emperor of No," *Boston Globe*, March 18, 2012.

11. Swidey, "Grover Norquist, Emperor of No."

12. Susanna McBee, "Nov. 7 Shaping Up as a Series of Prop 13 Look-Alike Contests," *Washington Post*, September 10, 1978.

13. "'Statement of Account' Takes Taxpayer Liability," *Spokesmen Review*, September 25, 1978; "Bureaucratic Tax Issue," *Spokane Daily Chronicle*, October 28, 1978.

14. During the following two decades, Abramoff's fundraising and lobbying prowess morphed into fraud and tax evasion, ultimately resulting in his conviction and convictions of twenty-four others. Neil Lewis, "Abramoff Gets 4 Years in Prison for Corruption," *New York Times*, September 4, 2008.

15. Easton, *Gang of Five*, 143. Jim Baker refused to allow the College Republicans an audience with President Reagan. Norquist and Abramoff asked the president to address the group's 90th anniversary dinner in 1982, but the White House instead sent Vice President George H. W. Bush—a moderate Republican of the sort they despised. Ibid. See also ibid., 135–37. In May 1982 Grover became executive director of Americans for the Reagan Agenda, a group with Howard Jarvis, Milton Friedman, and other conservatives as figureheads, to build support for a balanced-budget amendment. In a memorandum to the White House, cosigned by conservative luminaries, including Jerry Falwell, Paul Weyrich, Phyllis Schlafly, and Howard Phillips, Norquist urged President Reagan to deliver a televised speech to the nation promoting the amendment. The president instead held a rally on the Washington Mall. Marcus Witcher, "Getting Right with Reagan: Conservatives and the Fortieth President, 1980–2016" (PhD diss., University of Alabama, 2017), 47–48.

16. Heather Cox Richardson, *To Make Men Free: A History of the Republican Party* (New York: Basic Books, 2014), 302.

17. Norquist briefed President Reagan in a meeting with Paul Weyrich and other conservatives in an unsuccessful effort to convince the president to switch his support for the socialist government in Mozambique to a militant resistance organization. The meeting on foreign policy with conservative leaders is noted on the White House schedule for September 22, 1987, but Norquist is not listed there. A photo of the meeting, however, includes him. See White House, *President's Schedule for September 22, 1987* (Washington, DC: Government Printing Office, 1987); David R. Ottaway, "Carlucci and the Mozambicans: A Tale of Two Viewpoints," *Washington Post*, November 10, 1987; Easton, *Gang of Five*, 161–67.

18. Ari Shapiro, "The Man behind the GOP's No-Tax Pledge," *All Things Considered*, July 14, 2011, radio, 4:31, https://www.npr.org/2011/07/14/137800715/the-man-behind-the-gops-tax-pledge.

19. Grover Norquist, interview by Jon Stewart, *Daily Show*, Comedy Central, March 12, 2012, https://www.cc.com/video/7617jv/the-daily-show-with-jon-stewart-exclusive-grover-norquist-extended-interview-pt-1; Grover G. Norquist and John K. Cott Jr., *Debacle* (Hoboken, NJ: John Wiley & Sons, 2012), 181. See also Bernard M. Shapiro, "Presidential Politics and Deficit Reduction: The Landscape of Tax Policy in the 1980s and 1990s," *Washington and Lee Law Review* 50 (1993): 441–47, 442; James M. Poterba, "Federal Budget Policy in the 1980s," in *American Economic Policy in the 1980s*, ed. Martin Feldstein (Chicago: University of Chicago Press, 1994).

20. Norquist, interview by Jon Stewart.

21. Norquist claims President Reagan asked him to create Americans for Tax Reform (ATR) to support the 1986 tax reform, but that is an overstatement. In 1985 the White House arranged for the creation of a coalition called "Americans for Tax Reform" to help with its legislative effort for tax reform. On September 10, President Reagan and Treasury Secretary Jim Baker met in the Cabinet Room with members of the Americans for Tax Reform Steering Committee consisting of more than twenty leaders of conservative and business organizations. Meeting with Members of the Americans for Tax Reform Steering Committee, September 10, 1985, photo C30766, White House Photo Collection Contact sheets, Ronald Reagan Library, Simi Valley, CA, https://www.reaganlibrary.gov/archives/photo/c30766-01. Chief of Staff Don Regan asked Bill Barr, a private lawyer who had served on Reagan's domestic policy staff, to create Americans for Tax Reform as a tax-exempt organization. Barr enlisted Peter Ferrara, who had also served on Reagan's staff, to assist in this effort, and Ferrara recruited Norquist to become ATR's executive director. Easton, *Gang of Five*, 161. John Cassidy, writing in the *New Yorker*, says that Don Regan recruited Norquist, but this is not right. But that may be what Grover told him. John

Cassidy, "The Ringleader," *New Yorker*, July 4, 2005. On September 12, 1985, Americans for Tax Reform held its only public rally for Reagan's tax-reform effort in Tampa, Florida. Reagan spoke for about fifteen minutes to an audience of a couple of thousand elderly residents, many bused there by ATR. The president said that he was "happy to have a few kids of my own age to play with." Ronald Reagan, "Remarks at a Senior Citizens Forum on Tax Reform" (speech, Tampa, FL, September 12, 1985), Ronald Reagan Library, https://www.reaganlibrary.gov/archives /speech/remarks-senior-citizens-forum-tax-reform-tampa-florida. Peter Ferrara served as the spokesman for ATR. Tom Scherberger and Harry Straight, "Martinez's Opponents Cry No Fair over Reagan's Tampa Visit," *Orlando Sentinel*, September 12, 1985; Bob Kowalski, "Reagan Enlists Tampa Seniors for Tax Reform," *Fort Lauderdale Sun Sentinel*, September 13, 1985. Norquist said he "discovered that there was no public interest in fundamental tax reform. We offered to pay for the public to send telegrams to congressmen demanding reform, but almost nobody sent one. People wouldn't even send a free letter." Cassidy, "The Ringleader." Peter Ferrara tells a different story about Norquist's tax-reform efforts. Ferrara says that beginning in 1985 Grover, at age twenty-nine, spent most of his time traveling to rebel camps in Africa in his quest to oppose communism. Ferrara adds, "He kept taking off and going to Africa and the [ATR] board of directors couldn't understand—'what the heck is he doing in Africa? He's supposed to be passing the Tax Reform Act.'" Ferrara spent 1985 and 1986 protecting Grover from the angry directors, adding, "I didn't fully understand why he always had to go to Africa, but I figured if Grover thinks it's important, I've got to cover for him as long as I can. There was a lot of pressure to get rid of him"; Easton, *Gang of Five*, 161–62.

22. Norquist, interview by Steve Kroft.

23. "About the Pledge," Americans for Tax Reform, https://www.atr.org/about-the-pledge.

24. "Take the Pledge," Americans for Tax Reform, https://www.atr.org/take-the-pledge ?cmp.

25. Grover Norquist, "Anti-Tax Pledge Takes on Urgency," *Human Events*, June 22, 2010.

26. Shapiro, "The Man behind the GOP's No-Tax Pledge."

27. Grover claims he thought of the pledge as a teenager in high school, when he saw the political influence of an antitax message in the campaign of Meldrim Thomson Jr., who ran successfully for governor of New Hampshire in 1972 with the slogans "Low taxes are the result of low spending" and "Ax the Tax." Swidey, "Grover Norquist, Emperor of No."

28. Jason Horowitz, "Grover Norquist, the Anti-tax Enforcer behind the Scenes of the Debt Debate," *Washington Post*, July 12, 2011.

29. Ball, "Grover Norquist, the Happiest Man in Washington."

30. "Locking in the Pols," *Wall Street Journal*, September 16, 1986.

31. Understating its purpose, Grover said, "The pledge is designed to protect the process of tax reform." "Group Announces List of No-Tax Increase Signers," *Atlanta Daily World*, October 21, 1986.

32. David M. Erdman, "Pulpit Politics Are Not Passe on the Campaign Trail," *Morning Call*, November 2, 1986.

33. Jane Mayer, "Ways and Means Panel's Tax-Overhaul Proposal Brings 'Family' Strife to Conservative Coalition," *Wall Street Journal*, November 27, 1985.

34. Cassidy, "The Ringleader."

35. Erdman, "Pulpit Politics."

36. See, e.g., Report, "Americans for Tax Reform," box 7, folder: Thompson Committee Final Report, Volume 2 [2], Clinton Presidential Records: White House Staff and Office Files, Office of General Counsel, Michael Imbroscio, Clinton Digital Library, https://clinton.presidential libraries.us/items/show/98312.

37. Michael J. Graetz and Ian Shapiro, *Death by a Thousand Cuts: The Fight over Taxing Inherited Wealth* (Princeton: Princeton University Press, 2005), 27–28.

38. Cassidy, "The Ringleader."

39. Ibid.

40. Transcript, "Domestic Third Way Meeting," July 8, 1998, box 11, folder: Third Way, Clinton Presidential Records: White House Staff and Office Files, First Ladies Office, Speechwriting, and Laura Schiller, Clinton Digital Library, https://clinton.presidentiallibraries.us/items/show/546589.

41. Bernard Schoenburg, "Norquist: Beware the 'Takings Coalition,'" *State Journal-Record*, September 24, 2007.

42. Cassidy, "The Ringleader."

43. See, e.g., Renee Prendergast, "The Concept of Freedom and Its Relation to Economic Development: A Critical Appreciation of the Work of Amartya Sen," *Cambridge Journal of Economics* 29, no. 6 (November 2005): 1145–70.

44. Swidey, "Grover Norquist, Emperor of No"; Graetz and Shapiro, *Death by a Thousand Cuts*, 29.

45. Cassidy, "The Ringleader."

46. Schoenburg, "Norquist: Beware the 'Takings Coalition.'"

47. Graetz and Shapiro, *Death by a Thousand Cuts*, 214.

48. E.g., Michael Scherer, "Grover Norquist: The Soul of the New Machine," *Mother Jones*, January/February 2004, https://www.motherjones.com/politics/2004/01/grover-norquist-soul-new-machine.

49. Graetz and Shapiro, *Death by a Thousand Cuts*, 9.

50. David R. Mayhew, *America's Congress: Actions in the Public Sphere, James Madison through Newt Gingrich* (New Haven: Yale University Press, 2002), ix.

51. Dale Russakoff and Dan Balz, "He Knew What He Wanted: Gingrich Forced Disparate Lessons into a Single-Minded Goal," *Washington Post*, December 19, 1994.

52. Julian E. Zelizer, *Burning Down the House: Newt Gingrich, the Fall of a Speaker, and the Rise of the New Republican Party* (New York: Penguin, 2020), 26.

53. David Osborne, "The Swinging Days of Newt Gingrich," *Mother Jones*, November 1, 1984.

54. Newt advanced a wide range of policy ideas, from tax credits to help low-income children have computers to a moon colony that would become a state. Amy Gardner, "Gingrich Pledges Moon Colony during Presidency," *Washington Post*, January 25, 2012. He authored books, such as *To Renew America* and *Window of Opportunity*, created a television course called *Renewing American Civilization*, and routinely offered broad manifestos on the demands of the "third-wave information age." John J. Pitney Jr., "Understanding Newt Gingrich" (paper presented at American Political Science Association Meeting, San Francisco, CA, September 1, 1996), 11–13.

55. Pitney, "Understanding Newt Gingrich."

56. See, e.g., Zelizer, *Burning Down the House.*

57. Osborne, "The Swinging Days of News Gingrich."

58. Craig Shirley, *Citizen Newt: The Making of a Reagan Conservative* (Nashville: Nelson Books, 2017).

59. Steven Roberts, "One Conservative Faults Two Parties," *New York Times*, August 11, 1983.

60. Peter Grier, "Washington Warms Up to Balanced Budget Laws," *Christian Science Monitor*, March 24, 1982.

61. Roberts, "One Conservative Faults Two Parties."

62. Zachary C. Smith, "From the Well of the House: Remaking the House Republican Party, 1978–1994" (PhD diss., Boston University, 2012), 226–28.

63. Newt Gingrich, "The Republican Proposition for the 1982 Election," July 15, 1982, box 48, folder 15 C, CC Record Group 1, Subgroup 2, Series 3, Conservative Caucus Files, Jerry Falwell

Library, Lynchburg, VA, https://cdm17184.contentdm.oclc.org/digital/collection /p17184coll12/id/50021/rec/2.

64. Barbara Roessner, "Comma Gives Pause in Battle over GOP Platform Plank," *Hartford Courant*, August 15, 1984. According to *Newsweek's* Jonathan Alter, Gingrich's "firebrands took over the platform committee, ramming through a document so close to the fringe that many Republicans—including Senator Dole—felt obliged to condemn it." "We got everything we wanted," Gingrich said. Everything, that is, except a commitment by President Reagan to adhere to it. Zelizer, *Burning Down the House*, 76.

65. "The Long March of Newt Gingrich," *Frontline*, PBS, January 16, 1996, 53:55, https://www .pbs.org/video/frontline-long-march-newt-gingrich-preview/.

66. Stephen Engelberg and Katherine Q. Seelye, "Gingrich: Man in Spotlight and Organization in Shadow," *New York Times*, December 18, 1994.

67. Zelizer, *Burning Down the House*, 294.

68. Another organization was the Progress and Freedom Foundation, a think tank funded by tax-deductible contributions raised from wealthy conservatives. Jeffrey Eisenach, Newt's close associate who became the head of both GOPAC and the foundation, described its ambitions in a fundraising letter to a Tobacco Institute lobbyist: "The goal of this project is simple: To train by April 1996, 200,000+ citizens into a model for replacing the welfare state and reforming our government." The foundation's partisan activities and its enabling its donors to advocate for policies that would benefit them financially spurred Newt's adversaries to advance (unsuccessful) ethical and legal complaints. Glenn Simpson, "Will Newt Fall?" *Mother Jones*, August 1, 1995.

69. David Hoffman, "Tout the Past or Trumpet an Agenda? Reagan Strategists Split," *Washington Post*, May 26, 1984.

70. Richard Reeves, "The Republicans," *New York Times*, September 9, 1984.

71. Jon Meacham, *Destiny and Power: The American Odyssey of George Herbert Walker Bush* (New York: Random House, 2015), 364.

72. Connie Bruck, "The Politics of Perception," *New Yorker*, October 9, 1995.

73. McKay Coppins, "The Man Who Broke Politics," *The Atlantic*, November 2018.

74. Ronald Brownstein, *The Second Civil War: How Extreme Partisanship Has Paralyzed Washington and Polarized America* (New York: Penguin Press, 2007), 137–38.

75. Steven Roberts, "House GOP Freshmen Are Speaking Up on Party Issues," *New York Times*, October 29, 1979. Gingrich bragged, "I was in the Washington news media enough to be a very well-known freshman." Zelizer, *Burning Down the House*, 44–45. In October 1979 Gingrich urged the House Democratic leadership to resign because of the poor economy and budget gridlock. He and Paul Weyrich tried but failed to build a coalition to replace Tip O'Neill with a more conservative Speaker.

76. Zelizer, *Burning Down the House*, 62.

77. The *Atlanta Journal-Constitution* called Newt "a walking media event." Howard Kurtz, "Spin Cycles: A Guide to Media Behavior in the Age of Newt," *Washington Post*, February 26, 1995.

78. Zelizer, *Burning Down the House*, 62, 67.

79. Kathleen Hall Jamieson and Joseph N. Cappella, *Echo Chamber: Rush Limbaugh and the Conservative Media Establishment* (Oxford: Oxford University Press, 2008), 3.

80. Marc Fisher, "Rush Limbaugh, Conservative Radio Provocateur and Cultural Phenomenon, Dies at 70," *Washington Post*, February 17, 2021.

81. Ibid.; Adam Epstein, "Rush Limbaugh's Short-Lived TV Show Was the Gateway Drug to Fox News," *Quartz*, February 17, 2021, https://qz.com/1973960/rush-limbaughs-short-lived -tv-show-helped-usher-in-fox-news.

82. Stephen Talbot, "Wizard of Ooze," *Mother Jones*, May/June 1995.

83. See Brian Rosenwald, *Talk Radio's America: How an Industry Took Over a Political Party That Took Over the United States* (Cambridge, MA: Harvard University Press, 2019), 37.

84. Conor Friedersdorf, "How Rush Limbaugh Keeps His Listeners in Fantasy Land," *The Atlantic*, July 28, 2011.

85. David J. Hoaas, Lori D. Zimbelman, and Harold R. Christensen, "The Economic Pronouncements of Social Philosophies: Rush Limbaugh and Will Rogers," *Studies in Popular Culture* 17, no. 2 (April 1995): 94.

86. Jamieson and Cappella, *Echo Chamber*, 70.

87. Robert D. McFadden and Michael M. Grynbaum, "Rush Limbaugh Dies at 70; Turned Talk Radio into a Right-Wing Attack Machine," *New York Times*, February 17, 2021.

88. For vivid description, see Linda Shrieves, "Dittoheads: Limbaugh's Faithful," *Orlando Sentinel*, August 28, 1993.

89. See Fisher, "Rush Limbaugh, Conservative Radio Provocateur"; McFadden and Grynbaum, "Rush Limbaugh Dies at 70."

90. Rosenwald, *Talk Radio's America*, 36.

91. Phillip Seib, *Rush Hour: Talk Radio, Politics and the Rise of Rush Limbaugh* (Fort Worth: Summit Group, 1993), 118.

92. Rosenwald, *Talk Radio's America*, 77.

93. Randall Strahan and Daniel J. Palazzolo, "The Gingrich Effect," *Political Science Quarterly* 119, no. 1 (2004): 98.

94. Delaware Constitution, Article VIII, Section 6, and Section 10. (Uniquely among the states, two-thirds of the Delaware state legislature can amend the state's constitution without any vote of the people. Delaware Constitution, Article XVI.) Robert D. McFadden, "Pete du Pont, Ex–Delaware Governor Who Ran for President, Dies at 86," *New York Times*, May 17, 2021.

95. David Hoffman and Edward Walsh, "Bush and Dole Parry Attacks from Rivals," *Washington Post*, February 15, 1988. Another report quotes Dole as saying, "I'll never sign—I'd have to read it first. Maybe George . . ." Domenico Montanrro, "Read Their Lips: No New Taxes. Pledge Season Is Officially Open," NPR, April 24, 2015, https://www.npr.org/sections /itsallpolitics/2015/04/24/402013487/read-their-lips-no-new-taxes-pledge-season-is -officially-open.

96. Michael Grunwald, "Grover Norquist Isn't Finished," *Politico*, October 15, 2015, https:// www.politico.com/agenda/story/2015/10/grover-norquist-tax-interview-00288.

97. Dick Gephardt said that Democrats viewed Jim Wright's move into the Speaker's office as signaling the end of the Reagan era. On Jim Wright as Speaker, see Zelizer, *Burning Down the House*, 82–124; Smith, "From the Well of the House," 194–218.

98. After Wright manipulated a budget bill in October 1987, Dick Cheney, second in the House Republican leadership, said, "The degree of partisanship, the strength of feeling, is more than it has been. . . . We had our problems with Tip O'Neill, too, but with Wright it is somehow more personal." Noah M. Weiss, "The Republican Revolution? The Transformation and Maturation of the House Republican Party, 1980–1995" (undergraduate thesis, University of Pennsylvania, 2009), https://repository.upenn.edu/cgi/viewcontent.cgi?article=1013&context=uhf _2009.

99. Richard Corliss, "Conservative Provocateur or Big Blowhard," *Time*, October 26, 1992.

100. Zelizer, *Burning Down the House*, 88. In June 1987 Newt Gingrich, despite hesitancy from his close House allies Vin Weber of Minnesota and Pennsylvania's Bob Walker, began attacking Wright for corruption, claiming that he had violated House ethics rules. When Newt decided to file an ethics complaint against Wright in December 1987, he compared his clash with Wright to Martin Luther's sixteenth-century battle with the Roman Catholic Church. Invoking his own messianic zeal, Gingrich quoted Luther, "Here I stand. I can do no other. God help me."

101. Ibid., 88–89.

102. Brownstein, *The Second Civil War*, 139.

103. Zelizer, *Burning Down the House*, 132–35, 159–61. In April 1989 a Democratic congressman, supported by Common Cause, filed ethics charges against Newt for his book deal's financial arrangements similar to Wright's—charges that later were expanded to include campaign finance violations and other matters. Newt said the complaints against him were a "political witch hunt." He escaped wounded but unbowed. Charles Babcock, "Gingrich's Book Venture," *Washington Post*, March 20, 1989; Tom Kenworthy, "Gingrich Faces New Ethics Charges: GOP Whip Accused of Breaking House Rules, Laws on Use and Funds," *Washington Post*, October 29, 1989.

104. Zelizer, *Burning Down the House*, 206–10.

105. Ibid., 266–76. Newt told *Los Angeles Times* reporters that Coelho's resignation confirmed charges that Democrats had become corrupt having held power in the House for so long: "I think the fact that the No. 1 and No. 3 Democrats apparently will both leave in June says something about 35 years of monopoly power." Ibid., 239.

106. Ibid., 273.

107. Tom Shales, "Jim Wright's Final Hour in the Spotlight," *Washington Post*, June 1, 1989. Examining this conflict thirty years later, the historian Julian Zelizer blamed Newt for the vicious partisanship, the "mindless cannibalism." Gingrich's allies naturally told a different story. Pennsylvania congressman Bob Walker insisted Wright's "arrogance" and House Republicans' resentment at being frozen out of decision making galvanized their opposition. Walker said Wright "became a catalyst for bringing the whole Republican Party over to our side. . . . Wright made them so mad they accepted what we'd been saying about the majority." Mel Steely, *The Gentleman from Georgia: The Biography of Newt Gingrich* (Macon, GA: Mercer University Press, 2000), 188.

108. Emily Langer, "Thomas S. Foley, Former House Speaker, Dies at 84," *Washington Post*, October 18, 2013. Not long after Foley moved into the Speaker's office, some Republicans started spreading false rumors that he was gay. The Republican National Committee put out a memo challenging the new Speaker to come "out of the liberal closet." The *New York Daily News* quoted a Gingrich aide as saying, "We hear it's little boys." Gingrich described the aide's comments as "unforgiveable and destructive" but refused to fire the aide, who had spent two years investigating Jim Wright. "I would have forgiven any person with that track record one major mistake," Gingrich said. Dan Balz and Serge F. Kovaleski, "Gingrich Divided GOP, Conquered the Agenda; Revolt Gave Party a Glimpse of Its Future," *Washington Post*, December 21, 1994.

109. Martin Tolchin, "John G. Tower, 65, Longtime Senator from Texas," *New York Times*, April 6, 1991; Meacham, *Destiny and Power*, 363–64.

110. Brownstein, *The Second Civil War*, 139.

111. Newt began by consolidating the support of the 55 to 60 conservatives aligned with the Conservative Opportunity Society that he and Vin Weber, Dan Lungren, and Bob Walker had led since the early 1980s. Walker said, "There was a group of us who spent the weekend on the phone calling. By Monday morning, we had 60 people committed to vote for Newt for whip. . . . The last 30 or 35 votes came real hard." Memo, "Conservative Opportunity Society," August 11, 1983, box 10, folder: Newt Gingrich, Blackwell, Morton C.: Files, 1981–1984, Ronald Reagan Library, Simi Valley, CA, https://www.reaganlibrary.gov/public/digitallibrary/smof/publicliaison/blackwell/box-010/40_047_7006969_010_011_2017.pdf; Balz and Kovaleski, "Gingrich Divided GOP." Gingrich gathered additional support from a group of moderate Republicans frustrated with their inability to influence legislation in the Democratic House. He promised them power if they supported his candidacy and argued that his confrontational tactics, rather than the conciliatory pragmatism of Madigan, would create the best chance of capturing a Republican House majority. Smith, "From the Well of the House," 224, 226–28.

112. Newt was thrilled. "I came here [in 1978]," he said, "and the party would never elect Newt Gingrich to be whip, and for ten years I changed the party. I didn't run for leadership, I

just changed the party. In 1989 I went from being backbencher to the second-ranking Republican." Dan Balz and Ronald Brownstein, *Storming the Gates: Protest Politics and the Republican Revival* (Boston: Little, Brown, 1996), 134.

113. Smith, "From the Well of the House," 224; Robin Toner, "House Republicans Elect Gingrich of Georgia as Whip," *New York Times*, March 23, 1989.

114. Toner, "House Republicans Elect Gingrich of Georgia as Whip."

115. Meacham, *Destiny and Power*, 365.

116. Ibid.

Chapter 9

1. George H. W. Bush, "Address Accepting the Presidential Nomination at the Republican National Convention in New Orleans" (speech, New Orleans, LA, August 18, 1988), The American Presidency Project, https://www.presidency.ucsb.edu/documents/address-accepting-the-presidential-nomination-the-republican-national-convention-new.

2. On foreign policy issues, see Jon Meacham, *Destiny and Power: The American Odyssey of George Herbert Walker Bush* (New York: Random House, 2015), 367–89, 421–42, 482–96.

3. Ibid., 361.

4. Ibid.

5. Ibid., 409.

6. Sebastian Mallaby, *The Man Who Knew: The Life and Times of Alan Greenspan* (New York: Penguin, 2016), 372–90, 400–417.

7. Richard Darman, *Who's in Control? Polar Politics and the Sensible Center* (New York: Simon and Schuster, 1996), 187.

8. Meacham, *Destiny and Power*, 339.

9. Darman, *Who's in Control?* 191–92.

10. "Federal Deficit Hits a Record $211.9 Billion," *Los Angeles Times*, October 27, 1985; "Gross Domestic Product," Federal Reserve Bank of St. Louis, February 23, 2023, https://fred.stlouisfed.org/series/GDP. The federal government fiscal year ends on September 30. Deficit numbers generally refer to fiscal year deficits.

11. Phillip G. Joyce and Robert D. Reischauer, "Deficit Budgeting: The Federal Budget Process and Budget Reform," *Harvard Journal on Legislation* 29, no. 2 (Summer 1992): 433–34.

12. The Balanced Budget and Emergency Deficit Control Act, Public Law No. 93-344 (1985), *amended by* the Balanced Budget and Emergency Deficit Control Reaffirmation Act of 1987, Public Law No. 100-119 (1987).

13. Ibid. The 1985 Act delegated important judgments concerning deficit-reduction targets and sequestration to the Comptroller General of the United States, who serves at the pleasure of Congress. In 1986 the Supreme Court held that the Comptroller General's role violated the Constitution's separation of powers. Bowsher v. Synar, 478 U.S. 714 (1986). In 1987 Congress amended the law to transfer those functions to the president.

14. Statement of Senator Rudman, 99th Cong., 2nd sess., 132 Cong. Rec., pt. 13:18456.

15. Joyce and Reischauer, "Deficit Budgeting," 434. The crisis in the savings and loan industry, which began in 1986, cost the federal government nearly $125 billion and made meeting the GRH deficit targets more difficult.

16. Robert Reischauer, "Taxes and Spending under Gramm-Rudman-Hollings," *National Tax Journal* 43 (1990): 223–32.

17. Louis Uchitelle, "The Struggle in Congress; U.S. Deficit for 1990 Surged to Near-Record $220.4 Billion, but How Bad Is That?" *New York Times*, October 27, 1990.

18. Darman, *Who's in Control?* 206.

19. Michael J. Graetz, *The Decline (and Fall?) of the Income Tax* (New York: W. W. Norton, 1997), 162.

20. Susan F. Rasky, "Budget Tug of War Is About to Begin," *New York Times,* January 9, 1989.

21. Darman, *Who's in Control?* 202.

22. George H. W. Bush, "Address before a Joint Session of Congress" (speech, Washington, DC, February 9, 1989), The Miller Center, https://millercenter.org/the-presidency/presidential -speeches/february-9-1989-address-joint-session-congress. President Bush also emphasized freezing the military budget, maintaining Social Security benefits, and protecting the environment.

23. Sara Fritz and William Eaton, "Bush Budget Priorities: Democrats Reject Medicare Cuts, Accuse Bush of 'Voodoo Economics,'" *Los Angeles Times,* February 10, 1989.

24. Tom Kenworthy, "House Votes to Slash Capital Gains Taxes," *Washington Post,* October 29, 1989.

25. Jeffrey Birnbaum, "Merging a Lower Capital Gains Rate with a Rise in Gasoline Tax Would Leave the Poor the Losers," *Wall Street Journal,* May 8, 1989.

26. Public Law 101-239. The vote in the House was 333 to 91 and 87 to 7 in the Senate.

27. Tom Kenworthy, "$14.7 Billion Deficit-Reduction Bill Is Enacted," *Washington Post,* November 27, 1989.

28. Darman, *Who's in Control?* 218.

29. Ibid., 243, 245.

30. Meacham, *Destiny and Power,* 410.

31. Ibid., 412; Graetz, *Decline (and Fall?) of the Income Tax,* 163.

32. Meacham, *Destiny and Power,* 412.

33. Darman, *Who's in Control?* 259.

34. Ibid., 255, 260.

35. Ibid., 260.

36. John Yang, "Rep. Gingrich 'Prepared' to Back Increase in Taxes: GOP Whip Would Support Anti-Deficit Move," *Washington Post,* June 20, 1990.

37. Meacham, *Destiny and Power,* 414–15.

38. Oscar Wilde, "The Relation of Dress to Art: A Note in Black and White on Mr. Whistler's Lecture," *Pall Mall Gazette,* February 28, 1885.

39. Darman, *Who's in Control?* 261.

40. Ibid., 262.

41. Meacham, *Destiny and Power,* 414–15.

42. Andrew Rosenthal, "Bush Now Concedes a Need for 'Tax Revenue Increases' to Reduce Deficit in Budget," *New York Times,* June 27, 1990.

43. Meacham, *Destiny and Power,* 409; Craig Shirley, *Citizen Newt: The Making of a Reagan Conservative* (Nashville: Nelson Books, 2017), 254; John Robert Greene, *The Presidency of George Bush* (Lawrence: University Press of Kansas, 2000), 84.

44. Dan Balz and John E. Yang, "Bush Abandons Campaign Pledge, Calls for New Taxes," *Washington Post,* June 27, 1990; David Lauter and William J. Eaton, "Bush Breaks Campaign Vow, Says New Taxes Necessary," *Los Angeles Times,* June 27, 1990.

45. Patrick J. Buchanan, "The End of the Reagan Revolution," *Human Events,* October 13, 1990.

46. Meacham, *Destiny and Power,* 415.

47. Dan Quayle, *Standing Firm: A Vice-Presidential Memoir* (New York: HarperCollins, 1994), 192–93. Republican congressman Vin Weber, Newt's friend and ally, echoed Quayle's lament: "A lot of us were really committed supply-siders," he said. "We were of the belief that tax cutting was an indispensable element of our platform if we were going to win a Republican majority in the House. So there was just no way we were going to vote to raise taxes, even for a Republican president." Meacham, *Destiny and Power,* 415.

48. Darman, *Who's in Control?* 265.

49. Jon Meacham wrote, "Bush was more interested in the result, which he defined as responsible governance and sound financial stewardship, than he was in the political work of educating the country about the situation at hand." *Destiny and Power*, 417.

50. Ibid., 413.

51. Ibid., 418; Darman, *Who's in Control?* 266.

52. Noah M. Weiss, "The Republican Revolution? The Transformation and Maturation of the House Republican Party, 1980–1995" (undergraduate thesis, University of Pennsylvania, 2009), 51, https://repository.upenn.edu/cgi/viewcontent.cgi?article=1013&context=uhf_2009.

53. This discussion of the Andrews negotiations tracks Graetz, *The Decline (and Fall?) of the Income Tax*, 165–70. The author participated in the 1990 budget negotiations on behalf of the Bush administration.

54. Darman, *Who's in Control?* 272.

55. Ibid.

56. Ibid., 279.

57. Dan Balz and Serge F. Koveleski, "Gingrich Divided GOP, Conquered the Agenda; Revolt Gave Party a Glimpse of Its Future," *Washington Post*, December 21, 1994.

58. In addition to Gingrich's comments described in the text, on July 29 Gingrich said on NBC's *Meet the Press*, "I personally have been very clearly opposed to any increase in income taxes," and he said that he would not support a budget agreement unless it was a "very, very, good package." William Eaton, "Gingrich Sends Warning on Budget Deficit: House GOP Whip Won't Back It Unless It's 'A Very Good Package.' He Says Bush Made a Mistake When He Reversed Himself on Taxes," *Los Angeles Times*, July 30, 1990. The next day Gingrich said he would support tax increases only if there were spending cuts. David Wessel and Jackie Calmes, "In Budget Talks, Gingrich Plays Outsiders' Game While Gramm Is Fast Becoming a Team Player," *Wall Street Journal*, September 17, 1990. His 1990 Democratic congressional opponent said that Newt "changes his position on taxes more often than most people change socks." Ibid.

59. Wessel and Calmes, "In Budget Talks, Gingrich Plays Outsiders' Game."

60. Meacham, *Destiny and Power*, 444.

61. Shirley, *Citizen Newt*, 265.

62. Darman, *Who's in Control?* 279–80. Tom DeLay said, "The only way we could take over Congress . . . was to have a very clear distinction between the Democrats and the Republicans. The Bush administration muddled that distinction. The Bush administration wanted to work with Congress, rather than beat Congress. And so it was contrary to what we were doing." Ronald Brownstein, *The Second Civil War: How Extreme Partisanship Has Paralyzed Washington and Polarized America* (New York: Penguin Press, 2007), 198.

63. Quayle, *Standing Firm*, 197.

64. Brownstein, *The Second Civil War*, 148.

65. Ed Rollins, running the 1990 Republican Congressional Campaign Committee, described public perceptions that Republicans don't want to raise taxes as "the biggest difference between Republicans and Democrats." He publicly told congressional Republicans, "Do not hesitate to distance yourself from the president"—enraging Bush. Shirley, *Citizen Newt*, 246.

66. Meacham, *Destiny and Power*, 447.

67. Ibid.

68. In mid-October, Bush wrote in his diary, "I don't want a terrible deal to take place but [I] don't want to be off in some ideological corner falling on my sword and keeping the country from moving forward." Ibid., 448.

69. George H. W. Bush, "Statement on Signing the Omnibus Budget Reconciliation Act of 1990" (signing statement, Washington, DC, November 5, 1990), The American Presidency

Project, https://www.presidency.ucsb.edu/documents/statement-signing-the-omnibus-budget -reconciliation-act-1990.

70. Lois Romano, "Newt Gingrich, Maverick on the Hill," *Washington Post*, January 3, 1985; Gail Sheehy, "The Inner Quest of Newt Gingrich," *Vanity Fair*, September 1995, https://archive .vanityfair.com/article/1995/9/the-inner-quest-of-newt-gingrich.

71. Julian E. Zelizer, *Burning Down the House: Newt Gingrich, the Fall of a Speaker, and the Rise of the New Republican Party* (New York: Penguin, 2020), 293–95.

72. Mary McGrory, "Dems' Beaut: No Loot to Boot Newt," *Washington Post*, November 11, 1990.

73. Mel Steely, *The Gentleman from Georgia: The Biography of Newt Gingrich* (Macon, GA: Mercer University Press, 2000), 208–10.

74. For discussion of Newt's campaign and his role in the presidential campaign, see, e.g., Shirley, *Citizen Newt*, 304–14.

75. Patrick J. Buchanan, "1992 Presidential Announcement Speech: A Crossroads in Our Country's History" (speech, Concord, NH, December 10, 1991), 4President, http://www .4president.org/speeches/1992/patbuchanan1992announcement.htm.

76. Rick Perlstein, *Reaganland: America's Right Turn, 1976–1980* (New York: Simon and Schuster, 2020), 480.

77. Sean Wilentz, *The Age of Reagan: A History, 1974–2008* (New York: HarperCollins, 2008), 315.

78. E.g., Patrick J. Buchanan, interview by Bob Schieffer, *Face the Nation*, CBS News, February 4, 1992, https://www.youtube.com/watch?v=qBm7SZ_WjYY.

79. Kathleen Hall Jamieson and Joseph N. Cappella, *Echo Chamber: Rush Limbaugh and the Conservative Media Establishment* (Oxford: Oxford University Press, 2008), 106–7. The *Wall Street Journal* could not abide Buchanan's tariffs, criticizing him as the only candidate proposing a tax increase, "a massive government intervention in the economy," mentioning that Rush Limbaugh had also caught on to that, and quoting Limbaugh's criticism of Buchanan's willingness to "expand the role of government in people's lives." Ibid., 265n19.

80. Meacham, *Destiny and Power*, 501.

81. Robin Toner, "The 1992 Campaign: New Hampshire; Bush Jarred in First Primary; Tsongas Wins Democratic Vote," *New York Times*, February 19, 1992.

82. Ann Devroy, "Breaking Tax Pledge a Mistake, Bush Says," *Washington Post*, March 4, 1992. Bush's biographer Jon Meacham insisted that the president's "biggest mistake" remark was about "tactics, not substance." Meacham, *Destiny and Power*, 501.

83. Patrick J. Buchanan, "Campaign Speech" (speech, Norman, OK, March 5, 1992), C-SPAN, https://www.c-span.org/video/?25327-1/buchanan-campaign-speech.

84. In a misguided attempt to boost support from his right, Bush gave Buchanan a prime-time speaking slot the first night of the Republican convention. Buchanan declaimed a militant, populist, homophobic, racially coded attack on Bill and Hillary Clinton, insisting that there was a "religious war," a "cultural war, as critical to the kind of nation we shall be as the Cold War," a "war . . . for the soul of America." He urged Republicans to "take back our cities and take back our culture, and take back our country." Buchanan received a rousing ovation from the audience, but his speech was not lauded by the moderate and independent voters that George Bush needed to win. Patrick J. Buchanan, "Address to the Republican National Convention" (speech, Houston, TX, August 17, 1992), *Voices of Democracy*, https://voicesofdemocracy.umd .edu//buchanan-culture-war-speech-speech-text. Molly Ivins, a droll Texas political commentator, observed that "many people did not care for Buchanan's speech" and quipped it "probably sounded better in the original German." Molly Ivins, "Notes from Another Country (1992)," in *Letters to the Nation*, ed. Richard Lingeman (New York: The Nation, 2015).

85. Wilentz, *The Age of Reagan*, 321–22; Walter J. Stone and Ronald B. Rapoport, *Three's a Crowd: The Dynamics of Third Parties, Ross Perot, and Republican Resurgence* (Ann Arbor: University of Michigan Press, 2005).

86. Wilentz, *The Age of Reagan*, 322.

87. Brownstein, *The Second Civil War*, 148–49.

88. See, e.g., Grover Norquist, "It's My Party," *American Spectator* (January 1993): 28–31.

89. Glenn Kessler, "Grover Norquist's History Lesson: George H. W. Bush, 'No New Taxes,' and the 1992 Election," *Washington Post*, November 27, 1992.

90. Grover Norquist, interview by Jon Stewart, *Daily Show*, Comedy Central, March 12, 2012, https://www.cc.com/video/7617jv/the-daily-show-with-jon-stewart-exclusive-grover-norquist -extended-interview-pt-1.

91. John Cassidy, "The Ringleader," *New Yorker*, July 4, 2005.

92. Darman, *Who's in Control?* 299.

Chapter 10

1. Grover Norquist, "It's My Party," *American Spectator* (January 1993): 31.

2. Ibid.

3. Michael Kelly, "Gambling That a Tax-Cut Promise Was Not Taken Seriously," *New York Times*, February 18, 1993.

4. David E. Rosenbaum, "The 1992 Campaign: Clinton Promises to Protect Middle Class on Taxes," *New York Times*, October 31, 1992.

5. In addition to Bill Clinton, Hope, Arkansas, was the birthplace of Mike Huckabee, an Arkansas governor and candidate for the Republican presidential nomination, and his daughter Sarah Huckabee Sanders, who was elected governor of Arkansas in 2022. Frank Lockwood, "Upbringing Immersed in Arkansas Politics Prepared Sarah Huckabee Sanders for Role," *Arkansas Democrat-Gazette*, October 15, 2017, https://www.arkansasonline.com/news/2017/oct /15/sarah-huckabee-sanders-20171015-1/.

6. Bill Clinton, *My Life* (New York: Alfred A. Knopf, 2004), 58.

7. Sean Wilentz, *The Age of Reagan: A History, 1974–2008* (New York: HarperCollins, 2008), 326.

8. Clinton, *My Life*, 361.

9. Wilentz, *The Age of Reagan*, 318.

10. Robert B. Reich, "Movement Politics," *Boston Review* 29, no. 3–4 (Summer 2004): 18.

11. Bill Clinton, "The New Covenant: Responsibility and Rebuilding the American Community" (speech, Washington, DC, October 23, 1991), https://www.thetechnocratictyranny .com/PDFS/1991_Clinton_New_Covenant_Community.pdf.

12. In January 1992, just before the New Hampshire primary, Clinton flew back to Arkansas with great fanfare to oversee the execution of Ricky Ray Rector. Rector was an African American who had become severely mentally disabled after shooting himself in the head and destroying the front part of his brain, following his murder of a white police officer. Marshall Frady, "Death in Arkansas," *New Yorker*, February 22, 1993.

13. James Risen, "Clinton's Economic Ordeal: Promises Doomed by Math," *Los Angeles Times*, May 1, 1994.

14. Kelly, "Gambling That a Tax-Cut Promise Was Not Taken Seriously."

15. Sebastian Mallaby, *The Man Who Knew: The Life and Times of Alan Greenspan* (New York: Penguin, 2016), 420.

16. Ibid., 422.

17. Clinton, *My Life*, 459.

18. Mallaby, *The Man Who Knew*, 423.

19. Clinton, *My Life*, 463.

20. Bob Woodward, *The Agenda: Inside the Clinton White House* (New York: Simon and Schuster, 1994), 106.

21. Mallaby, *The Man Who Knew*, 429.

22. Woodward, *The Agenda*, 65.

23. Heather Stewart, Simon Goodley, and Katie Allen, "Why We All Get Burnt in the Bonfire of the Bond Markets," *The Guardian*, November 19, 2011.

24. Clinton, *My Life*, 460, 493–94.

25. Woodward, *The Agenda*, 104–5.

26. Clinton, *My Life*, 463.

27. Bill Clinton, "Address before a Joint Session of Congress" (speech, Washington, DC, February 17, 1993), The Miller Center, https://millercenter.org/the-presidency/presidential -speeches/february-17-1993-address-joint-session-congress.

28. Ibid.

29. Woodward, *The Agenda*, 153.

30. Ibid., 88–89, 217, 302.

31. The Omnibus Budget Reconciliation Act of 1993, Public Law, 103-56 (1993).

32. Woodward, *The Agenda*, 311.

33. Clinton, *My Life*, 522.

34. See Michael J. Graetz, *The End of Energy: The Unmaking of America's Environment, Security, and Independence* (Cambridge, MA; MIT Press, 2011), 179–95.

35. Matthew Rees, "How Whitman Did It," *Wall Street Journal*, November 9, 1993; Dan Balz, "Gov. Florio's Lead Slips as N.J. Contest Tightens," *Washington Post*, October 27, 1993; Tom Edsall, "Florio Runs Right Back into New Jersey Contest," *Washington Post*, September 27, 1993.

36. Woodward, *The Agenda*, 321.

37. Clinton, *My Life*, 629.

38. In May Dan Rostenkowski (along with a Democratic colleague from Pennsylvania) was indicted for embezzling House funds. Democratic leaders insisted he immediately resign his position as chairman of the Ways and Means Committee. Newt Gingrich quickly offered Rosty's indictment as further evidence of the Democratic Party's corruption. Rostenkowski was convicted in 1996 on mail fraud charges and served fifteen months in prison. In December 2000, Bill Clinton pardoned Rostenkowski, saying he had done a lot for his country and more than paid for his mistakes. Ibid., 940.

39. Ibid., 630–31.

40. David W. Brady, John F. Cogan, Brian J. Gaines, and Douglas Rivers, "The Perils of Presidential Support: How the Republicans Took the House in the 1994 Midterms," *Political Behavior* 18, no. 44 (December 1996): 361; Gary C. Jacobson, "The 1994 House Elections in Perspective," *Political Science Quarterly* 111, no. 2 (Summer 1996): 202–23; James E. Campbell, "The Presidential Pulse and the 1994 Midterm Congressional Elections," *Journal of Politics* 59, no. 2 (August 1997): 830–57.

41. Connie Bruck, "The Politics of Perception," *New Yorker*, October 9, 1995.

42. David Rosenbaum, "Republicans Offer Voters a Deal for Takeover of House," *New York Times*, September 28, 1994.

43. David Rosenbaum, "It's the Economy Again as Democrats Attack the Contract with America," *New York Times*, November 1, 1994; James Gimpel, *Legislating the Revolution: The Contract with America in Its First 100 Days* (Boston: Allyn and Bacon, 1996), 2.

44. Robin Toner, "The 1994 Campaign: Broadcaster; Election Jitters in Limbaughland," *New York Times*, November 3, 1994. See also David C. Barker, "Rushed Decisions: Political Talk Radio and Vote Choice, 1994–1996," *Journal of Politics* 61, no. 2 (May 1999): 527–39; Heather Cox Richardson, *To Make Men Free: A History of the Republican Party* (New York: Basic Books, 2014), 315–16.

45. Kevin Merida, "Rush Limbaugh Saluted as a 'Majority Maker,'" *Washington Post*, December 11, 1994.

46. Paul A. Gigot, "Dole Bows to GOP's New Powers: Potomac Watch," *Wall Street Journal*, April 14, 1995.

47. Gimpel, *Legislating the Revolution*, 153.

48. Eric Pianin, "Tax Cut Bill Passed by House," *Washington Post*, April 6, 1995. Families with incomes of $200,000 or less ($360,000 in 2021 dollars) would be given a $500 tax credit per child. Newt Gingrich told the 100 House Republicans who wanted to limit the credit to families with incomes no greater than $95,000 that such a limitation would inspire "every Republican in your district [to] ask you if you've lost your mind." Randall Strahan and Daniel J. Palazzolo, "The Gingrich Effect," *Political Science Quarterly* 119, no. 1 (2004): 89–114.

49. Eric Pianin, "House GOP Sticks with Tax Cut Plans, Despite Reagan Era Memories," *Washington Post*, April 2, 1995.

50. David Rosenbaum, "House Committee Supports Tax Cut," *New York Times*, March 15, 1995.

51. Robin Toner, "Washington Memo; Tax Cut Edges Out Deficit as GOP's Guiding Tenet," *New York Times*, April 3, 1995.

52. Steven A. Holmes, "Clinton Defines the Limits of Compromise with GOP; Gingrich Urges Dialogue," *New York Times*, April 8, 1995.

53. Ibid.

54. A balanced budget in seven years, House Budget Committee chairman John Kasich told Gingrich, required cuts in Medicare "unlike any this town has ever seen before." "Who said we have to do seven years?" Kasich asked. Newt responded that he was not going to "start accommodating to Washington realities." David Maraniss and Michael Weisskopf, *Tell Newt to Shut Up* (New York: Simon and Schuster, 1996), 37–38.

55. Several of Gingrich's former House allies were new senators, but the Senate had not changed as much as the House. On May 24 the Senate rejected, by a vote of 69–31, an amendment proposed by Phil Gramm that would have added $300 billion of tax cuts over seven years to a Senate Budget Committee deficit-reduction plan containing no immediate tax reductions. Twenty-three Republicans joined with all 46 Democrats to defeat Gramm's amendment. Bob Dole, who was competing with Gramm for the 1996 Republican presidential nomination, now recognized the power of tax cuts among Republican voters and supported Gramm's amendment. David E. Rosenbaum, "Gramm Proposal for Deep Tax Cut Killed by Senate," *New York Times*, May 24, 1995.

56. Thomas B. Edsall, "Hill Vote Is Milestone for Forces of Government Containment," *Washington Post*, June 30, 1995.

57. Ronald Brownstein, *The Second Civil War: How Extreme Partisanship Has Paralyzed Washington and Polarized America* (New York: Penguin Press, 2007), 162.

58. Elizabeth Drew, *Showdown: The Struggle between the Gingrich Congress and the Clinton White House* (New York: Simon and Schuster, 1996), 234.

59. Bill Clinton, "Presidential Budget Proposal," June 13, 1995, C-SPAN, https://www.c-span.org/video/?65710-1/presidential-budget-proposal.

60. Toner, "Washington Memo; Tax Cut Edges Out Deficit as GOP's Guiding Tenet."

61. Ibid. In October 1995 Senate Finance Committee Republicans agreed to a seven-year, $245 billion tax cut including a $500 child tax credit, a capital gains rate cut to 19.8 percent, increases in contribution limits to IRAs, and a rate cut for corporations from 35 to 28 percent. (The House bill would have cut the corporate rate to 25 percent.) The vote was purely partisan: the committee's eleven Republicans voted for it and its nine Democrats voted against. The Treasury indicated that the Republican bill would allocate 48 percent of its tax cuts to the top 12 percent of American households and increase taxes for 44 million households with incomes of $30,000 or less. Clay Chandler, "Senate Panel Passes $245 Billion in Tax Cuts for Families, Firms," *Washington Post*, October 20, 1995.

62. Maraniss and Weisskopf, *Tell Newt to Shut Up*, 146.

63. Steven Gillon, *The Pact: Bill Clinton, Newt Gingrich, and the Rivalry That Defined a Generation* (New York: Oxford University Press, 2008), 157–58.

64. Drew, *Showdown*, 275–76.

65. John E. Yang, "Underlying Gingrich's Stance Is His Pique about President," *Washington Post*, November 16, 1995.

66. Maraniss and Weisskopf, *Tell Newt to Shut Up*, 157.

67. Ibid., 153–56, 163–77.

68. Ibid., 178–79, 192.

69. Gillon, *The Pact*, 171.

70. Michael Allen Meeropol, *Surrender: How the Clinton Administration Completed the Reagan Revolution* (Ann Arbor: University of Michigan Press, 2000), 241.

71. E.g., Federal Reserve Bank of New York, *The Changing U.S. Income Distribution: Facts, Explanations, and Unresolved Issues*, by David Brauer, Research Paper No. 9811 (New York, April 1998), https://www.newyorkfed.org/medialibrary/media/research/staff_reports /research_papers/9811.html.

72. E.g., Internal Revenue Service, *Further Examination of the Distribution of Individual Income and Taxes Using a Consistent and Comprehensive Measure of Income*, by Tom Petska, Mike Strudler, and Ryan Petska (Washington, DC, 1999), https://www.irs.gov/pub/irs-soi/disindit.pdf.

73. Bill and Hillary Clinton's health-care debacle, his efforts to allow gay people in the military, and the assault weapons ban he had pushed through Congress shared in the blame. See, e.g., text at note 39; Brownstein, *The Second Civil War*, 150, 155–56.

Chapter 11

1. Michael J. Graetz, *100 Million Unnecessary Returns* (New Haven: Yale University Press, 2008), 36. The Gwinnett County rally occurred in May 2006.

2. Shawn Spohn and Korie Wilkins, "Flat Tax Recommended by GOP Leader," *The Lantern* (Ohio State University), August 2, 1998, https://www.thelantern.com/1998/08/flat-tax -recommended-by-gop-leader.

3. Alison Mitchell, "Two Republican Rivals, One Purpose on Taxes," *New York Times*, October 19, 1997.

4. Amy Fried and Douglas Harris, *At War with Government: How Conservatives Weaponized Distrust from Goldwater to Trump* (New York: Columbia University Press, 2021), 117–19.

5. William Saletan, "Debate and Switch," *Mother Jones*, March–April 1998. Dick Armey became president of CSE in 2003 after he retired from Congress; Billy Tauzin retired in 2005 and became the leader of the lobbying arm of the pharmaceutical industry at a reputed annual salary of $2 million.

6. Kathleen Hall Jamieson and Joseph N. Cappella, *Echo Chamber: Rush Limbaugh and the Conservative Media Establishment* (Oxford: Oxford University Press, 2008), 220, 225–26.

7. After Bill Clinton's 1992 election, Kemp helped form Empower America, a conservative "action group" that produced papers, op-eds, speeches, newsletters, and forums to advance conservative political ideas and oppose Clinton's policies. Morton Kondracke and Fred Barnes, *Jack Kemp: The Bleeding Heart Conservative Who Changed America* (New York: Sentinel, 2015), 252–56.

8. Jackie Calmes, "House GOP Leaders, Party Dissidents Reach Compromise on Tax-Cut Measure," *Wall Street Journal*, April 4, 1995.

9. "Full Text: Kemp Commission Report on Tax Reform," *Tax Notes*, January 17, 1996.

10. Associated Press, "GOP Panel Calls for Single-Rate Tax System: Kemp Commission Embraces Concept, but Steers Clear of Recommending It," *Chicago Tribune*, January 17, 1996;

U.S. Congress, Committee on Finance, *Report of the Activities of the Commission on Economic Growth and Tax Reform: Hearing before the Committee on Finance*, 104th Cong., 2nd sess., January 31, 1996.

11. "Kemp Commission: Damn the Deficit, Full Speed Backwards," *Citizens for Tax Justice*, January 17, 1996, https://ctj.org/kemp-commission-damn-the-deficit-full-speed-backwards.

12. Steven Pearlstein, "Turning the Tables in the Tax Code," *Washington Post*, April 15, 1995.

13. David Wessel and Greg Hitt, "Taxing Ideas: Anti-IRS Frenzy Gives Republicans a Chance to Road-Test Plans—Armey and Tauzin Debate the Merits of Flat Rate and Federal Sales Levy—Significance of the Alamo," *Wall Street Journal*, October 10, 1997.

14. U.S. Library of Congress, Congressional Research Service, *Tax Code Termination Act: A Fact Sheet*, by James M. Bickley, 98-548E (August 12, 1998); Graetz, *100 Million Unnecessary Returns*, 39.

15. Neal Boortz and John Linder, *The Fair Tax Book* (New York: Regan, 2005).

16. Jude Wanniski helped persuade Forbes to enter the 1996 presidential race touting this proposal, which Forbes described as if it was a flat-rate income tax. Elisabeth Bumiller, "In Political Quest, Forbes Runs in Shadow of Father," *New York Times*, February 11, 1996.

17. Douglas Turner, "Kemp Endorsed Forbes for Honorable Reasons," *Buffalo News*, March 18, 1996; John M. Border, "Campaign '96/Profile: Kemp Turns Heads with Late Cheer for Forbes: Timing of Endorsement Surprises Analysts. 'He Must Have Been on Another Planet Yesterday,' One Says," *Los Angeles Times*, March 7, 1996.

18. Jack Germond and Jules Witcover, "Flat-Tax Mania Enlivens the GOP Campaign," *Baltimore Sun*, January 22, 1996.

19. "The GOP Candidates' Positions," *USA Today*, January 18, 1996; Richard P. Wang, "The IRS and the Antitax Movement: Attacks on the IRS in the Wake of the 1994 Republican Revolution" (manuscript, Yale Law School, April 2023).

20. Howard Kurtz, "By Playing the Media, GOP Forced Clinton's Hand on IRS Overhaul," *Washington Post*, November 2, 1997.

21. *Seinfeld*, season 3, episode 2, "The Truth," aired September 25, 1991, NBC, https://www.youtube.com/watch?v=iNzAOKpo3CI&feature=youtu.be.

22. John Mintz, "Senate Panel to Hear Alleged IRS Abuse of Taxpayers," *Washington Post*, September 20, 1997.

23. Ibid.

24. John Broder, "Director of IRS Issues an Apology for Agent Abuses," *New York Times*, September 28, 1997.

25. Graetz, *100 Million Unnecessary Returns*, 37.

26. Ibid.

27. See, e.g., Rush Limbaugh speech at the annual Bakersfield Business Conference preceding a Scrap-the-Code debate between Dick Armey and Billy Tauzin. Rush Limbaugh, "Difference between Conservatives and Liberals," C-SPAN video, October 11, 1997, https://www.c-span.org/video/?93489-1/difference-conservatives-liberals.

28. Carl Weiser, "Real IRS Reforms Are Yet to Come, Agency-Rehash Measure That Won Senate Approval on Thursday Is Mostly Cosmetic," *Salt Lake City Tribune*, May 9, 1998.

29. "Clinton Signs IRS Reform Measure," *All Politics*, CNN, July 22, 1998, https://www.cnn.com/ALLPOLITICS/1998/07/22/irs.signing.

30. William V. Roth Jr. and William H. Nixon, *The Power to Destroy* (Washington, DC: Atlantic Monthly Press, 1999).

31. Graetz, *100 Million Unnecessary Returns*, 39.

32. Stefano DellaVigna and Ethan Kaplan, "The Fox News Effect: Media Bias and Voting," *Quarterly Journal of Economics* 122, no. 3 (August 2007): 1188.

33. Jamieson and Cappella, *Echo Chamber*, 48.

34. Ibid., 49.

35. DellaVigna and Kaplan, "The Fox News Effect," 1193–95; Heather Cox Richardson, *To Make Men Free: A History of the Republican Party* (New York: Basic Books, 2014), 318–19.

36. Kurtz, "By Playing the Media, GOP Forced Clinton's Hand on IRS Overhaul."

37. Jamieson and Cappella, *Echo Chamber*, 97.

38. Adrienne Gaffney, "The Improbable Rise of Matt Drudge, the Internet's Favorite News Scoundrel," *Town & Country*, September 21, 2021; "Matt Drudge, American Journalist," *Encyclopedia Britannica*, https://www.britannica.com/biography/Matt-Drudge.

39. Richardson, *To Make Men Free*, 318–19.

40. Sheryl Gay Stolberg, "Witty and to the Point, Dole Embodied 'Shared Values' in Washington," *New York Times*, December 5, 2021.

41. Maggie Astor, "A Chicken-Fried McGovern, Newt's Good Ideas and the Senate Zoo: A Dole One-Liner Sampler," *New York Times*, December 2, 2021. Dole's acerbic wit was legendary. In 1980, after Ronald Reagan won the presidency and Republicans captured a Senate majority, Dole said, "If we had known we were going to win control of the Senate, we'd have run better candidates." Dole's relationship with Newt Gingrich was strained. When Newt became Speaker in 1995, Dole told the *New York Times*, "You hear Gingrich's staff has five file cabinets, four big ones and one little tiny one. No. 1 is 'Newt's Ideas.' No. 2 'Newt's Ideas.' No. 3, No. 4 'Newt's Ideas.' The little one is 'Newt's Good Ideas.'" Ibid.

42. Thomas B. Edsall, "Right in the Middle of the Revolution," *Washington Post*, September 4, 1995; Gigot, "Dole Bows to GOP's New Powers," *Wall Street Journal*, April 14, 1995.

43. Massimo Calabresi, "The Revival of Trent Lott," *Time*, November 12, 2006.

44. John Yang, "House Reprimands, Penalizes Speaker," *Washington Post*, January 22, 1997; John Yang, "Gingrich Reelected Speaker Despite Defections," *Washington Post*, January 8, 1997; Mel Steely, *The Gentleman from Georgia: The Biography of Newt Gingrich* (Macon, GA: Mercer University Press, 2000), 345–49; James Carney, "Attempted Republican Coup," *Time*, July 28, 1997.

45. Robert Harris and Eric Pianin, "Bipartisanship Reigns at Budget Signing," *Washington Post*, August 6, 1997.

46. Bill Clinton, *My Life* (New York: Alfred A. Knopf, 2004), 743–45.

47. Jerry Gray, "Gingrich Suggests Removing Capital Gains and Estate Tax," *New York Times*, April 10, 1997.

48. Adam Clymer, "An Enthusiast Again, Gingrich Proposes a Tax Cut a Year," *New York Times*, July 12, 1997.

49. Clinton, *My Life*, 754; Matt Egan, Annalyn Kurtz, Tal Yellin, and Will Houp, "From Reagan to Trump: Here's How Stocks Performed under Each President," CNN Business, January 19, 2021, https://www.cnn.com/interactive/2019/business/stock-market-by-president/index.html.

50. For an insider's detailed description of the negotiations between the White House and Congress, see John H. Hilley, *The Challenge of Legislation: Bipartisanship in a Partisan World* (Washington, DC: Brookings Institution Press, 2008).

51. John E. Yang, "For Embattled Gingrich, Something to Celebrate," *Washington Post*, August 1, 1997. See also Gillon, *The Pact*.

52. Justin Elliott, Patricia Callahan, and James Bandler, "Lord of the Roths: How Tech Mogul Peter Thiel Turned a Retirement Account into a $5 Billion Tax-Free Piggy Bank," *ProPublica*, June 24, 2021, https://www.propublica.org/article/lord-of-the-roths-how-tech-mogul-peter-thiel-turned-a-retirement-account-for-the-middle-class-into-a-5-billion-dollar-tax-free-piggy-bank.

53. Congressional Budget Office, *An Economic Analysis of the Taxpayer Relief Act of 1997* (Washington, DC: Congressional Budget Office, 2000).

54. Elliott, Callahan, and Bandler, "Lord of the Roths."

55. Clinton, *My Life*, 754.

56. Comprehending the tax savings provided by these tax benefits for higher education, their various eligibility requirements, how they interacted, and their record-keeping and reporting requirements was mind-boggling. Each of the provisions has its own eligibility criteria and definition of qualified expenses. The various provisions did not provide consistent treatment of room and board, books, supplies and equipment, sports expenses, non-academic fees, or the class of relatives whose expenses may be taken into account. A student convicted of a felony for possession or distribution of a controlled substance was ineligible for one of the education credits but faced no bar to another. Graetz, *100 Million Unnecessary Returns*, 13.

57. Christopher Howard, *The Hidden Welfare State: Tax Expenditures and Social Policy in the United States* (Princeton: Princeton University Press, 1999). Tax expenditures are defined as "revenue losses attributable to provisions of the federal tax laws which allow a special exclusion, exemption, or deduction from gross income or which provide a special credit, a preferential rate of tax or a deferral of tax liability." They include "any reductions in income tax liabilities that result from special tax provisions or regulations that provide tax benefits to particular taxpayers." U.S. Congress, Joint Committee on Taxation, *Estimates of Federal Tax Expenditures for Fiscal Years 2020–2024*, 116th Cong., 2nd sess., November 5, 2020, JCX-23-20; Eric M. Patashnik, *Reforms at Risk: What Happens after Major Policy Changes Are Enacted* (Princeton: Princeton University Press, 2004), 37. There has been considerable debate in the tax literature over the concept and lists of tax expenditures.

58. Patashnik, *Reforms at Risk*, 46.

59. Eric Pianin and Clay Chandler, "Clinton, GOP Both Claim Budget Victories," *Washington Post*, August 5, 1997.

60. Harris and Pianin, "Bipartisanship Reigns at Budget Signing."

61. Nancy Gibbs and Michael Duffy, "Fall of the House of Newt," *Time*, November 16, 1998.

62. Ronald Brownstein, *The Second Civil War: How Extreme Partisanship Has Paralyzed Washington and Polarized America* (New York: Penguin Press, 2007), 172.

63. Thomas E. Mann and Norman J. Ornstein, *It's Worse than It Looks* (New York: Basic Books, 2012).

64. Robert B. Reich, "Movement Politics," *Boston Review* 29, no. 3–4 (Summer 2004): 18.

65. Gary Wills, "The Tragedy of Bill Clinton," *New York Review of Books* 51, no. 13 (August 15, 2004): 64.

Chapter 12

1. Bush v. Gore, 531 U.S. 98 (2000). In a 2013 interview retired Justice Sandra Day O'Connor, whom Ronald Reagan appointed as the first woman Supreme Court Justice and had cast a decisive vote for Bush, after previously defending the decision, expressed second thoughts: "Maybe the Court should have said 'We're not going to take it, goodbye.'" Jeffrey Toobin, "Justice O'Connor Regrets," *New Yorker*, May 6, 2013. "In all likelihood, George W. Bush still would have won Florida and the presidency last year if either of two limited recounts—one requested by Al Gore, the other ordered by the Florida Supreme Court—had been completed, according to a study commissioned by the *Washington Post* and other news organizations. But if Gore had found a way to trigger a statewide recount of all disputed ballots, or if the courts had required it, the result likely would have been different. An examination of uncounted ballots throughout Florida found enough where voter intent was clear to give Gore the narrowest of edges." Dan Keating and Dan Balz, "Florida Recounts Would Have Favored Bush," *Washington Post*, November 12, 2001. Even without Florida, if Gore had carried his home state of Tennessee or Bill Clinton's Arkansas, Gore, not Bush, would have been the forty-third president of the United States.

2. Charles Babington, "Bush Plans Response to Gore's Tax Jabs," *Washington Post*, October 9, 2000.

3. "Greenspan Testimony at Senate Budget Committee Hearing on the Economy," *Tax Notes*, January 25, 2001. Before the hearing Paul O'Neill, Greenspan's friend about to become Bush's treasury secretary, urged Greenspan to recommend a "trigger" mechanism to halt tax cuts if the predicted surpluses did not occur. Admitting "it's certainly not money in the bank," Greenspan agreed, but the trigger suggestion and his caveats were ignored by congressional Republicans, the press, and the public. Sebastian Mallaby, *The Man Who Knew: The Life and Times of Alan Greenspan* (New York: Penguin, 2016), 573–80. In January 2001 government forecasters did not foresee the massive drop in capital gains revenue from the stock market decline that began in March 2000, how sluggish the U.S. economy would become, or the massive increased spending on homeland security and the military after the September 11 attacks.

4. Patti Mohr, "Greenspan Endorses Tax Cuts, Social Security Privatization," *Tax Notes*, January 26, 2001.

5. "Text of President Bush's 2001 Address to Congress," *Washington Post*, February 27, 2001.

6. E.g., Congressional Budget Office, *The Budget and Economic Outlook: Fiscal Years 2005 to 2014* (January 2004), https://www.cbo.gov/sites/default/files/108th-congress-2003-2004/reports/01-26-budgetoutlook-entirereport.pdf.

7. Michael Kinsley, "Greenspan Shrugged," *New York Times*, October 14, 2007. Greenspan also subsequently described the 2001 tax cut "without the triggers" as "irresponsible fiscal policy." See also Ron Suskind, *The Price of Loyalty: George W. Bush, the White House, and the Education of Paul O'Neill* (New York: Simon and Schuster, 2004).

8. Michael J. Graetz and Ian Shapiro, *Death by a Thousand Cuts: The Fight over Taxing Inherited Wealth* (Princeton: Princeton University Press, 2005), 150. The team's leader was Karl Rove, a savvy Republican political strategist close to the Bush family. As his principal congressional liaison, Bush hired Nick Calio, a charming, well-connected Washington lobbyist, who headed congressional affairs under Bush's father. Bush's chief of staff, Andrew Card, also enjoyed important congressional relationships, having been General Motors' chief lobbyist. Bush's assistant treasury secretary for tax policy was Mark Weinberger, a talented former staffer for Kansas Republican senator Jack Danforth and a successful tax lobbyist for large multinational corporations. As Nick Calio remarked, "The Bush team was really unified on getting this bill through and worked well together. This was in sharp contrast to the first Bush administration, which suffered much well-publicized in-fighting."

9. Much of this section is adapted from Graetz and Shapiro, *Death by a Thousand Cuts* and Michael J. Graetz, "Death Tax Politics," *Boston College Law Review* 57, no. 3 (2016): 801–14.

10. Michael J. Graetz, "To Praise the Estate Tax, Not to Bury It," *Yale Law Journal* 93, no. 2 (December 1983): 259, 272.

11. See Graetz and Shapiro, *Death by a Thousand Cuts*, 76–82.

12. Ibid., 76–77.

13. There were additional rich families who contributed to the effort to repeal the estate tax. See Michael Crowley, "The 'Death Tax' Scam," *Rolling Stone*, June 11, 2009.

14. Graetz and Shapiro, *Death by a Thousand Cuts*, 62–66.

15. Ibid., 140–47.

16. Ibid., 13–14.

17. Ibid., 40; David Segal, "Lawmakers Strive to Reduce Estate Tax," *Washington Post*, July 28, 1997; Bob Thompson, "Sharing the Wealth," *Washington Post Magazine*, April 13, 2003.

18. Graetz and Shapiro, *Death by a Thousand Cuts*, 119.

19. Ibid. The previous discussion in this section is largely derived from ibid., 13, 69–70, 107–17, 122, 127, 231–32.

20. Ibid., 231–32.

21. Ibid., 159.

22. Ibid., 162–65.

23. Ibid., 166.

24. Hastert became Speaker in 1999 after Robert Livingston, the Republicans' first choice to replace Newt Gingrich, resigned from Congress after his marital infidelities became public. When Hastert became Speaker, many Washington insiders regarded his main qualifications as being neither Newt nor a philanderer. Hastert turned out to be worse. He resigned in 2007 and subsequently was convicted of a felony and imprisoned for structuring bank withdrawals to evade bank-reporting requirements. The withdrawals were used for payoffs to boys whom Hastert had sexually molested while coaching high school wrestling. Liam Stack, "Dennis Hastert, Ex-House Speaker Who Admitted Sex Abuse, Leaves Prison," *New York Times*, July 18, 2017. The Associated Press described Hastert as a "hide-bound, rock-ribbed, Illinois conservative" who "opposes abortion and advocates lower taxes, a balanced-budget amendment to the Constitution and the death penalty." Jennifer Loven, "Hastert a Conservative at Heart," *Associated Press News*, December 22, 1998. Writing in the *New Yorker*, Jonathan Franzen described Hastert as "an irrelevant, indispensable, modern, old-fashioned, moderate, conservative, nobody somebody." Jonathan Franzen, "The Listener: How Did a Former Wrestling Coach End Up Running the House of Representatives," *New Yorker*, October 6, 2003.

25. Graetz and Shapiro, *Death by a Thousand Cuts*, 147. A wild card in Hastert's strategy was the volatility of the new chairman of the House Ways and Means Committee, Californian Bill Thomas. Thomas was smart and hardworking but irascible. The *Los Angeles Times* wrote that Thomas was "known for his mastery of complex matters . . . but also for his occasional fits of temper." Richard Simon, "Californian Thomas Gets House Ways and Means Chairmanship," *Los Angeles Times*, January 5, 2001. On March 21, when the Ways and Means Committee met to consider estate tax repeal, Thomas told the committee, "The death tax should be repealed for one reason, which is simply that Americans should not be taxed when they die." Graetz and Shapiro, *Death by a Thousand Cuts*, 149.

26. Graetz and Shapiro, *Death by a Thousand Cuts*, 181–84. On March 1 the Ways and Means Committee approved an income tax rate cut costing $958 billion over ten years, nearly $150 million more than the president's plan. The bottom rate was higher than Bush had requested, 12 instead of 10 percent, and the top rate was lower, 33 rather than 35 percent. A week later the House passed the committee bill by a vote of 230 to 198 with 10 Democrats in favor. Three weeks later, the House voted overwhelmingly, 282 to 144, for the second installment of the Bush tax cuts. Sixty-four Democrats, nearly one-third of the total, voted for lowering taxes for families with children. This time the House exceeded the president's request by nearly $95 billion. Ways and Means chairman Bill Thomas told the press, "the smorgasbord has more food out there than you're going to eat." Lori Nitschke, "Tax Cut's Viability Lies in Deep Dealmaking," *CQ Weekly*, March 17, 2001. The House had passed $1.37 trillion in tax cuts, leaving $250 billion for everything else. President Bush had urged more than $100 billion in expanded charitable and education deductions, and increased tax credits for research and development. House Republicans had tax-cutting ideas of their own. A proposal to increase income tax benefits for retirement savings (costing more than $50 billion) passed the House by an overwhelming vote of 407 to 24. Several expiring provisions needed to be extended, and the rate cuts made it imperative to provide relief from minimum tax provisions or millions of middle-class families would face tax increases. Estate tax repeal was being squeezed despite its widespread support.

27. Graetz and Shapiro, *Death by a Thousand Cuts*, 184–85. One Republican, Amo Houghton of New York, a scion of the Corning Glass family and perhaps the wealthiest member of Congress, voted against repeal. The committee did not schedule repeal to take effect until 2011 and to offset the costs, the committee voted to eliminate the forgiveness of capital gains taxes for

heirs when they sell inherited assets worth more than $1.3 million. With this offset, a slow phased-in decline of estate tax rates, and long-delayed repeal, the cost was $193 billion over ten years—less than a quarter the costs of immediate repeal.

28. Senate elections in 2000 produced a Senate with 50 Republicans and 50 Democrats. On May 24, 2001, Vermont's senator Jim Jeffords, a lifelong Republican, became an independent and decided to caucus with the Democrats, but not until after the tax-cut legislation was sent to the president for his signature. Ibid., 180.

29. The Democrats' plan cost $900 billion, including about $150 billion of interest costs on the federal debt in their proposal. The $750 billion in tax cuts was nearly half of President Bush's $1.6 trillion proposal. President Bush's plan would have exceeded $2 trillion with the extra interest expense. Ibid., 178–79.

30. Ibid., 186. In May the House and Senate formally adopted budget resolutions calling for $100 billion of retroactive 2001 tax cuts to stimulate the economy, plus $1.25 trillion over the next decade, a total of $1.35 trillion, more than 80 percent of what Bush asked for and exactly the amount John Breaux wanted. The House vote was 221 to 201 with 6 Democrats joining the Republicans; the Senate tally was 53 to 47, with Republicans Chafee and Jeffords voting "no" and 5 Democrats in favor.

31. Shailagh Murray and Greg Hitt, "Senators Stall over Distributing Tax-Cut Spoils," *Wall Street Journal*, May 11, 2001.

32. Jake Thompson, "Grassley's Influence Set to Soar," *Omaha World Herald*, January 13, 2001.

33. This avoided a "Byrd rule" challenge on the Senate floor. The Byrd rule allows any senator to object to any provision that "would decrease revenues during a fiscal year after the fiscal years covered by the reconciliation bill." Sixty votes—which were not available—are necessary to override a Byrd-rule objection.

34. Graetz and Shapiro, *Death by a Thousand Cuts*, 200. After dinner the president's aides, Dick Armey, Phil Gramm, and Don Nickles, joined the group. The next morning President Bush—fearful that delay might unravel the legislation—called Grassley and Thomas urging them to compromise quickly. At about eight that evening, the four key congressional negotiators, Max Baucus, John Breaux, Chuck Grassley, and Bill Thomas, announced an agreement. An hour later the conference committee rubber-stamped it.

35. Vermont's Jim Jeffords voted in favor, fulfilling the promise he made to George W. Bush before leaving the Republican Party to join the Senate Democrats.

36. Graetz and Shapiro, *Death by a Thousand Cuts*, 203.

37. "Victory at a Price," *The Economist*, May 26, 2001.

38. Mallaby, *The Man Who Knew*, 607.

39. Ibid.

40. Suskind, *The Price of Loyalty*, 291–92. President Bush appointed John W. Snow, former CEO of CSX corporation, to succeed O'Neill. Snow became a vocal advocate of the Bush administration's 2003 tax cuts. He was forced to resign in 2006 when it became known that he had failed to pay income taxes on $24 million of loan forgiveness from CSX corporation.

41. U.S. Congress, Joint Committee on Taxation, *Estimated Budget Effects of the Revenue Provisions Contained in the President's Fiscal Year 2004 Budget Proposals*, 107th Cong., 1st sess., March 4, 2003, JCX-15-03.

42. U.S. Congress, Joint Committee on Taxation, *Estimated Budget Effects of the Conference Agreement for H.R. 2, The Jobs and Growth Tax Relief Reconciliation Act of 2003*, 107th Cong., 1st sess., May 22, 2003, JCX-55-03.

43. U.S. Congress, Joint Committee on Taxation, *General Explanation of Tax Legislation Enacted in the 108th Congress*, 108th Cong., 1st sess., May 31, 2005, JCS-5-05.

44. Thomas R. Oliver, Philip R. Lee, and Helene L. Lipton, "A Political History of Medicare and Prescription Drug Coverage," *Milbank Quarterly* 82, no. 2 (June 2004): 283–354.

45. William G. Gale and Peter R. Orszag, "Economic Effects of Making the 2001 and 2003 Tax Cuts Permanent," *International Tax and Public Finance* 12, no. 2 (March 2005): 192–232; William G. Gale, *Fiscal Therapy: Curing America's Debt Addiction and Investing in the Future* (New York: Oxford University Press, 2019), 46.

46. James T. Patterson, "Transformative Economic Policies: Tax Cutting, Stimuli and Bailouts," in *The Presidency of George W. Bush: A First Historical Assessment*, ed. Julian E. Zelizer (Princeton: Princeton University Press, 2010), 122.

47. Emily Horton, "The Legacy of the 2001 and 2003 'Bush' Tax Cuts," *Center on Budget and Policy Priorities*, October 23, 2017, https://www.cbpp.org/sites/default/files/atoms/files/3-31-17tax.pdf.

48. Gale and Orzsag, "Economic Effects," 225.

49. Patterson, "Transformative Economic Policies," 114.

50. Adam Tooze, *Crashed: How a Decade of Financial Crises Changed the World* (New York: Viking, 2018), 37.

51. President George W. Bush's State of the Union Address, February 2, 2005, https://georgewbush-whitehouse.archives.gov/stateoftheunion/2005/. Bush had endorsed this idea in his 1970 congressional race and mentioned it repeatedly during his 2004 reelection campaign. He told the press, "I earned capital in this campaign, political capital, and now I intend to spend it." William A. Galston, "Why the 2005 Social Security Campaign Failed, and What It Means for the Future," *Brookings Report*, September 2007, https://wagner.nyu.edu/files/performance/bush2005.pdf. The White House coupled its plan for private accounts with complex proposals cutting Social Security benefits. Bush's Social Security proposals quietly died.

52. Jon Meacham, *Destiny and Power: The American Odyssey of George Herbert Walker Bush* (New York: Random House, 2015), 560.

Chapter 13

1. As housing prices rose in the early and mid-2000s, financial institutions lent huge amounts for purchasing and refinancing homes, with increasing amounts for unconventional, risky "subprime" mortgages, especially in the housing-bubble states of Arizona, California, and Florida. Financial institutions sliced, diced, and repackaged these mortgages into mortgage-backed securities that obtained high credit ratings camouflaging their riskiness. Investment banks marketed profitable "collateralized debt obligations," involving more repackaging, further concealing the risks of the underlying mortgages. When housing prices collapsed, declines in values of these and related securities threatened the stability of financial institutions in America and around the world. See, e.g., Michael Lewis, *The Big Short: Inside the Doomsday Machine* (New York: W. W. Norton, 2010); Adam Tooze, *Crashed: How a Decade of Financial Crises Changed the World* (New York: Viking, 2018).

2. Barack Obama, *A Promised Land* (New York: Crown, 2020), 235.

3. Tooze, *Crashed*, 156–57; Michael J. Graetz and Ian Shapiro, *The Wolf at the Door: The Menace of Economic Insecurity and How to Fight It* (Cambridge, MA: Harvard University Press, 2020), chap. 3.

4. David Bernstein, "The Speech," *Chicago Magazine*, May 29, 2007.

5. See Stephen Skowronek, "Barack Obama and the Promise of Transformative Leadership," in *Obama's Fractured Legacy*, ed. Francois Vergniolle de Chantal (Edinburgh: Edinburgh University Press, 2020).

6. George W. Bush, "President Bush Signs H.R. 5140, the Economic Stimulus Act of 2008," press release, February 13, 2008, https://georgewbush-whitehouse.archives.gov/news/releases/2008/02/20080213-3.html.

7. Michael Cooper, "McCain Adviser Refers to 'Nation of Whiners,'" *New York Times*, July 11, 2008.

8. Carl Hulse and David M. Herszenhorn, "Defiant House Rejects Huge Bailout; Next Step Is Uncertain," *New York Times*, September 29, 2008; Alexandra Twin, "Stocks Crushed," *CNN Money*, September 29, 2008.

9. Joe Nocera, "First Bailout Formula Had It Right," *New York Times*, January 23, 2009; Wayne Duggan, "Financial Crisis Bailouts: What Did They Actually Cost Taxpayers?" *Yahoo Finance*, https://finance.yahoo.com/new/financial-crisis-bailouts-did-actually-184624029.html. Democrats voted 172 to 63 for the bill; Republicans opposed it 108 to 9. Ultimately, more than $400 billion was spent. By 2015 the government had recovered this money.

10. Michael Grunwald, *The New New Deal: The Hidden Story of Change in the Obama Era* (New York: Simon and Schuster, 2012), 113–14.

11. Peggy Noonan, "Turbulence Ahead," *Wall Street Journal*, November 28, 2008.

12. Obama, *A Promised Land*, 241–42.

13. Grunwald, *The New New Deal*, 92.

14. Eric Cantor, Paul Ryan, and Kevin McCarthy, *Young Guns: A New Generation of Conservative Leaders* (New York: Simon and Schuster, 2010), 21.

15. Grunwald, *The New New Deal*, 142–44.

16. Ibid., 248.

17. Joshua Green, "Strict Obstructionist," *The Atlantic*, January/February 2011.

18. Obama, *A Promised Land*, 244; Grunwald, *The New New Deal*, 162.

19. Grunwald, *The New New Deal*, 162.

20. Obama, *A Promised Land*, 248.

21. Grunwald, *The New New Deal*, 202.

22. Ibid.

23. Andy Barr, "Pence: GOP Won Stimulus Argument," *Politico*, February 26, 2009, https://www.politico.com/story/2009/02/pence-gop-won-stimulus-argument-019375.

24. Obama, *A Promised Land*, 258.

25. Ibid., 261–64.

26. Grunwald, *The New New Deal*, 207.

27. After enactment of the Recovery Act, House Democrats passed a bill taxing bonuses of financial institution executives at a 90 percent rate after it became known that AIG, an insurance company that took $170 billion in TARP funds, paid its executives bonuses totaling $165 million. The House legislation died in the Senate. This was the last real effort to hold any financial executives responsible for the economic crisis. Greg Hitt, "Drive to Tax AIG Bonuses Slows," *Wall Street Journal*, March 25, 2009.

28. David Brooks, "The Gang System," *New York Times*, February 5, 2009.

29. Heidi Przybyla and John McCormick, "Poll Shows Voters Don't Know GDP Grew with Tax Cuts," Bloomberg, October 29, 2009, https://www.bloomberg.com/news/articles/2010-10-29/poll-shows-americans-don-t-know-economy-expanded-with-tax-cuts#xj4y7vzkg.

30. Obama, *A Promised Land*, 266. The National Bureau of Economic Research later concluded the Great Recession ended in June 2009, but the nation's economy continued to struggle.

31. Grunwald, *The New New Deal*, 300.

32. "CNBC's Rick Santelli's Chicago Tea Party," Heritage Foundation, February 19, 2009, YouTube video, 4:36, https://www.youtube.com/watch?v=zp-Jw-5Kx8k&ab_channel=TheHeritageFoundation.

33. Jamilah King, "Rick Santelli: Tea Party Rant: Best Five Minutes of My Life," *Colorlines*, September 20, 2010, https://www.colorlines.com/articles/rick-santelli-tea-party-rant-best-five-minutes-my-life.

34. Obama, *A Promised Land*, 273.

35. Theda Skocpol and Vanessa Williamson, *The Tea Party and the Remaking of Republican Conservatism* (New York: Oxford University Press, 2012), 7.

36. Obama, *A Promised Land*, 274, 276–77.

37. See Nate Silver, "Tea Party Nonpartisan Attendance Estimates: Now 300,000+," 538, April 16, 2009, https://fivethirtyeight.com/features/tea-party-nonpartisan-attendance. Grover Norquest's estimate was a bit lower.

38. Christopher S. Parker and Matt A. Barreto, *Change They Can't Believe In: The Tea Party and Reactionary Politics in America* (Princeton: Princeton University Press, 2013), 1.

39. Skocpol and Williamson, *The Tea Party and the Remaking of Republicanism Conservatism*, 22.

40. Ibid., 21–82.

41. Ibid., 64–69, 77–78.

42. Parker and Barreto, *Change They Can't Believe In*, 51.

43. Ibid., 15.

44. Ibid., 191.

45. Ibid., 244 (emphasis added). Skocpol and Williamson provide anecdotes illustrating that some members of the Tea Party were not racist but, like Parker and Barreto, found anti-immigrant and anti-Muslim attitudes to be prevalent. Skocpol and Williamson, *The Tea Party and the Remaking of Republican Conservatism*, 68–72, 200–201.

46. Robb Willer, Matthew Feinberg, and Rachel Wetts, "Threats to Racial Status Promote Tea Party Support among White Americans" (SSRN working paper, May 4, 2016), https://papers.ssrn.com/sol3/papers.cfm?abstract_id=2770186.

47. Parker and Barreto, *Change They Can't Believe In*, 209–12.

48. Jane Mayer, *Dark Money: The Hidden History of the Billionaires behind the Rise of the Radical Right* (New York: Doubleday, 2016), 183–84.

49. Skocpol and Williamson, *The Tea Party and the Remaking of Republican Conservatism*, 121–53.

50. Ibid., 121.

51. Ibid., 131.

52. Ibid., 136–37.

53. Charles Koch claims the New Deal "prolonged and deepened" the Great Depression, which he insists was caused by government interference in the economy. In 2009 the billionaire Koch brothers were supporting thirty-four right-wing policy and political organizations. Mayer, *Dark Money*, 171.

54. Ibid., 180.

55. Skocpol and Williamson, *The Tea Party and the Remaking of Republican Conservatism*, 86.

56. Mayer, *Dark Money*, 181.

57. Ibid., 182.

58. Ibid., 183.

59. Ibid., 182. For Skocpol and Williamson's take, which emphasizes local organizations but also examines the roles played by the media and the billionaires' organizations, see Skocpol and Williamson, *The Tea Party and the Remaking of Republican Conservatism*, 83–120 (billionaires) and 121–52 (media).

60. Skocpol and Williamson, *The Tea Party and the Remaking of Republican Conservatism*, 23–24.

61. "Democratic Presidential Candidates Debate in Philadelphia," The American Presidency Project, April 16, 2008, https://www.presidency.ucsb.edu/documents/democratic-presidential-candidates-debate-philadelphia.

62. As an example, during his campaign Barack Obama described climate change as "melting our glaciers and setting off dangerous weather patterns as we speak." He claimed he wanted to end "the age of oil." "It will require nothing less than a complete transformation of our

economy," he said. Michael J. Graetz, *The End of Energy: The Unmaking of America's Environment, Security, and Independence* (Cambridge, MA: MIT Press, 2011), 160–61. But Obama's promise took a carbon tax, perhaps the most effective tool for addressing climate change, off the table. President Obama also eliminated any potential gas tax increases.

63. Obama, *A Promised Land*, 399.

64. Mayer, *Dark Money*, 194.

65. Ibid., 246.

66. Steve Benen, "On Groundhog Day, Republicans Vote to Repeal Obamacare," MSNBC, February 2, 2016, https://www.msnbc.com/rachel-maddow-show/groundhog-da-repubicans -vote-repeal-obamacare-msna787106.

67. Mayer, *Dark Money*, 247; Eliana Johnson, "Inside the Koch-Funded Ads Giving Dems Fits," *National Review*, March 31, 2014, https://www.nationalreview.com/2014/03/inside-koch -funded-ads-giving-dems-fits-eliana-johnson/.

68. Johnson, "Inside the Koch-Funded Ads Giving Dems Fits"; Mayer, *Dark Money*, 248–50.

69. Mayer, *Dark Money*, 410 (note to page 254).

70. See, e.g., Michael J. Graetz, "Should Carried Interest Be Taxed as Ordinary Income, Not as Capital Gains?" *Wall Street Journal*, May 14, 2012.

71. Mark DeCambre, "Schwarzman Likens Bam to Hitler over Taxes," *New York Post*, August 17, 2010; see also Mayer, *Dark Money*, 253–56.

72. Mayer, *Dark Money*, 257–58.

73. Teddy Davis, "Tea Party Activists Unveil 'Contract from America,'" ABC News, April 14, 2010, https://abcnews.go.com/Politics/tea-party-activists-unveil-contract-america/story?id =10376437&page=2. The document claimed to be based on the principles of individual liberty, limited government, and economic freedom. It contained ten items selected by 450,000 people in seven weeks of online voting.

74. "A Pledge to America," *Scribd*, https://www.scribd.com/document/37958976/GOP -Pledge-to-America#; Brian Montopoli and Jill Jackson, "Pledge to America Unveiled by Republicans," CBS News, September 23, 2010, https://www.cbsnews.com/news/pledge-to -america-unveiled-by-republicans-full-text.

75. Lucy Madison, "Obama's 2010 'Shellacking' Is Like Bush's 2006 'Thumping,'" CBS News, November 2, 2010, https://www.cbsnews.com/news/obamas-2010-shellacking-is-like-bushs -2006-thumping.

76. Jackie Calmes, "Demystifying the Fiscal Impasse That Is Vexing Washington," *New York Times*, November 15, 2012.

77. For single individuals, $200,000 a year. Obama, *A Promised Land*, 604.

78. Ibid., 605.

79. Ibid., 603.

80. Ibid., 605–19.

81. Ibid., 606.

82. Michael J. Graetz, "'Death Tax' Politics," *Boston College Law Review* 57, no. 3 (2016): 801–14.

83. Stephen Dinan, "Capitol Hill Least Productive Congress Ever: 112th Fought 'About Everything,'" *Washington Times*, January 9, 2013.

84. William G. Gale, *Fiscal Therapy: Curing America's Debt Addiction and Investing in the Future* (New York: Oxford University Press, 2019), 47; Leonard E. Burman, Jeffrey Rohaly, Joseph Rosenberg, and Katherine C. Lim, "Catastrophic Budget Failure," *National Tax Journal* 63, no. 3 (September 2010): 561–84.

85. Vanessa Williamson, "The Tea Party and the Shift to Austerity by Gridlock" (paper presented at the American Political Science Association Annual Conference, Chicago, August

29–September 1, 2013), https://scholar.harvard.edu/files/williamson/files/investment_or_austerity_in_the_united_states_williamson_apsa.pdf.

86. Calmes, "Demystifying the Fiscal Impasse That Is Vexing Washington."

87. Gale, *Fiscal Therapy*, 48.

88. Limitations on itemized deductions and personal exemptions, originally enacted in 1990 and repealed in 2001, were restored for married couples with incomes of $300,000 or more ($250,000 for singles). A new tax-saving opportunity was created for high-income individuals, allowing retirement savings plans to be converted into Roth IRAs.

89. For further details, see U.S. Library of Congress, Congressional Research Service, *An Overview of the Tax Provisions in the American Taxpayer Relief Act of 2012*, by Margot L. Crandall-Hollick R42894 (2013). The Senate passed the bill on New Year's Day by an overwhelming vote of 89 to 8. Only five Republicans and three Democrats voted against it. House Republicans, however, were disappointed that the legislation extended unemployment benefits and eliminated previously enacted cuts in payments to doctors and other health-care providers serving Medicare patients. Nearly two-thirds of House Republicans, 151 of 236, opposed the bill, even though they did not want the scheduled tax increases to go into effect. With 85 Republicans and all but 3 Democrats in support, the bill passed the House by a vote of 257 to 167. Jennifer Steinhauer, "Divided House Passes Tax Deal in End to Fiscal Standoff," *New York Times*, January 1, 2013.

90. Jonathan Weisman, "Lines of Resistance on Fiscal Deal," *New York Times*, January 1, 2013.

91. Janet Hook, Corey Boles, and Siobhan Hughes, "Congress Passes Cliff Deal," *Wall Street Journal*, January 7, 2013.

92. Paul Krugman, "That Bad Ceiling Feeling," *New York Times*, January 2, 2013.

93. Lori Montgomery and Rosalind Helderman, "Congress Approves 'Fiscal Cliff' Measure," *Washington Post*, January 1, 2013.

94. Josh Feldman, "Grover Norquist: Voting for Fiscal Cliff Compromise 'Technically' Not a Violation of the Pledge," *Mediaite*, https://www.mediaite.com/tv/grover-norquist-voting-for-senate-fiscal-cliff-compromise-technically-not-a-violation-of-the-tax-pledge.

95. Erin Delmore, "Norquist: 'No Republican Voted for a Tax Increase' in Fiscal Cliff Deal," MSNBC, January 2, 2013, https://www.msnbc.com/msnbc/amp/msna17382.

96. Parker and Barreto, *Change They Can't Believe In*, 3.

Chapter 14

1. E.g., Adam Serwer, "Birtherism of a Nation," *The Atlantic*, May 13, 2020.

2. See, e.g., "Trump Promised Over and Over to 'Save' Medicare, Medicaid, and Social Security. Will He?" *Washington Post*, February 12, 2018, video, 2:33, https://www.washingtonpost.com/videopolitics/trump-promised-over-and-over-to-save-medicare-and-social-security-will-he/2016/12/01/9f209386-b7e5-11e6-939c-91749443c5e5_video.html.

3. John Sides, Michael Tesler, and Lynn Vavreck, *Identity Crisis: The 2016 Presidential Campaign and the Battle for the Meaning of America* (Princeton: Princeton University Press, 2019), 70.

4. Katherine J. Cramer, *The Politics of Resentment: Rural Consciousness in Wisconsin and the Rise of Scott Walker* (Chicago: University of Chicago Press, 2016).

5. Arlie Russell Hochschild, *Strangers in Their Own Land: Anger and Mourning on the American Right* (New York: New Press, 2016); Sides, Tesler, and Vavreck, *Identity Crisis*. Julian Zelizer observed that Trump's "version of conservative populism played into the nativism, racism, sexism, insular xenophobic nationalism, and White rage that all had deep histories in this country." Julian E. Zelizer, ed., *The Presidency of Donald J. Trump: A First Historical Assessment* (Princeton: Princeton University Press, 2022), 22.

6. Howard Schneider, "Much of 'Trump Country' Was in Recession during 2016 Campaign," *Reuters*, December 18, 2019.

7. Michael Scherer, Josh Dawsey, Caroline Kitchener, and Rachel Roubein, "A 49-Year Crusade: Inside the Movement to Overturn Roe v. Wade," *Washington Post*, May 7, 2022.

8. Paul Ryan, *The Way Forward: Renewing the American Idea* (New York: Twelve, 2014), 13–15.

9. Ibid., 40–46.

10. Ibid., 54–60.

11. Nate Silver, "A Risky Rationale behind Romney's Choice of Ryan," *New York Times*, August 11, 2012.

12. Craig Gilberg, "Ryan's Conservatism Influenced by Free Market Economists," *Milwaukee Journal Sentinel*, August 11, 2012, https://archive.jsonline.com/news/statepolitics/ryans -conservatism-influenced-by-free-market-economists-1k6f813-165868526.html.

13. Nolan D. McCaskill and Kyle Cheney, "Paul Ryan Says He's Not Ready to Support Trump," *Politico*, May 5, 2016. In May 2016 Ryan wondered aloud whether Trump shared Republican values, including "adherence to the Constitution." The next month in a column for the *Janesville Gazette*, Ryan endorsed Trump, extolling the opportunity a Republican president would offer "to move ahead on the ideas that I—and my House colleagues—have invested so much in through the years." Dan Shafer, "Paul Ryan Endorses Donald Trump," *Milwaukee Magazine*, June 2, 2016, https://www.milwaukeemag.com/paul-ryan-endorses-donald-trump/.

14. Jennifer Steinhauer, Jonathan Martin, and David M. Herszenhorn, "Paul Ryan Calls Donald Trump's Attack on Judge 'Racist,' but Still Backs Him," *New York Tines*, June 7, 2016.

15. David A. Farenthold, "Trump Recorded Having Extremely Lewd Conversation about Women in 2005," *Washington Post*, October 8, 2015.

16. Mike DeBonis and Abby Phillip, "Ryan Cancels Plans to Campaign with Trump; GOPers Rush to Distance Themselves," *Washington Post*, October 7, 2016.

17. Dan Mangan, "Trump Brags about Not Paying Taxes: 'That Makes Me Smart,'" CNBC, September 26, 2016, https://www.cnbc.com/2016/09/26/trump-brags-about-not-paying-taxes -that-makes-me-smart.html.

18. "Rush Limbaugh Celebrates Trump's Tax Avoidance: 'He's a Master at This,'" *Media Matters*, September 28, 2020, https://www.mediamatters.org/rush-limbaugh/rush-limbaugh -celebrates-trumps-tax-avoidance-hes-master.

19. Gerry Mullany, "Donald Trump Claims His Wealth Exceeds 'Ten Billion Dollars,'" *New York Times*, July 15, 2015. In September 2021, *Forbes* estimated Donald Trump's net worth to be $2.5 billion. *Forbes* estimated his net worth to be as much as $4.5 billion in 2015. "Donald Trump Falls off the Forbes 400 for First Time in 25 Years," October 5, 2021, https://www.forbes.com /sites/danalexander/2021/10/05/donald-trump-falls-off-the-forbes-400-for-first-time-in-25 -years/?sh=1e82f641f62b.

20. David Barstow, Suzanne Craig, and Russ Buettner, "Trump Engaged in Suspect Tax Schemes as He Reaped Riches from His Father," *New York Times*, October 2, 2018.

21. According to the *Times*, tax experts briefed on its findings concluded that given "the pattern of deception . . . the Trumps appeared to have done more than exploit legal loopholes." Donald Trump's brother and lawyer insisted that there "was no fraud or tax evasion by anyone" (ibid.). The schemes involved numerous transactions between Fred and his children—especially Donald—which saved millions in income, estate, and gift taxes, frequently by manipulating valuations. For instance, in 1987 Fred Trump bought a 7.5 percent interest in Trump Palace, a 55-story Manhattan condominium, for $15.5 million and sold the interest to Donald four years later for $10,000, avoiding gift taxes up to 55 percent and deducting a loss even though the tax law prohibits deductions for losses on sales between family members. In 1995 Fred Trump valued apartments worth $900 million in 2004 as worth $41.4 million on his gift tax returns

according to the *Times*. The *Times* estimated that "hundreds of millions of dollars that otherwise would have gone to the United States Treasury, instead went" to Fred Trump's children. In another scheme, Fred Trump created an entity owned by his children that marked up equipment purchased by Fred's employees for his apartments by 20 to 50 percent. This not only inflated deductions against the apartment's rental income and avoided gift taxes on transfers to the children but also permitted Fred to increase the regulated rents of his low-income tenants. Ibid.

22. The Trump Organization falsely characterized Trump's payments totaling $420,000 to Karen McDougal and Stephanie Clifford ("Stormy Daniels") for their silence about sex with him as deductible legal expenses. Trump organizations treated $26 million in payments to Trump's family, including Ivanka Trump, as deductible "consulting fees." Donald Trump also deducted $70,000 for haircuts and styling; not even military officers are allowed deductions for haircuts. See "The President's Taxes: A Reader's Guide," *New York Times*, October 31, 2020; Russ Buettner, Suzanne Craig, and Mike McIntire, "Long-Concealed Records Show Trump's Chronic Losses and Years of Tax Avoidance," *New York Times*, September 27, 2020. An evaluation of New York State's investigation of Donald Trump and the Trump Organization for tax fraud and other violations of state law is Norman Eisen et al., *New York State's Trump Investigation: An Analysis of the Reported Facts and Applicable Law* (Washington, DC: Brookings Institution, 2021), https://www.brookings.edu/research/new-york-states-trump-investigation-an-analysis-of-the-reported-facts-and-applicable-law. On April 4, 2023, Manhattan District Attorney Alvin L. Bragg announced an indictment of Donald Trump for falsifying New York business records in connection with the payment of hush money to Stormy Daniels and another woman, which included a claim that the participants in the scheme mischaracterized, for tax purposes, the true nature of the payments. Press release, "District Attorney Bragg Announces 34-Count Felony Indictment of Former President Donald J. Trump," April 4, 2023, https://manhattanda.org/district-attorney-bragg-announces-34-count-felony-indictment-of-former-president-donald-j-trump/; Charlie Savage, "Analysis: A Surprise Accusation Bolsters a Risky Case against Trump," *New York Times*, April 4, 2023.

23. Fred T. Goldberg Jr. and Michael J. Graetz, "Trump Probably Avoided His Medicare Taxes, Too," *New York Times*, November 2, 2016; Steven M. Rosenthal, "Did Donald Trump Take Advantage of the Gingrich-Edwards Payroll Tax Loophole?" Tax Policy Center, October 7, 2016.

24. Charlie Savage, "In Blow to Trump, Supreme Court Permits House to Obtain His Tax Returns," *New York Times*, November 22, 2022.

25. Charlie Savage, Emily Cochrane, Stephanie Lai, and Alan Rappeport, "Despite Mandate, IRS Delayed Auditing Trump in Office, House Panel Finds," *New York Times*, December 20, 2022.

26. David Barstow, Mike McIntire, Patricia Cohen, Susanne Craig, and Russ Buettner, "Donald Trump Used Legally Dubious Method to Avoid Paying Taxes," *New York Times*, October 31, 2016. The tax law does not include borrowed funds in income, but if a borrower fails to repay loans, the canceled debt is taxed as income. Internal Revenue Code, section 108. Many middle-class Americans who have experienced home foreclosures or have been unable to repay student debts or credit cards have had to pay income taxes despite their financial straits. When Trump's Atlantic City casinos failed, he convinced his lenders to forgive hundreds of millions of dollars of debt but never reported the debt cancellations as income. Tax lawyers told Trump that this gambit would not succeed if challenged by the IRS, warning there was no statute, regulation, or judicial opinion approving his position. Trump's deductions allowed the losses to be deducted twice: once by the lenders who actually lost money and by Donald Trump who did not.

27. Joint Committee on Taxation, *Report to Richard Neal*, December 15, 2022, 5, https://int.nyt.com/data/documenttools/house-ways-and-means-trump-tax-report/ee70519acd75513e/full.pdf. An internal IRS memo described "animosity" between the IRS counsel and Trump's counsel, noting that Trump's team failed to provide facts necessary to resolve issues.

28. Ibid.; Alan Rappeport, "Trump Audit Shows Depths of IRS Funding Woes," *New York Times*, December 22, 2022.

29. Joint Committee on Taxation, *Report to Richard Neal*, 5–9; Catherine Rampell, "Why Did the IRS Drop the Ball on Trump's Tax Audits?" *Washington Post*, December 22, 2022. Donald Trump claimed large charitable deductions—totaling nearly $120 million—for "conservation easements" on property he owns. Such easements are allowed as charitable deductions, but Trump's deductions were almost certainly overvalued. For example, after years of unsuccessful efforts to develop property called Seven Springs that he purchased (along with a 60-room mansion) in Westchester County for $7.5 million, Trump claimed a $21.1 million deduction for agreeing to preserve 158.6 acres of the property. One independent appraiser described the valuation as "crazy." After first deciding not to question the well-publicized Seven Springs deduction, the agent auditing Trump's return reversed direction and decided that either the entire deduction should be disallowed or it should be reduced to $8.95 million along with possible penalties for a gross overvaluation. Joint Committee on Taxation, *Report to Richard Neal*, 5–6. In 2014, after abandoning plans to develop an 11.5-acre property used as a driving range at his Los Angeles golf club, he took an easement deduction of $25.1 million.

30. Trump's foundation paid Trump's debts to advance his political interests, bought portraits of Trump that he displayed at his private properties, and funded settlements of lawsuits against him. The *Washington Post* articles are collected in David A. Fahrenthold, *Uncovering Trump: The Truth behind Donald Trump's Charitable Giving* (New York: Diversion Books, 2017); Susanne Craig, Russ Buettner, and Mike McIntire, "Trump's Philanthropy: Big Tax Write-offs and Claims That Don't Always Add Up," *New York Times*, October 23 and November 1, 2020; Joshua Partlow, Jonathan O'Connell, and David A. Fahrenthold, "Trump Got a $21 Million Tax Break for Saving the Forest Outside His N.Y. Mansion: Now the Deal Is Under Investigation," *Washington Post*, October 9, 2020.

31. Shane Goldmacher, "Trump Foundation Will Dissolve, Accused of 'Shocking Pattern of Illegality,'" *New York Times*, December 18, 2018.

32. David Cay Johnston, *The Big Cheat: How Donald Trump Fleeced America and Enriched Himself and His Family* (New York: Simon and Schuster, 2021), 33–43; Fahrenthold, *Uncovering Trump*.

33. "Trump Accountants Say Financial Reports Unreliable," BBC News, February 15, 2022.

34. A twenty-five-page indictment on fifteen charges of tax fraud, grand larceny, and falsifying business records detailed how the Trump Organization compensated Mr. Weisselberg for a wide range of personal expenses without paying taxes due to the IRS, New York, and New York City. Daniel Hemel, "The Trump Organization Is in Big Trouble," *The Atlantic*, July 2, 2021.

35. Jonah E. Bromwich, Ben Protess, and William K. Rashbaum, "Inside the Negotiations That Led a Top Trump Executive to Plead Guilty," *New York Times*, August 18, 2022.

36. Ben Protess, Jonah E. Bromwich, and William K. Rashbaum, "Trump's Longtime Finance Chief Sentenced to Five Months in Jail," *New York Times*, January 10, 2023.

37. Alia Shoaib, "Trump Questions Whether Tax Fraud Is 'Even a Crime' after Ex-CFO Jailed," *Business Insider*, January 21, 2023.

38. Lisa Mascaro, "Trump Answers Romney: 'I Try to Pay as Little Tax as Possible,'" *Los Angeles Times*, January 24, 2016.

39. Justice Holmes certainly said the second sentence: "Taxes are what we pay for civilized society." Compania General de Tabacos de Filipinas v. Collector of Internal Revenue, 275 U.S. 87, 100 (1927). The first sentence was included in an anecdote about Holmes in a book by Justice Felix Frankfurter. Felix Frankfurter, *Mr. Justice Holmes and the Supreme Court* (Cambridge, MA: Harvard University Press, 1938), 42–43. Vanessa Williamson suggests that, like Holmes, many Americans view paying taxes as a civic duty and a patriotic act—a "badge of pride." Vanessa Williamson, *Read My Lips: Why Americans Are Proud to Pay Taxes* (Princeton: Princeton

University Press, 2017), 182. This implicitly raises questions about the political successes of the antitax movement. On the other hand, Williamson also describes American attitudes as a "paradox," in which people view taxpaying as virtuous and necessary but also are resentful that others are not paying their "fair share" and believe that the government wastes their tax dollars, attitudes consistent with antitax sentiments.

40. Russell Berman, "Donald Trump's Amazingly Conventional Tax Plan," *The Atlantic*, September 28, 2015; Alan Cole, *Details and Analysis of Donald Trump's Tax Plan* (Washington, DC: Tax Foundation, 2015), https://taxfoundation.org/details-and-analysis-donald-trump-s-tax-plan.

41. Philip Bump, Amber Phillips, and Callum Borchers, "Donald Trump's Economic Speech, Annotated," *Washington Post*, August 8, 2016.

42. Alan Cole, *Details and Analysis of Donald Trump's Tax Plan*, September 2016 (Washington, DC: Tax Foundation, 2016), https://taxfoundation.org/details-analysis-donald-trump-tax-plan-2016.

43. Paul Ryan's *Roadmap for America's Future* (introduced in 2008 and updated in 2010) would have turned Medicare into a limited health-insurance voucher, transferred Medicaid to the states with reduced federal funding and no coverage requirements, and lowered Social Security benefits and limited them to low-income retirees. Ryan, a committed supply-sider, would have lowered the top income tax rate to 25 percent, exempted capital gains, dividends, and interest from income taxation, repealed the estate tax, and substituted a sales tax for the corporate income tax. See, e.g., William Voegeli, "Paul Ryan's Roadmap," *Claremont Review of Books* 10, no. 3 (Summer 2010): 1–15, https://claremontreviewofbooks.com/paul-ryans-roadmap; Paul H. VanDeWater, "The Ryan Budget's Radical Priorities," Center on Budget and Policy Priorities, July 7, 2010, https://www.cbpp.org/research/the-ryan-budgets-radical-priorities#_ftn1. House Republicans approved Ryan's plan in 2009 when it had no prospect of becoming law in a Democratic Congress. Ryan, along with two other Republican representatives, voted in 2010 against a budget reduction plan proposed by the eighteen-member bipartisan National Commission on Fiscal Responsibility and Reform (the "Bowles-Simpson Commission") because it would have increased taxes. Grover Norquist agreed. In 2011 Ryan replaced the *Roadmap* with his *Path to Prosperity*, which would also have reduced income taxes, cut Medicare, Medicaid, and Social Security, and repealed Obamacare. Paul Ryan, *Fiscal Year 2012 Budget Resolution: The Path to Prosperity*, report prepared for the use of the House Committee on Budget, 112th Cong., 1st sess., April 5, 2011, https://www.kff.org/wp-content/uploads/sites/2/2011/05/pathtoprosperityfy2012.pdf; Paul Ryan, "The GOP Path to Prosperity," *Wall Street Journal*, April 5, 2011.

44. Howard Gleckman, "The Ryan Roadmap: Assume a Can Opener II," *Tax Vox*, Tax Policy Center Blog, February 9, 2010, https://www.taxpolicycenter.org/taxvox/ryan-roadmap-assume-can-opener-ii. The Congressional Budget Office (CBO) suggested that Ryan's *Roadmap* would create budget surpluses over two decades and eliminate the federal debt by 2080, but CBO's analysis assumed (as directed by Ryan's staff) that Ryan's tax proposals would generate revenues of 19 percent of GDP each year, rather than the 14 to 16 percent anticipated. Congressional Budget Office, "An Analysis of the Roadmap for America's Future Act of 2010," January 27, 2010, https://www.cbo.gov/sites/default/files/111th-congress-2009-2010/reports/01-27-ryan-roadmap-letter.pdf.

45. Paul Ryan, "The Case for Real Security and a Path to Prosperity" (speech, Washington, DC, April 5, 2011), *American Enterprise Institute*, https://www.aei.org/research-products/speech/the-path-to-prosperity.

46. Carl Hulse, "House Approves Republican Budget Plan to Cut Trillions," *New York Times*, April 5, 2011; Grover Norquist, "Why Republicans Will Support the Ryan Plan—and Win," *The Guardian*, June 3, 2011; Will Dobbs-Allsopp, "Before Ryan Was against Big Promises He Was for Them," *Morning Consult*, April 1, 2016, https://morningconsult.com/2016/04/01/paul-ryan-house-gop-budget-history/.

47. Alex Brill, *Tax Reform: Ryan-Brady Plan Is a Better Way* (Washington, DC: American Enterprise Institute, 2016), https://www.aei.org/wp-content/uploads/2016/10/Tax-reform -Ryan-Brady-plan-is-a-better-way.pdf.

48. Michael Devereux et al., *Taxing Profit in a Global Economy* (New York: Oxford University Press, 2021); Michael J. Graetz, "The Known Unknowns of the Business Tax Reforms Proposed in the House Republican Blueprint," *Columbia Journal of Tax Law* 8, no. 2 (2017): 117–69.

49. Graetz, "The Known Unknowns." The Ryan-Brady plan would have lowered the top individual income tax rate to 33 percent, taxed capital gains, dividends, and interest income at half the normal rates, repealed the minimum tax, doubled the standard deduction to $24,000 for married couples ($12,000 for single individuals), eliminated all itemized deductions except for mortgage interest and charitable deductions, and repealed the estate tax. The plan would have cut tax rates on non-corporate businesses, such as partnerships, to a maximum of 25 percent and repealed the tax provisions that funded Obamacare.

50. Peter Cary and Allan Holmes, "The Secret Saga of Trump's Tax Cuts," *Center for Public Integrity*, April 30, 2019, https://publicintegrity.org/inequality-poverty-opportunity/taxes /trumps-tax-cuts/the-secret-saga-of-trumps-tax-cuts.

51. On February 1, 2017, 100 large importers, like Nike, Target, Best Buy, and Walmart, announced opposition to the Ryan-Brady BAT. A few weeks later, South Carolina Republican senator Lindsay Graham, President Trump's golfing buddy, said the House BAT "won't get ten votes in the Senate." Cary and Holmes, "The Secret Saga of Trump's Tax Cuts." In April Secretary Mnuchin said, "We don't think it works in its current form, and we're going to have discussions with them about revisions." Jacob Pramuk, "The White House Just Outlined Its Tax Plan. Here's What's in It," CNBC, April 26, 2017, https://www.cnbc.com/2017/04/26/the-white-house-just -outlined-its-tax-plan-heres-whats-in-it.html. In May Koch-financed Americans for Prosperity published an anti-BAT video titled "The Truth about the Made in America Tax." Ways and Means Committee Republicans expressed concerns that the BAT "has the potential to pass on significant costs to the consumer." The *New York Times* pronounced the border-adjustment tax "finally dead." Alan Rappeport, "Border Tax's Apparent Demise Jeopardizes GOP Overhaul Plan," *New York Times,* May 23, 2017.

52. Cary and Holmes, "The Secret Saga of Trump's Tax Cuts."

53. Portions of this section are adapted from Michael Graetz, "Foreword—The 2017 Tax Cuts: How Polarized Politics Produced Precarious Policy," *Yale Law Journal Forum*, October 25, 2018, https://www.yalelawjournal.org/forum/foreword-the-2017-tax-cuts.

54. "The 1-Page White House Handout on Trump's Tax Proposal," CNN, April 26, 2017, https://www.cnn.com/2017/04/26/politics/white-house-donald-trump-tax-proposal/index .html.

55. Pramuk, "The White House Just Outlined Its Tax Plan."

56. Bob Woodward, *Fear: Trump in the White House* (New York: Simon and Schuster, 2018), 290.

57. U.S. Department of the Treasury, "Joint Statement on Tax Reform," press release, July 27, 2017, https://home.treasury.gov/news/press-releases/sm0134. Utah's Orrin Hatch chaired the Senate Finance Committee, but at age eighty-three he wasn't prepared to produce a complicated tax bill. So he deputized four Republican committee members: Rob Portman of Ohio, the most knowledgeable Republican on taxes; Pennsylvania's Pat Toomey, a long-time antitax advocate; John Thune of South Dakota, a member of the Republican leadership close to Mitch McConnell; and South Carolina's Tim Scott, a conservative African American supporter of the so-called "Fair Tax" (a proposal to replace all federal taxes with a 30 percent national sales tax).

58. Ed Markey, "Senate Democrats Lay Out Key Principles for Tax Reform," press release, August 1, 2017, https://www.markey.senate.gov/news/press-releases/senate-democrats-lay-out -key-principles-for-tax-reform.

59. U.S. Department of the Treasury, "Unified Framework for Fixing Our Broken Tax Code," press release, September 27, 2017, https://home.treasury.gov/news/press-releases/sm0166.

60. "Tax Reform Frame Released—Picture Missing," *Debevoise and Plimpton*, September 28, 2017, https://www.debevoise.com/insights/publications/2017/09/Tax-Reform-Frame-Released-Picture-Missing.

61. Jim Tankersley, "A 'Main Street' Tax Speech Becomes a Trump Riff on the Rich," *New York Times*, November 29, 2017.

62. Ibid. Donald Trump's business organization is composed of hundreds of "limited liability corporations" treated as partnerships under the tax law.

63. Ibid.

64. Bob Salsberg, "Pelosi Tax Overhaul Has Cast a 'Dark Cloud' over Washington," *Real Clear Politics*, February 2, 2018, https://www.realclearpolitics.com/articles/2018/02/02/pelosi_tax_overhaul_has_cast_a_dark_cloud_over_washington_136179.html; Mike Lillis, "Pelosi Denounces GOP Tax Reform as 'Armageddon,'" *The Hill*, December 4, 2017, https://thehill.com/homenews/house/363238-pelosi-denounces-gop-tax-reform-as-armageddon/.

65. Tara Golshan, "How Trump Broke Paul Ryan," *Vox*, April 12, 2018. Ryan subsequently joined the Board of Directors of Fox Corporation, became a vice chairman at Teneo, a global communications and consulting firm, and founded a nonprofit organization called the American Idea Foundation.

66. Erica Werner, "Fiscal Hawk Ryan Leaves behind Growing Deficits and a Changed GOP," *Washington Post*, April 11, 2018.

67. David Jackson, Herb Jackson, and Deirdre Shesgreen, "House Speaker Paul Ryan's Retirement Sparks Debate about Successor and Party's Future," *USA Today*, April 11, 2018.

68. "Tax Cut and Spending Bill Could Cost $5.5 Trillion through 2029," Committee for a Responsible Federal Budget, February 27, 2019, https://www.crfb.org/blogs/tax-cut-and-spending-bill-could-cost-55-trillion-through-2029.

69. This is how people often refer to the law, but the final legislation had a more cumbersome title: An Act to Provide for Reconciliation Pursuant to Titles II and V of the Concurrent Resolution on the Budget for Fiscal Year 2018; Pub. L. No. 115-97; Woodward, *Fear*, 294.

70. Scott Horsley, "After 2 Years, Trump Tax Cuts Have Failed to Deliver on GOP's Promises," NPR, December 20, 2019, https://www.npr.org/2019/12/20/789540931/2-years-later-trump-tax-cuts-have-failed-to-deliver-on-gops-promises.

71. "Distributional Analysis of the Conference Agreement for the Tax Cuts and Jobs Act" (Washington, DC: Tax Policy Center, 2017), https://www.taxpolicycenter.org/publications/distributional-analysis-conference-agreement-tax-cuts-and-jobs-act/full.

72. Russell Berman, "Trump Passed the Tax Cuts. Now He's Undermining Them," *The Atlantic*, August 9, 2019.

73. U.S. Library of Congress, Congressional Research Service, *Recent Changes in the Estate and Gift Tax Provisions*, R42959 (2021), https://sgp.fas.org/crs/misc/R42959.pdf; "2017 Tax Law Weakens Estate Tax, Benefitting Wealthiest and Expanding Avoidance Opportunities," Center on Budget and Policy Priorities, June 1, 2018, https://www.cbpp.org/research/federal-tax/2017-tax-law-weakens-estate-tax-benefiting-wealthiest-and-expanding-avoidance.

74. U.S. Congress, Joint Committee on Taxation, *Present Law and Data Related to the Taxation of Business Income*, 115th Cong., 1st sess., September 15, 2017, JCX-42-17, 50, 56; Internal Revenue Service, *Statistics of Income—Individual Income Tax Returns* (Washington, DC, 2022), table 1.4, https://www.irs.gov/pub/irs-pdf/p1304.pdf.

75. Under prior law, people could avoid capital gains taxes by using the proceeds from an asset sale to purchase another asset of "like-kind." The 2017 law eliminated this break for all assets but real estate, allowing real estate investors to continue avoiding capital gains taxes by reinvesting sales proceeds in other buildings or land. Even if they change their investments, by

holding property until they die, real estate investors can escape a lifetime of capital gains taxes. See Internal Revenue Code § 1031. E.g., Jim Tankersley, "A Curveball from the New Tax Law: It Makes Baseball Trades Harder," *New York Times*, March 19, 2018.

76. David Wessel, *Only the Rich Can Play: How Washington Works in the New Gilded Age* (New York: Hachette Book Group, 2021).

77. Ibid., 116–17. See also Michael J. Graetz and Ian Shapiro, *The Wolf at the Door: The Menace of Economic Insecurity and How to Fight It* (Cambridge, MA: Harvard University Press, 2020), 229–38; Raj Chetty et al., "The Opportunity Atlas: Mapping the Childhood Roots of Social Mobility" (National Bureau of Economic Research, working paper, no. 25147, January 2020), https://www.nber.org/papers/w25147.

78. Wessel, *Only the Rich Can Play*, 117–42, 256–77. According to the Tax Foundation, "Given that there is no consensus on the efficacy of place-based incentive programs, gathering data on opportunity zones is crucial. Senators Cory Booker (D-NJ) and Tim Scott (R-SC) had originally included provisions for annual data collection beginning five years after the bill passed, but those provisions were dropped in the final version of the TCJA." Scott Eastman and Nicole Kaeding, *Opportunity Zones: What We Know and What We Don't* (Washington, DC: Tax Foundation, 2019), https://taxfoundation.org/opportunity-zones-what-we-know-and-what-we-dont.

79. Michael Cohn, "IRS and Treasury Preview Postcard-Size Form 1040," *Accounting Today*, June 29, 2018.

80. Kelly Phillips, "Here's How the New Postcard-Sized Form 1040 Differs from Your Current Tax Return," *Forbes*, June 30, 2018.

81. Phillip Levine, "The University Endowment Income Tax: Who Will Pay It and Why Was It Implemented?" *Econofact*, https://econofact.org/the-university-endowment-tax-who-will-pay-it-and-why-was-it-implemented.

82. Both Mitch McConnell and Paul Ryan opposed trade barriers. At a Republican retreat for donors in August 2016, Ryan, his party's most prolific fundraiser, reiterated his commitment to free trade, suggesting Republicans should repudiate "trade protectionism." Theodore Schleifer, "Paul Ryan Praises Free Trade at Koch Retreat," CNN, August 2, 2016; Doug Palmer, "Ryan Brings Free Market Zeal to Trade Debate," *Politico*, February 5, 2015. In 2019 Senate Finance Committee chairman Chuck Grassley insisted Republicans "are still a party of free trade." Phil Levy, "Is the GOP Still the Party of Free Trade?" Reagan Presidential Foundation and Institute, https://www.reaganfoundation.org/reagan-institute/publications/is-the-gop-still-the-party-of-free-trade.

83. See Section 232 of the Trade Expansion Act of 1962, 19 U.S.C. § 1862.

84. E.g., Grant W. Gardner and Kent P. Kimbrough, "Tax Regimes, Tariff Revenues, and Government Spending," *Economica* 59, no. 233 (February 1992): 75–92.

85. President Reagan made this observation in his Thanksgiving address in 1988. Levy, "Is the GOP Still the Party of Free Trade."

86. Gary Hufbauer and Zhiyao (Lucy) Lu, *Policy Brief 17-16: The Payoff to America from Global Integration: A Fresh Look with a Focus on American Workers* (Washington, DC: Peterson Institute for International Economics, 2017).

87. Government efforts to protect such workers through "trade adjustment assistance" have been ineffectual. Graetz and Shapiro, *The Wolf at the Door*, 152–60.

88. Lawrence Summers, "Trump's Trade Policy Violates Almost Every Strategic Rule," *Washington Post*, June 4, 2018.

89. Catherine Rampell, "So You're Telling Me My Subaru Is a National Security Threat?" *Washington Post*, May 24, 2015.

90. Mark Landler and Ana Swanson, "Trump Sees a China Trade Deal through a New Prism: The 2020 Election," *New York Times*, May 10, 2019.

91. P. J. Huffstutter, "US Farm Income Expected to Rise in 2019, but Only Because of Government Aid," Reuters, November 27, 2019, https://www.reuters.com/article/usda-farming/u-s-farm-income-expected-to-rise-in-2019-but-only-because-of-government-aid-idUSL1N28714L. Many companies and communities were harmed by Trump's tariffs: Harley-Davidson, the iconic American motorcycle manufacturer, said it was moving some manufacturing to Thailand and Europe. The Missouri Mid-Continent Nail company, the nation's largest nail manufacturer, laid off 50 of its 600 workers and threatened to move to Mexico unless it was exempted from the steel tariffs. Rick Barrett, "Trump Responds as Harley Davidson Announces Plans to Move More Motorcycle Products Overseas," *Milwaukee Journal-Sentinel*, June 6, 2018; Chris Isidore, "Largest U.S. Nail Manufacturer on the Brink of Extinction Because of Steel Tariffs," *CNN Money*, June 26, 2018. In New Hampshire, China's 25 percent retaliatory tariff on lobsters shifted Little Bay Lobster Company's 50,000 pounds of weekly orders from China to a less expensive Canadian lobster supplier.

92. Woodward, *Fear*, 177; Jane C. Timm, "Fact Check: Trump Says China Is Paying for His Tariffs. He's Wrong," NBC News, August 2, 2019.

93. Some of the discussion in this section is derived from Graetz and Shapiro, *The Wolf at the Door*, chap. 6.

94. Matthew J. Belvedere, "Influential Anti-Tax Activist Grover Norquist to Trump: 'Tariffs Are Taxes'—Leverage World Outrage over China Trade Instead," CNBC, December 7, 2018.

95. "Foreign Trade: Trade in Goods with China," U.S. Census Bureau, https://www.census.gov/foreign-trade/balance/c5700.html#2021; James Mann, "Trump's China Policy: The Chaotic End to the Era of Engagement," in *The Presidency of Donald J. Trump: A First Historical Assessment*, ed. Julian E. Zelizer (Princeton: Princeton University Press, 2022), 268–71.

96. Steve Liesman, "Trump's Tariffs Are Equivalent to One of the Largest Tax Increases in Decades," CNBC, May 16, 2019, https://www.cnbc.com/2019/05/16/trumps-tariffs-are-equivalent-to-one-of-the-largest-tax-increases-in-decades.html (using estimate by the Tax Foundation). President Biden kept President Trump's tariffs in force.

97. Pablo D. Fajgelbaum et al., "The Return to Protectionism" (National Bureau of Economic Research, working paper, no. 25638, March 2019), 25, 27, https://www.nber.org/system/files/working_papers/w25638/revisions/w25638.rev0.pdf.

98. David Dollar, "How Have Trump's Trade Wars Affected Rust Belt Jobs," October 19, 2020, in *Dollars & Sense*, produced by the Brookings Institution, web, 27:29, https://www.brookings.edu/podcast-episode/how-have-trumps-trade-wars-affected-rust-belt-jobs; Aaron Flaaen and Justin R. Pierce, "Disentangling the Effects of the 2018–2019 Tariffs on Globally Connected U.S. Manufacturing Sector" (Board of Governors of the Federal Reserve System Finance and Economics Discussion Series 2019-086 working paper, Washington, DC, December 2019), https://doi.org/10.17016/FEDS.2019.086.

99. Heather Long, "Trump's Steel Tariffs Cost U.S. Consumers $900,000 for Every Job Created, Experts Say," *Washington Post*, May 7, 2019.

100. Niv Elis, "Corker: Tax Cuts Could Be 'One of the Worst Votes I've Made,'" *The Hill*, April 11, 2018, http://thehill.com/policy/finance/382663-corker-tax-cuts-could-be-one-of-worst-votes-ive-made.

101. Bob Bryan, "Treasury Secretary Steven Mnuchin Doubled Down on a Claim about the Tax Bill That Almost Every Independent Group Says Is Wrong," *Business Insider*, August 28, 2018, http://www.businessinsider.com/mnuchin-gop-trump-tax-law-pay-for-itself-deficit-rising-debt-2018-8.

102. Harvard economists Robert Barro and Jason Furman estimated that for 2020–27, the predicted impact of the 2017 legislation on GDP growth is 0.04 to 0.13 percentage points per year. Robert J. Barro and Jason Furman, *Brookings Papers on Economic Activity* (Spring 2018): 260. The Joint Committee on Taxation, which used a weighted average of three macroeconomic models, reached a similar conclusion. Ibid., 301, 318; see also Alan J. Auerbach, William G. Gale, and Aaron Krupkin, *The Federal Budget Outlook—Even Crazier After All These Years* (Washington, DC: Tax Policy Center, 2018), https://www.brookings.edu/research/the-federal-budget

-outlook-even-crazier-after-all-these-years; William G. Gale et al., *Effects of the Tax Cuts and Jobs Act: A Preliminary Analysis* (Washington, DC: Tax Policy Center, 2018), https://www.brookings.edu/research/effects-of-the-tax-cuts-and-jobs-act-a-preliminary-analysis.

103. Allan Sloan and Cezary Podkul, "Trump's Most Enduring Legacy Could Be the Historic Rise in the National Debt," *Washington Post*, January 14, 2021.

104. Ibid. Trump's tariffs raised $71 billion in 2019, an increase of $36 billion from President Obama's last year in office. Grover Norquist, unsurprisingly a strong supporter of the tax cuts, blamed the 2019 slowdown in economic activity and business investments on Trump's tariffs. Berman, "Trump Passed the Tax Cuts."

105. Congressional Budget Office, *Monthly Budget Review: Summary for Fiscal Year 2019* (November 2019), https://www.cbo.gov/publication/55824.

106. Brian Riedl, "Trump's Fiscal Legacy: A Comprehensive Overview of Spending, Taxes and Deficits," Manhattan Institute, May 12, 2022, https://www.manhattan-institute.org/trumps-fiscal-legacy.

107. Sloan and Podkul, "Trump's Most Enduring Legacy Could Be the Historic Rise in the National Debt." The pandemic added $3.9 trillion in debt. Riedl, "Trump's Fiscal Legacy." Both George W. Bush and Barack Obama had faced costly crises, from terrorism and the financial crisis, respectively. There are various ways to measure how much a president added to the federal debt. For example, the five presidents with the largest percentage increase in the federal debt during their presidencies were Franklin Roosevelt, Woodrow Wilson, Ronald Reagan, George W. Bush, and Barack Obama. Donald Trump did not even make that list (although he had fewer years in office than those who did). Kimberly Amadeo, "U.S. Debt by President: By Dollar and Percentage," *The Balance*, March 31, 2023, https://www.thebalancemoney.com/us-debt-by-president-by-dollar-and-percent-3306296.

108. Riedl, "Trump's Fiscal Legacy"; Congressional Budget Office, *The 2020 Long-Term Budget Outlook* (September 2020), https://www.cbo.gov/publication/56516.

109. Sloan and Podkul, "Trump's Most Enduring Legacy Could Be the Historic Rise in the National Debt."

110. Tony Romm, "Trump Promises Permanent Cut to Payroll Tax Funding Social Security and Medicare If He's Reelected," *Washington Post*, August 8, 2020; Jim Tankersley, "Trump's Payroll Tax 'Cut' Fizzles," *New York Times*, September 11, 2020.

111. "Trump Holds White House News Conference," *PBS NewsHour*, August 12, 2020, YouTube video, 1:03:22, https://www.youtube.com/watch?v=zydur7nz5Xs&ab_channel=PBSNewsHour.

112. On December 14, 2014, the outgoing Republican Ways and Means chairman, Dave Camp of Michigan, released a final draft of a massive tax-reform plan that he had been working on for several years. Camp's bill would have achieved many of the economic and simplification benefits of the 2017 legislation without costing significant revenue or providing large tax cuts for the highest earners. Joint Committee on Taxation, "Technical Explanation, Estimated Revenue Effects, Distributional Analysis and Macroeconomic Analysis of the Tax Reform Act of 2014, A Discussion Draft of the Chairman of the House Committee on Ways and Means to Reform the Internal Revenue Code," September 2014, https://www.jct.gov/publications/2014/jcs-1-14/.

Chapter 15

1. Michael Batty et al., "The Distributional Financial Accounts of the United States" (Washington, DC: Board of Governors of the Federal Reserve, 2020), 17–19, https://www.aeaweb.org/conference/2021/preliminary/paper/ANrhSBKE.

2. Bernie Sanders, "A Threat to American Democracy" (speech, United States Senate Floor, March 27, 2014), YouTube video, 22:11, https://www.youtube.com/watch?v=fQOCfweYLrE.

3. Brad Tuttle, "Most Americans Want the Rich to Pay Higher Taxes, According to Every Poll Everywhere," *Money Magazine*, January 20, 2020; Howard Schneider and Chris Kahn, "Majority of Americans Favor Wealth Tax on Very Rich: Reuters/Ipsos Poll," Reuters, January 10, 2020; Tim Ryan Williams, "Americans Are Ready to Tax the Rich," *Vox*, October 16, 2021; Amina Dunn and Ted Van Green, "Top Tax Frustrations for Americans: The Feeling That Some Corporations, Wealthy People Don't Pay Fair Share," Pew Research Center, April 30, 2021, https://www.pewresearch.org/fact-tank/2021/04/30/top-tax-frustrations-for-americans-the-feeling-that-some-corporations-wealthy-people-dont-pay-fair-share; Frank Newport, "U.S. Public Opinion and Increased Taxes on the Rich," Gallup, June 4, 2021, https://news.gallup.com/opinion/polling-matters/350555/public-opinion-increased-taxes-rich.aspx.

4. Newport, "U.S. Public Opinion and Increased Taxes on the Rich."

5. Glenn Kessler, "Fact Checker: Joe Biden's Claim That He Won't Raise Taxes on People Making Less than $400,000," *Washington Post*, August 31, 2020.

6. Ibid. The Tax Policy Center estimated that Biden's proposals would increase taxes by $2.1 trillion over the next decade, cut taxes for the bottom 60 to 80 percent of households, and substantially increase taxes for those with the most income. As numerous economists pointed out, Biden's promise not to raise taxes on anyone earning less than $400,000 ignored any indirect burdens that increasing corporate taxes would have over time on workers. For more details and an analysis of Biden's proposals, see, e.g., Gordon B. Mermin et al., *An Updated Analysis of Former Vice President Biden's Tax Proposals* (Washington, DC: Tax Policy Center, 2020), https://www.taxpolicycenter.org/publications/updated-analysis-former-vice-president-bidens-tax-proposals/media.

7. Joe Biden, "Get It Done: Joe Biden for President 2020," October 10, 2020, YouTube video, 1:00, https://www.youtube.com/watch?v=vagDx0-USUA.

8. Susan Cornwell and Trevor Hunnicutt, "Biden Campaign Tees Up Trump Tax Issue on Eve of First Debate," Reuters, September 28, 2020.

9. See, e.g., Grover Norquist, "6 Ways Biden's Corporate Tax Hike Will Hurt Businesses," *Fox Business*, July 20, 2021, https://www.foxbusiness.com/markets/biden-corporate-tax-hike-hurt-america-grover-norquist.

10. The initial legislation passed unanimously in the Senate and by a voice vote in the House, and was signed into law by Donald Trump on March 27, 2020. This included cash payments to individuals and families, more comprehensive and greater unemployment benefits, loans to businesses, including hundreds of billions in forgivable loans, and large payments to state and local governments. See "Breaking Down $3.4 Trillion in COVID Relief," Committee for a Responsible Federal Budget, January 7, 2021, https://www.crfb.org/blogs/breaking-down-34-trillion-covid-relief#:~:text=Of%20the%20%243.4%20trillion%20in,from%20the%20other%20two%20bills.

11. Howard Gleckman, "Pandemic Bill Would Cut Taxes by an Average of $3,000 with Most Relief Going to Low- and Middle-Income Households," Tax Policy Center, March 8, 2021.

12. "Expanded Child Tax Credit Continues to Keep Millions of Children from Poverty in September," Center on Poverty and Social Policy at Columbia University, October 27, 2021, https://www.povertycenter.columbia.edu/publication/monthly-poverty-september-2021; Ben Casselman, "Child Tax Credit's Extra Help Ends Just as Covid Surges Anew," *New York Times*, January 2, 2022; Daniel Hemel, "Want to Improve the Lives of Children? Expand the Child Tax Credit," *Washington Post*, August 18, 2022.

13. Ian Prasad Philbrick, "Why Isn't Biden's Expanded Child Tax Credit More Popular?" *New York Times*, January 5, 2022 (updated January 10, 2022).

14. The Rescue Act explicitly prohibited states from using its funds "to directly or indirectly" finance tax cuts, but this restriction was impossible to enforce and federal judges blocked its enforcement in at least fifteen states. See, e.g., Kayla Goggin, "Treasury Department Can't Enforce American Rescue Plan Tax Cut Rule, 11th Circuit Says," *Courthouse News*, January 20, 2023.

15. Catherine Rampell, "Democrats Accidentally Made It Easier for Republicans to Cut Taxes This Year, Oops," *Washington Post*, January 31, 2022.

16. Some economists, notably including former treasury secretary Lawrence Summers who headed the National Economic Council under President Obama, warned that the $1.9 trillion American Rescue Act was too large relative to the shortfall in economic output and likely to generate inflationary pressures. Lawrence H. Summers, "The Biden Stimulus Is Admirably Ambitious. But It Brings Some Big Risks, Too," *Washington Post*, February 4, 2021. Inflation then was less than 2 percent, but a year later neared 8 percent. Some economists disputed Summers's suggestion that Biden's Rescue legislation was responsible for the inflation that emerged, blaming supply chain and labor supply issues resulting from the Covid pandemic and the Federal Reserve's exceptionally expansionary monetary policy. They noted inflation has spiked elsewhere, hitting 7.5 percent in Europe, for example. John Cassidy, "Was Larry Summers Really Right about Inflation and Biden?" *New Yorker*, April 8, 2022.

17. Biden's proposals included universal pre-kindergarten and large childcare subsidies, paid family and medical leave, free community college, expanded health insurance subsidies, and energy subsidies. Lindsey McPherson, "How 'Build Back Better' Started, and How It's Going: A Timeline," *Roll Call*, July 21, 2022.

18. "The Biden Administration Has Approved $4.8 Trillion of New Borrowing," Committee for a Responsible Federal Budget, September 13, 2022, https://www.crfb.org/blogs/biden-administration-has-approved-48-trillion-new-borrowing.

19. Scott Rasmussen, "61% Say Biden Likely to Raise Middle Class Taxes," August 10, 2021, https://scottrasmussen.com/61-say-biden-likely-to-raise-middle-class-taxes.

20. U.S. Department of the Treasury, *General Explanations of the Administration's Fiscal Year 2022 Revenue Proposals* (Washington, DC, 2021), 60–67, 82–84, https://home.treasury.gov/system/files/131/General-Explanations-FY2022.pdf.

21. Internal Revenue Code, § 6103. See, e.g., Jonathan Weisman and Alan Rappeport, "An Exposé Has Congress Rethinking How to Tax the Superrich," *New York Times*, June 16, 2021.

22. Jesse Eisinger, Jeff Ernsthausen, and Paul Kiel, "The Secret IRS Files: Trove of Never-Before-Seen Records Reveal How the Wealthiest Avoid Income Tax," *ProPublica*, June 8, 2021, https://www.propublica.org/article/the-secret-irs-files-trove-of-never-before-seen-records-reveal-how-the-wealthiest-avoid-income-tax.

23. Rachel Louise Ensign and Richard Rubin, "Buy, Borrow, Die: How Rich Americans Live Off Their Paper Wealth," *Wall Street Journal*, July 13, 2021.

24. Justin Elliott, Patricia Callahan, and James Bandler, "Lord of the Roths: How Tech Mogul Peter Thiel Turned a Retirement Account for the Middle Class into a $5 Billion Tax-Free Piggy Bank," *ProPublica*, June 24, 2021, https://www.propublica.org/article/lord-of-the-roths-how-tech-mogul-peter-thiel-turned-a-retirement-account-for-the-middle-class-into-a-5-billion-dollar-tax-free-piggy-bank.

25. Naomi Jagoda, "Republicans Open New Line of Attack on IRS," *The Hill*, June 13, 2021.

26. Jonathan Weissman, "For Schumer and Pelosi, the Challenge of a Career with No Margin for Error," *New York Times*, September 26, 2021.

27. Ben Steverman, Anders Melin, and Devon Pendleton, "The Hidden Way the Ultrarich Pass Wealth to Their Heirs Tax Free," *Bloomberg Business Week*, October 21, 2021. For a more general discussion of estate tax avoidance, see Evan Osnos, "Trust Issues: Confessions of a Disgruntled Wealth Manager," *New Yorker*, January 23, 2023, 30–41.

28. The legislation also included universal pre-kindergarten, paid family leave, and a variety of health, climate change, housing, and immigration provisions. Nik Popli and Abby Vesoulis, "The House Just Passed Biden's Build Back Better Bill. Here's What's in It," *Time*, November 19, 2021.

29. Ibid.; Sarah Ewall-Wice et al., "House Passes Build Back Better Bill after Overnight Delay," CBS News, November 19, 2021, https://www.cbsnews.com/live-updates/build-back -better-passes-house.

30. Editorial, "'Only Morons Pay the Estate Tax,'" *New York Times*, November 20, 2017.

31. In March 2022, President Biden released updated tax proposals, including many from the previous year that were not included in the House bill, including an increase in the corporate tax rate. The Biden administration knew it was just making a political point by renewing its calls for a higher corporate rate.

32. U.S. Department of the Treasury, *General Explanations of the Administration's Fiscal Year 2023, Revenue Proposals* (Washington, DC, 2022), 34–36, https://home.treasury.gov/system /files/131/General-Explanations-FY2023.pdf.

33. Ibid., 111. This income tax recommendation was different and much smaller but related to Elizabeth Warren's proposals to impose a 2 percent annual tax on the 75,000 households with net wealth above $50 million—a tax she estimated would produce $3.75 trillion of additional taxes in a decade. Elizabeth Warren, "Ultra-Millionaire Tax," Warren Democrats, https:// elizabethwarren.com/plans/ultra-millionaire-tax. It is not clear whether either Warren's or Biden's proposal would be upheld by the current Supreme Court as constitutional. See National Federation of Independent Business v. Sebelius 567 U.S. 519 (2012) (citing Eisner v. Macomber, 252 U.S. 189 (1920)).

34. Emily Cochrane and Lisa Friedman, "Manchin Pulls Plug on Climate and Tax Talks, Shrinking Domestic Plan," *New York Times*, July 14, 2022. A spokeswoman for Senator Manchin said, "Political headlines are of no value as inflation soars to 9.1 percent. Senator Manchin believes it's time for leaders to put political agendas aside . . . and adjust to the economic realities the country faces to avoid taking steps that add fuel to the inflation fire." She added, "Senator Manchin has not walked away from the table." Tony Romm and Jeff Stein, "Manchin Says He Won't Support New Climate Spending or Tax Hikes on the Wealthy," *Washington Post*, July 14, 2022.

35. Ewan Palmer, "Democrats Just Beat Mitch McConnell at His Own Game," *Newsweek*, July 28, 2022.

36. Jeff Stein, Maxine Joselow, and Rachel Roubein, "What's in the Charles Schumer-Joe Manchin 'Inflation Reduction Act,'" *Washington Post*, July 28, 2022.

37. Benjamin Guggenheim, "Reconciliation Tax Reform Limited by Delicate Negotiations," *Tax Notes*, July 29, 2022.

38. Jeff Stein, "With Sinema's Help, Private Equity Firms Win Relief from Proposed Tax Hikes," *New York Times*, August 7, 2022.

39. Massachusetts's Richard Neal, chairman of the House Ways and Means Committee, said, "You're reminded of how difficult legislating is when you have big majorities, never mind when you have a tiny one." Emily Cochrane, "House Passes Sweeping Climate, Tax and Health Care Package," *New York Times*, August 12, 2022.

40. Tony Romm, "Corporate America Launches Massive Lobbying Blitz to Kill Key Parts of Democrats' $3.5 Trillion Economic Plan," *Washington Post*, August 31, 2021.

41. A similar minimum tax was included in the 1986 Tax Reform Act in response to well-publicized reports that some companies, like General Electric, had paid no tax despite reporting large profits to shareholders. The 1986 provision was scheduled to terminate after three years, and it did.

42. Alan Rappeport, "Democrats Eye a Major Shift in How Corporations Are Taxed," *New York Times*, August 6, 2022. Treasury Secretary Janet Yellen urged Congress to enact a broader 15 percent corporate minimum tax advanced by the OECD and agreed to by many other countries. Editorial, "The Schumer-Manchin Double Tax," *Wall Street Journal*, August 3, 2022.

43. William J. Gale and Samuel J. Thorpe, *Rethinking the Corporate Income Tax: The Role of Rent Sharing* (Washington, DC: Tax Policy Center, 2022), https://www.brookings.edu/wp-content/uploads/2022/05/Rethinking-the-Corporate-Income-Tax-Formatted.pdf.

44. David Lawler, "IRS Chief Says $1 Trillion in Taxes Goes Uncollected Every Year," Reuters, April 13, 2021. Other estimates suggested the number was closer to $600 billion, still a healthy sum.

45. Jonathan Swan and Alayna Treene, "GOP Tax Attack," *Axios*, June 30, 2021, https://www.axios.com/2021/07/01/gop-tax-irs-infrastructure.

46. Alan Rappeport and Tiffany Hsu, "More Money for IRS Spurs Conspiracy Theories of 'Shadow Army,'" *New York Times*, August 19, 2022.

47. Laura Saunders, "The Saturday I Spent Five-and-a-Half Hours in Line Waiting for the IRS," *Wall Street Journal*, May 20, 2022.

48. Laura Saunders, "What $80 Billion More for the IRS Means for Your Taxes," *Wall Street Journal*, August 19, 2022.

49. Ibid.

50. Alan Rappeport, "Janet Yellen Pledges 5,000 New IRS Hires to Bolster Taxpayer Responsiveness," *New York Times*, September 15, 2022.

51. Rappeport and Hsu, "More Money for IRS"; Dana Milbank, "Another Republican Lie Is Born," *Washington Post*, August 24, 2022.

52. Alex Isenstadt, "RNC Chief on Tape to Donors: We Need Help to Win the Senate," *Politico*, August 24, 2022.

53. Milbank, "Another Republican Lie Is Born."

54. Editorial, "The IRS Is About to Go Beast Mode," *Wall Street Journal*, August 16, 2022.

55. Rappeport and Hsu, "More Money for IRS."

56. Jacob Bogage, "IRS Launches Safety Review after Right-Wing Threats," *Washington Post*, August 23, 2022.

57. Ibid.

58. Mike Palicz, "First GOP Bill Rolls Back Biden's 87,000 IRS Agents," Americans for Tax Reform, January 7, 2023, https://www.atr.org/first-gop-bill-rolls-back-bidens-87000-irs-agents; Tony Romm, "House GOP Votes to Slash IRS Funding, Targeting Pursuit of Tax Cheats," *Washington Post*, January 9, 2023.

59. Jason Smith, "Opening Statement: 118th Congress Organizational Meeting, Ways and Means Committee," January 31, 2023, https://waysandmeans.house.gov/chairman-smith-opening-statement-118th-congress-organizational-meeting/.

60. H.R. 25, Fair Tax Act of 2023, 118th Cong., 1st sess., introduced January 9, 2023. Business and state government purchases would be exempt from the sales tax.

61. Natasha Sarin, "There's Nothing Fair about Republicans' FairTax Proposal," *Washington Post*, February 13, 2023.

62. Amy B. Wang, "Democrats Hammer GOP Plan to Impose National Sales Tax, Abolish IRS," *Washington Post*, January 5, 2023.

63. John H. Cochrane, "A Consumption Tax Is the Shock Our Broken System Needs," *Wall Street Journal*, February 2, 2023.

64. Howard Gleckman, "Making the TCJA's Individual Tax Cuts Permanent Would Add More than $3 Trillion to the Federal Debt, Mostly Benefit High-Income Households," Tax Policy Center, November 30, 2022, https://www.taxpolicycenter.org/taxvox/making-tcjas-individual-tax-cuts-permanent-would-add-more-3-trillion-federal-debt-mostly. The Congressional Budget Office estimated extending these tax cuts would add $2 trillion to federal deficits by 2032, and much more after that. Congressional Budget Office, *The Budget and Economic Outlook: 2022 to 2032* (May 2022), 88, https://www.cbo.gov/publication/58147; Congressional Budget Office, *The 2022 Long-Term Budget Outlook* (July 2022), https://www.cbo.gov/publication/57971.

65. Eric Revell, "GOP Lawmakers Propose Balanced Budget Amendment as US Nears Debt Ceiling," *Fox Business*, January 18, 2023, https://www.foxbusiness.com/politics/gop-lawmakers -propose-balanced-budget-amendment-us-nears-debt-ceiling.

66. Mark Zandi, Christian Deritis, and Bernard Yaros, "Going Down the Debt Limit Rabbit Hole," *Moody's Analytics*, March 2023, https://www.moodysanalytics.com/-/medis/article /2023/going-down-the-debt-limit-rabbit-hole.pdf; Leonard E. Burman et al., "Catastrophic Budget Failure," *National Tax Journal* 63, no. 3 (September 2010): 561–84; Alan Rappeport and Emily Cochrane, "What Happens Next in the Debt Limit Debate?" *New York Times*, February 1, 2023.

67. Hans Nichols, "Yellen Warns of Debt Ceiling 'Catastrophe' for U.S. and Beyond," *Axios*, January 28, 2023, https://www.axios.com/2023/01/28/yellen-debt-ceiling-nervous-default-recession.

68. Burgess Everett and Olivia Beavers, "Schumer Plots Debt Ceiling Course against McCarthy: 'We'll Win,'" *Politico*, January 30, 2023, https://www.politico.com/news/2023/01/30 /schumer-debt-ceiling-mccarthy-00080025.

69. Zandi, Deritis, and Yaros, "Going Down the Debt Limit Rabbit Hole," 1–4.

70. Office of Management and Budget, *Budget of the U.S. Government, Fiscal Year 2024*, https://www.whitehouse.gov./omb/budget.

71. Jim Tankersley, "In Budget Talks, Biden Rejects Hard Choices of the Past," *New York Times*, March 13, 2023.

72. "What Would It Take to Balance the Federal Budget?" Committee for a Responsible Federal Budget, January 12, 2023, https://www.crfb.org/blogs/what-would-it-take-balance-budget.

73. Cody Stanton, "McCarthy Debt Limit Bill Would Repeal IRA Green Energy Credits," *Tax Notes*, April 20, 2023; David Harrison, "House Republicans Unveil Bill to Raise Debt Ceiling, Cut Spending," *Wall Street Journal*, April 20, 2023.

74. "What's in the Limit, Save Grow Act?" Committee for a Responsible Federal Budget, April 20, 2023, https://www.crfb.org/blogs/whats-limit-save-grow act; E. J. Dionne Jr., "McCarthy's Debt Ceiling Plan Is Theater Unworthy of a High School Gym, *Washington Post*, April 23, 2023.

75. Christian Datoc, "White House Claims Debt Ceiling Plan Passed by House Violates No-Tax-Hike Pledge," *Washington Examiner*, April 26, 2023.

76. Ibid.

77. Ibid.; Richard Rubin, "Republicans Effectively Voted to Raise Taxes. They're Fine with That," *Wall Street Journal*, April 29, 2023.

78. Harrison, "House Republicans Unveil Bill to Raise Debt Ceiling, Cut Spending."

79. John Wagner, "Biden Rejects GOP Spending Cuts, Warns of Catastrophic Government Default," *Washington Post*, April 19, 2023.

80. Stanton, "McCarthy Debt Limit Bill Would Repeal IRA Green Energy Credits."

81. Alexander Bolton, "Manchin Slams Biden for 'Deficiency of Leadership,' Applauds McCarthy Debt Limit Plan," *The Hill*, April 20, 2023.

82. H.R. 3746, Fiscal Responsibility Act of 2023, 118th Cong., 1st sess., 2023. The repurposing of $20 billion of IRS funding was not included in the text of the legislation but was agreed to by President Biden and Speaker McCarthy. See Katherine Doyle and Zoe Richards, "Biden Touts Bipartisanship in Oval Office Speech on Debt Ceiling Deal," NBC News, June 2, 2023; Michael D. Shear, " 'The Stakes Could Not Have Been Higher': Biden Praises Debt-Ceiling Deal," *New York Times*, June 2, 2023; Alex Gangitano, "Biden Commends McCarthy for Debt Ceiling Deal: 'We Were Able to Get Along and Get Things Done,' " *The Hill*, June 2, 2023.

83. Phillip L. Swagel, director, Congressional Budget Office, to Speaker Kevin McCarthy, May 30, 2023, https://www.cbo.gov/system/files/2023-05/hr3746_Letter_McCarthy.pdf; Penn Wharton Budget Model, "The Fiscal Responsibility Act of 2023: Budget Cost Estimates of the Debt Ceiling Agreement," May 31, 2023, https://budgetmodel.wharton.upenn.edu/issues /2023/5/31/the-fiscal-responsibility-act-of-2023; Glenn Kessler, "McCarthy Hypes 'Largest

Cut' to Sell Debt-Ceiling Deal," *Washington Post*, May 31, 2023; Greg Ip, "A Debt Deal That Doesn't Deal with Debt," *Wall Street Journal*, May 31, 2023; Tony Romm et al., " 'You Don't Have Another Option': Inside the Biden, McCarthy Debt Ceiling Deal," *Washington Post*, June 3, 2023; Jim Tankersley, "Biden's Debt-Deal Strategy: Win in the Fine Print," *New York Times*, June 3, 2023.

Chapter 16

1. See, e.g., Michael J. Graetz and Ian Shapiro, *The Wolf at the Door: The Menace of Economic Insecurity and How to Fight It* (Cambridge MA: Harvard University Press, 2020).

2. On February 3, 2023, for example, Americans for Tax Reform reported that 42 of the Senate's 49 Republicans, 189 House members, and 15 governors had signed pledges never to raise taxes. "About the Pledge," Americans for Tax Reform, https://www.atr.org/about-the-pledge/.

3. Bruce Bartlett, a former staffer for Jack Kemp and economist in the Reagan *and* George H. W. Bush administrations, described how Republicans use the "starve the beast" strategy to enact large tax cuts when they are in power and urge large spending cuts for deficit reduction when Democrats are in charge. Bruce Bartlett, "The Republicans' Familiar, Troubling Plan to Torpedo Biden's Presidency," *New Republic*, October 26, 2020.

4. Martin Feldstein and Charles Y. Horioka, "Domestic Savings and International Capital Flows," *Economic Journal* 9, no. 358 (June 1980): 314–29.

5. William G. Gale, "What the Kansas Tax-Cut About-Face Means," *Brookings*, June 13, 2017, https://www.brookings.edu/blog/up-front/2017/06/13/what-the-kansas-tax-cut-about-face-means; William G. Gale, "The Kansas Tax Cut Experiment," *Brookings*, July, 11, 2017, https://www.brookings.edu/blog/unpacked/2017/07/11/the-kansas-tax-cut-experiment.

6. Robert Frank and Philip J. Cook, *The Winner-Take-All Society: Why the Few at the Top Get So Much More than the Rest of Us* (New York: Penguin Books, 1995).

7. Katharina Pistor, *The Code of Capital: How the Law Creates Wealth and Inequality* (Princeton: Princeton University Press, 2019).

8. See, e.g., Graetz and Shapiro, *The Wolf at the Door*, 137–69.

9. E.g., Trevon D. Logan, "Whitelashing: Black Politicians, Taxes, and Violence" (National Bureau of Economic Research, working paper, no. 26014, June 2019).

10. Michael Leachman et al., "Advancing Racial Equity with State Tax Policy" (Washington, DC: Center on Budget and Policy Priorities, 2018), https://www.cbpp.org/research/state-budget-and-tax/advancing-racial-equity-with-state-tax-policy.

11. E.g., Robin L. Einhorn, *American Taxation, American Slavery* (Chicago: University of Chicago Press, 2006); Camille Walsh, *Racial Taxation* (Chapel Hill: University of North Carolina Press, 2018); Dorothy A. Brown, *The Whiteness of Wealth* (New York: Crown, 2021).

12. Internal Revenue Code, § 199A.

13. Steve Mullis, "Leaked Video Shows Romney Discussing 'Dependent' Voters," NPR, September 18, 2012, https://www.kcur.org/2012-09-18/leaked-video-shows-romney-discussing-dependent-voters.

14. "Non-Payers by State," Tax Foundation, September 18, 2012, https://taxfoundation.org/nonpayers-state-2010.

15. Mark Memmott, "Romney's Wrong and Right about the '47 Percent,'" NPR, September 18, 2012, https://www.npr.org/sections/thetwo-way/2012/09/18/161333783/romneys-wrong-and-right-about-the-47-percent; Garrett Watson, "COVID-19 Tax Relief Added to Increasing Share of Households Paying No Income Tax," Tax Foundation, August 20, 2021, https://taxfoundation.org/us-households-paying-no-income-tax/.

16. For an accessible explanation and analysis, see Jonathan Gruber and Botond Koscegi, "A Modern Economic View of Tobacco Taxation" (Paris: International Union against Tuberculosis

and Lung Disease, 2008), https://untobaccocontrol.org/taxation/e-library/wp-content/uploads/2020/06/A-modern-economic-view-of-tobacco-taxation.pdf.

17. If the public wants to conserve energy, produce more energy-efficient products, or move from fossil fuels to less environmentally damaging sources of energy, and energy taxes are unavailable, only two other policy options (other than the government purchasing different products) are available: subsidizing behavior to be encouraged or limiting through regulations or mandates behavior to be curtailed. In 2009 President Obama and House Democrats tried but failed to enact legislation regulating carbon dioxide emissions. Michael J. Graetz, *The End of Energy: The Unmaking of America's Environment, Security, and Independence* (Cambridge, MA: MIT Press, 2011), 197–216. The 2022 Inflation Reduction Act contains a variety of costly subsidies for moving energy consumption away from fossil fuels to less-damaging renewable energy sources. Subsidies increase the profits of producers of favored products and may lower costs for those who use them. It is practically impossible to design subsidies to avoid providing unnecessary benefits for behavior people would have done without the subsidy; limiting subsidies to genuinely incremental activities is nearly always impossible. Moreover, in subsidizing activities it wants to encourage, Congress frequently picks winners and rewards favored constituents and contributors. In 2022 large subsidies were enacted to address climate change.

18. U.S. Congress, Joint Committee on Taxation, *Estimates of Federal Tax Expenditures for Fiscal Years 2020–2024*, 116th Cong., 2nd sess., November 5, 2020, JCX-23-20.

19. Ibid.

20. See Allison Rogers and Eric Toder, "Trends in Tax Expenditures, 1985–2016" (Washington, DC: Tax Policy Center, 2011), https://www.urban.org/sites/default/files/publication/27561/412404-Trends-in-Tax-Expenditures---.PDF; Tom Neubig and Agustin Redonda, "Tax Expenditures: The $1.5 Trillion Elephant in the Room," *Bloomberg Tax*, September 7, 2021, https://news.bloombergtax.com/daily-tax-report/tax-expenditures-the-1-5-trillion-elephant-in-the-budget-room.

21. Each estimate is separate and adding them together misstates the amount of revenues that would be gained from their repeal.

22. See, e.g., "The Biden Administration Has Approved $4.8 Trillion of New Borrowing," Committee for a Responsible Federal Budget, September 13, 2022, https://www.crfb.org/blogs/biden-administration-has-approved-48-trillion-new-borrowing.

23. Congressional Budget Office, *The Budget and Economic Outlook: 2022 to 2032* (May 2022), 5–7, https://www.cbo.gov/publication/58147. The total federal debt of about $31.5 trillion in January 2023 includes debt owed by Treasury to other federal agencies as well as debt owed to the public. Some economists believe the CBO estimates are overly optimistic. See, e.g., Martin A. Sullivan, "CBO Updated Forecast Still Outdated and Likely Too Optimistic," *Tax Notes*, May 22, 2023; Larry Summers, "Rethinking Fiscal Policy: Keynote at the Peterson Institute," June 1, 2023, https://larrysummers.com/2023/06/01/rethinking-fiscal-policy-keynote-by-lawrence-h-summers-at-the-peterson-institute/.

24. In states where constitutions require balanced budgets, an unwillingness to tax means basic public needs, like healthy drinking water and functioning electricity, sometimes go unmet.

25. Burman et al., "Catastrophic Budget Failure," 576–77: "In modern times, no country as economically dominant as the United States has suffered such a series of macroeconomic setbacks at the magnitudes that would likely occur under [a debt-ceiling crisis.] . . . [I]f the crisis forced the U.S. government to close a budget gap of, for example, 10 percent of GDP, the resulting fall in output might approach 25 percent—a decline not seen since the Great Depression."

26. Congressional Budget Office, *The Budget and Economic Outlook: 2022 to 2032*, 80–81.

27. Martin A. Sullivan, "Escalating Interest Costs Will Squeeze Congress," *Tax Notes*, February 7, 2023 (based on May 2022 projections by the Congressional Budget Office).

28. Congressional Budget Office, *The Budget and Economic Outlook: 2018 to 2028* (May 2018), https://www.cbo.gov/publication/53651.

29. Edward Meadows, "Laffer's Curveball Picks Up Speed," *Fortune*, February 23, 1981.

30. Frederico Cingano, "Trends in Income Inequality and Its Impacts on Economic Growth," Figure 3, p. 19 (OECD Social Employment and Migration Working Paper No. 163, December 2014), https://doi.org/10.1787/5jxrjncwxv6j-en; Christopher Ingraham, "How Rising Inequality Hurts Everyone, Even the Rich," *Washington Post*, February 6, 2018.

31. E.g., Editorial, "How America Soaks the Affluent," *Wall Street Journal*, March 4–5, 2023.

32. Congressional Budget Office, *The Distribution of Household Income, 2019*, November 15, 2022, Data Underlying Exhibits: Exhibits 11 and 12, https:www.cbo.gov/publication/58353.

33. See, e.g., Congressional Budget Office, *Trends in the Distribution of Family Wealth, 1989 to 2019*, September 27, 2022, https://www.cbo.gov/publication/57598.

34. Rising health-care costs have also been important.

35. Congressional Budget Office, *Options for Reducing the Deficit, 2023–2032, Volume 1: Larger Reductions*, December 7, 2022, https://www.cbo.gov/budget-options/58630.

36. See, e.g., Jane Meyer, *Dark Money: The Hidden History of the Billionaires behind the Rise of the Radical Right* (New York: Doubleday, 2016); Larry M. Bartels, *Unequal Democracy: The Political Economy of the New Gilded Age*, 2nd ed. (Princeton: Princeton University Press, 2016).

37. OECD, Centre for Tax Policy and Administration, "Revenue Statistics 2022: The United States," https://www.oecd.org/tax/revenue-statistics-united-states.pdf.

38. "Americans' Views of Government: Decades of Distrust, Enduring Support for Its Roll," Pew Research, June 6, 2022, https://www.pewresearch.org/politics/2022/06/06/americans-views-of-government-decades-of-distrust-enduring-support-for-its-role.

39. U.S. Congress, Joint Economic Committee, *A Symposium on the 40th Anniversary of the Joint Economic Committee Hearings: Hearings before the Joint Economic Committee*, 99th Cong., 1st sess., January 16, 1986, 262.

40. McCulloch v. Maryland, 17 U.S. 316, 431 (1819).

Index

abortion movement, 43, 264

Abramoff, Jack, College Republicans and, 117–18

Adams, Samuel, as Boston tax collector, 2

Adams, Thomas Sewall, tax policy advisor, 14

affirmative action, 5; college admissions, 273–74n38; discord over, 10–11; higher education, 29–30

Affirmative Action Compliance, Los Angeles County Office, 30

Affordable Care Act, Obama's, 209, 222

African Americans, Phillips on voting of, 11–12

Agnew, Spiro, resignation of, 6

Aid to Families With Dependent Children, poor people's budget, 286n9

Ailes, Roger: Fox News with Murdoch, 174; Limbaugh and, 127; rehearsing Bush, 135

Allott, Gordon, Weyrich and, 43

American Bankers Association, 63

American Conservative Union, 41, 119

American Council for Capital Formation (ACCF), 17, 63, 74

American dilemma, race relations as, 8–11

American Dream, 28

American Economic Association, 14

American Enterprise Institute (AEI), 17, 55

American Idea Foundation, 326n65

American Legislative Exchange Council (ALEC), 43, 122

American Presidency Project, 289n55, 291n11, 302n1

American Rescue Act (2021), 233–34, 330n14, 331n16

American Revolution, 2; Proposition 13 as second, 22

Americans for Prosperity, 204, 207

Americans for Tax Reform (ATR), 114, 116, 119, 120, 210, 244, 248

Americans for the Reagan Agenda, 296n15

American Taxpayer Relief Act (2012), 214, 320n89

Anarchy, State, and Utopia (Nozick), 16

Anderson, Jack, uncovering Jarvis scam, 24

Andrews Air Force Base, 142, 160

Anthony, Beryl, on Gingrich, 132

antitax movement: classing interests and ideologies, 14–17; distrust of government, 4–7; elite admiration for Ayn Rand, 16; Jarvis as antitax, 34; Jarvis' Proposition 13 and, 35; modern, 1; property taxes and, 18; racial resentment and, 12, 256; resistance to taxes, 2–4; stagflation and, 7–8

Apolinsky, Harold, on death tax repeal, 184

Apprentice, The (television show), 219

Archer, Bill: on income tax, 170; IRS hearings on Fox News, 174; on Laffer Curve, 158

Armey, Dick: budget negotiations and, 141; on Bush's tax plan, 192; Contract with America, 156; on Democratic ads, 160; on Forbes's flat tax, 171; FreedomWorks and, 207; Gingrich and, 132, 158; K-Street Project, 175; Norquist applauding, 149; Tauzin and, 167, 309n5, 310n27

A NOTE ON THE TYPE

This book has been composed in Arno, an Old-style serif typeface in the classic Venetian tradition, designed by Robert Slimbach at Adobe.